Fifth Edition

A BECOMING AWARE

A LOOK AT HUMAN RELATIONS AND PERSONAL ADJUSTMENT

VELMA WALKER

Tarrant County Junior College

LYNN BROKAW

Portland Community College

KENDALL/HUNT PUBLISHING COMPANY

2460 Kerper Boulevard P.O. Box 539 Dubuque, Iowa 52004-0539

Do you know that you are the only one of you? You are absolutely unique. There is no one like you. *You* are the original article. God only made *one,* and you are *it.*

Think what this means! You are completely in charge of your own life. *You* determine what happens to *you* by being true to that self which you really are. Shakespeare said, "To thine own self be true, and it must follow as the night the day, thou can not then be false to any man."

So be yourself today! The world is waiting for *you!* Do what *you* have to do, joyously and with all your heart!

Anonymous

Cover art by Kenneth Ley, Dubuque, Iowa.

Interior photos by Nancy Anne Dawe, Decatur, Georgia.

Copyright © 1976, 1977 by Velma Walker

Copyright © 1981, 1986, 1992 by Kendall/Hunt Publishing Company

ISBN 0–8403–6741–4

Printed in the United States of America

10 9 8 7 6 5 4 3 2 1

CONTENTS

2   Self-Awareness 45

7 Resolving Interpersonal Conflict 259

8   Managing Stress 305

9 What Is Important to Me 351

10 Life Planning 385

PREFACE

Becoming Aware: A Look at Human Relations and Personal Adjustment is written for college students of any age and for all others who wish to expand their self-awareness and explore avenues for personal growth and development. The topics discussed include: meeting people and forming relationships; self-awareness or who am I?; shaping and controlling our own destiny; achieving a balance between emotional expression and control; learning effective communication skills; establishing intimate relationships; resolving interpersonal conflicts, learning how to manage stress; the significance of choosing our values and developing a lifestyle with meaning; and the importance of choosing a direction for our life.

We have tried in every way possible to make this a personal book. Within each chapter, we encourage readers to examine relevant issues pertaining to their understanding of self and their relationships with others. The book is designed to be a personal workbook as well as a classroom text. Each chapter has a minimum of four activities for the reader to pause and reflect on the personal application of the concepts presented in the chapter. Each chapter also contains a Learning Journal for the reader to write and assess the personal value or meaning gained from the concepts presented. The activities, as well as the Learning Journal, have perforated pages, specifically designed for more convenient classroom participation or work outside of class that can be used for evaluation and assessment. Additionally, there are over 150 thought-provoking quotes, from well-known sources, and over 20 short poems designed to further promote insightful awareness.

The fifth edition of *Becoming Aware* reflects significant changes. Each chapter has been extensively expanded and updated to give the reader a greater opportunity for self-exploration: For example, the organization of the chapters has been revised to reflect a more meaningful flow of concepts; the poems are being integrated into the text to increase reader applicability; and thought-provoking short quotes are being graphically presented to add some balance to the written text. Furthermore, a complete glossary and index have been included in the revised edition. And, the interior of the book has been given a new "eye-appealing" dimension.

We are fortunate to have received some excellent suggestions from reviewers for this edition and have incorporated many of their suggestions into this revision. A major addition is a new chapter on resolving interpersonal conflict. Unlike previous editions, this topic has been separated from the stress management chapter and now includes a greater focus on developing assertiveness skills for win-win problem solving.

As mentioned earlier, the reader will find new material and revised sections in all chapters. The major changes are: More attention to the dynamics involved in establishing interpersonal relationships has been included in the chapter on getting acquainted with ourselves and others; theories related to the development of the self-concept have been expanded in the self-awareness chapter; and the popular "Self-Change Project" in Chapter 3 has been given greater emphasis with a more simplified outline, along with an updated discussion of the theory of locus of control.

In addition, a more thorough and practical discussion of the primary emotions and how to deal with them in our relationships with others has been included in the chapter on becoming emotional; the chapter on communication will reflect new sections on nonverbal communication, communication spoilers, and active listening; and new sections pertaining to the theories of interpersonal attraction, mate selection, marital adjustment, and relationship dependency and co-dependency have been included in the chapter on becoming intimate. Also, the theory of RET has been added to the stress management chapter, along with expanded coverage of strategies for coping and managing stress; greater emphasis on assessing our values by how we spend our time has been added to the chapter on meaning and purpose; and, the life planning chapter now includes new sections on the importance of taking risks and developing a balanced life.

Our approach in *Becoming Aware* is humanistic and personal; that is, we stress the healthy and effective personality and the common struggles we all have in developing a greater awareness of self and establishing more meaningful relationships with others. We especially emphasize taking risks in accepting personal responsibility for achieving a greater awareness of self and deciding whether and how we want to change our life.

We wrote this book for students who were looking for a *practical* course: one that dealt with issues in everyday living and would also provide a catalyst for their own personal growth. *Becoming Aware* has been adopted in courses dealing with the psychology of adjustment, human relations, applied psychology, personal growth and awareness, etc. We have also been fortunate to have had numerous adoptions from technical and vocational programs, ranging from nursing to electronics. In addition, instructors in teacher-training courses, as well as management development courses, have found *Becoming Aware* a practical guide for their students.

It has been our experience that active, open, practical, and personal participation in these courses has led to greater self-awareness, enhanced relationships with others, and increased control over choosing a direction for one's life.

An updated and expanded Instructor's Resource Manual accompanies this textbook. It includes more test items (multiple-choice, true–false, and short answer essays for each chapter); additional activities and exercises for classroom participation; suggested films for each chapter; guidelines for using the book and teaching the course; examples of course syllabi with various grading scales; a lecture outline for each chapter; and a student-evaluation instrument to assess the impact of the course.

ACKNOWLEDGMENTS

We are grateful for the insightful suggestions and innovative ideas received from David Stanton of Tarrant County Junior College, Pam Gasper of Portland Community College, Tobin Quereau of Austin Community College, Rich Reiner of Rogue Community College, and Carol Shapiro of South West State University.

We are also indebted for those who reviewed the earlier editions and made suggestions that have been included in this revision: Dr. Mary Jane Dickson, Eddie Sandoval, and Mary Ann Lee, Tarrant County Junior College; Lynn Godat and George Vaternick, Portland Community College; Jo Carolyn Miller, in private practice in Dallas, Texas; Minister and former Human Relations Professor, J. D. Phillips; and Jeannene Cox Ward, a Human Relations seminar instructor.

In addition, we are grateful for the suggestions and creativity of artist Stephen Andrews.

Also, we would like to thank our families, Danny, David, Judy, Chad, and Brett, who endured the irritating and constant sounds of keyboards and printers, patiently tolerated the late-night hours of work and research, and were always giving us their moral support and encouragement.

Finally, we would like to acknowledge those individuals and publishers who kindly gave us their permission to reprint their materials. In several instances, we regret that even after diligent searching, we have not been able to properly credit material being used and have listed the author as anonymous. Some of our material has been used for many years in classes and workshops with the result that proper identification has been lost, or we no longer are able to provide source information as we would like. Because the material has proved to be of great value, we have included it in our book. We trust that eventually we will be able credit these authors with proper recognition for their work.

Velma Walker

Lynn Brokaw

INTRODUCTION

If you cannot risk, you cannot grow,
If you cannot grow, you cannot become your best,
If you cannot become your best, you cannot be happy,
If you cannot be happy, what else matters?

David Viscott, M.D.
(from *Risking,* 1977)

Thank you for joining us as we explore avenues to new and greater beginnings in our lives. The title, *Becoming Aware: A Look at Human Relations and Personal Adjustment,* is descriptive. The basic element in this class is you and your relationship with others. Therefore, it is important that we begin this book with you as the subject.

You are probably varied and complex. You have needs and wants, feelings and fears, problems and anxieties, goals and ambitions, prejudices and priorities, and accomplishments and potentials.

You are also constantly adapting to changes. Life, then, requires a continuous adjustment. Adjustment is perhaps synonymous with coping and adapting to change, which are significant parts of the process of growth and development. Therefore, adjustment might be referred to as *the process of achieving a satisfactory relationship between oneself and one's environment.*

You are also a unique individual, but at the same time, you share a common struggle of wanting to be a healthy, happy, and more fully functioning individual. What does this mean? What kind of person are you trying to become?

Psychologists Abraham Maslow and Carl Rogers have devoted much of their lives researching and describing a healthy, happy, and more fully functioning individual. Carl Rogers calls this person "the fully functioning person" whereas Maslow calls this person "the self-actualizing person" and the "fully-human person." Do these individuals have common characteristics? Let's see.

A MODEL FOR PERSONAL GROWTH

Throughout this book, there will be frequent references to "growth as a person," and much will be said about the necessity of self-awareness and interpersonal encounter as a means to this growth. We will also be emphasizing that each individual has to grow into his or her own person, *not become "like"* anyone else. While it is difficult to describe what "growth as a person" really means, we have tried to focus the contents of this book around the following common characteristics of healthy, happy, and more fully functioning individuals: (1) an ability to accept oneself and others, (2) an efficient perception of reality, (3) close, caring interpersonal relationships, (4) autonomy and independence, (5) a strong ethical sense, and (6) willingness to continue to grow as a person. We will now explain these characteristics more fully.

1. **An Ability to Accept Oneself and Others**
   Happy, healthy individuals like themselves—they have a positive *self-concept.* Feeling good about themselves, they can also accept others, even when they are different. Healthy individuals tend to view themselves as people who are acceptable and capable of making a valuable contribution to the world in which they live.

2. **An Efficient Perception of Reality**

   Having a good self-concept, happy and healthy individuals do not have to hide behind a mask through which they filter reality. They see the world as it really is, rather than the way "it ought to be," and people as they really are, rather than the way "they ought to be."

3. **Close, Caring Interpersonal Relationships**

   Happy and healthy individuals are not afraid to be open and let others see how they feel. Because they feel good about themselves, they can afford to have deep human relationships with others. However, these strong ties are usually to only a few people, for a deep involvement with even one person takes considerable time.

4. **Autonomy and Independence**

   They trust themselves and rely on their own insights about what is right, what is wrong, and about what should be done in a given situation. Thus, happy and healthy individuals are independent in thought and action, relying more on their own standards of behavior and values rather than overemphasizing what others expect of them.

5. **A Strong Ethical Sense**

   They are as much concerned with the rights of others as they are with their own rights. They believe in honesty for all, kindness for all, and respect for all, regardless of nationality, race, religion, political beliefs, or whether relative, friend, or enemy.

6. **Willingness to Continue to Grow as a Person**

   Happy and healthy people tend to understand that being alive means allowing oneself to grow and to change, rather than reaching some end point and standing there. They tend to know where they are going, and consequently, have developed a sense of meaning or mission in their life. Thus, they enjoy and appreciate the fullness of life.

It is important to emphasize that the characteristics above represent a guide in our own search for happiness and fulfillment. It is also important to note that personal growth and development is a life-long process. We don't suddenly arrive at a certain point and then relax and quit. Rather, we are on a never-ending journey, with each day offering new experiences, contacts with new people, and new opportunities for personal enrichment.

Therefore, personal growth, as well as meaningfull relationships, does not just happen. We must be aware of the dynamics involved in acquiring the awareness and skills necessary to develop and expand our lives. We then must be willing to take some risks to incorporate what we have learned into *our own unique personalities*. It is to this end that we, the authors, commit the contents of this book.

ORGANIZATION OF BECOMING AWARE

Using the above characteristics of healthy, happy, and more fully functioning individuals as a model for this book, we have attempted to include concepts which we hope will assist you in becoming the person you want to be. We have chosen to explain a brief overview of the book by asking you some thought-provoking questions.

Chapter 1:   Am I an Open or Closed Person?

In order for growth to take place and for effective relationships to be established, you must be willing to share your thoughts, feelings, and values with others. You must be open with what you love, hate, feel, desire, and what you are committed to. If you are feeling lonely in spite of being surrounded by people, it may be possible that you are keeping your *real* self hidden from others. Are you ready to take some risks and explore some avenues for learning to be more open and honest about yourself?

If you have the desire to form special, close relationships with others, the prerequisite is knowing, accepting, and appreciating yourself.

Chapter 2:   Who Am I?

Obviously, all growth begins with self-acceptance. The more we approve and accept ourselves, the less concerned we are whether others will approve and accept us. We are then able to be ourselves with confidence. In order to connect with others, we must have a clear sense of who we are, what we want, our strengths and weaknesses, likes and dislikes, our values and priorities in life. A strong identity is part of the foundation of intimate relationships. Are you ready to take the risks necessary to discover **Who Am I?**

After you have developed a personal identity and a deeper appreciation for yourself, you are then more equipped to exercise control over your life.

Chapter 3:   Am I in Control of My Life?

Fortunately, life is filled with both the freedom and the opportunity to make choices. Some people feel that they are in control of their own destinies. They believe that what happens to them and what they achieve in life are due to their own abilities, attitudes, and actions. These people are happier, more fully functioning people. However, some people see their lives as being beyond their control. They believe that what happens to them is due to fate, luck, or even other people. Consequently, such people never really actualize their potential. Are you ready to take the risk in learning to accept the responsibility for shaping your own destiny?

Not only do happier and healthier people have control over their behavior and what they become, they also have control over what they "do with their emotions."

Chapter 4:   How Do I Express My Emotions?

As we go through adulthood, we have the opportunity to experiment with a full range of behaviors and a full range of emotions. Emotional health includes experiencing the full spectrum of human feelings from love and excitement to anger and despair. The ability to express feelings rather than squelching them is also important. Stored-up hurt, fear, or anger may result in emotional numbness, shutting off positive as well as negative feelings. Are you ready to take some risks in learning how to achieve a balance between emotional expression and control?

The full and free experience and expression of all our feelings is necessary for personal peace and meaningful relationships. Happy, healthy people realize the tremendous benefits of being able to communicate what they are feeling.

Chapter 5:   How Well Do I Communicate?

A significant part of the entire growth process is learning effective communication skills. In fact, communication is extremely important in almost every aspect of our lives. We need to become aware of the conditions that are interfering with the communication process and make an attempt to modify our behavior in such a way that real meaning and understanding are communicated. This can lead to establishing and maintaining more satisfying relationships with others, which is the basic goal of communication. Are you ready to take the risk of learning how to communicate more effectively?

It is through communication that we begin the process of becoming acquainted with others. It is also through communication that special relationships are formed.

Chapter 6:   What is the Role of Love in My Life?

As we begin to openly and honestly share ourselves with others, we find that others will begin to share themselves with us. This will be the beginning of beautiful friendships and intimate relationships. There is an inescapable law built into human nature that reads: We are never less than individuals but we are never merely individuals. No man is an island. Fully functioning people have learned to move the focus of their attention and concern from themselves to others. They care deeply about others. Are you ready to take the risks of learning how to "move out of yourself" into genuine love relationships?

As we develop special relationships and learn to deal with our emotions, we will inevitably experience some interpersonal conflicts.

Chapter 7: How Can I Solve My People Problems?

There is really no end to the numbers and kinds of disagreements possible since people are different, think differently, and have different needs and wants that sometimes do not match. Likewise, there are a wide range of feelings and emotions that accompany the conflict. However, *how* you resolve your interpersonal conflicts is the single most important factor in determining whether your relationships will be healthy or unhealthy, mutually satisfying or unsatisfying, friendly or unfriendly, deep or shallow, intimate or cold. Are you ready to take some risks in learning how to approach your interpersonal conflicts differently—do you realize that there doesn't have to be a winner and a loser?

Sometimes interpersonal conflicts, as well as some of the adjustments we have to make in life, become difficult situations for us to deal with.

Chapter 8: How Am I Coping with the Stress in My Life?

A fact of life experienced by everyone, at one time or another, is that of stress. There are potentially negative and positive effects that can result from stress. Therefore, it is extremely important, not only that we recognize stress, but that we learn how to handle it, live with it and make it work for us. Frequently, our stress is created by our own thoughts and feelings. You will recall from our earlier discussion that one of the characteristics of fully functioning people is that they accept reality for what it is, rather than what it "ought to be." Are you ready to take some risks in learning to identify your stressors, as well as finding the level of stress at which you are most comfortable?

When you have learned how to manage the stress in your life, you are then free to prioritize your values and develop a lifestyle with meaning.

Chapter 9: What Is Important to Me?

A well-defined value system is basic to personal motivation, self-determination, and a lifestyle with meaning. Fully alive people are committed to a cause in which they can believe and to which they can be dedicated. Their value system is the control point of their life, helping them to choose their direction in life. When we can control the direction of our life, rather than allowing it to be controlled by forces and values outside ourselves, a feeling of self-affirmation is created. Are you ready to risk clarifying your values, and in return, finding meaning and a sense of mission to which you can direct your life?

You are now ready to deal with where you want to go with your life.

Chapter 10: Where Do I Want to Go with My Life?

As we experience growth and depth in our personal life and in our relationships, we begin to plan where we want to go with our life. Effective life planning begins with an answer to these questions: What are my needs? What are my wants? What are my priorities? Once we have arrived at the answer, a well-defined, implemented course of action is essential—keeping in mind that life is a process and we must remain open to change as we move through our daily experiences. Are you ready to risk getting in touch with your needs and wants and begin exploring ways in which you can meet them?

A LAST THOUGHT

If you are going to become a happier, healthier, and more fully functioning individual, you'll have to take risks. There is simply no way you can grow without taking chances. Because your personal growth and development are important to us, we have created personalized activities in each chapter for the sole purpose of encouraging you to begin taking risks. As you read each chapter, we encourage you to *think* about how the different concepts presented relate to you in your search to become a healthier, happier, and more fully functioning individual. Then, we ask you to reflect on what you have learned in your personal Learning Journal. Our desire is that you will risk and grow in your understanding of self and how you relate with others.

We hope to motivate you with these words from an anonymous author:

RISKS

To laugh is to risk appearing the fool.
To weep is to risk appearing sentimental.
To reach out for another is to risk involvement.
To expose feelings is to risk exposing your true self.
To place your ideas, your dreams, before a crowd is to risk their loss.

To love is to risk not being loved in return.
To live is to risk dying.
To hope is to risk failure.
But risks must be taken,
because the greatest hazard
in life is to risk nothing.

The person who risks nothing, does nothing, has nothing, and is nothing.
They may avoid suffering and sorrow,
but they cannot learn, feel,
change, grow, love, live.
Chained by their attitudes, they are a slave;
They have forfeited their freedom.
Only a person who risks is free.

Anonymous

It is now time to begin your journey to a happier, healthier, and more fully functioning individual.
Are you ready to become free to be the person you want to be?

Ten Commandments of Human Relations

1. **SPEAK TO PEOPLE.**   There is nothing so nice as a cheerful word of greeting.
2. **SMILE AT PEOPLE.**   It takes 72 muscles to frown, only 14 to smile.
3. **CALL PEOPLE BY NAME.**   The sweetest music to anyone's ears is the sound of his own name.
4. **BE FRIENDLY AND HELPFUL.**   If you would have friends, be a friend.
5. **BE CORDIAL.**   Speak and act as if everything you do is a genuine pleasure.
6. **BE GENUINELY INTERESTED IN PEOPLE.**   You can like almost everybody if you try.
7. **BE GENEROUS** with praise—cautious with criticism.
8. **BE CONSIDERATE** with the feelings of others. There are usually three sides to a controversy; Yours, the other fellow's, and the right side.
9. **BE ALERT** to give service. What counts most in life is what we do for others.
10. **ADD TO THIS** a good sense of humor, a big dose of patience and a dash of humility, and you will be rewarded many-fold.

Anonymous

1

Getting Acquainted With Ourselves and Others

ME—A QUESTION

Am I afraid to be me?
Why?
Why am I afraid to be
the only thing I can be?
Am I afraid that if I am me,
if I find out who me is
I will be disappointed?
Am I afraid that the
person I think is me is
someone else?
Why?
Why don't I know who the
real me is?
Why?
Why have I tried
to fool so many people that
I have fooled myself?
Who?
Who is me? I am me.
How?
How will I find me? By looking.
When?
When will I find me? Now.
Why?
Why must I find me? To be free.

Dorothy Dickson
(Written in 1968, at the age of 9. Dorothy completed
her Ph. D. in Clinical Psychology in 1992).
*Used with permission of Dorothy Dickson Rishel, Gulfport, MS.

What would you do without friends? What would it be like?
Where would you go? Would you have fun? Would you know what love is? Would life have any meaning?
Have you ever had a close friend or relative die? How did you feel when it happened?
Have you ever experienced, or had close friends or relatives experience, a divorce? Did they feel lonely? Were they depressed? What did they experience?
How did you feel when your best friend or lover returned after being gone for a long period of time? Overjoyed? Excited?

It's obvious that personal relationships and friendships are important to us. We need merely to reflect for a moment on the source of our greatest pleasure and pain to appreciate that nothing else in our life has aroused the extremes of emotion than the relationships that we have experienced with other human beings.

How would you answer the following question? What is it that makes your life meaningful? Research has shown us that most people answer this question by saying, "personal relationships." Argyle (1987) confirms this and notes that, by contrast, money, career, and religion are relatively less important for people than are their personal relationships.

Because relationships are so important in our lives, why do many of us find it so difficult to *get acquainted* with other people? Psychologists have found that a person must gain an understanding of himself or herself before they can become acquainted with others. Let's discover some ways to find the person within yourself.

SELF-DISCOVERY

To become acquainted, to get to know another person, requires a shared giving and taking regarding what we know about ourselves. We also need to know how we are reacting to the present situation and how we feel about something the other person has done or said.

Accept me as I am, only then will we discover each other.

Frederico Fellini

Getting to know other people is important, but getting to know yourself is more important. It's not until you can understand yourself that you can understand others. It's not until you can learn to accept yourself for who you are that you can accept others for being the person they are. How can I do this? I've heard these words so many times. It seems kind of crazy, because I've also heard that in order to understand myself I need feedback from others. If I don't get feedback from others, I don't know if I'm a good person or a jerk. Sidney Jourard (1971) states "that a maladjusted person is a person who has not made himself or herself known to another human being and thus, does not know or understand themselves." We need relationships in order to discover who we are, but we need to understand ourselves first in order for our relationships to grow from acquaintances, to friendships, and ultimately to intimate relationships (this topic will be discussed in-depth in the chapter Becoming Intimate). In order to become a healthy and happy person, an individual needs to form close, caring, inter-personal relationships. How do we learn to do this?

There are some basic questions concerning self-discovery and getting acquainted with others that you can ask yourself. "How well do I know myself? Is it easy for other people to get to know me? How well do other people really know me? How much of myself do I reveal to those with whom I want to have a close, personal relationship? How much do I want them to know about me regarding my innermost thoughts, feelings, and actions?" You also have to ask yourself, "How interested am I in learning the innermost thoughts, feelings, and ac-tions of those with whom I desire to have a close relationship?" As you read on, you will discover the importance of revealing the "real you" to other people.

SELF-DISCLOSURE

The revealing of the inner self is called self-disclosure—this means talking to another person about your innermost thoughts and feelings, your aspirations and dreams, your fears and doubts. It's talking about things you're ashamed of and proud of. Self-disclosure is a critical part of relationship building.

The evolution of a relationship, getting acquainted, becoming friends, and developing intimacy is based on how much you are willing to disclose about yourself and how much the other person is willing to disclose about themself to you. The more you know about another person and the more he or she knows about you, the more effective and efficient the relationship will be. People who share their ideas, interests, experiences, expectations, and feelings with others generally will have more friends and develop long lasting relationships easier than those who do not (Cozby, 1973). A lack of self-disclosure will make people suspicious and uncomfortable around us. In turn, they will not talk about themselves and finding common interests on which to base a relationship becomes difficult.

Good self-disclosure skills are fundamental to relationships for many reasons (Nelson & Jones, 1990). These reasons include the fol-lowing.

If I tell you who I am, you may not like who I am, and it's all that I have.

John Powell

Defining Yourself. Disclosing personal information lets you be known to others. If you do not define yourself, misunderstandings are more likely to occur. Others may perceive you based on their own interpretation rather than on information you give them.

Knowing Yourself. As you disclose information about yourself, you can get deeper insights and understandings about the kind of person you are. You also give others the opportunity to give you feedback.

Getting Acquainted. Talking about yourself and letting other people talk about themselves gives each of you the opportunity to understand and know the other as an individual. Each is given the opportunity to understand and trust the other.

Developing Intimacy. As you begin to share and receive, a deeper feeling of trust and understanding will evolve and a mutual feeling of closeness will develop.

Sidney Jourard (1964) has investigated the process of self-disclosure in detail. In THE TRANSPARENT SELF, he writes:

You cannot collaborate with another person towards some common end unless you know him. How can you know him, and he you, unless you have engaged in enough mutual disclosure of self to be able to anticipate how he will react and what part he will play? Self-disclosure, my communication of my private world to you, in language, which you clearly understand is truly an important bit of behavior for us to learn something about. You can know me truly only if I let you, only if I want you to know me. Your misunderstanding of me is only partly your fault. If I want you to know me, I shall find means of communicating myself to you. If you want me to reveal myself, just demonstrate your goodwill—your will to employ your power for my good and not for my destruction.

If I expose my nakedness as a person to you, do not make me feel shamed.

John Powell

Before we can engage in *self-disclosure,* there must be an atmosphere of goodwill and trust. An individual is not likely to engage in much *self-disclosure* if the situation involves too much personal threat, or even threat to anyone with whom he or she is closely associated. Jourard feels that it sometimes takes a form of self-disclosure to stimulate goodwill in other people. For example, a little *self-disclosure* establishes your goodwill, which encourages the other person to some *self-disclosure,* thus establishing his or her goodwill, which reassures you about further *self-disclosure,* and so on.

Self-disclosure usually involves the sharing of private information, and it is generally of such a nature that it is not something you would normally disclose to everyone who might inquire about it. Therefore, you are not expected to bare the innermost secrets of your soul to casual acquaintances; you can save that information for the *significant others* in your life. However, if you are to communicate effectively with others, some degree of *self-disclosure* is required:

What Kind of Things Can You Reveal to Another Person? A few examples might be:

- Likes and dislikes
- Fears and anxieties
- Feelings and reactions about something another person has said or done
- Attitudes and opinions
- Tastes and interests
- Ideas about money
- Work perceptions
- Personality choices
- Feelings and reactions about events that have just taken place
- Perceptions of self and others

There are some disadvantages to self-disclosure, particularly if there is too much of it (Wortman, 1976). Talking too much about ourselves early in a relationship may not facilitate the development of friendship. People might attribute your high self-disclosure as an indication that you are too immature, insecure, phoney, or that you tell everyone such things. Other people like to think that they are special to you.

Self-disclosure involves taking risks. The greatest risk is one of rejection—not being liked or accepted. This may cause us to hide behind a mask, a facade, and try to be something we know we are not. In this state, effective communication cannot occur, and the growth and maintainance of those deep, special, and meaningful relationships with friends and spouses cannot occur. Risk nothing, gain nothing. You have a choice: to withdraw from honest encounters, to hide your feelings, to falsify your intentions—or to be transparent, open, and real through *self-disclosure.*

Two Advantages of Self-Disclosure. One advantage is that *self-disclosure improves relationships.* We prefer to be with people who are willing to disclose to us and we are more willing to be open with them. Self-disclosure is a reciprocal process. Disclosure leads to trust and trust leads to more disclosure; thus, the relationship will grow and develop into a mature and long lasting, loving interaction. There is a strong positive correlation between self-disclosure and marital satisfaction (Miller and Lefcourt, 1982). Research has shown that the more a couple is willing to disclose about themselves, the greater the marital satisfaction and the greater the chance the marriage will last over a longer period of time.

Before you go on, refer to Table 1.1.

Only in the part of us that we share, can we understand each other.

Anonymous

No one can develop freely in this world and find a full life without feeling understood by at least one person.

Paul Tournier

Table 1.1
Women Talk More Than Men

Research has shown that women disclose more than men (Cline, 1986). If you are a female, please do not be offended; this is a positive statement. It has been found that it is to a woman's benefit that she is more open and willing to disclose than a man. Women tend to have more friends and closer relationships than men. These friendships tend to provide her with more social support.

Within families, parents tend to disclose more to their daughters than to their sons (Daluiso, 1972). Because we learn through modeling, females would be more likely to be open and share their feelings with others. Males are socialized not to disclose and so build up more tension and anxiety in their daily lives and thus would be more likely to experience stress-related problems—ulcers, heart attacks, early death, and so on. Women tend to have fewer stress-related problems.

Males tend to disclose more to strangers than females do and are more willing to disclose superficial things about themselves, such as their work, accomplishments, attitudes, and opinions. Males are also less intimate and less personal than females. Males are expected not to disclose, it's not ''manly.'' Men are socialized to compete, and sharing private information can seem to be incompatible with winning (Lewis, 1978).

One finding is that both men and women generally prefer self-disclosure with members of the opposite sex (Rosenfeld, 1981). Women say to the men, ''let's talk.'' Men communicate to women by ''telling'' them what to do and giving directions. As many of you have discovered, this creates communication problems within many male-female relationships.

Men need to learn to talk more; it will improve their relationships with members of both sexes.

What does the baby chicken know which we overlook? The shell around us won't crack at its own accord.

Anonymous

The second advantage is that *self-disclosure promotes mental health.* Withholding important information can create stress and thus leads to less-effective functioning and even possible physical problems (Jourard, 1971). We all need a release and for many of us "talking-out" our feelings, problems and thoughts relieves us of the stresses and anxieties that are interfering with our everyday functioning. *This release of emotional tension through talking is known as a catharsis.* As many of you have discovered, you feel relieved after sharing your problems with another person. This is the reason counseling and therapy is so effective for many individuals.

We all need to discover new ways to communicate our feelings and thoughts to others. One way to illustrate how self-disclosure operates in communication is to look at Figure 1.1 (The Johari Window).

THE JOHARI WINDOW

The Johari Window (1969), developed by and named after psychologists Joseph Luft and Harry Ingram, can be looked upon as a communication window through which you become more aware of yourself and your potential as a communicator as you give and receive information about yourself and others. In order for a relationship to develop into a quality relationship, there needs to be trust and mutual sharing of information and feelings, also known as *openness*. An *open* communicator is one who is willing to seek feedback from others and to offer information and personal feelings to others. Open communication involves both giving and receiving. According to the Window, a person's communication behavior can be viewed by looking at the size of each of the four windowpanes—Open, Hidden, Blind, and Unknown. These four quadrants, illustrated in Figure 1.1, represent the whole person in relation to others.

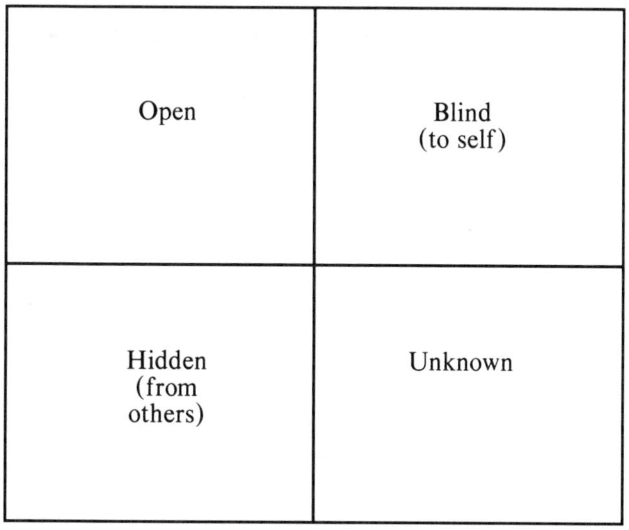

Open	Blind (to self)
Hidden (from others)	Unknown

Figure 1.1. Adapted from Joseph Luft, OF HUMAN INTERACTION, by permission of Mayfield Publishing Co., Copyright 1969 by the National Press.

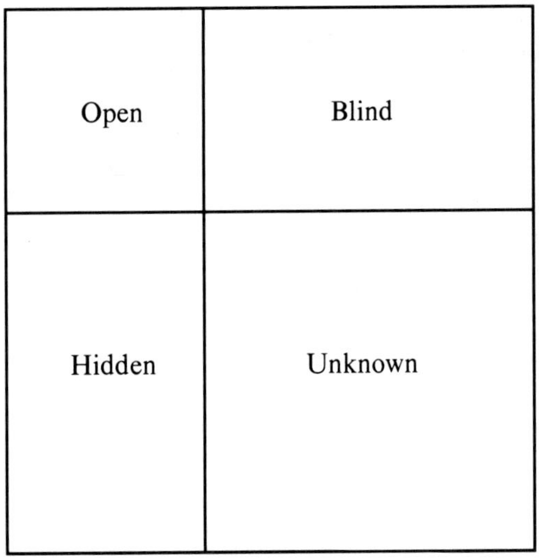

Figure 1.2.

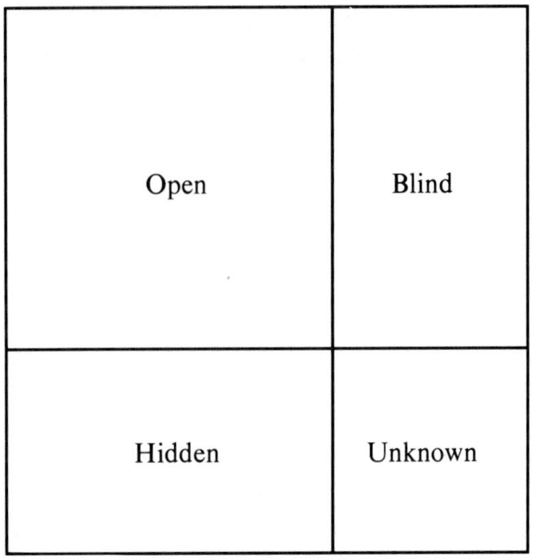

Figure 1.3.

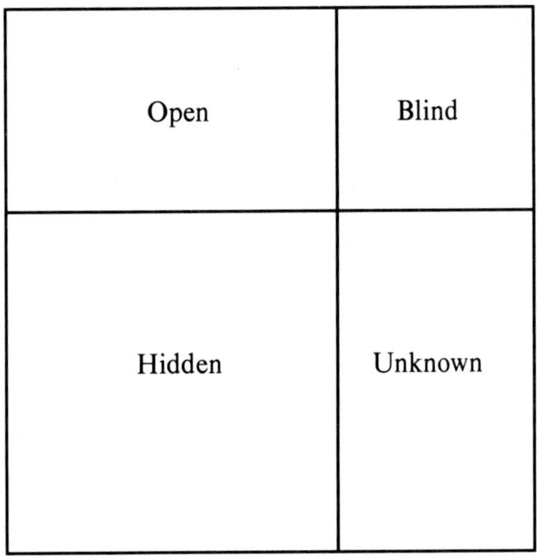

Figure 1.4.

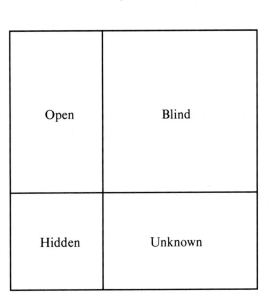

Figure 1.5.

The *Open area represents information, feelings, and opinions that you know about yourself and that others know about you.* This area also includes feelings that others have about you, perhaps a mutual friend of yours and another person, of which you are aware. Communication in this open area is free and open.

The *Blind area represents information about you of which you are unaware but is easily apparent to others.* An example would be a mannerism in speech or gesture of which you are unaware but that is quite obvious to others, such as constantly saying, "You know" or constantly "playing with your keys." Communication in this area is not free and open.

The *Hidden area represents information and personal feelings that you keep hidden from others.* Consequently, communication in this area is restricted. The only way others can learn of this information is if you decide to participate in self-disclosure. This area is quite large with a new acquaintance because we do not feel safe in revealing our true selves and feelings.

The *Unknown area represents information about you that is unknown to self or others*. For example, you may have an aptitude or skill of which you and others are completely unaware. Communication in this area is impossible, since it is totally unknown. Information in this area may take years to be known. However, as you try to gain insight into your *real, true* self, you may be able to add to this area.

The size of each windowpane varies depending on your communication behavior and the quality of your relationship. When you first meet someone, the area of common knowledge is minimal. Likewise, your communication with that individual would be represented by a small open windowpane and a large unknown area. Also, if you find it difficult to share your ideas and feelings with others, as well as to receive feedback from others, you would tend to have a small open windowpane, as illustrated in Figure 1.2.

As a relationship grows and the trust level increases, you will be more likely to share more information and feelings. Consequently, others will respond by giving you more feedback. Therefore, your communication behavior should be represented by a much larger open windowpane and a smaller unknown pane. See Figure 1.3.

If you are receptive to feedback but are basically unwilling to share information and feelings with others, your communication behavior will be represented by a fairly large hidden pane and a smaller open pane, as illustrated in Figure 1.4.

On the other hand, you may find it very difficult to receive criticism or suggestions from others, but it may be easy for you to share information and feelings with others. Consequently, your communication behavior would be represented with a large blind pane, as illustrated in Figure 1.5.

As we can see, interpersonal communication of any significance is virtually impossible if the individuals involved have little or no open windowpane. So, ideally, we strive to make the open window the largest area, which would indicate the extent to which two or more persons can give and take, work together, and enjoy experiences together. By improving the use of feedback in our communication with others, we begin to expand our open windowpane.

Some people may get along fine with others without insight or awareness. However, such lack of awareness inhibits our communication effectiveness and thus impedes our personal growth.

Now that we understand the importance of *self-disclosure* in the development of a relationship, we need to understand why relationships are so important. We are all social beings and seek social relationships. We all have a need for other people. Relationships satisfy needs. We are motivated not only to seek the company of others, but to form close and lasting relationships. Many people have difficulty forming relationships and don't seem to have any friends. What happens to these people?

WILL YOU BE MY FRIEND?

Will you be my friend?
There are so many reasons why you never should:
I'm sometimes sullen, often shy, acutely sensitive,
My fear erupts as anger, I find it hard to give,
I talk about myself when I'm afraid

And often spend a day without anything to say.
   But I will make you laugh
   And love you quite a bit
   And hold you when you're sad
I cry a little almost every day
Because I'm more caring than the strangers ever know,
And if at times, I show my tender side
(The soft and warmer part I hide)
   I wonder,
   will you be my friend?
A friend
   Who far beyond the feebleness of any vow or tie
   Will touch the secret place where I am really I,
   To know the pain of lips that plead and eyes that weep,
   Who will not run away when you find me in the street
   Alone and lying mangled by my quota of defeats
   But will stop and stay—to tell me of another day
   When I was beautiful.

Will you be my friend?
There are so many reasons why you never should:
Often I'm too serious, seldom predictably the same,
Sometimes cold and distant, probably I'll always change.
I bluster and brag, seek attention like a child,
I brood and pout, my anger can be wild,
   But I will make you laugh
   And love you quite a bit
   And be near when you're afraid.
I shake a little almost every day
Because I'm more frightened than the strangers ever know
And if at times I show my trembling side
(The anxious, fearful part I hide)
   I wonder,
   Will you be my friend?
A friend
   Who when I fear your closeness, feels me push away
   And stubbornly will stay to share what's left on such a day,
   Who, when no one knows my name or calls me on the phone,
   When there's no concern for me—what I have or haven't done—
   And those I've helped and counted on have, oh so deftly, run,
   Who when there's nothing left but me, stripped of charm and
   subtlery,
   Will nonetheless remain.

Will you be my friend?
   For no reason that I know
   Except I want you so.

LONELINESS

The lack of relationships creates *loneliness*. *Loneliness occurs when a person has fewer interpersonal relationships than desired or when the relationships are not as satisfying as desired. Loneliness* is one of the most serious problems in our society today. Harry Stack Sullivan (1953) considered loneliness to be the worst emotional experience imaginable. He stated that the deepest problem of people is loneliness, isolation, and difficulty with self-esteem. Research has shown that loneliness leads to depression and depression can cause psychological and physiological problems.

Most of you have observed many of your friends and relatives going through some form of transition in their life—the breaking up of a long-term relationship or marriage, death of a loved one, and so on, that has caused them to be in a state of need. Most of us, at one time or another in our life have also experienced this feeling, that something is lacking in our life and there doesn't seem to be anything to live for. What is this feeling? It is the feeling of loneliness. *Loneliness is a feeling of longing and emptiness, that is caused by the lack of emotional attachment and/or social ties.*

Being lonely is not the same as being alone. Many of us have a need to be alone at times in order to maintain our mental health. Some people can feel lonely even when surrounded by others. Some people prefer solitude and are content with fewer social interactions. *Loneliness* is a highly subjective and personal feeling.

Loneliness is most prevalent among teenagers, unmarried young adults, the divorced, and the widowed. Research has shown that loneliness leads to depression and depression leads to many psychological and physiological problems. *Loneliness* makes a person vulnerable to many different situations. This may include the use of drugs or alcohol, suicide, sexual promiscuity, mental illness, and negative relationships.

Loneliness is something that will affect most of us at one time or another in our life. What can we do to help ourselves and others to prevent this feeling of loneliness from taking over our lives? Robert Weiss (1974) has found that the satisfying of *two relationship needs* will help us overcome the feeling *of loneliness;* (1) *the need for emotional attachments*; and (2) *the need for social ties.* If one or both of these needs are not satisfied, loneliness will exist. What are these needs and why do we really need relationships?

WHAT SHOULD A RELATIONSHIP PROVIDE?

Why does our society and many other cultures put so much emphasis on marriage? Why are there clubs for single people; escort services; single's bars; dating services; and, more recently, people advertising for partners in local newspapers and 1-900 telephone services to meet new people? Because people are lonely. We have a strong need for relationships. The following needs must be satisfied in order to have a fulfilling life and overcome the feeling of loneliness.

Happiness may be had only by helping others to find it.

Napolean Hill

People are lonely because they build walls instead of bridges.

Joseph Newton

Emotional Attachments. *We all need to know that no matter what the situation is, or whatever we do, good or bad (for better or worse, in sickness or in health), that there will be someone around to take care of us or help us out.* As long as we know this, we feel comfortable and secure. A child who knows that mother or father is available whenever he or she needs one of them will feel secure enough to explore the world. This child will be willing to take some chances and risks in life. A child that is insecure and not sure whether the parents will be available when needed will be clinging and unsure of other people. How would you feel if you were told by your parents, "If you ever get in trouble with the law," or "If I ever hear about you taking drugs," or "If you ever get someone pregnant or get pregnant, don't step a foot back in this house?" Most people who have been told this when they were young feel insecure and very lonely, because they are not sure anyone will be there in a time of need.

Most people will receive their *emotional attachment* from their parents, especially during their early years of development. And if you think about it, many individuals continue to rely on their parents for this support for most of their lives. This is why in some married couples who are having marital problems, the husband or wife goes back to the parents' home: The parents still provide the individual with the feeling of security. As we tend to mature, start to "cut the apron strings," and become more independent, we begin to find this emotional support from others—our best friend, boyfriend, girlfriend, spouse, pastor, and so on. For some people their dog or cat will provide them with this feeling of security, especially if the pet is the only being they have ever been able to rely on. Is this the reason for the following saying, *a dog is man's best friend?*

Inanimate objects, such as teddy bears, dolls, imaginary companions; certain belief systems, such as religious beliefs or philosophies of life; or confidence within one's self may also satisfy the need for *emotional attachments* for some people. A young child's blanket or teddy bear is security for some. As you know, if you take the blanket or bear away for a short time, just to be washed, the child can go into a rage and become very insecure and lonely.

What happens to a person who has been relying, solely, on his or her spouse for the satisfaction of this need, especially when the spouse announces that the relationship is over? This person will become insecure, lonely, and vulnerable. A newly divorced or separated individual who has lost his or her emotional support is very open and vulnerable to another person or belief system that tends to show the individual this support. This is why many individuals end up in a negative relationship or some type of cult or gang that purports to provide emotional support.

Teenagers are another group of people who are very vulnerable. Teenagers are attempting to become independent and no longer want to rely on their parents for emotional support. They seek satisfaction of this need through other means—peer group, boyfriend or girl-friend, drugs, religion, cults, gangs, and so on. They will continue to seek emotional support until it is satisfied. Most individuals will satisfy this through positive means, but others may end up in negative situations, such as membership in a gang or cult, use of drugs, and so on.

As you can see, the satisfaction of the *emotional attachment* need is vital in order to overcome loneliness. We have also discovered another need that must be satisfied in order for us to overcome the feeling that something is missing in our life. What is it?

Social Ties. *Social ties provide us with the feeling of belonging, a feeling that we are part of a group and have an identity.* During early childhood this feeling of belonging and developing an identity is, for most children, provided by their parents—"I'm a member of the Smith family or Walker family or Sanchez family." Later in childhood the peer group becomes more important to children than the family, especially during adolescence. Special groups, clubs, teams, and religious organizations such as Boy Scouts, Bluebirds, Indian Guides, little league, church youth groups, pep clubs, gangs, and fraternal organizations provide many young people with the feeling of identity. Have you ever observed children walking down the street in their scout uniforms or team uniforms? They really think they are "special," These uniforms make them feel like they are part of a group and they have an *identity*. We all need an *identity*.

How does the person feel who is not able to join a club or be a member of a team? This person feels left out and that there is something missing in life. This person will do whatever it takes to satisfy this need. The end result of not having this need satisfied is the same as for those whose *emotional attachment* needs are not satisfied. This person will feel lonely, depressed, and vulnerable.

Social ties may be satisfied through positive as well as negative means. Social ties may be satisfied through marriage—a legal bonding that makes you feel like you belong to another person and have a recognized identity. A person's job or career may give some people a feeling of identity or belonging. Ask a person the question, "Who are you?" and the response is generally, "I'm a student, a banker, a plumber, a salesperson, an attorney." The title gives the individual an identity and the organization the person works for gives the person a feeling of belonging.

During the high school and college years, a person's identity may be found in many different ways. Some students find their identity by being on an athletic team, being an excellent student, playing in a band or orchestra, dating a cheerleader, or being in a sorority or fraternity. If a student does not find his or her identity or feeling of belonging through "normal" or acceptable means, he or she will attempt to satisfy this need through other means, such as drugs, bizarre clothing, a unique hairstyle, promiscuous behavior, gang activity, or delinquent behavior.

It is difficult to give attention to yourself and to others at the same time.

Dale Carnegie

A man who talks only of himself and thinks only of himself is hopelessly uneducated.

Murray Butler

Emotional support and *social ties* are not only important to young people but are vital to all of us and will be throughout our lives. We will be in a constant state of stress and anxiety if our emotional support and social ties change too much. Divorce, death of a loved one, changing jobs or being fired from a job, retirement, breaking up with a boyfriend or girlfriend, or a serious illness may cause our needs to change.

Having enjoyed the friendship of many people in many places for many years—I have learned that, in the main, people are as we choose to find them.

Doris Schary

How Do You Satisfy These Needs? Where do you get emotional support? Who or what provides you with an identity or feeling of belonging? Most of you have heard the stories about couples who have been married for many years when suddenly one of the two dies, and within a few hours or days the other one dies. A similar situation is when a long-term employee retires from a firm and within a year passes away. What has happened in both of these situations? For some individuals their spouse becomes their sole emotional support and identity, and when their needs are no longer being satisfied they become *lost*. The person becomes lonely, insecure, and depressed and says, "What's there to live for?" and just *gives up*. In the retirement situation, the same thing happens; the job becomes the individual's security and identity, and all of a sudden when the individual retires, both needs are lost, and then the person *gives up psychologically and physiologically*.

These examples should demonstrate to all of us that we *should not* rely only on one person or one source for the satisfaction of these needs. We all need to work at developing a good support system. We also need to make sure our loved ones, including children, parents, spouses and friends, have a good support system that satisfies all of their needs.

Now that we understand the need for relationships, many of us still find it difficult to get to know other people and develop good relationships. Why do we fear getting acquainted?

THE FEAR OF GETTING ACQUAINTED

Meeting people and forming relationships should be fun, but for a lot of people it's a difficult process, full of stress and anxiety. "It seems so easy for other people, but for me, it's one of the most difficult things I do in life." Because of the complexity of our society we have made the process of getting acquainted and developing relationships an involved process. "How can I make meeting people and forming relationship more fun and less stressful"? Why do I feel so uncomfortable meeting people?

How Do You Feel in the Following Situations?

Meeting people for the first time.
Asking someone for a date.
Giving a talk in front of a group of people.
Going to a party.
Asking someone for help—for example, from your boss or
  professor.
Being interviewed.
Situations requiring assertiveness—for example, asking for your
  money back.
Participating in a discussion group.
Showing your body in a nonsexual context.
Going to a dance or nightclub.

Am I Shy? How did you answer the questions just listed? If your answer to any of the questions is that you feel uncomfortable, anxious, inhibited, or cautious, you showed signs of shyness. Don't feel bad: *Shyness* is *universal.* It affects the young and the old, men and women, celebrities and people like you and me. It is a very common problem. A study by Phillip Zimbardo (1977, 1987) indicates that 40 percent of the respondents were currently troubled by shyness and that 80 percent had reported being shy during some stage in their lives. Most shy people reported that they do not like being shy. Shy people find it difficult making friends and they tend to be sexually inhibited. They tend to be lonelier and more depressed than others. *Loneliness* and *shyness* are closely related. Shyness leads to loneliness and loneliness leads to shyness.

What Is Shyness? Shyness involves *feelings, physical reactions,* and *thoughts,* that create a state of anxiety, discomfort and inhibition. Let's discuss each one.

- *Feelings.* Feelings associated with shyness include anxiety, insecurity, stress, loneliness, mistrust, embarrassment, tension, fear, confusion, and so on.
- *Physical reactions.* Physical reactions associated with shyness include nausea, butterflies in the stomach, shaking, perspiring, pounding heart, feeling faint, blushing, and so on.
- *Thoughts.* Thoughts associated with shyness include: "I'm not an interesting person," "I'm not as good as they are," "They won't like me," "I lack self-confidence," "I don't have the social skills," and so on.

Consequences of Shyness. For some people, shyness may become a "mental handicap" that is as crippling as the most severe of physical handicaps. Its consequences can be devastating. What are the consequences of shyness? (Zimbardo, 1978)

1. *Shy people become preoccupied with themselves and thus self-conscious.* Because of this, they are not aware of other people's feelings and needs. For example, if such people have a facial blemish or their hair is not "just right," they know everybody will notice so they won't go to school or to a party.
2. *Shyness makes it difficult for us to become acquainted with new people and thus make new friends.* At a party these people would not introduce themselves to others but would say to themselves, "Nobody is interested in me; I must be a boring person. Nobody would want to get to know me anyway."
3. *Shyness keeps us from experiencing new situations.* A new experience is a risk that may result in failure, so it seems easier not to take the chance.
4. *Shyness prevents people from standing up for their own rights and thus keeps them, as individuals, from expressing their own feelings and beliefs.* If other people don't know how you feel and what you want, how do you expect them to make decisions that will benefit you?
5. *Shy people tend not to demonstrate their personal strengths and capabilities and thus prevent others from making positive evaluations.* If you have two employees, equal in all abilities except that one is shy and the other is not shy, which of the two would you promote? In most situations the nonshy person would be promoted since we are more aware of his or her potential than that of the shy person.

As you have observed, shyness can have some very negative effects on us.

What Is the Difference Between a Shy and Nonshy Person? It may come as a surprise to many of you that the major difference between the two individuals is just a matter of *self-evaluation.* How do you compare yourself to others? Do you see yourself as capable, as intelligent, or as attractive as the person next to you? If the answer is no, would you interact with them? Or, if you did have to interact with them, how would you feel? Would you feel inferior or inadequate? Most people would feel this way. Why? As we stated earlier, *shyness is a matter of self-evaluation*—how you compare yourself with others. Actually this should tell you how ridiculous shyness really is, because we are all capable human beings. Just because the other person is a doctor, lawyer, teacher, or engineer doesn't make that person superior to you. The other person may have more formal education than you or more money than you, but you may have more common sense or *real-life* education. You are just as good as the other person.

What Causes Shyness? Competition seems to create shyness. We live in a very competitive society and because of that have a high incidence

Mutual confidence is the foundation of all satisfactory human relationships.

Napolean Hill

of shyness as compared to other cultures. Beginning at birth people start comparing us: "Why don't you act like your sister?" or "Why don't you get good grades like your brother?" Because other people compare us with others, we begin to compare ourselves with others and what do we discover? There is always someone who we perceive that is better than us. Thus, we begin to feel inferior and then begin to act inferior. Consequently, *shyness* is created. Once we begin to see ourselves as shy, we begin to act shy and now the *self-fulfilling prophecy* begins. We will see how the *self-fulfilling prophecy* influences us later in this chapter.

Overcoming Shyness. How can a person overcome shyness? It would be naive to pretend that shyness can be overcome easily. However, it is important to emphasize that shyness *can* be overcome successfully. There are three steps in the process of dealing with *shyness* (Zimbardo, 1987). (1) *Analyzing your shyness,* (2) *Building your self-esteem,* and (3) *Improving your social skills.*

Steps In Overcoming Shyness

Analyzing Your Shyness	Building Your Self-Esteem	Improving Your Social Skills
1. Try to pinpoint exactly what social situations tend to elicit your shy behavior. 2. Try to identify what causes your shyness in each situation. Use a diary or journal to keep track of the times you experience this feeling. 3. Have a friend or relative give you feedback. Discuss how you interact with others and how you can improve.	1. Recognize that you ultimately control how you see yourself. 2. Set your own standards. Don't let others tell you how to live your life. 3. Set realistic goals. Don't set your goals too high or too low. Many people demand too much of themselves. 4. Talk positive to yourself. Tell yourself that you can do it, that you are a good person, and so on.	1. Follow a role model. Select someone you respect and observe how they interact. Imitate their behavior. 2. Learn to listen. 3. Smile. 4. Reinforce yourself for each successful interaction. 5. Use your imagination. Rehearse in your mind new situations and how you will respond in each. 6. Practice with a friend-interviews, dating situations, and so on.

Overcoming shyness is an ongoing process. Many of the projects at the end of the chapter will help you in this process. The Self-Change Project in the Learning chapter could be used to help a person overcome shyness. If shyness is creating a problem in your life, we recommend that you consult a professional counselor at the local college or workplace who may be able to provide some new insights into helping you overcome shyness.

As we begin to reach out and meet new people in the process of overcoming shyness, we attempt to sift through the millions of people in the world to select the individuals that will eventually become our friends and lovers. How do we do this? We begin the process of getting acquainted and finding friends through *people perception.*

Most of us feel that others will not tolerate emotional honesty in communication. We would rather defend our dishonesty on the grounds that it might hurt others; and having rationalized our phoniness into nobility, we settle for superficial relationships.

John Powell

PEOPLE PERCEPTION

Imagine yourself at a large party that you are attending alone. You look around and see nothing but unfamiliar faces. As you look at each individual, you immediately make a judgment of what you think each person is like. Your perception of each individual is based on many things, such as your past experience, your prejudices, and stereotyping. Because your past experiences, prejudices, and stereotypes are different from those of others, your perception of each individual will be different from other people's interpretation. You may perceive someone as serious and studious, whereas someone else may perceive the same individual as depressed and slow intellectually. Sometimes we discover that our perception is not always accurate. Some recent psychological studies indicate that our perception may be distorted at the time of perception, because we are using our own past experiences, prejudices, and stereotyping to make the interpretation.

As we encounter people each day, we form impressions or perceptions of them. The term *social perception describes the way we perceive, evaluate, categorize, and form judgments about the qualities of people we encounter.* These social perceptions have a critical influence on our interactions. In fact, they are more important in guiding our feelings, thoughts, and behaviors than the actual traits or attitudes of the people around us. The factors that seem to influence our *social perceptions* are *first impressions, stereotyping* and *prejudices.*

First Impressions. First impressions can have a tremendous influence on our perception of others. The initial impression we have of another person may have a strong impact on our future interactions with the person. If you go to a party and see someone that looks just like the boss who just fired you last week, what is your impression of that person? What's the likelihood of you approaching that person? You will most likely avoid that person even though he or she seems to be very friendly and not at all like your boss. The *primary effect* occurs when the *first impression* carries more weight than subsequent information. That first impression of the person that looks like your previous boss will be difficult to change even if you see the person in a new and different situation.

DON'T BE FOOLED BY ME

Don't be fooled by me.
Don't be fooled by the face I wear.
For I wear a thousand masks, masks that I'm afraid to take off, and none of them are me.
Pretending is an art that's second nature with me, but don't be fooled, for God's sake, don't be fooled.

I give the impression that I'm secure, that all is sunny and unruffled with me, within as well as without, that
    confidence is my name and coolness my game; that the water's calm and I'm in command, and that I need
    no one.
But don't believe me.
Please.

My surface may seem smooth, but my surface is my mask.
Beneath this lies no complacence.
Beneath dwells the real me in confusion, in fear, and aloneness,
But I hide this. I don't want anybody to know it.
I panic at the thought of my weakness and fear of being exposed.
That's why I frantically create a mask to hide behind, a nonchalant, sophisticated facade, to help me pretend,
    to shield me from the glance that knows.
But such a glance is precisely my salvation. My only salvation.
And I know it. That is if it's followed by acceptance, if it's followed by love. It's the only thing that will
assure
    me of what I can't assure myself, that I am worth something.

But I don't tell you this. I don't dare. I'm afraid to.
I'm afraid you'll think less of me, that you'll laugh at me, and your laugh would kill me.
I'm afraid that deep-down I'm nothing, that I'm no good, and that you will see this and reject me.
So I play my game, my desperate game, with a facade of assurance without, and a trembling child within.
And so begins the parade of masks. And my life becomes a front.

I idly chatter to you in the suave tones of surface talk. I tell you everything that is really nothing, and nothing
    of what's everything, of what's crying within me; so when I'm going through my routine do not be fooled
    by what I'm saying. Please listen carefully and try to hear what I'm not saying, what I'd like to be able to
    say, what for survival I need to say, but what I can't say.

I dislike hiding. Honestly!
I dislike the superficial game I'm playing, the phony game.
I'd really like to be genuine and spontaneous, and me, but you've got to help me. You've got to hold out your
    hand, even when that's the last thing I seem to want.
Only you can wipe away from my eyes the blank stare of breathing death.
Only you can call me into aliveness. Each time you're kind and gentle, and encouraging, each time you try to
    understand because you really care, my heart begins to grow wings, very small wings, very feeble wings,
    but wings. With your sensitivity and sympathy, and your power of understanding, you can breathe life into
    me. I want to know that.
I want you to know how important you are to me, how you can be the creator of the person that is me if you
    choose to.
Please choose to. You alone can break down the wall behind which I tremble, you alone can remove my mask.
    You alone can release me from my shadow-world of panic and uncertainty, from my lonely person.
Do not pass me by. Please . . . do not pass me by.

It will not be easy for you. A long conviction of worthlessness builds strong walls.
The nearer you approach me, the blinder I strike back.
I fight against the very thing I cry out for.
But I am told that love is stronger than walls, and in this lies my hope.
Please try to tear down those walls with firm hands, but with gentle hands, for a child is very sensitive.
Who am I, you may wonder. I am someone you know very well.
For I am every man you meet, and I am every woman you meet.

Author Unknown

Disclosing To Her Best Friend About The Date She Had Last Night

He was late for our first date. What an unreliable flake he must be.
What do you think?

Our *first impressions* are formed quite rapidly—within a matter of seconds (Berscheid & Graziano, 1979). Research indicates that negative first impressions are often quickly formed and hard to overcome. This is why they say "getting-off on the wrong foot" may be particularly damaging to a person. The opposite tends to be true of positive first impressions, which are often hard to earn but easily lost (Rothbart & Park, 1986). If the person you are going out with for the first time is late, what is your impression? Would you think that he or she is unreliable and must be a flake—*a negative first impression?* Many of you would feel this way and this impression would be difficult to change. If your new date is on time are you willing to say this person is reliable and conscientious? Most of us will take more time to make that judgment, even though the first impression was positive.

While you are walking down the street one day, you notice a person that you have never seen before. In your mind, you immediately form an impression of what you think this person is like. What had the greatest impact on the formation of your opinion? Was it the way the person was dressed, the hairstyle, size or shape, facial expression, or physical attractiveness? A recent survey indicated that women are most impressed by the way the man dresses, whereas men seem to be influenced most by the physical attractiveness of the women. Overall, we seem to be influenced more by *physical appearance* than anything else. This may be due to the fact that mass media puts too much emphasis on these factors and thus has a great influence on our perception of the world.

Other factors that seem to have an impact on our first impressions of others include what the individuals are doing (their *behavior*) at the time you perceive them and what the *interactional possibilities* are with that person (whether or not they would be a good date or tennis partner, or study partner, and so on). If you see someone acting weird at your first encounter, what kind of person do you think he or she is? What will you think of that person the next time? Most of us would continue to perceive the person as weird, because of what we observed them doing the first time we saw him or her. If you see someone you think that would be fun to date, will you approach the person. If you think the person sitting in the corner would help you study psychology, will you ask him or her to help you? If you perceive someone as "stuck-up," will you approach the person? Based on your first impression of these individuals you have already determined how you will respond or not respond to them. You are making your decision based on how you perceive the *interactional possibilities.*

When you go to a rock concert and look at all the different people attending, what other factors influence your perception of them? Are you making judgments about individuals without knowing anything about them because of the way they're dressed, or their hairstyle, or their race? Or, could it be that you have preconceived beliefs about people who attend rock concerts? Are you prejudiced, or is it that you are stereotyping people? Prejudices and stereotyping have a great influence on our perception of others.

Prejudices. Our perception of other people may be influenced and distorted by our prejudices. *Prejudices* predispose us to behave in certain ways toward other people and groups. Prejudice is prejudgment of a person or group of people without having all known information and facts. Being prejudiced does not always have a negative meaning, it can be positive. You see someone dressed as a nurse. You automatically perceive that person as kind and generous, even though you do not know anything about the individual. It's too bad that most of us allow our prejudices to affect our interaction with others negatively.

Stereotyping. Many people think people with red hair have hot tempers, that all police officers are mean, that all Irish people drink a lot, that all Japanese are intelligent, that all Jewish people are rich. These are all *stereotypes*—preconceived, inaccurate, rigid beliefs about individuals or groups of people. The habit of stereotyping people is so common that almost any personal characteristic leads to the formation of stereotypes. For example, what are your feelings about overweight people, people who wear glasses, short people, black people, women, or homosexuals?

Did you know that tall people are more apt to get hired first and get paid more than short people? Did you know that attractive students tend to get better grades than less attractive students? Are you aware that women are paid sixty-five percent of what men are paid for doing the same job? Is this because tall people are better qualified than short people, attractive students are more intelligent than the less attractive students, and women are not as good employees? No, it's because we have allowed our *prejudices* and *stereotyping* to influence our behavior. We must learn to overcome these influences and accept people as they are and not how we learned to perceive them. We must work together to reduce prejudices and break down the assumptions that one group is better than or inferior to others. We must work to develop positive interactions among all individuals no matter what size, shape, or color the person is.

As we continue the process of people perception, we discover that it is common for us to make many mistakes and errors in our perceptions of others (Buckhout, 1980). We have found that our prejudices and our stereotypes often lead to unfair treatment of others. Let's take a look at another characteristic that seems to have the greatest impact on our perception of others, without substantial evidence to support its accuracy.

Physical Attractiveness. Are you more likely to seek out an attractive person as a friend or someone who is perceived as less attractive? If you were an employer, would you be more likely to hire the most attractive applicant? Do you perceive physically attractive people to be more poised, likeable, sexy, competent, happy, interesting, and socially skilled than people of average or unattractive appearance? Many of you would answer no to these questions, but when it came time for you to act on these questions, it would be a different story. Research indicates that *physical attractiveness* has a profound influence on our impression of others and our interaction with them (Dion & Berscheid, 1974; Baron, 1986; Dion & Dion, 1987; Solomon, 1987).

In general, people tend to believe that what is beautiful is good (Dion, 1980). This stereotype seems to start early in life. When preschool children were asked to pick whom they liked best and who is the best behaved in their class, they selected for both categories those of their classmates whom adults judged to be the most attractive physically (Dion & Berscheid, 1972).

The only way to live happily with others is to overlook their faults and admire their virtues.

David Goodman

We have all been told *beauty is only skin deep; it's what's inside the person that counts.* A person's character and behavior are more important than looks. Most of us would probably agree that *physical attractiveness* should not be a major factor in *interpersonal attraction.* Then, why is physical beauty such a powerful influence in attracting us to others?

One reason is that we all want to be accepted and liked, and we perceive attractive people as being more friendly and liked more by others. Thus, if we hang around them more, we will also be perceived in the same way. People tend to see themselves as being more similar to attractive people than to unattractive people. Another reason is that since early in life we have been told that beautiful things are good and that ugly things are bad, so we have generalized that to include our perception of people. Finally, we discover that attractive people tend to receive more positive reinforcement than less attractive individuals and thus will be more likely to feel good about themselves. And, if they feel good about themselves, other people will perceive them as more positive and they will continue to receive more and more reinforcement.

What about dating? When you select a date, does physical attractiveness influence your selection? Research has shown that people desire to date the most attractive person possible. But when given the opportunity to choose a date, people tend to choose someone of attractiveness nearly equal to their own (Berscheid et al., 1971). We may desire the more attractive date, but we are afraid that they would reject us. In order to maintain a positive self concept, we are more likely to select someone we think would be more likely to say "yes." That person will most likely be someone who we perceive as equal to us in physical attractiveness. *The matching hypothesis proposes that people of similar levels of physical attractiveness gravitate toward each other.* There seems to be evidence to support this in regards to selecting friends, dating partners, and marriage partners. Look around, look at your friends and mates—are they similar to you?

Your best friend wants to get a date for you. Your friend asks you to list the three most important characteristics you would like that date to have. What are the three characteristics you would list? Most people would say, intelligence, friendliness, and sincerity are the most important qualities. But when you actually make your selection, you base your selection on physical appearance.

The more we become aware that characteristics like physical attractiveness influence our perception of one another, the less chance these characteristics will have of influencing our perception of others. Thank goodness that *beauty is in the eye of the beholder* and what is beautiful to one person is not considered beautiful to another person. This gives all of us a chance.

Perception is an interesting subject. The better we get to know someone, the more beautiful he or she becomes in our eyes. We often perceive the people we love as being beautiful, regardless of what anyone else may think.

Another important aspect of people perception is the judgment we make about why people behave as they do. Our responses to other people are strongly influenced by these judgments, and we are constantly attempting to understand the reasons for other people's behavior. This leads us to the *attribution process.*

The Attribution Process. Attributions allow us to make sense out of other people's actions, figure out their attitudes and personality traits, and ultimately gain some control over subsequent interactions with them through our increased ability to predict their behaviors.

Treasure life in yourself and you give it to others, give it to others and it will come back to you. For life, like love, cannot thrive inside its own threshold, but is renewed as it offers itself. Life grows as it is spent.

Ardis Whitman

What would you do and think in the following situation? Class is over and you are walking to your next class and you see your boyfriend or girlfriend on the other side of campus talking to a member of the opposite sex. Many of you would feel your emotions take control of your mind and body and react aggressively toward your partner and accuse him or her of flirting with the other person. Are you jealous? What would you say when your boyfriend or girlfriend finds you talking to a member of the opposite sex? It tends to be a different story when the shoe is on the other foot, doesn't it? Why? Attribution theory shows that we frequently overestimate the influence of a person's personality and underestimate the impact of the situation he or she is in. In the above situation, you attributed your girlfriend's or boyfriend's behavior to his or her personality, such as not being a trustworthy person. You forgot to consider the *situation* she was in. Remember, yesterday she was sick and missed her classes and she was talking to the other person in order to get the notes for class. Your response to this event was inappropriate because you didn't consider the situation your girlfriend was in. Have you ever done this? Hopefully you are secure enough in your relationship with your boyfriend or girlfriend that you would trust them talking to a person of the opposite sex.

If you observed people you don't know donating blood, what would you say about them? Most of us would say that they are kind, generous, considerate people. Do we really know what kind of people they are? If you see someone cheating on a test, what do you think? Is he or she a bad person? Do you know why the people were giving blood or the person was cheating, or did you make an inference based on personality? Perhaps the people giving blood were really being paid for donating. Does that make them kind, generous people? The person cheating was told by his parents that if he didn't earn an "A" in his psychology class they would no longer fund his college education, so he felt the pressure to get a good grade. That doesn't make cheating right but, you can now understand why he was cheating. If you found yourself in a similar situation where you were cheating, would you tell yourself that you were a bad, no good person for cheating, or would you justify your behavior based on the situation? Most of us attribute our own behavior to the situation and attribute other people's behavior to their personality. When we do this, we are in error in our perception of others and this misperception creates problems in our interaction with them.

While you observe other people in the future, think before you determine what type of person you are watching. You need to ask yourself, "Would I behave that way if I were in that situation?" Remember, put yourself in the other person's shoes before you form an opinion about another person.

Another variable has a powerful influence on our perception of others and our interaction with them: the power of expectations.

The Self-Fulfilling Prophecy. *We see what we want to see; we become what others expect of us.* This is the premise of the *self-fulfilling prophecy.* This is such a powerful force in life that it not only determines how you see yourself in the present but can actually influence your future behavior and that of others. A self-fulfilling prophecy occurs when a person's expectations of an event makes the outcome more likely to happen than would otherwise have been true. Self-fulfilling prophecies occur all the time, although you aren't always aware of them. For example,

- You hate math, but you register for a math class anyway, knowing that you will have difficulty learning the material. You end up dropping out because you're failing the course.
- You expect to become nervous and not do well in a job interview and later did so.
- Your boss assigns you a new task, saying that you will have difficulty completing it. You proved him right and didn't complete it.
- A father keeps telling his daughter that she is a brat. She proves him right and keeps causing problems.
- You anticipated having a good (or terrible) time at a social affair and your expectations came true.

Get on good terms with yourself and see how quickly others get on good terms with you.

Napolean Hill

In each of these cases, there is a good chance that the event happened because you expected it to happen. Rosenthal and Jacobson (1968) found that a teacher's expectations can have a tremendous affect on his or her students. A teacher was told that certain students had more intellectual potential than the other students in the class, although results of a test prior to the teacher's first day of class indicated that all the students started with about the same potential. The students who were recognized as having "high potential" by the teacher showed much greater achievement on a test a few months later than those recognized as "average" students—apparently as a result of the teacher's higher expectations.

Parents, as well as teachers, can convey their expectations in indirect and subtle ways. A frown could be interpreted as an indication that children are not liked or their performance is not acceptable. A pat on the back may indicate that they did a good job or their performance was good. These subtle and indirect messages are being interpreted constantly by the people around us. What kind of messages are you sending? Are they positive expectations or negative? Be careful, because the people around you may be interpreting your responses differently than you think you are sending. These prophecies that others are imposing on you subtly or directly contribute to your *self-concept.* A child is constantly being berated by his parents— "you're such a brat, you never do anything right, you're such a cry baby, you're so dumb, nobody will ever want to marry you." How will this child feel about himself or herself? What are the parents doing to this child's self-concept? If the child perceives himself or herself as a failure or as a brat or as a person nobody will want to marry, eventually the person will prove to be that kind of person.

Expectations are the basis of the self-fulfilling prophecy. We also find that expectations are the foundation of our success, but they can also be the basis of our failure. If we believe that we can succeed, we can do it. If we believe that we are incompetent and not capable, we will be a failure. Which do you want to become?

Can I change my image? Can I change how others perceive me? Can I change my expectations? It's not easy, but you can change. How can you do this? You are constantly projecting yourself to others as being a capable, good, bad, inferior, successful, dumb, happy, sad, depressed, superior person. Do you like the way others perceive you as a person? You can change your image through *impression management.*

Impression Management. There is a strong correlation between the self-fulfilling prophecy and *impression management.* If you project yourself as being a successful person, others will perceive you as being successful, and if they expect you to be successful you become more successful. *Impression management* refers to our conscious efforts to present ourselves in socially desirable ways.

Have you ever been interviewed for a job? How did you dress? Did you project yourself in a positive way? Did you relate to an interviewer differently than you do with your friends? Most of you would dress differently for the interview. You would make sure that you say the "right" things and respond positively to the interviewer. You are doing what we call *impression management.* You are attempting to portray yourself in a way you think the interviewer *expects* you to be. *Impression management* is necessary if we want people to like us, respect us, hire us, buy something from us, etc.

What kind of image do you project? How do others perceive you? Remember, if you don't like how others are perceiving you, you can change the image. You can change the way you dress, the way you act, your hairstyle, your posture—whatever it takes to change the image. You can do it.

As we begin to understand the process of people perception we are now ready to begin the process of getting acquainted. What are the stages in the development of a friendship? See Table 1.2.

Life is now in session. Are you present?

B. Copeland

A man without a smiling face must not open a shop.

Ancient Chinese Proverb

Table 1.2
Stages in the Development of a Friendship

1. *Awareness.* We become aware of each other in a social setting—first impressions. Without talking or letting other people know we are interested in them, we begin to evaluate them. What are the interactional possibilities? If we think there are possibilities, we are ready for the next step.
2. *Breaking the Ice.* This is a difficult step for most people. Talk about the weather, hobbies, school, new movies in town, politics, or other relatively superficial issues. As we begin to get to know each other, we begin to disclose more and more about ourselves. Disclosure leads to trust, trust leads to disclosure, and it all leads to discovering more about each other.
3. *Mutuality.* As the relationship evolves, we disclose more about our personal lives and begin to share hopes, dreams, and fears with each other. If we discover that we have some common interest and desires, the relationship will continue to develop (Levinger & Snoek, 1972).

Think of several people you have met recently. Did you go through these stages?

Unfortunately, it is not easy to meet or get acquainted with others. If we wait for others to initiate the encounter, we may become very lonely. It is up to you—and only you—to initiate the encounter and get the ball rolling in order for your friendships to grow and develop into a long-lasting relationship.

If we understand what steps are involved in initiating new relationships we will be more likely to begin to incorporate them into our everyday life. What are these steps?

Steps in Initiating New Relationships. Here are four steps you can take to initiate new relationships.

1. *Communication* underlies all relationships, but in order to communicate with others we must first make contact with them. Whatever the nature of the situation, an encounter usually begins with some communicative act that invites a response from another person. In order to do this, we must develop good communication skills. We find that the people who seem to have lots of friends, also seem to have good communication skills. These skills can be learned. Chapter 5 will help you learn these skills.

2. *Exposing yourself* may give you the opportunity to get acquainted with someone you would like to get to know. When we say *exposing yourself,* we don't mean by showing parts of your body. We mean allowing the people you want to get to know to see you more often. The more familiar you become with someone, the more apt you are to interact with that person. The first time you walk by a stranger, what do you do? Most of us would ignore the stranger. The next time you walk by the stranger you may smile. The next time you see one another you say, "Hi," and from then on, the more you encounter this person the more you begin to interact, and all of a sudden you are friends.

Student Story

One of my students came to my office one day for counseling. He said he was depressed and said that he didn't have any friends. He said that there was something missing in his life. I asked about his daily activities. He had an early morning class where he sat in the front corner seat. After class he went to the library to study, then on to his next two classes, where he sat in the front corner seat. Then he would go to his job and finally home. This was his daily routine. Was he giving himself the opportunity to meet new friends? No wonder he was lonely and depressed. We discussed some alternatives to his daily routine. What would you recommend?

Some alternatives would be for him to sit near other students, go to where the other students socialize between classes, and expose himself to other students.

It took some effort on his part as he slowly started to reach out to get acquainted with others. To his surprise, within one week, he began to make new friends.

If this student can change his behavior, so can you. How often have you heard about people marrying the person next door? You are constantly being *exposed* to that person. You see each other on a regular basis and without any real effort on your part, all of a sudden you are friends and begin dating. The more we see someone, the less we will be influenced by first impressions.

Where Did You Meet Your Friends? Was it school, church, near where you live, at your place of employment, the grocery store, at the athletic club? Research reveals that most people are most likely to like, and even marry, those individuals who live, work, or go to school within a close proximity to them. *Proximity—geographical nearness—*is perhaps the most powerful predictor of friendship. Of course, *proximity* also provides opportunities for fights, assaults, rapes, and murders. But much more often, it instigates liking.

A study of college students living in a dormitory found that students were more likely to become friends with the person next door than with the person living two doors down the hall. They were more likely to become friends with the person two doors away than the person living on the floor above them (Priest & Sawyer, 1967).

What about the saying, *Absence makes the heart grow fonder?* As long as you isolate yourself from other prospective dates or mates, the saying is accurate. But for most of us, the saying goes, *Absence make the heart grow fonder of someone else.* There is another saying that is appropriate here, *When I'm not with the one I love, I love the one I'm with.* What happens when friends and lovers move away? Eventually, most relationships slowly dissolve to nothing more than a periodic phone call or card.

Evidence shows that familiarity does not breed contempt; it breeds fondness. The more we are exposed to novel stimuli—a new person or new product, and so on, our liking for such stimuli increases. This phenomenon, called the *mere exposure effect,* explains in part why we are attracted to people in close proximity to us (Brooks & Watkins, 1989; Moreland & Zajonc, 1982). If it seems as though you are having difficulty getting acquainted with others, you may want to join a single's club, try a dating service, join an exercise club, take a special interest class, or even advertise in a newspaper. These are only a few of the possibilities of exposing yourself to others. Be careful when you join a club or dating service. Check its references. How long have they been established? How much will they cost you? Talk to others who have joined or used their services. You want to make sure that you can benefit from their services and not let them take advantage of you.

3. *Social skills* enable you to create the situations in which you can meet new people and maintain their friendship. How can you learn these skills? Practice makes perfect. Practice the skills you observe other people use that enable them to interact well among others. Practice role playing with a friend—your friend will be able to provide you with feedback that will be beneficial to enable you to change. Practice different situations in your mind. Picture yourself asking someone out for a date or imagine yourself being interviewed for a job. The more you practice, the better you will be able to handle the situation. Practice verbal and nonverbal skills. Another idea would be to have someone video tape you in different situations. This is a lot of fun and great feedback when you watch yourself on film.

4. *Classes* in communication skills, human relations, or assertiveness skills will provide you with new techniques and skills that you can apply in developing new relationships and improving your present relationships.

These are just a few steps you can use in initiating new relationships. There are many other techniques that will facilitate the process that are included throughout the text. We hope they will work for you.

Become acquainted with your other self; it may be better than the one you know best.

Napolean Hill

A LAST THOUGHT

Is it any wonder that many of us feel lonely in spite of being surrounded by people? We are lonely because we keep our real selves hidden, and keep operating next to people, and not with people, in order to make them like us and to keep them at a safe distance. Hence, no one really contacts us or we them. We don't have genuine relationships with people—instead, we bump shells with others.

Therefore, if we want other people to be open with us, we must begin by carefully opening up ourselves to them, by telling them honestly and openly of our feelings. Then, we have given them the courage to share their own feeling with us.

If you have the desire to form special, close relationships with other people, remember that the prerequisite is knowing, accepting, and appreciating yourself.

You can learn to make your social life rich and rewarding by taking an active role in changing yourself. Your knowledge and beliefs about relationships will influence your enjoyment. You learn from experience, so take charge of your life, take a few risks and chances. Enjoy life and appreciate each and every relationship you have.

CHAPTER DISCUSSION QUESTIONS

1. What are some of the risks involved in getting acquainted with others?
2. What can you do to overcome shyness?
3. Why is self-disclosure so important in a relationship?
4. What can you do to help yourself establish more interpersonal relationships?
5. How has the self-fulfilling prophecy influenced you?
6. What are the qualities necessary to have a close, personal relationship with another person?
7. What are the two factors that must be met within a relationship in order to overcome loneliness?
8. Explain the four steps in initiating new relationships.
9. Explain Impression Management and give examples of when you have used it.
10. Give some examples of how first impressions have influenced your interactions with others? Were they accurate or not?

KEY TERMS

Self-Disclosure
Loneliness
Johari Window
Openness
Open Area of Johari Window
Blind Area of Johari Window
Hidden Area of Johari Window
Unknown Area of Johari Window

Emotional Attachments
Open Communicator
Stereotyping
Social Ties
Shyness
Social Perception
Primacy Effect
Prejudice

REFERENCES

Argyle, M. and Henderson. "The Rules of Friendship." *Journal of Social and Personal Relationships,* (1984): 211–237.

Baron, R. (1986). Self-presentation in job interviews: When there can be "too much of a good thing." *Journal of Applied Social Psychology,* 16, 16–28.

Berscheid, E., Dion, K., Walster, E. and Walster, G. W. (1971): Physical attractiveness and dating choice: A test of the matching hypothesis. *Journal of Experimental Social Psychology,* 7, 173–189.

Berscheid, E., and Graziano, W. The Initiation of Social Relationships and Interpersonal Attraction. In R. L. Burgess and T. L. Hustom (eds.), *Social Exchange in Developing Relationships.* New York: Academic Press, 1979.

Berscheid, E. Physical Attractiveness. In L. Berkowits (ed.) *Advances in Experimental Social Psychology,* vol. 7. New York: Academic Press, 1974.

Brooks-Gunn, J., and Watkins, M. (1989) Recognition, memory and the mere exposure effect. *Journal of Experimental Psychology: Learning, Memory and Cognition* 15, 968–976.

Buckhout, R. (1980) Nearly 2,000 witnesses can be wrong. *Bulletin of Psychonomic Society,* 16, 307–310.

Coleman, J., *Intimate Relationships, Marriage, and Family.* Indianapolis, Indiana: Bobbs-Merrill Co., 1984.

Cozby, P. C. "Self-Disclosure: A Literature Review." *Psychological Bulletin* 79 (1973); 73–91.

Dion, K., and Berscheid, E. (1974). Physical attractiveness and peer perception among children. *Sociometry,* 37, 1–12.

Dion, K. L., and Dion, K. K. (1987). Belief in a just world and physical attractiveness stereotyping. *Journal of Personality and Social Psychology,* 52, 775–780.

Jourard, S. M., *The Transparent Self,* 2nd ed. Princeton, N.J.: Van Nostrand, 1971.

Jourard, S. M., *The Transparent Self,* Ontario, Canada: Van Nostrand, 1964.

Levinger, G., and Snoek, D. J. (1972). Attraction in relationships: A new look at interpersonal attraction. Morristown, N.J.: *General Learning Press.*

Lewis, Michael and Brooks, Jeanne (1978): Self-knowledge and emotional development. In Michael Lewis and Leonard Rosenblum (eds.) *The development of affect.* New York: Plenum, 205–226.

Miller, R. S., and H. M. Lefcourt, "The Assessment of Social Intimacy." *Journal of Personality Assessment* 46 (1982): 514–518.

Moreland, R., and Zajoac, R. (1982). Exposure effect in person perception: Familiarity, similarity and attraction. *Journal of Experimental Social Psychology* 18, 395–415.

Rosenthal R., and L. Jacobson, *Pygmalion in the classroom.* New York: Holt, Rinehart and Winston, 1968.

Rothbart, M. and Park, B. (1986). On the confirmability and disconfirmability of trait concepts. *Journal of Personality and Social Psychology,* 50, 131–142.

Sullivan, H. S. *The Interpersonal Theory of Psychiatry,* New York, 1953.

Weiss, R. S., The Provisions of Relationships. In Z. Rubin (ed.) *Do Unto Others: Joining, Molding, Conforming, Helping, Loving.* Englewood Cliffs, N.J.: Prentice Hall, 1974.

Wortman, D. B., P. Adosman, E. Herman and R. Greenberg. "Self-Disclosure: An Attributional Perspective." *Journal of Personality and Social Psychology* 33 (1976): 184–191.

Zimbardo, P. *Shyness, What it is, What to do about it,* Reading, Mass, Addison-Wesley, 1977.

Zimbardo, P. G., (1987) *Shyness,* New York: Jove.

HUMAN BINGO*

Purpose: To provide an opportunity for participants to get to know each other in a unique way.

Instructions:

1. Find a person who meets the qualification of one item below and write the person's name in any blank of your bingo card. (You cannot use a person more than once.) Use these questions or make up questions that are appropriate for your group. This is a good ice-breaker and does not have to be used in conjunction with the bingo game. Another way to use this activity is to have each person sign their name next to the item that applies to them.
   a. A person whose last name begins with the same letter as yours.
   b. A person who has the same number of brothers or sisters as you.
   c. A person born in a different state.
   d. A person who owns a dog.
   e. A person whose favorite TV program is the same as yours.
   f. A person whose favorite food is the same as yours.
   g. A person who has the same color shoes as you.
   h. A person whose first name begins with the same letter as yours.
   i. A person who likes country western music.
   j. A person who lives within a hundred miles of you.
   k. A person who has an uncle or aunt living over 1000 miles away.
   l. A person who owns cats.
   m. A person who owns tropical fish.
   n. A person who owns a Ford Motor product.
   o. A person who lives in an apartment.
   p. A person who admits to being over 39.
   q. A person who sings in a church choir.
   r. A person who took French in high school.
   s. A person who plays tennis.
   t. A person who belongs in a service club.
   u. A person who graduated in a class over 300.
   v. A person who really enjoys opera.
   w. A person who likes to hunt and fish.
   x. A person who attends church regularly.
   y. A person who owns a "CB."

II. After you have found the person who qualifies for one of the items above, ask that person the following questions, using the blank to record your short answers:
   a. What do you do professionally?
   b. Why did you take this class?
   c. What do you hope to take home with you as a result of being here?
   d. Ask a final question of your own—such as (can be serious or silly):
      What would you do with a million dollars?
      Who is the most important person in your life?
      What animal best represents you?
      What kind of car would you like to drive?
      What person from history would you like to be?

*Submitted by Dr. Joseph D. Dameron, Professor of Counselor Education, North Texas State University, Denton, Texas.

III. After you have interviewed the person who qualifies and have recorded short answers to the questions, have that person sign his or her blank—and move on to someone else. Remember—you can only use a person once on your card.

IV. When the participants have completed every square on their Bingo card, it's time to play Human Bingo.
   a. The facilitator begins by having one person read the name and information from one of the squares and introduce this individual.
   b. All participants who have a square containing the same name will cross that square out.
   c. Then, the person whose name was in the first square used will choose the next person to introduce, and so on until someone "Bingos" by having four squares—in either a vertical, horizontal, or diagonal line—filled.
   d. The game can continue until others have "Bingoed" if time permits.

V. Facilitator might want to have small prizes for winners.

VI. This exercise may be done exclusively until completed or integrated with other activities over a number of class periods.

HUMAN BINGO

Name _____

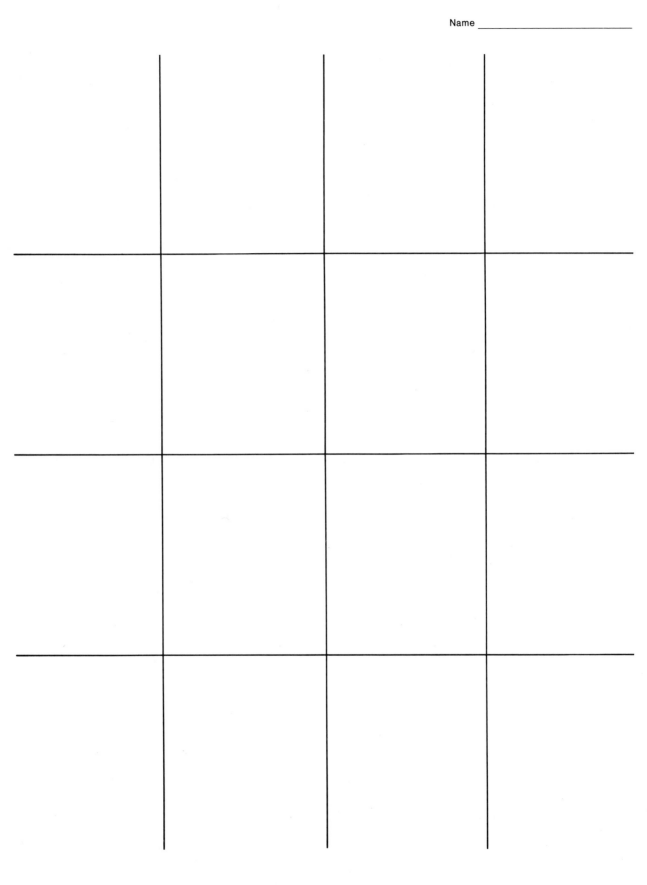

FIRST IMPRESSIONS

Purpose: To discover how our perception of an individual compares with other people's perception of the same individual. First impressions can have an important impact on our relations with others. This activity will allow you to see that these impressions differ among individuals and the impact of the first impression should not influence you as much in the future.

Instructions:

I. Divide the class into small groups of three to four individuals.

II. Have each group go somewhere on campus where they can observe other students.

III. Each student will take paper and something to write with.

IV. Each group will select three individuals, one at a time. Each member of the group will look, not stare, at the individual selected and then write down how he or she perceives this person, based on the first impression. Write down no more than six characteristics about the person you are observing. Do not discuss this with any members of your group, yet. Do this for the other two individuals your group has selected.

V. After you have written down characteristics about all three of the individuals you observed, compare your perceptions of each individual with the other members of your group. Are your perceptions similar or different? How do they compare?

VI. After about twenty minutes, go back to your classroom and discuss this with the other groups.

Discussion:

1. How did your perceptions compare with other members of your group?

2. How do you feel first impressions affect your perception of others?

3. How can we keep first impressions from having such a great influence on us?

WHO AM I COLLAGE

Purpose: To help students put their concept of *self-image* into a more definite form and enable each person to know something about all the other people in the class—including the teacher.

Instructions:

I. Construct out of class a self-image collage by pasting or gluing fragments, pictures, or words torn out of magazines, newspapers, and so on, on a large piece of poster board (or other chosen object) to form an abstract "picture" or composition. This will represent your view of the self.

II. Each individual is asked to compose the collage around the following ideas:
    a. At least three people most influential in your life.
    b. Hobbies and interests you have.
    c. Three words you would like to have said about you.
    d. The part of your personality you are the most proud of.
    e. Other personality traits.
    f. Likes and dislikes.
    g. Goals and values for your life.
    h. Background, family, and friends.
    i. Any other pertinent information.

III. Show your collage to the rest of the class, commenting on the various pictures or meanings reflected.

IV. The instructor may wish to give the class members a pad of small sheets of paper to write individual comments on the members of the class as they give their collage. This feedback should be based on how the class members see each other in their presentation.

Discussion:

1. If you were to do your collage again, what changes would you make?

2. What was the *most* difficult part of this assignment? Why?

HOW DO OTHERS PERCEIVE ME?

Purpose: To gain a better understanding of yourself and to discover how others perceive you.

Instruction:

I. Write a description of yourself in 50 words or less.

II. After you have completed your description have someone close to you, such as a parent or gaurdian (someone who has known you for at least 10 years) write a description of you in 50 words or less.

III. Have a friend or acquaintance (someone you have known for less than a year) write a description of you in 50 words or less.

IV. Read each of the descriptions and compare how similar or different they are in comparison to your own description.

Discussion:

1. How did your personal description differ from how the person who has known you for many years describe you? Explain. How does it differ from the person who has known you for less than a year? Explain.

2. How is your personal description similar to the other two descriptions? Explain.

3. What surprised you about the way the other people described you? Explain.

4. Do you think their perception of you is accurate? Explain.

5. What would you like to change about how they perceive you? Explain.

6. How would you like people to perceive you?

YOUR INTERPERSONAL STYLE

Purpose: To enable you to "get in touch" with your own interpersonal style.

Instructions: Interpersonal style may be defined as your characteristic ways of thinking and feeling about how you interact with other people, together with your interpersonal skills (and lack of skills), and your characteristic success and failures in relationships.

I. After giving some thought to the above definition, consider the categories below and ask yourself the questions within these categories.

II. *Categories*

Extensiveness. How extensive is my interpersonal life? How much of my day is spent with people? Do I seek out opportunities for being with people? Do I have many friends and acquaintances or few? Are my contacts with others planned or left up to chance? Is my life too crowded with people? Are there too few people in my life? Do I prefer smaller gatherings or larger groups? Do I have a need for quiet time away from people? Am I outgoing or introverted or somewhere in between?

Needs and wants. What are my interpersonal wants and needs? How do I express them? Directly? Indirectly? Do I like to be challenged? Complimented? Reassured? Left alone? Treated like a child? Like a parent? Do I like to be responsible and assertive? Do I want others to control me? With what kind of people do I associate? Are they like me? By what criteria do I choose my friends and acquaintances: chance, intelligence, physical attractiveness, good-naturedness, values, social position?

Caring. How caring am I in my interactions with others? Do others know that I care? Is it obvious in my behavior? Do I sometimes wonder whether I care at all? Do I take others for granted? Who really cares for me? How do I show care? How is care shown to me? In what ways am I self-centered? Am I a generous person? How do I express my generosity?

Competence. What are my interpersonal skills? Am I good at communicating understanding to others? Am I appropriately warm? Do I communicate to others that I respect them? Am I my real self when I am with others—that is, do I communicate genuineness? Am I open, willing to talk about myself appropriately? Can I challenge others and invite them to explore my relationships directly with others? What skills do I want to acquire? How well do I meet strangers? Am I awkward, embarrassed, resentful? Or enthusiastic, poised, confident?

Emotions. What do I do with my emotions in interpersonal situations? Do I swallow them? Or some of them? Do I wear my emotions on my sleeve? Is it easy for others to judge what I am feeling? Am I moody? To what extent am I ruled by my emotions? How do I make my emotions public? How do I feel about being emotional in interpersonal situations? How perceptive am I of the emotional states of others? How do I react to others when they are emotional? What emotions do I enjoy in others? What ones do I fear? What do I do when others keep their emotions to themselves?

Intimacy. How intensive is my interpersonal life? Do I actively pursue intimacy with others? Do I encourage others to get close to me? If so, how? Are there people with whom I would like to be more intimate? Are there people who will not allow me to be intimate with them? What does intimacy mean for me? Do I see that there are a variety of ways of being intimate with others? What kind of people are attracted to me? What forms of intimacy do I find most rewarding? Most threatening?

Rejection and alienation. Is loneliness ever a problem for me? If so, how do I handle it? Do others see me as lonely at times? If so, how do they react to me? What do I do when I see that others are lonely? Am I easily threatened by others? How do I react when I am threatened? What threatens me in interpersonal situations? Have I experienced rejection? How do I handle being ignored or left out or rejected? Do I ignore or reject others? How do I handle the problem of not wanting to relate to people who want to relate to me?

Interpersonal influences. What demands do I place on my friends and/or acquaintances? Am I manipulative in my dealings with others? If so, with whom and how? Do others try to manipulate me? Who and how? What demands do my friends place on me? Do I tell others explicitly what I expect from them, or do I assume that they know what I want? Do I see that giving and receiving influence can under certain conditions be proper and growthful in my interpersonal life? If so, under what conditions? Am I either dominant or submissive in my relationships to others? When and under what conditions?

Mutuality. Do I allow for give and take in my relationships with others? Am I authoritarian or parental? Am I democratic? Am I laissez-faire? Am I willing to compromise? Do I take responsibility for what happens in my relationships, or do I "let things take their course"? Do I encourage mutuality in decision making? Do I encourage dialogue? Do I expect to be treated as an equal? Do my relationships involve mutual responsibilities?

Work relationships. How do I get along in my work relationships? Do I treat people at work as people or as roles? Do I assert myself with my superiors (including teachers)? Am I understanding with my subordinates? Do I have prejudices toward people in certain "inferior" roles? Am I overpersonal at work? Am I a loner at work?

Values. What are my principle interpersonal values? How open to interpersonal growth am I? What am I willing to risk with others? In what areas am I not willing to take risks? Do I allow ambiguity and uncertainty in my interpersonal life? Am I tolerant of others whose opinions differ from mine? What are my prejudices? Am I willing to change my own values, beliefs, and behaviors when in my dealings with others it seems appropriate to do so? How rigid or flexible am I in my relationships with others? Do I seek out ways to grow with others? Do I share my values with others? Can I put my interpersonal relationships into perspective by putting them into the wider contexts of work, world conditions, and so on?

III. Pick out the questions in the list above that you would like to answer for yourself in more detail. Share these with your fellow group members without making any extensive attempt now to answer them.

IV. Make a list of questions or categories, or both, that you think are missing in the listings above. Try to think of questions that, if answered, would help you get a better perspective on your own interpersonal style. Share these new categories and/or questions with your fellow group members.

LEARNING JOURNAL FOR GETTING ACQUAINTED

Select the statement below that best defines your feelings about the personal value or meaning gained from this chapter and respond below the dotted line.

I LEARNED THAT I	I WAS SURPRISED THAT I
I REALIZED THAT I	I WAS PLEASED THAT I
I DISCOVERED THAT I	I WAS DISPLEASED THAT I

....

2

Self-Awareness

THE MAN IN THE GLASS

When you get what you want in your struggle for self,
And the world makes you king for a day,
Just go to a mirror and look at yourself,
And see what that man has to say.

For it isn't your father, or mother, or wife,
Whose judgement upon you must pass;
The fellow whose verdict counts most in your life,
Is the one staring back from the glass.

He's the fellow to please, never mind all the rest,
For he's with you right up to the end,
And you've passed your most dangerous difficult test,
If the man in the glass is your friend.

You may fool the whole world down the path way of years
And get pats on the back as you pass,
But your final reward will be heartaches and tears,
If you've cheated the man in the glass.

Author Unknown

MY "SELF-IMAGE"

In my memories of when I was a "little" kid, between the ages of two and four, it seemed like everything I would attempt would be a "No, No," "No" to this, and "No" to that, and "No" to everything. For awhile I almost thought my name was "NoNo." I soon learned that my life was much easier if I just sat and watched television.

Life was not much fun because I was afraid to try anything, because I thought I would get in trouble. I didn't think I was a very good kid, because most of the people around me kept telling me that I wasn't capable of doing anything. I thought it was because I was "no good" and "inferior," but in reality I just wasn't old enough to do what I wanted to do. I didn't realize that.

When I turned six, I was excited because it was time to go to school like the "big kids." It was a new life and I needed a change. It didn't take long for me to realize that I was not as good as the rest of the kids. They laughed at my overalls and shiny shoes. When it came time to select teams, I was the last to be picked, because I was short, skinny, and wore glasses.

I wanted to be liked by the other students and my teachers, so I became the "class clown." I needed attention and I got it, but it was the wrong type of attention. I became depressed and felt inferior to the people around me, so I withdrew into my own little world and isolated myself as much as I could. I would sit in the corner at school and at home I would go to my room and draw.

My early school years were not fun. In middle school I got mixed up with the "wrong crowd." I wanted to be accepted, so I thought I had to be like everyone else. I wanted to be part of a group with an identity so I got involved in a gang. In the meantime I tried a few drugs and got in trouble. It wasn't a happy time in my life.

In ninth grade, I registered for an art class, not knowing what art was all about. The teacher asked the students to draw a picture. I turned mine in and the teacher thought it was great. The teacher thought that I had talent, but I knew better. I have been told that I am "dumb, inferior and not capable of accomplishing anything," so why try. My teacher encouraged me and kept telling me how good I really was, so I kept trying. All of a sudden the other students were also telling me that I was good and I began to believe it. I became motivated to succeed in the field of art. I overcame my depression, set some goals, and found some friends that accepted me for being me and not because of my size or looks.

I am now a professional artist and feel good about myself and my life. I like people and accept them as they are and will allow them the freedom to grow and develop as an individual. I hope you will too.

"SELF-IMAGE" DEVELOPMENT

Reviewing the preceding story, we realize that people acquire a sense of self throughout their life. It is an ongoing process that evolves from our experiences and interactions with others within the environment. Significant adults in their life also provide us with feedback as to who we are. This is the beginning of *self-image development*. In this chapter you can learn ways in which you can identify and better understand your *real self* and learn strategies to improve your self-esteem.

Was I Born This Way? Are you born with a *self-image* or is it acquired? Most psychologists say that it is acquired. Our self-image is affected by all the experiences we have had—successes and failures, compliments and "put downs," happy times and sad times, personal thoughts and experiences, our own expectations and others' expectations of us, and the way other people have reacted to us—especially in our early adulthood.

A man has to live with himself, and he should see to it that he always has good company.

C. E. Hughes

SIGNIFICANT OTHERS

We learn who we are from the way we are treated by the important people in our lives. Harry Stack Sullivan (1953) calls these important people *significant others*. Sullivan goes to the extent of saying that "a person is nothing more than the reflected appraisal of significant others." From the verbal or non-verbal communication of these significant others, we learn whether we are liked or disliked, accepted or unaccepted, worthy of respect or disdain, a success or a failure. If we are to have a strong self-concept, we need love, respect, and acceptance from the significant others in our life. In essence, our self-image is shaped by those who have loved—or have not loved us.

Who Are the Significant Others in Your Life? How have they affected your self-image? Who are you a significant other to? Think about the kind of influence you are having on their self-image. Is it a positive or negative effect? You may be surprised to find that if you are a parent, a spouse, a boyfriend or girlfriend, a teacher, a son or daughter, a brother or sister, or a person that can have any impact on another individual, you are a significant other.

A parent says to a child, "you'd better not try that; I don't think you can do it." You tell your husband, "Can't you ever do anything right?" A teacher tells a student, "Everyone else in the class understands it; what's wrong with you?" A son tells his mother, "You're a 'rotten' parent; you made me this way." Have you heard any of these comments? If we hear these comments too often, we soon begin to believe them, especially if the person saying them is important or significant to us.

From all of these experiences, you construct a mental blueprint of the sort of person you are. Once an idea or belief about ourselves goes into this mental picture, it becomes true as far as we are personally concerned. We generally do not question its validity but proceed to act upon it as if it were true. Most of our actions, feelings, responses, and even our abilities are consistent with this self-image. If we see ourselves as incapable as we enter a math class, we will most likely experience difficulty and failure. If you view yourself as well qualified and capable as you are interviewed for a job, the interviewer will evaluate you on a positive basis, and this will improve your prospects of getting the job. This is often called the *self-fulfilling prophecy.*

Self-respect is the best means of getting the respect of others.

Napolean Hill

Must we have all the answers before we begin? If we have all the answers, there is little beginning.

Leonard Andrews

When our *self-concept* is intact and secure, we feel good. When it is threatened, we feel anxious and insecure. When it is adequate and one that we can be wholesomely proud of, we feel self-confident. We feel free to be ourselves and to express ourselves. When it is inadequate and an object of shame, we attempt to hide it rather than express it—we withdraw inside ourselves. If we have strong, positive feelings about ourselves, we want and feel that we deserve a good love relationship, a good job, a feeling of freedom—whatever we think of as the highest good for us. On the other hand, if we have a poorly developed, negative, or inferior self-image, we may expect very little for ourselves. We may settle for second or third best because we feel that is all we deserve. In essence, we project to others the way we feel about ourselves. If we cannot like and respect ourselves, how can we ever hope other people will see us as worthy individuals who have something to contribute to the world in which we live.

To gain a better understanding of how the "self-image" evolves over a life span, we need to study some of the traditional theories of personality that will provide us with a foundation of how we become aware of who we really are.

THEORIES OF PERSONALITY

Throughout our lives we will be attempting to understand other people, such as our boyfriends or girlfriends, our bosses, our husbands or wives, our teachers, etc. In addition, we will also be attempting to understand ourselves. The following theories will help us gain an understanding of ourselves and the people around us. We will consider a variety of theories that will help you in the journey of finding yourself and answering the question, who am I.

The theory that has had the greatest impact on the field of psychology was developed by Sigmund Freud. This theory has created a lot of controversy, not only within the realm of psychology, but also within our everyday lives—in literature, movies, child-rearing practices, the feminist movement, etc. Let's take a look at this theory.

Sigmund Freud. Freud's theory of personality development lays the foundation for most other personality theories. Freud (1920) states that a person's personality is made up of three distinct but interrelated parts: the *id,* the *ego,* and the *superego.*

The *id* is composed of the basic biological drives that motivate an individual. This includes the hunger drive, the thirst drive, sexual impulses, and other needs that assure survival and bring pleasure. The id is present at birth and remains an active force throughout our life. We are not consciously aware of the actions of our id. Freud has received much of his criticism because of the emphasis he puts on the sexual impulses and pleasure drives and their control over our behavior.

The *superego* begins to develop after the age of four and is acquired from the environment around us. It consists of our values, morals, religious beliefs, and ideals of our parents and society. Another name for the superego would be our conscience. The superego tells us what is right and wrong, what we should do and should not do—the ideal rather than the real. The superego attempts to limit the sexual and aggressive impulses of the id. As you can observe, the id and the superego are in conflict. Each characteristic is trying to take control of your life.

The *ego* to the rescue. Thank goodness for the ego and the fact that it develops before the superego. The ego begins to develop after the first year of life and begins to moderate and restrain the id by requiring it to seek gratification of its impulses through realistic and socially acceptable means. The ego is the rational, logical, and realistic part of your personality that attempts to maintain balance between the id and superego. The conflict between the id and the superego causes anxiety, which in turn leads the ego to create defense mechanisms to control the anxiety. Defense mechanisms will be discussed in chapter 8.

Becoming is superior to being.

Paul Klue

Freud theorized that the core of personality is formed before the age of six in a series of *five psychosexual stages*. These stages put emphasis on the biological controls of our behavior, especially the sex drive.

Freud's Five Stages of Psychosexual Development

1. The oral stage: Emphasizes satisfying the basic biological drives, specifically the need for oral gratification, which is usually satisfied via sucking. If a child does not satisfy this during the first year of life, he or she will be insecure and continue to try to satisfy this stage later in life through nail biting, finger sucking, cigarette smoking, drinking too much, and so on. This behavior will become dominant when a person experiences anxiety.

2. The anal stage: Evolves around toilet training and the child's attempts to become a capable, somewhat independent being. If too much emphasis is put on such things as toilet training, the child may become obstinate, stingy, too orderly or disorderly, compulsively clean or messy, destructive, or cruel. A child who learns to control his or her basic physiological functioning without too much anxiety will feel comfortable and secure as a capable individual.

3. The phallic stage: Considered to be the most crucial stage in an individual's development. This is when an individual will gain his or her identity, specifically the sex role identity. This is also where Freud receives the greatest amount of criticism. During this stage males learn to be "men" and females learn to be "women."

4. The period of latency: From six to puberty is considered to be a quiet time in a child's development. Psychosexual development is on "hold." This could be considered to be a continuation of the identity stage, as boys continue to play with other boys with emphasis on male type games, and girls find out what it is like to be a woman. You can see why parts of Freud's theory of personality development are criticized today.

5. The genital stage: Beginning at puberty, a time when a person has to take this new-found sex drive, which cannot be exhibited directly at this young age, and learn to control it through some form of socially acceptable activity. As a person becomes capable of doing this, he or she becomes more comfortable with the self and thus is able to develop a mature and responsible social-sexual relationship with others.

Most psychologists today think that Freud put too much emphasis on the biological drives, specifically the sex drive—the id. Erik Erikson, an original follower of Freud, realized that the biological drives are important, but that the effects of the environment on us and our development are as important if not more important. Erikson's first five stages correspond closely with Freud's five stages but with extra emphasis on the environment.

Eric Erikson: Erikson (1950) has identified *eight stages of psychosocial development* that each individual experiences throughout his or her life. Each state is characterized by specific tasks that must be mastered. If these tasks are not satisfied, an unfavorable outcome throws us off balance and makes it harder to deal with later crises. As each stage is completed, we continue to build toward a positive, healthy development and a satisfying life. Those who are plagued with unfavorable outcomes will continue to face frustration and conflict while striving to develop as a person. A brief description of Erikson's eight stages of psychosocial development follows.

Erikson's Eight Stages of Psychosocial Development

1. Trust vs mistrust: During the first years of life, a child is completely dependent on others for the satisfaction of his or her needs. If these needs are satisfied on a consistent basis, the child will feel comfortable and secure. If the child's needs are not satisfied on a regular basis, mistrust will develop and this may become the core of later insecurity and suspiciousness. This child will become mistrusting and fearful of others and have difficulty developing close, trusting relationships with others in the future.

2. Autonomy vs. doubt: During the ages from one through three, children are attempting to become more independent. They are learning to walk, talk, explore, and become toilet trained. The people around them, especially their parents, help the children develop *a sense of independence and autonomy* by encouraging them to try new skills and by reassuring them if they fail. Consistent discipline is also important during this time. If the parents are inconsistent, overprotective, or show disapproval while children are attempting to do things on their own, they will become doubtful, unsure, and ashamed of themselves. If children are told by a significant other that they should be able to read or be toilet trained, they wonder, "What is wrong with me? My parents say I should be able to do that but I can't do it." This child will feel doubtful and shameful of himself or herself and thus feel negative about their capabilities. A child that has accomplished some of these tasks and is given encouragement and positive reinforcement will feel confident and independent.

3. Initiative vs. guilt: During the ages of three through five, the child moves from simple self-control to an ability to take control. This is the questioning and exploring stage when a child wants to try anything and everything. The child becomes very curious about the world around him or her. If the child is encouraged to take the initiative and explore the world, the child will feel good about himself or herself and will continue to be curious in the future. If the parents inhibit the child's activities and curiosity, the child will feel guilty whenever he or she takes the initiative and thus cause the individual to become passive. Why try to do something if your parents keep showing disapproval?

4. Industry vs. inferiority: Let's assume that the child is between the ages of six and eleven and is excited about life, motivated to solve problems, and set to accomplish tasks. These are the early school years when the child should be making new friends, joining clubs and teams, and succeeding in school. When a child has a task to complete, such as a homework assignment, cookies to sell, or a wood car to make, the child should attempt to accomplish the task with encouragement from others. The parents should not intervene and complete the task for the child. Otherwise, the child will quickly learn that the parents will always complete the task, so why try? Or possibly the child will feel inferior and incapable, because his or her parents always end up completing the tasks. Many parents feel like they are being responsible parents by helping their children learn, but in reality, they are hindering their development. During this stage the child is becoming involved in the outside world, and other people such as teachers, classmates, and other adults who can have a great influence on the child's attitude toward himself or herself.

Caring sometimes hurts, but not as much as the alternative—not caring.

Anonymous

5. Identity vs. role confusion: Between the ages of twelve and eighteen a person is caught between childhood and adulthood. The major task to accomplish during this stage is to answer the question, "who am I?" Adolescence is a turbulent time for many individuals. Mental and physical maturation brings on new feelings and new attitudes that people are unsure of. Should these new feelings and new attitudes be expressed or inhibited, such as one's new-found sex drive?

Our identity evolves from our self-perceptions and our relationships with others. People need to see themselves as positive, capable, and lovable individuals as well as having the feeling that they are accepted by others. Otherwise, they will experience *role confusion,* an uncertainty about who they are and where they are going. Role confusion may lead to a constant searching for acceptance and a feeling of belonging. This search can lead people to unhealthy relationships and to alternatives such as drugs and gangs.

Caring in an adult relationship is helping each other grow by receiving and not denying each other's authentic feelings . . . caring thus is encouraging someone to do something he wants to do, not what you want him to do—encouraging him to act the way he feels, not the way you think he should feel.

Nena and George O'Neill

6. Intimacy vs. isolation: Now that we feel good about ourselves and have an identity, we are ready to form meaningful relationships and learn to share with others. During the young adult years we must develop the ability to care about others and a willingness to share experiences with them. Marriage and sexual intimacy does not guarantee these qualities. Failure to establish intimacy with others leads to a deep sense of isolation. The person feels lonely and uncared for in life. A person that satisfies this stage is capable of developing close, intimate, and sharing relationships with others and feels comfortable and secure in these relationships.

7. Generativity vs. self-absorption: Until middle age we seem to be preoccupied with ourselves. Even the intimacy stage is primarily for the self to prevent loneliness. Now, we are ready to look beyond the self and look to the future, not only for ourselves, but also for others. This seems to be the best time to establish a family, because we are concerned about the development and welfare of others. This is the time in our life when we feel productive and are concerned for the benefit of humankind.

What about the individual who does not feel productive and also feels like he or she is not accomplishing any goals in life? This person feels trapped. Life loses its meaning and the person feels bitter, dreary, unfulfilled, and stagnant. This person becomes preoccupied with the self and personal needs and interests.

8. Integrity vs. despair: Old age should be a time of reflection, when a person should be able to look back over the events of a lifetime with a sense of acceptance and satisfaction. This is the type of person who has tried to live life to its fullest. The individual who wished he or she could live life over again and also feels cheated or deprived of any of the breaks in life will live a life of regret and failure. This is the person who keeps saying, *"What if. . . ?* or *"If I would have taken that opportunity"* and because of this, feels depressed and will be unhappy the rest of his or her life.

As most people continue through this stage, they reevaluate the meaning of life for themselves and ideally find a new meaning that will help reduce fear and anxiety and help prepare them for facing death.

As you observe these eight stages, you notice that there is a positive and negative aspect of each stage. Are you able to identify the stage you are in right now? Are you able to identify the stages some of your friends are in? Erik Erikson was one of the first psychologists to put some emphasis on the fact that we continue to go through developmental stages throughout our lives. Freud emphasized that the first six years of life were the most important years.

Life is an echo. What you send out—Comes back. What you sow—You reap. What you give—You get. What you see in others—Exists in you.

Zig Ziglar

STAGES OF ADULT DEVELOPMENT

Most psychologists ignored the adult years until Daniel Levinson (1978) did an intensive study of the lives of forty men. Levinson's study indicates that we all, at least men, continue to go through developmental stages our entire lives and some of these stages we experience may be as traumatic as some of the stages we experienced earlier in life, such as in adolescence. These stages seem to alternate between relatively stable periods and periods of transition. Levinson's study begins to look at men who are between the ages of seventeen and twenty-two while the individual is still struggling with his or her identity. This is a continuation of the *adolescent identity crisis stage,* in which the individual is still striving to become independent. During this age range the individual is attempting to break the apron strings between the self and the parents. This is easier for some individuals than for others.

This is a period of time for searching, not only for your own personal identity, but for your career and social identity. Money seems to be an important factor in developing independence. Not until a person feels economically independent will he or she feel like an independent individual.

Persons becoming comfortable with the self and their own identity are ready to enter the adult world. For most individuals this stage takes place between the ages of twenty-two and twenty-eight. This is the time the individual is getting established in the game of life. During this period the individual finds his or her first real job, the one that has the potential for a future career. Permanent relationships are being formed, including marriage and the beginning of a family. This seems to be a good period of time for most individuals. They feel like they are really becoming established and they are on the road to success.

During the previous two stages of life, most people have been setting goals for the future. Some of these goals are realistic and others are unrealistic fantasies. During the ages of twenty-eight and thirty-three, we begin to evaluate what we are doing and where we are going. We begin to ask ourselves some questions such as, "Is this the type of job and career I want to be involved in the rest of my life?" or "Is this the person I want to be married to the rest of my life?" After evaluating yourself and your life, you need to make some major decisions that may affect you the rest of your life. This is not an easy period for many people, because many decisions need to be made. This is why this period is considered *the wavering and doubt stage.* "Should I change jobs, or should I get a divorce? Should I do this, or should I do that? If I make this decision, what will the result be?" We keep wondering whether or not we are making the right decision. Some individuals will make major transitions during this stage, such as changing careers or getting divorced. Life becomes more serious; now it's for real. Other individuals evaluate their lives during this period and decide that they are happy with their career and happy with their spouse and will continue to be motivated to succeed in both.

We are now ready *to establish a place for ourselves* in society, solidify our family life, and succeed in the world of work. We are between the ages of thirty-three and forty and are striving to reach our goals that we have set for ourselves and our family. We are interested in making the world a better place to live, especially for our immediate family. We are willing to join service clubs, be on the school board, run for political office, or do what it takes to help make the world a better place to live. We are finally getting settled in what society has been telling us to do for the last thirty-some years. We now want to *establish roots* and make sure we live in an area that is "best" for our family and our career. We are beginning to feel good about our life and the direction it is taking.

As we approach the age between forty and forty-five we begin to ask ourselves questions about our lives. We realize that life is half over. We ask ourselves, "what have I accomplished so far in my life? Have I reached the goals I have set for myself? Am I going to be president of the corporation?" This is a time for re-evaluation of our lives and what we want out of them. According to Levinson, if people do not go through *a midlife transition,* they will live a life of staleness and resignation.

This is the time in life when individuals may experience a major transition, or they may decide they like what they are doing and are happy with the relationships they are involved in and become re-motivated to succeed in what they are doing. Some of the transitions that are common during this time are changes in career and marriage. Some individuals experience a painful and disruptive struggle which is called the *midlife crisis*. This is similar to the *adolescent identity crisis,* in which the individual seeks a new identity. Because these individuals have not satisfied the goals that they had set for themselves, they experience frustration. In order to overcome this frustration and depression, they attempt to find their identity through radical and extreme means. Some will quit their jobs, divorce their spouses, and attempt to start all over again. Some men will leave their wives, sell the family station wagon, buy a sports car, and start dating twenty-year-old women. They are trying to prove to themselves that they are still capable as "men."

During the *midlife transition* years, the female is not as concerned about her sexual capacity as the male. For women, who have primarily been mothers, this is a time for an emerging identity; Their children are becoming adults and more independent. It is a bittersweet time in which a woman who has not established a career or other outside interests begins to experience the empty-nest syndrome and at the same time begins to look at available options for redirecting her talents and energy. As the woman continues through this stage, depression and listlessness are common but temporary feelings. These vulnerable feelings may be followed by, or coincide with, the menopausal years and thus become a particularly trying period.

The career oriented woman who postpones motherhood or decides not to have children may experience similar feelings—either guilt for not having children and being unfulfilled as a woman or anxiety to reconfirm her work identity. As an extreme example, consider a woman between forty and fifty years of age who has two children, age twenty and eighteen, respectively. Both children are becoming independent, and the mother is no longer feeling needed. Twenty years ago she was told by society that her goal in life was to get married and have children. She has done both and now what is there left for her to do? Her body is beginning to change, and she can no longer reproduce. She may feel as though she is no longer attractive to the opposite sex. Because of the culture she grew up in and the physiological changes that are taking place, she becomes depressed. She feels worthless as a person, she has reached her goals, and she feels that she is no longer a "sexual being." She has no identity. This is generally a temporary condition and after adjusting to the physiological changes within her body and reevaluating her life, she sets new goals and begins to strive toward them.

Most people go through the transition stage without any real problems and are able to adjust to these problems without experiencing a major crisis. Other individuals experience major transitions that result in positive changes, whereas still others will have negative experiences that could result in such things as depression and suicide.

All of us need to continue to evaluate our lives on a regular basis. As long as we do this we won't experience any traumatic transition that will disrupt our lives.

TRANSACTIONAL ANALYSIS

Transactional Analysis (Berne, 1961, 1964) teaches people a theory of personality to use in becoming more aware of themselves, their interactions with others, and their life patterns or scripts. Berne says that the personality has three basic parts or ego states known as the Parent, the Adult, and the Child. These are very closely associated with Freud's id, ego, and supergo.

The *Child* is learned during childhood and may continue throughout life. The Child is primitive, demanding, impulsive, playful, creative, and manipulative. The *Parent* is a recording that we acquired from our parents or other authority figures. The Parent evaluates, nurtures, and judges. The Parent says "you should, you ought to, why don't you, you can't do it, thats good" etc. The *Adult* is the mature and rational decision making part of the personality. With the Adult in charge, a person can explore alternatives and their consequences and decide which ego state is needed. According to TA, people get in trouble when they use inappropriate ego states. Which ego state do you use, especially in your interaction with others?

Strokes are a special form of stimulation one person gives to another. Strokes are essential to a person's life. Strokes can vary from actual physical touch to praise or just recognition. Negative strokes are painful or unpleasant forms of recognition and make the person who receives them feel not OK. Positive strokes are helpful or pleasant forms of recognition that gives the person who receives them a feeling of being OK.

It has been said that small children need actual physical strokes in order to remain alive. As we get older, we do not need as much cuddling as when we were young, but we always need someone who cares about us and tells us so. Unless we have this, we face "emotional death" of our mind, body, and spirit. The craving to be appreciated is the deepest principle in human nature.

Who's OK? The quantity and quality of strokes we have received during our lifetime help us to formulate our attitudes about ourselves and others (Harris, 1969). We may decide, "I'm not OK—you're OK."

This position says, "I don't like myself—I'm a big mistake, but everyone else is OK." The second attitude we may form is "I'm not OK, you're not OK." The position says "I'm not good and everyone else is just as bad—I wish I weren't even here and you're not worth being with either." We may decide, "I'm OK—you're not OK." This position says, "I'll be OK if you leave me alone—you hurt me—you are not OK." The position of hope is "I'm OK—you're OK." This is the outlook of a mature adult at peace with himself or herself and others, a person who can have relationships with others without manipulating them, using them, or putting them down. It is the ultimate position based on faith, hope, work, dedication, and commitment. This position says, "I count on me and you count on you."

CARL ROGERS: SELF THEORY

Carl Rogers (1951) defines the development of the self-concept in terms of *self-actualization,* which is defined as the fulfillment of one's own completely unique potential. The key to self-actualization is the self-concept. Rogers maintains that the way we regard ourselves depends largely on the kind of regard given by others. In the ideal situation love is given freely and does not depend on any specific aspects of behavior. Rogers calls this *unconditional positive regard.* Unconditional acceptance leads to unimpaired growth and the development of positive characteristics. Individuals who have received unconditional positive regard have a positive realistic self-concept, high self-esteem, and feelings of self respect. Rogers believes that a fully functioning person lives totally in the present and is continually changing to make full use of her potential.

The difficulties in functioning are caused by a lack of unconditional acceptance by others starting at birth. Many parents make their affection and approval conditional on certain kinds of behavior. If the child does what the parent says, the parent will love the child. If the child does not live up to parental expectations, the parent may show disapproval and withhold affection. Consequently, the child attempts to live up to his parents expectations but can't always be successful. This is the beginning of an unrealistic self concept.

In order to become *a self-actualized individual,* we must accept ourselves as we are, the positive and the negative, with the potential to grow as a person and accept others as they are rather than wishing they were somehow different. We all need to learn to place a high value on the individuality and uniqueness of ourselves and others.

THE SELF-ACCEPTING PERSON*

The self-accepting person is a participant in life rather than a spectator.

He is inclined to be objective, spontaneous, and emotionally and intellectually honest.

He tries to understand the interpersonal and environmental problems he faces, but he also accepts his limitations in gaining true insight concerning them.

He works out the best adjustment to life of which he is capable, often without fully understanding all that is involved.

However, he is willing to experience the pleasures and discomforts of self-revelation: i.e., he accepts the mixed pain and joy that accompanies each change in his attitude and feeling toward himself and others.

His claims on life are, for the most part, reasonable. If he wants to be a member of the Country Club and yet cannot afford it, he finds other social and recreational outlets in keeping with his budget.

The self-accepting person without special talent or ability is able to share emotionally in the gifts of others without undue regret about his own inborn deficiencies.

He does not brood about missed opportunities, lost causes, errors, and failures. Rather, he looks on them for what they can contribute to his doing things differently or better in the future.

He does not get stuck in the rut of irrational feelings of love, hate, envy, jealousy, suspicion, lust, and greed, because he lets each feeling spell out its special message for him.

VICTOR FRANKL: SEARCH FOR MEANING

As humans, we are capable of self-awareness that allows us to reflect and to decide. With this awareness, we become free beings who are responsible for choosing the way we live and thus influence our own destiny.

This awareness of freedom and responsibility gives rise to existential anxiety, which is a basic human condition. Whether we like it or not, we are free, even though we may seek to avoid reflecting on this freedom. The knowledge that we must choose leads to anxiety. Facing the inevitable prospect of eventual death gives the present moment significance, for we become aware that we do not have forever to accomplish our projects.

Our task is to create a life that has meaning and purpose. (Meaning, purpose, and self-actualization will be discussed in more detail in Chapters 9 and 10.) As humans, we are unique in striving

Really now, what is the rush, are you passing up yourself? Look back for a moment, you may find parts of you scattered along the trail.

Anonymous

*From SELF-ACCEPTANCE by McDonald, Smith, and Sutherland. Copyright by The Hogg Foundation for Mental Health, The University of Texas, Austin, Texas.

toward creating purposes and values that give meaning to living. In order to increase our capacity to live fully, we must become aware that:

- We are finite, and we do not have an unlimited time to do what we want to do with our life.
- We have the potential to take action or not to act; inaction is a decision.
- We choose our actions, and therefore we can partially create our own destiny.
- Meaning is not automatically bestowed on us but is the product of our searching and of our creating a unique purpose.
- Existential anxiety, which is basically a consciousness of our own freedom, is an essential part of living; as we increase our awareness of the choices available to us, we also increase our sense of responsibility for the consequences of these choices
- We are subject to loneliness, meaninglessness, guilt, and isolation.
- We are basically alone, yet we have an opportunity to relate to other human beings.

This is an existential view of human nature that states that the significance of our existence is never fixed once and for all. Rather, we continually recreate ourselves through our goals. Humans are in a constant state of transition, emerging, evolving, and becoming. Being a person implies that we are discovering and making sense of our existence.

VIRGINIA SATIR: SELF-WORTH

Virginia Satir (1972) indicates in her writing that the crucial factor in *interpersonal relations*—what happens inside people and between people—is the picture of the individual worth that each person carries around. A person who can appreciate his or her *own self-worth* is able to see and respect the worth of others. Satir describes a human being who is living humanly, as a person who understands, values, and develops his or her body finding it useful and beautiful. This is a person who is honest about himself or herself and others, who is willing to take risks, to be creative, embrace change, who is feeling, loving, playful, authentic, and productive. Satir says that the person who is living humanly can stand on his or her own two feet, love deeply, fight fairly and effectively, and can be on equally good terms with both his or her tenderness and his or her toughness.

Self-worth is learned, and the family is where it is basically acquired. There is always hope that your life can change because you can always learn new things. Human beings can learn, grow, and change all their lives. Every person has a feeling of worth, positive or negative. The question is, which one is it, *positive or negative*?

Do You Have High or Low Self-Worth? If you have *low self-worth* or know someone with *low self-worth,* you can change or help the other person change. Don't blame other people for your problems or faults. You are already that way, but you can change. Look to the

Get plenty of psychological sunshine. Circulate in new groups. Discover new and stimulating things to do.

David Schwartz

future. For others to change, a nurturing environment needs to be provided; and for you to change, a new environment is also needed. You will be able to develop and grow in an atmosphere where individual differences are appreciated, mistakes are tolerated, communication is open, and rules are flexible—this is a nurturing environment. Satir describes the main points that help a human being change and grow:

1. Communication of feelings; all feelings are honorable—express your feelings—no one knows how you feel if you don't disclose them.
2. Belief that a person is able to grow and change—if you believe you can change, you can.
3. Restoring the use of the senses—take in the world and see freely, touch freely, and hear freely.

What's in the "Pot of Self-Worth"? Finally, it is essential that people are able to be in contact with themselves on *a human* basis. Unfortunately, people are often dominated by some kind of idea of "what is right" that is actually *not right*. Satir uses a big pot that was used on her farm when she was a child as an analogy. There were times when the pot was used for soup, soap, and fertilizer. There were always two questions one had to ask about that pot to find out if you could use it or whether you wanted to put your energy into cleaning it out. (1) What is it full of? and (2) How full is it? Satir uses this "pot concept" to refer to how you feel about yourself, your self-worth.

Suppose your "pot" is full of a feeling you have had since childhood, such as hostility toward one of your parents because they abused you. Your inner thoughts say, "I must be a bad person, because my parents always beat me. I'm no good. I must have deserved the abuse." Your pot of self-worth is low, because of your past experience. You are experiencing "self-defeating" thoughts. You can learn to change these feelings. You can change your *self-talk,* and tell yourself that you are a "good person." You can read a good self-help book that may help you or you may seek professional counseling.

How Full Is Your Pot Of Self Worth?

36 oz. —
27 oz. —
18 oz. —
9 oz. —

What will it take to fill your pot?

Your self-worth pot is constantly changing. One day you get an "A" on a test and you feel great, your pot of self-worth is full of good feelings. The next day you don't make the basketball team and your pot of self-worth is low, it has a lot of negative feelings in it. Knowing that you are a "good" person no matter what happens to you will help you maintain a full pot of good feelings and help you succeed in life.

You must learn to free yourself of any rule decreeing that some feeling you have is not a human feeling. Then you are free to function fully and free to make choices about what you want for your life.

THE SELF

The Nature of the Self. One of the main factors differentiating humans from other animals is awareness of "self." As human beings, we can think, feel, and reflect on who we are. We form an identity and attach a value to it.

Who are YOU?
Where are you headed?
Does it make a difference that you exist?

Over 2000 years ago, the Greek philosopher Socrates advised all seekers of wisdom, "know thyself." What Socrates realized and we have discovered since is the most vibrant, compelling, and baffling reality we can know, the self. It is difficult to define and even more difficult to measure or investigate. Yet, such awareness of self is vital in knowing how people adjust to life.

Many ideas about the self have sprung from the humanistic-existential perspective. Carl Rogers (1959) has summarized a number of important characteristics of the self as follows:

1. It is organized and consistent.
2. It includes one's perceptions of all that comprises I or me.
3. It includes the relationship among I or Me and other people and features of life, as well as the value and importance of these relationships.
4. The self is available to consciousness (we can become aware of it) but it is not always conscious at any given moment.
5. The shape of the self is constantly changing, yet always recognizable.

Don't sell yourself short. Conquer the crime of self-deprivation. Concentrate on your assets. You're better than you think you are.

David Schwartz

We are human. We wrestle with our humanness. Some of us struggle with insecurity or inferiority, some deal with emotional, mental or sexual problems. Poverty, illness, and physical disabilities test us. Many feel the pain of sexual, racial, or ethnic prejudice. It is as if each of us is given a special task or challenge to work on as part of life and part of what will enhance our growth as an individual. It is the joy of discovering ourselves as human beings, our personal growth, sharing our love with others, and the contribution we make to others' lives that makes the process of life so exciting. The journey inward is life. Each of us must find his or her own way.

MYSELF

I have to live with myself, and so
I want to be fit for myself to know,
I want to be able, as days go by,
Always to look myself straight in the eye;
I don't want to stand, with the setting sun,
And hate myself for things I have done.

I don't want to keep on a closet shelf
A lot of secrets about myself,
And fool myself, as I come and go,
Into thinking that nobody else will know
The kind of man I really am;
I don't want to dress up myself in sham.

I want to go out with my head erect,
I want to deserve all men's respect;
But here in the struggle for fame and self
I want to be able to like myself.
I don't want to look at myself and know
That I'm bluster and bluff and empty show.

I can never hide myself from me;
I see what others may never see;
I know what others may never know,
I never can fool myself, and so.
Whatever happens, I want to be
Self-respecting and conscience free.

Edgar A. Guest

FIND YOUR TRUE SELF

The personal self-image is the part of self that includes physical, behavioral, and psychological characteristics that establish uniqueness. It also includes gender, racial or ethnic identity, age, and status. Your personal self-image, who you think you are, is literally a package you put together from how others have seen and treated you and from your conclusions as you compared yourself to others. Your sense of identity is the end result of the interaction between your uniqueness and how others have reacted to it. It is the package you call *me*. But it is not the real self.

It is never who you are that hangs you up, but rather who you THINK you are. To discover your real self it is important to separate the Real You from your personal self-image. Lining up your self picture to fit the Real You is of utmost importance. There is probably no more exciting journey than that of real self-discovery. Once your self-belief system is accurate, you are free of the trap of low self-esteem. You are free to be the real you.

Where Did Your "Personal Self-Image" Come From? Your personal self-image includes past teachings about yourself. As a child, you build your sense of self based on what others told you about you. If you were exposed to large doses of put downs and belittlers, your personal self-image doesn't feel very pleasant. If you grew up in a very positive climate, your me package feels good to live in. Your personal self-image is simply a belief system you have constructed about yourself. These past learnings jell into a self which may or may not be accurate. But once past learnings are part of your self-image, you see the package you have put together as accurate regardless of the facts.

Tom for instance was repeatedly told as a child that he was dumb because he was slow to learn to read. Because he bought that label, he ignored or denied any evidence of his academic ability and creativity. "Dumb" and "smart" don't mix, they are mutually exclusive. Tom held onto those negative messages he received from significant people in his life such as his parents and teachers. He also ignored any contrary evidence, because it didn't fit the "dumb" profile.

As an adult, Tom's past learning limited the accuracy of his "personal self-image." He saw only evidence of being academically inferior. Years later, despite a college degree and a successful career, Tom still sees himself as "dumb."

Each of us identifies whatever qualities we learn to place after the words *I am.* Like Tom, we see such traits as truths about ourselves. These truths or self-beliefs literally screen out any messages to the contrary. In this way, past teachings can limit our options. If your self-worth is low or shaky, you are still believing things about yourself that are untrue, negative ideas programmed into you about you.

There was a prisoner who spent years in his cell totally unaware that the door was unlocked. At any point he could have walked out. But because he assumed there was a lock on the door, he remained trapped. His false belief limited his behavior.

Once you become aware that you are not locked into a prison of self-doubt, whole new sets of choices open up. You become aware of new ways to see yourself, new ways you can behave, and new ways to relate. Of course, such choices and behaviors have been available to you all along. The problem has been you did not fully appreciate your capabilities and potential.

Lack of awareness, of course, is the same as having no choice. It is up to you to increase your awareness about the *real you* so you can experience inner freedom. By increasing your awareness about yourself, you increase your choices in life. Carl Rogers (1971) described such a person as a *fully functioning person* who feels inwardly free to move in any direction. Being a *fully functioning person* can be a reality for you. If you strive to such an inner freedom, little can hold you back.

Accept human differences and limitations. Don't expect anyone to be perfect. Remember, the other person has a right to be different. And don't be a reformer.

David Schwartz

HOW WE GET OUR SELF-IMAGE FROM OTHERS

"There's no doubt about it, kids come into this world with different personalities. Take my youngest, sweet good-natured boy, he'd give you the shirt off his back. But the oldest won't part with a dime. He's a born miser."

"I know what you mean. I've got one at Princeton, and another who'll be lucky if he gets out of high school. He'll never be a student that's for sure. I've told him, "You're not stupid, just lazy." "You should meet my daughters. You wouldn't know they are related. The little one is graceful, moves like a ballerina. The big one can't walk into a room without knocking something over. We call her "the klutz."

If I were able to express myself, I could have told them: "Dear Friends, what you are making jokes about is no laughing matter. Children see themselves primarily through their parents' eyes. They look to us to tell them not only who they are, but what they're capable of becoming. They depend on us for a larger vision of themselves and for the tools to implement that vision."

I also could have given them the following quote by an anonymous writer:

There is no such thing as a child who is selfish. There is only a child who needs to experience the joys of generosity. There is no such thing as a child who is lazy. There is only a child who is unmotivated, who needs some one to believe that he can work hard when he cares enough. There is no such thing as a child who is clumsy. There is only a child who needs to have his movements accepted and his body exercised. Children—all children—need to have their best affirmed and their worst ignored or redirected.

SELF-ESTEEM

How to Appreciate Your True Self. This chapter began with a description of the nature of self. Remember that as human beings, we have the ability to reflect on who we are. We are aware of a unique identity. But we are not only aware of ourself, we attach a value to that self. So we can decide whether we will accept or reject our self, whether we are OK or not OK, whether we are good or bad. You are either a self-hater, self-doubter, or a self-affirmer.

So this unique human ability we have, the ability we have to attach a value to our self, can lead to self-rejection and tremendous emotional pain. The term *self-esteem* refers to overall evaluation of oneself, whether one likes or dislikes who one is, believes or doubts oneself, and values or belittles one's worth. How you evaluate yourself is critical to your psychological adjustment. Table 2.1 illustrates characteristics of low self-esteem and high self-esteem.

Table 2.1	
High Self-Esteem Traits	**Low Self-Esteem Traits**
Perceive reality	Avoid reality to avoid anxiety
Relatively undefensive	Defensive
Spontaneous	Reserved
Natural	Plays a role
Task-centered	Self-centered
Enjoys being alone	Oriented toward approval of others
Self-reliant	Dependent
Feels kinship with humankind	Us vs. them
Relationships intimate	Relationships casual
Nonjudgmental of others	Critical of others
Acceptant	Strikes to be perfect and avoid mistakes
Well-developed value system	Values not clarified
Philosophical sense of humor	Hostile
Creative	Creativity perceived as risky
Cooperative with others	Views self as different from others
Makes growth choices	Makes fear choices
Dares to be unpopular	Conforming
Experiences w/o self-consciousness	Considers what others think

Just knowing what traits a high self-esteemer has is not enough for most of us to embark upon the philosophical, emotional, and behavioral change necessary to increase our self-esteem. On the following page is a list of strategies that provide a good start. This list is by no means complete, because this process is an ongoing one that will continue your entire lifetime. Remember also that this is not an easy process. It not only takes work but requires the inner strength to put up with the anxiety that goes along with making change and making mistakes. And remember, too, that not all these strategies will work for you. Think of this list as a menu from which you choose what you like and what fits, and from which you reject what you don't like and what doesn't fit. So here goes. This is no easy fix, just an aid or guideline for you. And just because you are willing to try to judge yourself less often means you are a courageous person.

A walk in the valley, I came in from the night. I was lonely your light was on, you were there. Thanks. A friend.

Robert Cummings

STRATEGIES TO IMPROVE SELF-ESTEEM

1. Reject Parts of Your Personal Self-Image That Does Not Represent Your Real Self. Be objective about yourself. Review all those old learning messages and discard the old false negative tapes. Your personal self-image and your real self should be close to the same.

2. Be Able to Accept All Parts of Your Physical Appearance Now! Describe your age, height, weight, facial appearance, skin, hair, and specific body areas such as chest, waist, and legs. Then accept your body. Treasure it. It is what you have and it works. Stand before a mirror and say out loud, "I love you. You are all I have and I will take care of you." Judy started working on appreciating her body by completing an appearance inventory as follows:

```
       middle age
    +large brown eyes
    +dark curly hair
       black complexion
    +clear, young looking skin
    −buckteeth
    −fat stomach
    −fat hips
    +large breasts
       slim legs
    −big nose
    −no chin
       5′5″
    −150 lbs
    +nice teeth
    −too many fat cells
```

Then she went back over her list and put a plus next to descriptions that represented strengths to her, a minus by items she wanted to change, and did not mark the items she considered to be neutral. She also reworded those minus statements to more accurate, less judgmental statements:

Minus Statement	Less Judgmental Statement
buckteeth	Prominent front teeth
fat belly	32 inch waist
fat hips	40 inch hips
big nose	distinctive nose
no chin	smaller chin
too many fat cells	slightly overweight

Remember, *low self-esteemers* put off *self-acceptance* until they get that perfect body. It is imperative you treasure your body the way it is now.

3. Affirm Your Strengths. This is not an easy task. The American culture has a degree of ambivalence about boasting. In addition to cultural prohibition, you may have had experiences in your own family that make you reluctant to acknowledge your positive side. Critical parents often punish children for speaking well of themselves. Also while growing up, children experience hundreds and hundreds of interactions like these:

Heather: I got a 100 on my spelling test.
Dad: Great. But what are you going to do about that D in Math?
Jason: I made my own bed.
Mom: Yes, but it is hard to tell. Your room is such a mess.
Mike: I came in second place at the district track meet and got my best time.
Dad: Who came in first?

As a result of cultural and parental conditioning, you may find it anxiety provoking to give yourself credit for your assets. However, it is now time to toot your own horn. Get a BIG piece of blank paper. List all your strengths. Think of all parts of your real self-image.

- Your physical appearance
- How you relate to others
- Your personality
- How others see you
- Your work/school/daily task performance
- Your mental functioning
- Your sexuality

It takes a concentrated effort to make this list. If you are having difficulty thinking of strengths, think of how your best friend would describe you in each of these areas. Your list of strengths will be long if you are willing to put forth the effort and willing to experience the anxiety. Once you've listed many of the qualities in yourself you appreciate doesn't mean you will remember them. Remembering your strengths, particularly at the times when you feel most down on yourself requires a system. The following three strategies may help you really believe your positive qualities:

People can be terribly brutal with themselves. Out of the whole animal kingdom, only humans are endowed with this capacity to make themselves miserable.

S. A. Bower and Gordon G. Bower

A. Daily affirmations. Write affirmations for yourself each day. Make them believable, comforting, and supportive.

B. Reminder signs and notes. Many people who post positive messages report they reinforce and strengthen their personal sense of adequacy.

C. Active integration. Recall specific examples and times when you clearly demonstrated your strengths. Transform your strengths into specific memories. This process will help to convince you that your list of positive qualities actually applies to you.

4. List Your Faults. There is nothing wrong with having faults. Every human being has them. The problem is not with your faults, but how you overrate them. The problem is that people use their faults for destructive self-attack and to condemn themselves. There are four basic rules to acknowledging weaknesses:

A. *Use nonpejorative language*—language that does not make a bad situation worse. Go through your list and eliminate all the words that have negative connotations. For example; fat, ugly, dumb, blabbermouth, etc. Banish these words from your self descriptive vocabulary.
B. *Use accurate language.* Confine yourself to the facts.
C. *Be specific rather than general.* Eliminate words such as always, never, everything, etc.
D. *Find exceptions or corresponding strengths.* This is essential for any item you feel particularly bad about.

5. Find Your Defense Mechanisms and Use Them Less Often. Even if we have developed a reasonable healthy self-concept there will always be frustrations, conflicts, and problems in our lives that interfere with our ability to maintain a healthy self-concept. We are extremely sensitive to threats to our ego. We will do almost anything to avoid, escape, or shield ourselves from the anxieties elicited by these threats. In order to protect our feeling of self-esteem and self-respect from unwelcomed information about ourselves, we unconsciously resort to various distortions of reality (Freud, 1936). Defense mechanisms do not eliminate the problems that are the cause of the anxiety, but they help us live and cope with reality and hopefully maintain our mental health while we defend ourselves from this unwanted information. Defense mechanisms have two primary characteristics.

• They distort reality.
• They operate unconsciously.

Defense mechanisms are designed to help us escape the pain of anxiety. Most of us would have difficulty maintaining our mental health without resorting to such defenses. The trouble is that these defenses can become common patterns of behavior for reacting to conflict. As a result, defense mechanisms prevent us from looking at ourselves on a realistic basis. They distort our self-concept. As we become more aware of ourselves as unique individuals with potential for growth, the greater the possibility is for us to become consciously aware of the defense mechanisms we use to escape reality. The more aware we become of using them, the more aware we become of ourselves as unique individuals and the less we need them in order to face reality openly and honestly. (Defense mechanisms are discussed in Chapter 8.)

6. Listen to Your Inner Voice. We pay attention to other people so that we can learn best how to gain their acceptance, love, respect, and protection and at that same time avoid their rejection. As a result, we tend not to pay enough attention to our inner voices. Abraham Maslow (1971) suggests that one way to promote our own growth is to pay attention to our own values and tastes. Carl Rogers (1961) tells us to trust ourself. We must trust our ability to live our own life, to discover and follow our own standards. He reminds us that it is all right to become more like the person we want to be. If we value our own judgments more highly, become more self-directing, we will become more self confident.

We are free to go where we wish and to be what we are.

Jonathan Livingston Seagull

7. Make the Growth Choice Rather Than the Fear Choice. Reject rigidity. Take responsibility to direct your own life. If you are dissatisfied with your life as it is now, be willing to accept change. You promote your growth or fail to do that every time you make a decision. We are constantly making decisions whether to be honest or to lie, to try new things or be safe, to be open or be defensive. If you make each decision a choice for growth, you manifest courage.

8. Shed Perfectionistic Demands. Realize that you are human and that you do have faults. Don't expect always to live up to your own ideals or those of others. By accepting your faults, you can begin to examine them without being afraid of what you might find. Come to grips with the fact that everyone can't like you, or you will spend your life trying to please others. Although there is nothing wrong with pleasing others, you must first of all be true to yourself.

9. Become More Synergistic. Maslow describes *this as being involved with others.* Become involved with other people and your work and leisure time will become more valuable to you. Make a commitment. Alfred Adler (1927) points out that we greatly promote our health and functioning by cooperation with others.

10. Don't Overburden Yourself with Work. Take time for the pleasures in life. Enjoy the present and expand it. Plan for the future but don't live it.

11. Keep a Diary. Record what you enjoy about your day. You may be doing things out of habit rather than because you enjoy them. By keeping a diary you may discover that some of your activities don't make you happy. If this is the case, you can actively make the attempt not to do these things any longer.

12. Keep a Sense of Humor. Laugh easily, enjoy a good joke, get fun out of life. Some of us don't know how to play. We take our life and ourselves too seriously. Perhaps we grew up in families in which there wasn't much fun and happiness. Remember to keep a balance in your life between work and play.

13. Make Mistakes. You will make thousands of mistakes during your lifetime if you plan to live up to your creative potential. Do a personal mistake check, then increase the number of mistakes you make each day by 10 percent. You will take more risks, stretch, grow, and enjoy life more. You learn through experience. If you don't try something you may lose out on a lot of experiences in your life.

Everyone makes mistakes; don't worry about them. Forgive yourself for making mistakes. If you don't make mistakes, you're not trying.

So, there you have it. The thirteen strategies listed here to help you to improve your self-esteem will give you a good start. As your work progresses you may come up with a few of your own that are not listed here. Just remember that as a child you were told all about who you were. Your sense of self came from others. As an adult it is up to you to develop a realistic positive sense of self. To do this you must be dedicated to the effort for a lifetime. It is not enough to just say you will love yourself. Your assumptions about yourself and about your world must be positive, healthy, and realistic ones.

MY DECLARATION OF SELF-ESTEEM

I am me.

I was uniquely created by God. There's not another human being in the whole world like me—I have my very own fingerprints and I have my very own thoughts. I was not stamped out of a mold like a Coca-Cola top to be the duplicate of another.

I own all of me—my body, and I can do with it what I choose; my mind, and all of its thoughts and ideas; my feelings, whether joyful or painful.

I own my ideals, my dreams, my hopes, my fantasies, my fears.

I reserve the right to think and feel differently from others and will grant to others their right to thoughts and feelings not identical with my own.

I own all my triumphs and successes. I own also all my failures and mistakes. I am the cause of what I do and am responsible for my own behavior. I will permit myself to be imperfect. When I make mistakes or fail, I will know that *I* am not the failure—I am still O.K.—and I will discard some parts of me that were unfitting and will try new ways.

I will laugh freely and loudly at myself—a healthy self-affirmation.

I will have fun living inside my skin.

I will remember that the door to everybody's life needs this sign: Honor Thyself.

I have value and worth.

I am me, and I am O.K.

ANONYMOUS

THE JOURNEY

Growth and change is not a destination but rather a journey. All through our lives, if we are to function fully, we will continue to grow and change. Our basic psychological need is *the need to feel that we are worthwhile to ourselves and others.* A person who realizes he or she does have worth is usually someone who can give love and receive love. However, an important part of fulfilling our need to be worthwhile depends upon our ability to see that even though we are the object of someone's love, this does not in itself give us worth. We have worth whether or not someone loves us. We can journey alone in life, but we do need to love one person, ourselves.

A LAST THOUGHT

In the process of becoming able to see ourselves more realistically, two stages seem to develop. We accept ourselves and we grow. In the acceptance stage, we realize that there are some features of ourselves that need modification, and some features of ourselves are unchangeable and must be accepted as such. The growth stage occurs when we realize that past experiences are good teachers and we build upon these past experiences for growth. Personal growth and self-awareness involve accepting ourselves and enjoying our relationships with others. Only *you* can choose whether you will live an enjoyable and fulfilling life or one of stagnation.

The first mile of the most important journey into growth and change must be a journey within one's self—a deeper self awareness. *Happy traveling!*

CHAPTER DISCUSSION QUESTIONS

1. Do we have a choice in determining who we become?
2. How do interactions with others help in discovering who we are?
3. How does past learning sometimes lead to self put-downs?
4. How does striving for perfection lead to emotional pain?
5. Why is it so difficult to make changes in our self-concept?
6. How can we learn to accept our mistakes?
7. What does Carl Rogers mean when he says that "it is a courageous person who seeks to understand the self?"
8. Who are the significant others in your life? What impact have they had on your life, good or bad?
9. What are your feelings about Freud's stages of psychosexual development? Can you relate your life to these stages? Explain.

KEY TERMS

Self-Awareness	Personal Self-Image
Self-Image	Self-Esteem
Significant Others	Stages of Psychosocial Development
Id	Trust vs Mistrust
Ego	Autonomy vs Doubt
Super-ego	Initiative vs Guilt
Stages of Psychosexual Development	Industry vs Inferiority
Oral Stage	Identity vs Role Confusion
Anal Stage	Intimacy vs Isolation
Phallic Stage	Generativity vs Self-Absorption
Latency Stage	Integrity vs Despair
Genital Stage	Stages of Adult Development
Getting Established Stage	Adolescent Identity Crisis Stage
Getting Settled Stage	Wavering and Doubt Stage
Mid-Life Crisis	Mid-Life Transition
Child	Transactional Analysis
Adult	Parent
Unconditional Positive Regard	Strokes
Search for Meaning	Self Theory
Self-Worth	Pot of Self-Worth
Real Self	

REFERENCES

Adler, Alfred. *What Life Should Mean to You.* Boston: Little Brown, 1931.

Briggs, Dorathy Corkille. *Celebrate your self. Enhancing Your Own Self Esteem.* New York: Doubleday, 1977.

Brooks-Gunn, J. and Lewis, M. *Mirror Image Stimulation and Self-Regulation in Infancy.* Presented at the meeting of the Society for Research in Child Development. Denver, 1975.

Frankl, Viktor. *Man's Search for Meaning.* New York: Simon & Schuster, 1959.

Harris, Thomas A. *I'm OK—You're OK.* New York: Harper & Row, 1969.

James, Jennifer. *Success Is the Quality of Your Journey.* Seattle: James Inc., 1983.

James, Jennifer. *The Slug Manual: The Rise and Fall of Criticism.* Seattle: Bronwen Press, 1986.

James, Jennifer. *You Know I Wouldn't Say This If I Didn't Love You.* New York: Newmarket Press, 1990.

James, Muriel and Jongeward, Dorothy. *Born to Win.* Nass Addison-Wesley, 1973.

Levinson, Daniel J. *The Seasons of a Man's Life.* New York: Ballantine Books, 1978.

Maslow, Abraham. *The Healthy Personality.* New York: Can Nordstrand Reinhold, 1969.

McKay, Mathew. *Self Esteem.* Oakland: New Harbinger, 1987.

Newman, Mildred and Berkowitz, Bernard. *How to Be Your Own Best Friend.* New York: Ballantine Books, 1978.

Rogers, Carl and Stevens, B. *Person to Person: The Problems of Being Human.* New York: The Pocket Book, 1972.

Rogers, Carl. *On Becoming a Person.* Boston: Houghton Mifflin, 1970.

Satir, Virginia. *Peoplemaking.* Palo Alto: Science & Behavior Books, 1972.

Satir, Virginia. *Self Esteem.* Berkeley: Celestial Arts, 1975.

Satir, Virginia. *Your Many Faces.* Berkeley: Celestial Arts, 1978.

Viorst, Judith. *Necessary Losses.* New York: Fawcett Gold Medal Books, 1986.

WHO DO YOU THINK YOU ARE?

Purpose: To help you identify your own self-concept.

Instructions:

  I. For each category below supply the words or phrases that describe you best.
 II. After filling in the spaces within each category, organize your responses so that the most fundamental characteristic is listed first, with the rest of the items following in order of descending importance.

Part A: *Identifying the elements of your self-concept*

  1. What moods or feelings best characterize you (cheerful, considerate, optimistic, and so on)?

   a. _____

   b. _____

   c. _____

  2. How would you describe your physical condition and/or your appearance (tall, attractive, weak, muscular, and so on)?

   a. _____

   b. _____

   c. _____

  3. How would you describe your social traits (friendly, shy, aloof, talkative, and so on)?

   a. _____

   b. _____

   c. _____

  4. What talents do you possess or lack (good artist, lousy carpenter, competent swimmer, and so on)?

   a. _____

   b. _____

   c. _____

  5. How would you describe your intellectual capacity (curious, poor reader, good mathematician, and so on)?

   a. _____

   b. _____

   c. _____

6. What beliefs do you hold strongly (vegetarian, Christian, passivist, and so on)?

   a. _____

   b. _____

   c. _____

7. What social roles are the most important in your life (brother, student, friend, bank teller, club president, and so on)?

   a. _____

   b. _____

   c. _____

8. What other terms haven't you listed so far that describe other important things about you?

   a. _____

   b. _____

   c. _____

Part B: *Listing self-concept elements in order of importance*

1. _____   13. _____

2. _____   14. _____

3. _____   15. _____

4. _____   16. _____

5. _____   17. _____

6. _____   18. _____

7. _____   19. _____

8. _____   20. _____

9. _____   21. _____

10. _____   22. _____

11. _____   23. _____

12. _____   24. _____

III. Give this list (part B) to another person (classmate). This list will describe to your partner how you perceive yourself as a person.

Discussion:

A. Does this list describe you as a person? If not, tell your partner more information about you that describes the *real* you.

B. Tell your partner what you like about yourself as a person. Use the characteristics from your list.

C. Tell your partner what element or elements you listed that you would like to change.

D. Discuss with your partner how important a person's self-concept is and how a person's self-concept affects his or her personality.

E. Discuss with your partner what you learned about yourself from this activity.

ADJECTIVE CHECKLIST

Purpose: To provide an opportunity for the class members to reveal themselves to the other group members and to receive feedback on how the other group members perceive them.

Instructions:

I. Go through the list of adjectives and check the four adjectives you think are most descriptive of yourself.

II. Divide into groups of three or four.

III. Each member of the group then shares with the group the adjectives he or she checked. Members of the group then share with the person what adjective they would have checked if they were to describe him or her. Try not to spend more than five to ten minutes on each person in the group.

_____ accepting	_____ effervescent	_____ unpredictable
_____ self-accepting	_____ thoughtful	_____ patient
_____ anxious	_____ lazy	_____ extroverted
_____ aggressive	_____ dependable	_____ hostile
_____ original	_____ mystical	_____ questioning
_____ happy	_____ inconsiderate	_____ remote
_____ vain	_____ understanding	_____ shy
_____ conforming	_____ sarcastic	_____ warm
_____ irritable	_____ dreamy	_____ withdrawn
_____ worried	_____ silly	_____ bitter
_____ rigid	_____ selfish	_____ independent
_____ brave	_____ carefree	_____ naive
_____ responsible	_____ determined	_____ complex
_____ simple	_____ spontaneous	_____ sensitive
_____ proud	_____ tense	_____ insensitive
_____ adaptable	_____ certain	_____ nervous
_____ dependent	_____ sentimental	_____ loving

Discussion:

1. What did you find out about yourself as a result of this activity?

2. What is the one adjective that causes you the greatest amount of difficulty in relationships with other people?

ACCEPTING MYSELF

Purpose: To demonstrate the value of feeling positive about yourself and to demonstrate the value of accepting yourself with your strengths and your weaknesses.

Instructions:

   I. The participants will number themselves, 1, 2, 3 until every participant has a number.

  II. All the ones, twos, threes, will get together and form a group.

 III. The participants will then answer the following questions, with *all* participants answering question (a) first.

     a. *Three* things I like about myself.

       _____

       _____

       _____

     b. *Two* things I would like to change about myself.

       _____

       _____

  IV. When the participants have completed the questions, share the answers with your group. Give examples so that your partners will understand you better.

   V. Your partners will ask at least two questions about each of your statements. Then, each partner will have a turn to share and be asked questions.

 VI. Group members might want to discuss how they feel each other might change the aspects of themselves that they feel need some modification.

Discussion:

A. Which answer was harder for you to reveal? Why?

B. Discuss the following statement: Accepting ourselves means to accept our strengths and our weaknesses and make every effort to change the weaknesses into strengths, if *possible* and *desirable* to the individual.

I AM A PERSON WHO CONVEYS

Purpose: To become more aware of how you are perceived by others and how accurate you are in your perceptions of others.

Instructions:

I. Each person responds to the scale by circling the number on the continuum that indicates the way you convey yourself to others. Do not mark this the way you see yourself but the way you feel you come across to others.

I AM A PERSON WHO CONVEYS . . .

Personal warmth	1 2 3 4 5 6 7 8 9	Aloofness, coldness
Neat appearance	1 2 3 4 5 6 7 8 9	Careless appearance
Cheerful disposition	1 2 3 4 5 6 7 8 9	Unhappy disposition
Sincerity Genuineness	1 2 3 4 5 6 7 8 9	Insincerity, artificiality
Insecurity in behavior	1 2 3 4 5 6 7 8 9	Confidence in behavior
Reluctancy to talk with others	1 2 3 4 5 6 7 8 9	Eagerness to talk with others
Desire to listen	1 2 3 4 5 6 7 8 9	No interest in listening
Primary concern for self	1 2 3 4 5 6 7 8 9	Primary concern for others
Ability to express ideas and feelings	1 2 3 4 5 6 7 8 9	Difficulty in expressing ideas and feelings
Awareness of what is happening	1 2 3 4 5 6 7 8 9	Lack of awareness of what is happening
Difficulty in making other people comfortable	1 2 3 4 5 6 7 8 9	Ease in making other people comfortable

Talk too much	1 2 3 4 5 6 7 8 9	Talk too little
Not intelligent	1 2 3 4 5 6 7 8 9	Intelligent
Excitement, enthusiasm	1 2 3 4 5 6 7 8 9	Dullness, apathy

II. Then, pair off with another person and write that person's name in the space provided in the heading

(_____ Is a Person Who Conveys).

III. Without any discussion, mark the responses as to how you perceive your partner.

IV. _____ IS A PERSON WHO CONVEYS . . .

Personal warmth	1 2 3 4 5 6 7 8 9	Aloofness, coldness
Neat appearance	1 2 3 4 5 6 7 8 9	Careless appearance
Cheerful disposition	1 2 3 4 5 6 7 8 9	Unhappy disposition
Sincerity Genuineness	1 2 3 4 5 6 7 8 9	Insincerity, artificiality
Insecurity in behavior	1 2 3 4 5 6 7 8 9	Confidence in behavior
Reluctancy to talk with others	1 2 3 4 5 6 7 8 9	Eagerness to talk with others
Desire to listen	1 2 3 4 5 6 7 8 9	No interest in listening
Primary concern for self	1 2 3 4 5 6 7 8 9	Primary concern for others
Ability to express ideas and feelings	1 2 3 4 5 6 7 8 9	Difficulty in expressing ideas and feelings
Awareness of what is happening	1 2 3 4 5 6 7 8 9	Lack of awareness of what is happening

Difficulty in making other people comfortable	1 2 3 4 5 6 7 8 9	Ease in making other people comfortable
Talk too much	1 2 3 4 5 6 7 8 9	Talk too little
Not intelligent	1 2 3 4 5 6 7 8 9	Intelligent
Excitement, enthusiasm	1 2 3 4 5 6 7 8 9	Dullness, apathy

V. Exchange the scale, " ＿＿＿＿＿＿＿＿＿ Is a Person Who Conveys." Each participant now has two scales, one of which is your self-evaluation, and the other your partner's evaluation of you. Looking at both scales, identify any discrepancies between the two.

VI. Then, discuss the discrepancies in terms of:
(1) "I see you this way because . . . " and
(2) "I feel I convey this trait to others because . . . "

Discussion:

1. Many times we feel we convey a particular characteristic to others because that is the way we see ourselves. What does this activity show us about our awareness and honesty in conveying our true self to others?

2. Did you have a realistic perception of yourself as compared to how the other person perceived you? Discuss the differences between your perceptions and the other person's perceptions.

3. Discuss how our perceptions of another person affect our interactions with them.

HUMAN RELATIONS POSITION PAPER

Purpose: To analyze your present position, based upon your past experiences and learning, in order to have a better idea of the direction in which you want to move in the future.

Instructions:

   I. A Human Relations Position Paper should represent a critical analysis of those factors that have brought you to this point in your life and have made you what you are. It should also include your plans for the future.

  II. No one but you and your instructor will read your position paper unless, of course, you choose to show it to someone else. Your instructor considers it completely confidential.

 III. As a guide for preparing your position paper, the following outline is suggested. This is intended only as a guide, and you may add or delete whatever items you choose.

  IV. Anything that helps you arrive at your *position* and chart your course of action (from poetry to pictures to words) is acceptable.

   V. Your instructor will determine the length of this paper. We suggest five pages.

THE OUTLINE

   I. The Person I Am (Include the influential factors which have contributed to making you what you are).
      A. Influence of Family Background
         1. Relationship with parents
         2. Relationship with siblings
         3. Socioeconomic setting
         4. Family's expectations
         5. Other
      B. Adolescence
         1. School experience
         2. Peer Group (Left out/included—Why?)
         3. Successes/Failures and their effect
         4. Influential adults other than parents
         5. Other
      C. Personal Sexuality
         1. Dating experiences and its effect
         2. "Facts of life" information or misinformation and its effect
         3. My "role" as a man/woman
         4. My attitudes toward the opposite sex
         5. Other
      D. Goals for Future
         1. How have I arrived at my goals?
         2. Occupational choice—Why?
         3. Feelings of personal adequacy or inadequacy
         4. Degree of flexibility
         5. Influential people
         6. Other

II. Where Do I Go From Here?
  A. Summary of Present Position
    1. How do I see myself/how do others see me
    2. How well do I communicate
    3. Value system
    4. Relationships with others (OKness)
    5. My view of a meaningful occupation
      a. What I expect
      b. What's expected of me
      c. My chances for success
    6. How I view my sexuality
      a. In relation to marriage
      b. "Role" expectations
      c. Understanding of needs
  B. Plans for Future
    1. What is the Good Life for me?
      a. How I will achieve it
      b. How it relates to my value system
      c. How it relates to my chosen occupation
    2. What are my priorities for future?
    3. Do I want to "go it alone" or build relationships with others?
      a. How I will do this
    4. Do I want to share my life with someone else in marriage?
      a. My responsibilities
      b. What I expect of others
    5. What will my biggest problems be?

LEARNING JOURNAL FOR WHO AM I

Select the statement below that best defines your feelings about the personal value or meaning gained from this chapter and respond below the dotted line.

I LEARNED THAT I   I WAS SURPRISED THAT I

I REALIZED THAT I   I WAS PLEASED THAT I

I DISCOVERED THAT I   I WAS DISPLEASED THAT I

....

3

Who's In Control

CHILDREN LEARN WHAT THEY LIVE

If a child lives with criticism. He learns to condemn.
If a child lives with hostility. He learns to fight.
If a child lives with ridicule. He learns to be shy.
If a child lives with shame. He learns to feel guilty.
If a child lives with tolerance. He learns to be patient.
If a child lives with encouragement. He learns confidence.
If a child lives with praise. He learns to appreciate.
If a child lives with fairness. He learns justice.
If a child lives with security. He learns to have faith.
If a child lives with approval. He learns to like himself.
If a child lives with acceptance and friendship. He learns to
find love in the world.

How am I ever going to stop smoking? I've tried hundreds of times.

I need to lose 15 pounds. I lose 5 pounds then gain back 10 pounds. How can I lose weight and make sure that I can keep it off?

I need to study more. My grades aren't too good. How can I get myself to sit down and study more?

I would sure like to have more dates, I haven't had a date for two months. How can I get more dates?

My boss is always so critical. Why can't she be more positive?

Most of us have either asked one or more of these questions or we have heard many of our friends ask them. Now the question is "If I want to change, can I? Am I in control of my own behavior, or is someone or something else in control of me? How can someone change?" As we all know change is not easy.

B. F. Skinner (1972), a well known psychologist, has indicated in much of his writing that all of our behavior is controlled and that there is no such things as "free will." Do you agree? This is a philosophical question that people have been discussing for years. We will not attempt to answer this question in this book, but we will be referring to it, directly or indirectly, throughout the book. Who is in control? You? Me? Someone else? Our environment? Psychologists have come up with a number of theories to explain how we can develop the capacity to control our own behavior and to develop the capacity to influence other people's behavior. Many psychologists believe that learning theory is the answer to all our questions. Learning theory underlies all relationships, good relationships, bad relationships, happy ones, and sad ones.

SELF-CONTROL OR EXTERNAL CONTROL

Self-control is often considered the opposite of external control. *In self-control,* individuals set their own standards for performance and will then reward or punish themselves for meeting or not meeting these standards. In external control, on the other hand, someone else sets the standards and delivers or withholds the rewards or punishment.

Both Angie and Beth took a Psychology test last Friday. Angie studied two hours every night for the last five nights, and it paid off for her: She received an "A" grade. Angie knows that she earned her grade, it took a lot of work. On the other hand, Beth only studied two hours total for her test and she also received an "A" for her grade. Beth knows how hard she really studied and that she was really lucky to receive such a good grade. How hard will Beth study for her next test? Who will be more motivated to study, Beth or Angie? Which person will be most likely to succeed in school and everyday life?

Perceived Locus of Control. People differ markedly in their feelings about their capacity to control life situations. Some people feel that they are in control of their own destinies. Their general expectancy is that which happens to them and what they achieve in life is due to their own abilities, attitudes, and actions. In contrast, other people see their lives as being beyond their control. They believe that what happens to them is determined by external forces, whether it be luck or fate, other people, "Mother Nature," or the stars. According to Julian Rotter (1966), these two types of people are said to be identified as having either an *internal* or an *external* "locus of control." Angie would be said to have an *internal locus of control* and Beth would have an *external locus of control.*

Internals perceive that their efforts make a difference when they are facing a difficult situation, so they try to cope with it. They take whatever action seems appropriate to solve the problem.

Externals perceive that their efforts won't make a difference, so naturally they don't attempt to cope with threatening situations.

The difference in *perceived locus of control* is important for personal adjustment to the world. People who believe they can control events in their environment will respond to stress quite differently from those who believe the opposite. Rotter indicates that these attitudes are learned from experience prior to the age of nineteen. If you discover that your efforts are repeatedly rewarded, you will believe that you will be able to exert control over your outcomes in the future. If you discover that your efforts are to no avail, you will become resigned to the lack of control.

Internals are more apt to become *activists,* because they feel their efforts will have an effect on the outcome. Smokers who successfully quit smoking have been found to be more *internal* than those who were unsuccessful (James, Woodruff, & Werner, 1965). Externals who attempt to stop smoking are apt to say, "It's no use. I'm hooked and there is nothing I can do about it."

ARE YOU AN INTERNAL OR EXTERNAL?

What implications does research on the locus of control have for you? The most important point is that there is a link between your beliefs about the locus of control and your behavior. If you believe your experience is beyond your own control, you may expend less effort than you could. You may not try as hard as you are able, because you believe that your efforts won't make a difference. You may satisfy yourself with poor performance, figuring there's nothing you can do to improve the situation. Certainly some situations are more out of your control than others are, but your overall attitude about challenging situations affects every aspect of your life.

To help you assess your own locus of control we suggest that you identify who or what controls different aspects of your life by doing the exercise at the end of the chapter, WHAT CONTROLS YOUR LIFE?

Internals seem to be more successful in most aspects of life than *externals*. Although an internal locus of control does not ensure success, those who believe they can influence life events tend to be the best life managers. This is true for several reasons. For one thing, these people are more likely to consider the possibility of doing something differently in their lives than people with an external orientation.

Internals are more curious than externals about ways to improve their lives. They see that education and knowledge are personal power. They are more likely to read about problem areas in their lives and attend workshops and classes related to solving these problems. Internals are also better listeners than externals (Lefcourt et al., 1985). They are more likely to ask questions, give others time to speak, and accurately interpret what others are saying.

Concerning relationships, internals tend to fare better than externals, especially considering the fact that internals tend to be better listeners and are more willing to work at improving their relationships. During stressful times in life, internals are more likely to seek social support than externals (Lefcourt et al., 1984).

Are you an internal or an external? Which of these do you want to be? Can you change your behavior? Who's in control? As you continue to read this chapter you will discover new ways to take control of your life. One of the ways that you will discover to take control of your own life is by developing a high level of self-efficacy.

What one single ability do we all have? The ability to change.

L. Andrews

Self-efficacy is our belief about our ability to perform behaviors that should lead to expected outcomes. Believing that you can control your behaviors is fundamental to self-management. Individuals having *high* self-efficacy for particular behaviors or skills are likely to work longer and try more strategies to develop these skills than those with *low* self-efficacy (Bandura 1986). When self-efficacy is high, we feel confident that we can execute the responses necessary to earn reinforcers. When self-efficacy is low, we worry that the necessary responses may be beyond our abilities. Perceptions of self-efficacy are subjective and specific to different kinds of tasks. For instance, you might feel extremely confident about your ability to handle different social situations but very doubtful about your ability to handle academic challenges. Perceptions of self-efficacy can influence which challenges we tackle and how well we perform.

Increasing your self-efficacy about behaviors you wish to change is very much tied to the recall of past successes (Goldfried & Robins, 1982). The more successes you recall, the more likely you are to believe that you can change other behaviors. On the other hand, recalling failures is very debilitating to self-efficacy (Kirsch, 1986). Having a sense of self-efficacy is important in taking the active approach to life for successful adjustment.

How did you become an internal or external? Where did your high level or low level of self-efficacy come from? How can you take control of your life? These are not easy questions to answer. In order to understand yourself better and to discover different ways to improve your life, psychologists have developed many different theories. Many of these theories evolve around *learning theory*.

THE BOTTOM LINE

Face it, nobody owes you a living,
What you achieve or fail to achieve in your lifetime,
    is directly related to what you do,
    or fail to do.

No one chooses his parents or childhood,
    but you can choose your own direction.
Everyone has problems and obstacles to overcome,
    but that too is relative to each individual.

Nothing is carved in stone,
    you can change anything in your life,
    if you want to badly enough.

Excuses are for losers:
    Those who take responsibility for their actions
    are the real winners in life.
Winners meet life's challenges head on,
    knowing there are no guarantees,
    and give all they've got.

And never think it's too late or too early to begin,
    Time plays no favorites
    and will pass whether you act or not.

Take control of your life.
    Dare to dream and take risks . . .
    Compete.

Anonymous

SOCIAL LEARNING THEORY

Albert Bandura is one of several behaviorists who has added a cognitive flavor to learning theory. Bandura points out that humans obviously are conscious, thinking, feeling beings. He feels that some psychologists like B. F. Skinner ignore these cognitive processes. An important aspect of *social learning theory* that may have an important impact on our lives is *observational learning*.

Observational Learning. This occurs when an individual's behavior is influenced by the observation of others, who are called *models*. Observational learning requires that you pay attention to someone who *is significant* to you, a parent, friend, and so on. Observe his or her behavior and understand its consequences, and then store this information in your memory.

Some models are more influential than others. Children and adults tend to imitate people they like and respect more so than people they don't. We also are especially prone to imitate the behavior of people that we consider attractive or powerful, such as rock stars, movie stars, sports heros or politicians. It's a bit scary to discover that we are also more likely to model after the individual who is the most aggressive, especially if that aggression leads to positive reinforcement. If you observe your mother yelling at your father in order to get him to do something, and he does do it, you are more likely to yell at someone the next time you want something. Prior to that experience you most likely would have not yelled at someone in order to get your way. A five-year-old boy goes to the store with a seven year old. The older boy picks up a candy bar and doesn't pay for it and on the way home shares it with his friend. Did he get positive reinforcement for stealing? What's the likelihood that the younger boy will attempt to pocket a candy bar the next time he goes to the store? What we learn through modeling is not always positive. That's why our parents keep saying, "Do what I say, not what I do".

According to *social learning theory,* modeling has a great impact on personality development. Children learn to be assertive, conscientious, self-sufficient, aggressive, fearful, and so forth by observing others behaving in these ways.

What are some of the other theories of learning that may have an impact on my relationships? You will now get a chance to understand how learning theory applies to you and your life.

HOW DOES LEARNING THEORY INFLUENCE MY LIFE?

When you do something you enjoy, what is the likelihood that you will do it again?

If you try something and fail at it, what are the chances that you will attempt it again?

If you ask someone out for a date five times and the answer is "NO" each time, are you going to ask again?

If you make a comment to a member of the opposite sex who responds by slapping you, will you make that comment next time?

Someone you don't know very well embarrasses you in front of a large group, are you going to avoid that person in the future?

If you drink something that tastes good, will you drink it again?

You hate green peas because you were forced to eat them as a kid; do you eat them now?

All of these situations can be explained by learning theory.

In order to understand learning theory, we need to define the term, *learning:* Learning is defined in psychology as a relatively permanent change in behavior as a result of experience or practice.

Before you can begin the process of learning, you have to pay attention. Are you aware of all the different types of stimuli that gets your attention?

I was born a human being; I had to learn what being human is all about.

Rabbi Abraham Heschel

WHAT GETS YOUR ATTENTION?

You are concentrating on reading a book and the phone rings. What do you do? A person enters the room that you perceive as attractive. Do you notice that person? What gets your attention? Before you can learn something, you have to pay attention to it. Attention is the most important aspect of learning, because we have to pay attention to something before we can respond. Another aspect of attention that may surprise you is that you can only pay attention to one thing at a time. You can't watch TV and study at the same time. Again, what do you pay attention to? We find that there are three kinds of stimuli that attract our attention. They are *novel stimuli, significant stimuli* and *conflicting stimuli*. We find that these three different kinds of stimuli are not only important to learning, but vital to our relationships with others.

Novel Stimuli. We tend to pay attention to people, places, or things that are new, different, unique, or original. You tend to pay more attention to the student who is new to your school than a student who has been going to your school for the past few years. When reading the newspaper, you tend to notice an advertisement that is in color more than in black and white, because the color ad is unique. The person with a mohawk haircut will generally be noticed before someone with a "normal" hairstyle. A person wearing the latest in fashionware will tend to get more attention than someone wearing last year's clothing. Why? Because it's unique, different or *novel*. The more familiar we become with the "new" person, the "unique" hairstyle, or the "latest" fashion, the less we are apt to pay attention. We tend to begin to take them for granted. When you begin to date someone you tend to give the individual a lot of special attention, but what happens after you have been dating that same individual for years? Many times you find that you begin to habituate or get bored with that individual when the novelty wears off and you no longer pay as much attention to him or her.

Teachers need to consider this as they attempt to get students to learn. A teacher needs to make material unique or *novel* to the students in order to get their attention so they can learn. A salesperson needs to market his or her product in a unique way in order to get the customer to pay attention to the product and not the competitor's product.

Eventually, the *novelty* or uniqueness of people or things will tend to fade away and we tend to pay less attention to them. Now, what can we do to continue to keep someone's attention and thus get people to learn? What else gets your attention?

Significant Stimuli. So, you like to listen to music? Do you like ice cream? Are you interested in sex? Do you like money? If your answer to all of these questions is yes, then all of these things are *significant* to you, and you will pay attention to them. If you are a teacher and want to get your students to learn, you better make sure the material is *significant* to your students. Otherwise, you may find it difficult to keep your students attention. You need to make the material relate directly to your student's needs, wants, interests, and desires. If you do this, you will be surprised to discover that your students are paying attention and thus learning.

When you start dating someone, do you consider your date's needs, wants, interests, and desires as you decide where to go and what to do? If you do, you will find that your date will respond more positively to you, and you both will be much happier. If you send your mate flowers for the first time and he or she likes them, will you receive more attention? Are the flowers *significant?* Are the flowers *novel?* Because they are both *novel* and *significant,* they should increase the attention paid to you by your friend. You reinforce your mate and your mate reinforces you. It tends to make life more interesting to you and your friends.

If you want a relationship to continue on a positive basis over a long period of time you must make sure that you provide *novel* and *significant* stimuli in the relationship; otherwise, the relationship will become stale and boring. This is why that old saying is appropriate here. "The grass always looks greener on the other side of the fence." You wonder why your boyfriend, girlfriend, husband, or wife is always looking at members of the opposite sex? You wonder why students aren't paying attention to the teacher? Could it be that the other people are novel and maybe even more significant?

Not too long ago, a colleague of mine told me it was her husband's birthday a few days before and she decided to surprise him. For your information, this couple has been married about ten years. The morning of her husband's birthday she packed a picnic-type lunch: cheese, wine, and so on. She put on her coat and nothing else, went to his office building at noon, and went into his private office and closed the door. She set up the picnic lunch and opened up her coat and said, "Happy Birthday, Dear!" Is this significant stimuli? Is it novel stimuli? It most definitely is, and if these two people continue to provide novel and significant stimuli in their relationship, it will continue on a positive basis for a long time. You don't have to do what this woman did, but you do need to continue to provide novel and significant stimuli in your relationships with others. Otherwise, you may discover that your friends and partners become bored with the relationship and then begin to form other relationships that will meet their needs and be more exciting. Is there anything else that seems to get our attention? When you have an argument with your mate, do you pay attention to them? Of course you do, but why?

The quality, not the longevity, of one's life is what is important.

M. L. King Jr.

Conflicting Stimuli. What if we were to tell you that all of your behavior is controlled!; that there is no "God"!; that it is all right to steal!; that it's okay to cheat on your spouse, boyfriend, or girlfriend? Are these statements in conflict with any of your beliefs? We have discovered that you will not only pay attention to *novel* and *significant* stimuli, but also anything that is in conflict with your values, needs, morals, etc. It has been found that in many relationships the only time that two people pay attention to one another is when they are in conflict—arguing, fighting, etc. We do not recommend this form of stimuli in order to get attention, because it can create more problems than it solves. If this is the only time you find that you and your partner pay attention to one another, you might want to change this by seeking counseling, reading a good self-help book, or changing your behavior in order to provide more novel or significant stimuli in your relationships.

With all the technology and equipment we have today and with all the activities available to us, many of us still get tired of just sitting around. We get bored with life. Why?

Boredom. Have you every heard someone say, "I sure am bored, there's nothing to do?"

We have TV's, VCR's, computers, video games, cable TV, the latest table games and there is still nothing to do. After playing a video game for two hours without any additional challenge, a person will finally get bored with the game. Your family has owned a full size pool table for the last eight years and you no longer get excited about playing pool, but when your friends come to visit you, all they want to do is play pool. Playing pool is boring to you, because it is always available, but to your friends, playing pool is exciting, it's novel, and also significant.

We all seek change in our lives. Kids get bored, teenagers get bored, and adults get bored. If you take your kids to the zoo every Saturday, eventually, they will not enjoy going any longer. If you take your date to the movie every Friday night, it just isn't as exciting as it use to be. You have your favorite dessert, a hot fudge brownie sundae, every night for two months. Believe it or not, even that sundae will not be enjoyed as much as it was when you could have it only once a month. Using novel and significant stimuli in your life will help you and those around you have an exciting nonboring life.

We learn throughout life. We all need to change in order to adapt to the world that we must live in. What we have learned in the past is not always the best for us in the future. Consider using novel and significant stimuli and sometimes conflicting stimuli as you relate to others in business situations, relationships, family situations, and in a teaching-learning environment—which is the laboratory of life. If you do, you will discover that your life and the lives of the people around you will improve.

Now that we have your attention, it's time to learn.

Life's greatest achievements is in the continual remaking of yourself so that at last you know how to live.

W. Rhodes

LEARNING THEORY

Why study learning theory? *Learning theory* is the basis of all interactions—we are applying it constantly and it is constantly being applied on us, most of the time without our knowledge. If you have a better understanding of learning theory, it will help you understand the relationships you have with others and thus, hopefully you will be able to improve the relationships you are involved in and help you acquire new relationships.

An understanding of learning theory will also allow you to understand yourself as well as others. You will learn how to manage your own behavior as well as discover ways in which you can influence other people's behavior.

Classical Conditioning. Why does Nick hate apple pie? Apple pie used to be Nick's favorite desert. One day Nick and his friend Ted ate seven pieces of apple pie for lunch. Later that day Nick got very sick. That was five years ago, and today Nick still will not consider eating another piece of apple pie, but Ted still loves apple pie. Why? Nick thinks the apple pie made him sick, but it was really the flu that made him sick. During that past week, all the members of Nick's family were sick because of the flu. As you can see from this example, Nick associated getting sick with apple pie, not the flu. This is an example of *classical conditioning. Classical conditioning* involves learning a connection between two stimuli, a *neutral stimulus* (apple pie) and a stimulus that already produces a response (the flu). Actually, the flu (unconditioned stimulus) caused Nick to get sick (unconditioned response), but Nick thinks that the apple pie (neutral stimulus) made him sick, and now Nick thinks he will get sick if he were to eat another piece of apple pie. He has been *conditioned* to dislike pie. Is there a change in Ted's behavior as a result of experience? If the answer is yes, then learning has taken place. How does classical conditioning work?

Ivan Pavlov, a Russian physiologist, is considered the founder of classical conditioning. To make a long story short, Pavlov was experimenting with the salivary response of dogs. At first a bell was rung and the dog emitted no response or an irrelevant response, such as the ears perking up. When the food was placed in the dog's mouth, the dog would automatically salivate. Food is called the *unconditioned stimulus,* because it is the cause of the salivation, the *unconditioned response.* After ringing the bell a few times prior to feeding the dog, Pavlov noticed that the dog was salivating in response to the bell before the food was brought in. The bell now becomes the *conditioned stimulus* and causes the dog to salivate, the *conditioned response.* Was there a change in the dog's behavior as a result of its experience? If the answer is yes, then learning has taken place and the dog has been conditioned. Do you salivate to the sight of food? This is a *conditioned response.*

CLASSICAL CONDITIONING

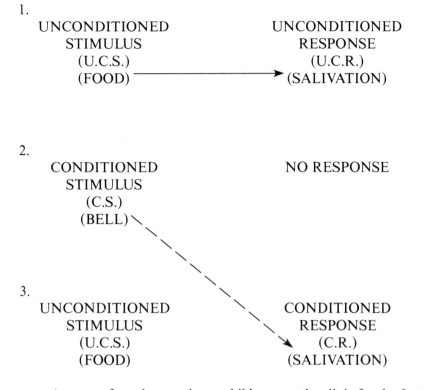

1.
UNCONDITIONED   UNCONDITIONED
STIMULUS   RESPONSE
(U.C.S.)   (U.C.R.)
(FOOD) ——————————→ (SALIVATION)

2.
CONDITIONED   NO RESPONSE
STIMULUS
(C.S.)
(BELL)

3.
UNCONDITIONED   CONDITIONED
STIMULUS   RESPONSE
(U.C.S.)   (C.R.)
(FOOD)   (SALIVATION)

As most of you know, when a child goes to the clinic for the first time for an injection, the child is not hesitant to go. As you know, the injection, the unconditioned stimulus, causes pain, the unconditioned response. Will the child, willingly, go to the clinic next time? The answer is, most likely, NO WAY!! As soon as the child sees the clinic or smells the odor in the clinic, the child will get very upset and attempt to get away from there as quickly as possible. The sight of the clinic or the odor is the conditioned stimulus that causes the child to try to avoid the pain of the injection, the conditioned response. Do you now understand why many children don't want to go to the clinic or doctor's office? They have been classically conditioned to fear these situations.

Did you ever drink too much of a specific kind of alcohol one evening and then later that night get very sick? As you may know, after such an experience you may never touch that kind of alcohol and most likely never will again, but you still drink other forms of alcohol. Why? You associated getting sick with a specific kind of alcohol, not alcohol in general. This one experience conditioned you to dislike that specific kind of alcohol. Sometimes you can be conditioned very quickly, as many of you have learned.

Most fears and phobias are learned through the process of classical conditioning. The famous experiment of John B. Watson and Rosalie Raynor (1920) demonstrates how fears and eventually phobias are easily learned.

I Can't Stand Those White "Little" Monsters!

Albert was classically conditioned to fear the white rat.

An eleven-month-old boy named Albert was classically conditioned to fear a variety of furry things. Before the experiment Albert enjoyed playing with a white rat. One day as the rat was handed to Albert the experimenters made a loud terrifying noise that startled Albert and made him cry. They continued to do this six more times, until Albert showed a strong fear of the rat, crying and shrinking away whenever the rat was placed near him. As the experiment continued, the experimenters presented Albert with other objects that were similar to the white rat, such as a white stuffed animal, a furry white blanket, and a Santa Claus mask. To their surprise, Albert showed the same fear response to the different white furry objects as he did the white rat. This process is called *stimulus generalization.* (A day later, Albert was released from the hospital where the experiment took place without further treatment.) So, if you are walking down the street one day wearing your white fur coat and a seventy-year-old man starts yelling and running the other way, say, "Hi Albert." Albert should have gone through *a reconditioning process* called *desensitization* in order to extinguish him of the fears.

Table 3.1 Classical Conditioning: Learning Through Associations					
	Neutral Stimulus	Pleasant or Painful Stimulus	Before Conditioning	Conditioning	After Conditioning
Pavlov's Experiment	Bell	Food	Bell elicits no response	Bell is paired with food, which elicits salivation	Bell alone, without food, elicits salivation
McDonald's Advertising goal	Golden arches	Food	Arches elicit no response	Arches are paired with tasty food, which elicits salivation	Arches alone, without sight of food, elicits salivation
A child learning	Dog	Dog-bite	Dog elicits pleasant response	Dog-bite is paired with pain	Sight of dog instills feeling of fear and avoidance

Classical conditioning helps explain the formation of fears, attitudes, prejudices, and feelings that may seem quite irrational. (See Table 3.1) You don't understand why you have such an uneasy feeling around your red-haired boss. You can't think of any logical, rational reason for this feeling. You have also noticed that you feel uneasy around other red-haired individuals. One day while you were reminiscing about elementary school, you remembered that your second-grade, red-haired teacher slapped your hands with a ruler every time you made a mistake. At that time it was a very painful, embarrassing experience to be hit in front of all your friends. This one early experience, that you repressed, is still having an effect on your present life, especially your interactions with red-haired individuals. You were conditioned to dislike red-haired individuals. Prior to second grade you liked people with red hair, but since this one experience, red-haired individuals have become the *conditioned stimulus* for your fear (uneasy feeling), the *conditioned response*. Have you ever had an experience like this?

Do you now understand how fears, prejudices, phobias, dislikes, stereotypes, and uneasy feelings can be learned through classical conditioning? Each one of these can have a negative effect on our relationships with others. The more we are aware of how these feelings develop, the greater the chance we have to unlearn them through the same conditioning process. Most aspects of learning begin with classical conditioning, but as learning evolves, classical conditioning develops into another form of learning—operant conditioning.

Operant Conditioning. Why do you work? If you didn't enjoy working and didn't earn money for doing it, would you still be working? Why do you continue going out with the person you are dating? Why do you still have certain friendships that remain strong over the years and other friendships that have waned? You receive *positive reinforcement* for working, so you continue to work. Your date satisfies your needs, so you continue to date that person. Your friends satisfy some of your other needs and in return you reinforce them. The friendship continues; the relationships that are not reinforcing or satisfying will wane over a period of time. All of these interactions involve *operant conditioning.*

Operant conditioning is based on the premise that we are controlled by the consequences of our behavior. Many psychologists say that most of our behavior is learned through operant conditioning. If you cry and then get what you want, are you going to cry the next time you want something? The cry was reinforced and thus the reinforcement will increase the probability of you crying the next time you want something. The class clown gets attention for acting out in class, even though it is considered by most of us as negative attention, so the individual continues acting out. If this person didn't get any attention, would he or she continue to be the class clown? Most likely, this individual would not. If you change your hair style and receive a lot of compliments, will you continue to wear it that way? If you receive a lot of stares or negative comments on your new outfit, will you wear it again? You will tend to like people who compliment you more than people who ignore you or make negative comments. These are all examples of operant conditioning. You make a response and the consequences of that response determines whether or not you make that response again.

WHAT ARE THE CONSEQUENCES?

Reinforcement. In behavioral terminology, pleasant or unpleasant stimuli that strengthen a behavior are called *reinforcers,* and their effect is called *reinforcement.* The simplest type of reinforcer, called a *primary reinforcer,* is a pleasant or unpleasant one to which we respond automatically without learning (food, drink, heat, cold, pain, physical comfort or discomfort). However, the vast majority of our reinforcers are not primary reinforcers, but *conditioned or secondary reinforcers:*—stimuli to which we have attached positive or negative value through association with previously learned conditioned reinforcers. For example, a kiss is a primary reinforcer. It can be pleasant or unpleasant, depending on who's doing the kissing—your sweetheart or Dracula.

Reinforcers act to strengthen behavior through two different types of consequences. These two consequences are *positive reinforcement* and *negative reinforcement.* Consequences can also weaken or eliminate a behavior through the use of *punishment.*

Positive Reinforcement. This is anything that increases a behavior by virtue of its presentation. If you help a stranger who responds by giving you five dollars, what's the chance of you helping other strangers?

You were given five dollars (positive reinforcement) for helping the stranger and that five dollars will increase the probability of you helping other strangers in the future. If you hadn't received the money, you are not as likely to help in the future. A child cries at the store, and the father gives the child a candy bar to be quiet. Now the father discovers that the child cries every time they go to the store. What is happening here? The father is giving the child positive reinforcement for crying. We need to be careful in what behavior we are reinforcing. As you can see, it's easy to reinforce improper behavior. Your spouse asks you very nicely for a favor, and you ignore the request. But later, when your spouse yells and screams at you to do something, you immediately respond and do it. What's happening here? You are positively reinforcing your spouse for yelling. And, now you wonder why your spouse is always yelling at you. Remember, positively reinforce the good responses, not the bad ones.

Negative Reinforcement. This is anything that increases a behavior by virtue of its termination or avoidance. My employer yells at me for not producing enough work, so now I work harder to produce more in order to avoid being yelled at. In this situation, the yelling would be defined as *negative reinforcement.* I received a ticket for speeding once, and now I find that I am obeying the speed limit more often in order to avoid getting any more tickets. The ticket is negative reinforcement. We avoid people who are not nice to us and avoid classes we have difficulty with because of negative reinforcement. Negative reinforcement may have positive consequences, because it allows us to avoid painful and dangerous situations. Can you think of any examples?

Punishment. This is anything that decreases a behavior by virtue of its presentation. A child runs across the street and then gets spanked. Now, the child no longer runs across the street. The spanking stopped or decreased the number of times the child runs across the street, so the spanking would be defined as *punishment.* You drink too much

What is the greatest motivator? Success! It works every time.

Anonymous

scotch one evening and get very sick. To your amazement, you don't ever want to drink scotch again. Getting sick is the *punishment* for drinking.

Punishment is considered to be the most effective, but not the best, means of stopping a response, and that is why so many of us continue to use it so often. We get positive reinforcement for using punishment. You spank your child for damaging your new stereo. Since the spanking, the child has not touched your stereo, so the spanking is defined as punishment and you discover you are spanking your child more often because it stops or decreases the child from emitting negative, unwanted responses. You, the punisher, are receiving *positive reinforcement* for punishing (spanking) your child.

Psychologists suggest that you don't need to use punishment as a means of disciplining your children, because positive reinforcement is the most effective and best means of controlling someone's behavior. But, if you find it necessary to use punishment, make sure you use some type of alternative form of behavior that will lead to positive reinforcement. If your child knows that it is wrong to run across the street, but still does it, you may use some form of punishment, but in order for the punishment to be effective, you must make sure the child knows that he or she will receive some type of positive reinforcement. Otherwise, the child will have no real reason to stay on your side of the street.

As you already know, we do not recommend using punishment, but many people do use it and many abuse it. The following guidelines summarize research evidence on how to make punishment effective while minimizing its side effects (Axelrod & Apsche, 1983: Parke 1977: Walters & Grusec, 1977).

Strengthen me by sympathizing with my strengths, not my weaknesses.

B. Alcott

GUIDELINES FOR PUNISHMENT

1. *Punishment should be timely.* It should take place as soon after the incident as possible. A delay undermines the impact. The old saying, "Wait until your father gets home," is not an effective means of using punishment. Quick punishment highlights the connection between the prohibited (inappropriate) behavior and its negative outcome (consequences).

2. *Punishment should be just severe enough to be effective.* Although more severe punishments tend to be more effective in eliminating and suppressing unwanted behavior, they also increase the likelihood of undesirable effects, such as aggression. Thus, it's best to use the least severe punishment that seems likely to have some impact.

3. *Punishment should be explained.* A person needs to know the reason why he or she is being punished. Explain, as fully as possible, the reason for the punishment. The more a person understands why they are being punished, the more effective the punishment tends to be.

4. *Punishment should be consistent.* If you want to eliminate an undesirable behavior, you should punish it each and every time it occurs. Inconsistency creates confusion.

5. *Make an alternative response available and reinforce it.* One shortcoming of punishment is that it only tells a person what *not* to do. People need to know what they *can* do. Most undesirable behaviors have a purpose. If you make another behavior available that leads to positive reinforcement, doing so should weaken the response being punished. For example, the class clown, mentioned earlier in the chapter, should receive positive reinforcement for being quiet and paying attention, and the need for clowning around will decrease.

6. *Physical punishment should be kept to a minimum.* A minimum amount of physical punishment may be necessary when children are too young to understand a verbal reprimand or the withdrawal of privileges. A light slap on the hand or bottom is adequate. Otherwise, physical punishment tends to lead to aggressive responses by the person being punished.

7. *Do not apply punishment to consummatory responses!* Consummatory responses (eating, drinking, sleeping, sex, studying, etc.) are very sensitive to punishment. When rats were shocked while they were consuming food, the experimenters were "shocked" to discover that the rats would never eat again. They starved to death. Could this be the cause of some eating disorders? Parents who force their child to study may be causing their child to hate school. The child may interpret the force as punishment. A woman who is raped may never enjoy sex again if she perceived the rape as punishment for having sex.

8. *Punishment suppresses behavior.* Research has demonstrated that when the punisher is not around or available, the person receiving the punishment will most likely start emitting the negative behavior again. While individuals are in prison for committing a crime, they cannot commit the crime again. Being in prison would be defined as punishment. But, as soon as the prisoners are released, we find that many of them commit the same crime again. Was punishment effective? If you didn't think the police officer would catch you speeding, would you speed again?

I expect to pass through this life but once; therefore if there be any kindness I can show or any good thing that I can do for any fellow being, let me do it now, not defer, or neglect it, for I shall not pass this way again.

Anonymous

What Kind of Reinforcement Do You Use? Many facets of your personality have been developed through operant conditioning. When children are being good, nobody pays attention. When children "act out," they get a lot of attention. They like attention so they "act out" more and we wonder why they are so "bratty." This behavior, then, becomes part of their personality. How was your personality formed? What kind of reinforcement did other people use on you? What kind of reinforcement are you using on other people? Is it effective? How does it affect your relationship with other people?

Positive reinforcement is generally much more effective than any other form of reinforcement. You will discover that if you use positive reinforcement on yourself and in your relationships with others, you will be much happier and those around you will be much happier. Your business relationships and your personal life will be richer, more positive, and effective.

SELF-CONTROL IN EVERYDAY LIVING

All of us are engaged in a variety of everyday activities simply to survive. We must eat, drink, sleep, and take care of basic biological needs. It turns out that all of these activities can pose challenges to a successful personal adjustment to our environment, and we must be careful to control them and not let them control us. Some people's eating, drug use, sleeping, or alcohol use controls their life.

Failure is positive feedback.

Anonymous

What other challenges do we have that seem to control our everyday lives? Do any of you need to study more? Would you like to stop smoking?

Would you like to exercise more? Do you watch TV too much? Are you shy? Would you like to make more friends? These and many of your other habits that you would like to change can be modified. You can do it! Let's find out how.

Psychologists have devised a number of different theories to explain how we develop the capacity for self-control. We have found one technique that has been very successful for many individuals. This technique includes the application of learning theory to improve your self-control. If you stop and think about it, self-control—or the lack of it—underlies many of the personal challenges that we struggle with in everyday life. *What we learn can be unlearned.*

A SELF-CHANGE PROGRAM

A Lesson in Self-Control: A Five Step Program

Step 1: Identify the behavior to be changed.
Step 2: Observe the behavior to be changed.
Step 3: Set your goal.
Step 4: Design your program.
Step 5: Monitor and evaluate your program.

Identify the Behavior to be Changed. The first step in any systematic program in self-modification is to identify the specific behavior that you would like to change. Many of us tend to be vague in describing our problems and identifying the exact nature of the behavior we want to change. You must be specific and define clearly the overt behavior to be changed. For example:

I want to lose weight.
I want to stop smoking.
I want to spend more time studying.
I want to exercise more.
I would like to have more dates.
I need to stop procrastinating.

Which of the above statements is too vague and would not be easy to observe? Can you measure and observe how much exercise you do? Definitely. But can you observe yourself procrastinating? You need to identify what things you are not doing, so you can get them completed in a timely manner.

Drug abuse, physical abuse, eating disorders and other serious negative habits that are detrimental to *your* health can be changed through the process of self-modification with a lot of willpower. But, we have found that it is easier to change these serious habits with benefit of professional help. So, please seek professional help or if you know anyone else having a serious problem, please help them find professional help. Talk to your instructor, counselor, pastor, or therapist.

Observe the Behavior to be Changed. The second step in your self-change project is to observe the behavior to be changed in order to discover your operant level (*baseline*), the number of responses prior to beginning the project. People are often tempted to skip this step and move ahead. In order to evaluate your progress you must not skip this step. You need to know the original response level, the starting point. You can't tell whether your program is working unless you have a baseline for comparison. While observing your behavior in order to find your *operant level,* you need to monitor three things: (1) the initial response level of the target behavior, (2) the events that precede the target behavior, (3) the typical consequences (reinforcement or punishment).

1. Initial Response Level. You need to keep track of each and every response, of the targeted behavior, that occurs within a specified period of time, usually five to seven days. Write down on a piece of paper attached to your cigarette package, each and every cigarette you have each day for a week. Keep a diary of the number of dates you have within a three-week period, the amount of time you study each day for five days, the number of times you yell at your kids, the amount of time you spend exercising each day for six days, or whatever the targeted behavior happens to be. As soon as you can identify a *pattern of behavior,* you are ready for the next step. If you discover that you don't exercise, there is nothing to observe. Your operant level for exercise is "0," no responses prior to conditioning. You may discover that your *operant level* for cigarette smoking is "23 cigarettes" per day, "42 minutes" of studying each day, "3,100" calories each day, or "2 dates" per month. Now, to the next step.

2. Events that Precede the Target Behavior. The events that precede the target behavior can play a major role in governing your target response. Where you study may affect how much time you actually study. When you study at the library, you find that you study more than when you study at home on the kitchen table or on your bed. You discover that you smoke more when you drink coffee. You may find that you may have to give up coffee in order to stop smoking, because coffee seems to create the urge to smoke. You find that you eat the greatest number of calories late at night after you have a couple of beers; the beers seem to stimulate the hunger drive. Once you are able to pinpoint the events that seem to cause the behavior, you can design your program to circumvent it or break it down.

3. Consequences. Finally, you need to identify the reinforcement that is strengthening the targeted behavior or the punishment that is decreasing or suppressing it. We eat because we like food—the food becomes reinforcing in itself, just like smoking: we enjoy it. It's easier not to study than to study. Bad habits are self-reinforcing. I don't have to worry about being turned down for a date if I don't ask anyone out. Most of the behaviors we would like to change are being reinforced and thus, very difficult to change.

Set Your Goal. The most important factor in the third step is that when you set your goal, make sure that it is a realistic goal that can be accomplished. Losing twenty pounds in four weeks is not realistic, but four to five pounds could be realistic. Studying five hours a day, seven days a week is not realistic for many students, but studying three hours a day, five days a week would most likely be accomplished by most students, depending on how many courses you are taking and how many hours you work per week.

Try to set behavioral goals that are both challenging and realistic. You want your goals to be challenging, so that they lead to improvement in your behavior. However, setting unrealistic high goals— a common mistake in self-modification—often leads to unnecessary discouragement.

If you aren't willing to work for your goals, don't expect others to.

Anonymous

Designing Your Program. Now that you have identified the targeted behavior to be changed, found your operant level, and set your goal, you are ready to design your program.

You have now discovered that many of your bad habits and behaviors that you have identified to change are self-reinforcing. In order for you to change you must find something that is more reinforcing to you than the previous reinforcement. You must find something that will motivate you and make you want to change. If you intend to reward yourself for increasing a response, you need to find an effective reinforcer. What is reinforcing to one individual may not be reinforcing to another. Your choice will depend on your unique personality and situation. How can you discover what is reinforcing to you?

Selecting reinforcers. What is reinforcing enough to you to motivate you to change? Is it money, sex, free time, compact discs, concert tickets, praise, or tickets to the ball game? An easy way to discover what is reinforcing to you is to observe your own behavior for awhile. (1) Observe what you enjoy doing for a few days. (2) Observe what you spend your money on each week? (3) What kind of praise do you like to receive from yourself and from others? (4) What are your major interests? (5) What do you do for fun? (6) What people do you like to be with? (6) What do you like to do with those people? (7) What would be a nice present to receive? (8) What makes you feel good? (9) What would you like to do for your next vacation? (10) What would you buy if you had an extra $20? $50? $100? (Watson & Tharp, 1989).

Any or all of these items could be used as reinforcers to motivate you to change.

Administrating the Reinforcers. Receiving the reinforcement has to be contingent upon your making the appropriate response first. Once you have chosen the reinforcer, you then have to set up reinforcement contingencies. Your reinforcement contingencies will describe the exact behavioral goals that must be met and the reinforcement that may then be awarded. Do not administer too much reinforcement and receive it too often. If you do, you soon get bored or habituate to it. If a chocolate milk shake was used as reinforcement five times a day for three weeks, you would soon get tired of having milk shakes. They would soon lose their reinforcing value.

Generally, rapid reinforcement works better than delayed reinforcement. If we delay reinforcement, we discover that we don't realize what behavior is being reinforced. You may find it easier to have a friend or relative administer the reinforcement. It may also commit you more to your project if you make up a *behavioral contract* for you to sign and give to your friend.

A Sample Contract

Target behavior: I lose five pounds in the next six weeks.

Contract between: Sally Sane
Amy Abler (roommate of Sally Sane)

Agreement: Sally Sane—I agree to stop eating candy bars and drinking pop between meals. I will write down each and every candy bar and soda pop that I consume for the next seven days. I will weigh myself each day and record my weight. After the observation period, for the following two weeks, I will eat only one candy bar each day and two cans of pop. During the second two weeks, I will eat one candy bar every other day and one soda pop each day. On the final two weeks, I will have only one candy bar and one soda pop every three days. From that day following I will substitute pieces of fruit and vegetables and glasses of water for my snacks between meals.

Agreement: Amy Abler—I agree to help Sally Sane lose five pounds and stop eating candy bars and drinking pop between meals. I will review her program with her weekly and do whatever I can to help her reach her goal.

Consequences: Sally Sane—For each week that I reach my goal, I will buy myself a new tape or CD. If I fail to reach my goal during the week, I do not get the new tape or CD and I will have to clean the apartment without Amy's help. When I reach my final goal, I will receive two tickets to the concert that I have been wanting to attend.

Consequences: Amy Abler—I will praise Sally for keeping her schedule and offer encouragement. I will review her program with her weekly and give her feedback. If she reaches her goal by the end of the six weeks, I will clean the apartment the next two weeks without Sally's help.

Signed: _____

_____

date _____

Trying to modify behavior is a difficult task. Sometimes it helps to have someone we can talk to or who might assist us to do this. It is difficult to change some of our actions by ourselves. We might benefit from a person who can offer advice or encouragement. Or we might need another person to know about our plan because it keeps us honest and committed to our project. It is sometimes easy to fool yourself about your progress, but another person may not be as easily deceived.

Just Do It—Monitor and Evaluate Your Program. Now that you have designed your project, you are ready to "do it." As you begin the project, you need to monitor your progress as you begin to achieve your goal. Monitoring your progress will allow you to assess whether your plan is working. Start with your *operant level* (baseline) and continue to accurately record the frequency of your targeted behavior so you can evaluate your progress. If your behavior shows improvement, keep up the good work. However, if there is no improvement or you begin to regress, you need to *reevaluate your reinforcers,* because they don't seem to be motivating you to improve. You may need to strengthen your reinforcement, or delay the time between you emit the behavior and the time you receive the reinforcement (it may be too lengthy). Do not reward yourself when you have not actually earned it. Many people end up giving themselves the reinforcers no matter what they do. They rationalize it by saying, "I needed that new dress anyway" or "I just need a vacation, even though I'm not going to stop smoking." Another problem you may have in not reaching your goal is that you are trying to do too much too quickly by setting unrealistic goals.

When set into action, self-modification programs often need some fine-tuning. So don't be surprised if you need to make a few adjustments. Often, a small revision or two can turn a failing program around and make it a success. Don't give up!

A Happy Ending. Often, a new and improved pattern of behavior becomes self-maintaining. When you feel good about yourself and know that you are successful, it becomes self-reinforcing. Responses such as eating right, not smoking, exercising regularly, or studying diligently may become habitual so that they no longer need to be supported by an elaborate program. But you may find it important to periodically reinforce yourself for *doing the right thing* and not slipping back to your old patterns of behavior. You did a good job, keep up the good work!

Once you learn to apply this process to yourself, you will discover that it can also be used in many different situations. Parents may apply it to their children. Teachers use it in the classroom. An employer may use these principles in the workplace. A wife may use it on her husband. Can you explain how it can be applied in these situations? Positive reinforcement is very motivating. Make sure it is applied appropriately.

A LAST THOUGHT

We learn throughout life. What we learn is not always positive, but we have also learned that we can take the negative and turn it into a positive and rewarding experience. It takes a lot of work and will power, but you can do it.

Learn to change your life and facilitate the changing of other people's lives through the use of learning theory. The use of positive reinforcement in your own life and applying it to those around you will enhance your relationships and make you feel better about yourself.

Who's in control? You're in control! Take the "steering wheel" of your own life and head it in the right direction.

CHAPTER DISCUSSION QUESTIONS

1. Do you agree with B. F. Skinner that all your behavior is controlled? Explain your answer.
2. What are the benefits of having an internal locus of control? What are the benefits of having an external locus of control?
3. What is self-efficacy and how can you increase your self-efficacy?
4. What people have been a model in your life? What influence have they had on you?
5. Why do we need a basic understanding of learning theory in order to understand human relations?
6. Explain how positive reinforcement, negative reinforcement, and punishment has affected your life.
7. What can you do to your relationships to make them more interesting and exciting?
8. If you were a teacher, what would you do in order to keep your student's attention?
9. Using operant conditioning, how would you change one of your bad habits?

KEY TERMS

Internal locus of control
External locus of control
Self-Efficacy
Social Learning Theory
Observational learning
Learning
Novel stimuli
Significant stimuli
Conflicting stimuli
Classical Conditioning
Unconditioned stimulus
Unconditioned response

Conditioned stimulus
Conditioned response
Stimulus generalization
Desensitization
Operant Conditioning
Reinforcers
Reinforcement
Primary reinforcement
Positive reinforcement
Negative reinforcement
Punishment
Conditioned reinforcement

REFERENCES

Axelrod, S. and Apsche, J. (1983). *The Effects of Punishment on Human Behavior,* New York: Academic Press.
Bandura, A. (1986). *Social Foundations of Thought and Action: A Social-Cognitive Theory.* Englewood Cliffs, N.J.: Prentice Hall.
Rotter, J. B. "Generalized Expectancies for Internal Versus External Control for Reinforcement" *Psychological Monographs* 80, No. 609 (1966).
Skinner, B. K. (1972). *Beyond Freedom and Dignity.* New York: Knopf.
Solomon, M. (December 1987) Standard issue. *Psychology Today,* pp. 30–31. (p. 597)
Watson, D. C. and Tharpe, G. G. (1989). *Self-directed behavior: Self-modification for personal adjustment.* Pacific Grove, CA: Brooks/Cole.
Watson, J. B. and Rayner, R. (1920). "Conditioned emotional reactions." *Journal of Experimental Psychology* 3, 1–14.

WHAT CONTROLS YOUR LIFE?

Purpose: This is a device to measure your attitudes toward rewards and punishments: do you feel that they come as a result of your own behavior or from outside sources? We have reproduced this device below so that you can measure yourself and determine your own beliefs. Read each set of two statements and decide which statement seems to you more accurate and place a check mark next to it. Read and answer carefully. There are no right or wrong choices. They are based on your *personal* judgments. Try to respond to each pair of statements independently, apart from your responses to other pairs of statements.

1. _____ a. A great deal that happens to me is probably a matter of chance.
   _____ b. I am the master of my fate.

2. _____ a. It is almost impossible to figure out how to please some people.
   _____ b. Getting along with people is a skill that must be practiced.

3. _____ a. People like me can change the course of world affairs if we make ourselves heard.
   _____ b. It is only wishful thinking to believe that one can really influence what happens in society at large.

4. _____ a. Most people get the respect they deserve in this world.
   _____ b. An individual's capabilities often pass unrecognized no matter how hard he or she tries.

5. _____ a. The idea that teachers are unfair to students is nonsense.
   _____ b. Most students don't realize the extent to which their grades are influenced by accidental happenings.

6. _____ a. If you don't get the right opportunities, one cannot become a good leader.
   _____ b. Capable people who fail to become leaders have not taken advantage of their opportunities.

7. _____ a. Sometimes I feel that I have little to do with the grades I get.
   _____ b. In my case the grades I make are the results of my own efforts; luck has little or nothing to do with it.

8. _____ a. Heredity plays the major role in determining one's personality.
   _____ b. It is one's experiences in life that determine what one is like.

9. _____ a. It is silly to think that one can really change another person's basic attitudes.
   _____ b. When I am right I can convince others.

10. _____ a. In my experience I have noticed that there is usually a direct connection between how hard I study and the grades I get.
    _____ b. Many times the reactions of teachers seem haphazard to me.

11. _____ a. The average citizen can have an influence in government decisions.
    _____ b. This world is run by the few people in power, and there is not much the little guy can do about it.

12. _____ a. When I make plans, I am almost certain that I can make them work.
    _____ b. It is not always wise to plan too far ahead because many things turn out to be a matter of good or bad fortune anyhow.

13. _____ a. There are certain people who are just no good.
    _____ b. There is some good in everybody.

14. _____ a. In my case, getting what I want has little or nothing to do with luck.
    _____ b. Many times we might just as well decide what to do by flipping a coin.

15. _____ a. Promotions are earned through hard work and persistence.
    _____ b. Making a lot of money is largely a matter of getting the right breaks.

16. _____ a. Marriage is largely a gamble.
    _____ b. The number of divorces indicates that more and more people are not trying to make their marriages work.

17. _____ a. In our society a man's future earning power is dependent on his ability.
    _____ b. Getting promoted is really a matter of being a little luckier than the next guy.

18. _____ a. Most people don't realize the extent to which their lives are controlled by accidental happenings.
    _____ b. There is really no such thing as luck

19. _____ a. I have little influence over the way other people behave.
    _____ b. If one knows how to deal with people, they are really quite easily led.

20. _____ a. In the long run, the bad things that happen to us are balanced by the good ones.
    _____ b. Most misfortunes are the result of lack of ability, ignorance, laziness, or all three.

21. _____ a. With enough effort, we can wipe out political corruption.
    _____ b. It is difficult for people to have much control over the things politicians do in office.

22. _____ a. A good leader expects people to decide for themselves what they should do.
    _____ b. A good leader makes it clear to everybody what their jobs are.

23. _____ a. People are lonely because they don't try to be friendly.
    _____ b. There's not much use in trying too hard to please people—if they like you, they like you.

24. _____ a. There is too much emphasis on athletics in high school.
    _____ b. Team sports are an excellent way to build character.

25. _____ a. What happens to me is my own doing.
    _____ b. Sometimes I feel that I don't have enough control over the direction my life is taking.

Scoring Key for Project: For each of the responses below, give yourself 1 point.

Item #	Response	Item #	Response	Item #	Response
1	a	10	b	19	a
2	a	11	b	20	a
3	b	12	b	21	b
4	b	13	a	22	b
5	b	14	b	23	b
6	a	15	b	24	a
7	a	16	a	25	b
8	a	17	b		
9	a	18	a		

Your total number of points indicates the degree to which you view control as external or internal. The higher the score (above 15), the more you perceive control as external. The lower the score (below 15), the more you perceive control as internal. Now that you have totaled your score, you may want to refer back to the chapter discussion on Internals and Externals in order to interpret your results.

Discussion:

1. Would you find it more beneficial to be an internal or an external? Why?

2. What did you learn from this activity?

SELF-CHANGE PROJECT

Purpose: To understand how learning theory applies to your life.

Instruction: Review the chapter on Learning Theory, specifically the Self-Change project explained in the chapter

1. Identify the target behavior you would like to change.

_____

_____

_____

2. Observe the target behavior for 5–7 days to get the operant level (baseline). Write it down.

_____

_____

_____

3. What is your goal and date to be completed.

_____

_____

_____

4. Identify the reinforcer, long-term and short term. What will motivate you to change?

_____

_____

_____

5. Make a plan.

_____

_____

_____

6. What are the results?

_____

Suggestion to Instructors: The authors suggest that this Self-Change Project be a major out-of-class assignment and that on completion, the projects are shared with the class or small group and the questions below are discussed.

Discussion:

1. What kinds of changes would you like to make about yourself?

2. What is motivating (reinforcing) enough to get you to change your behavior?

3. What could people use as reinforcers in order to facilitate the behavior change?

4. How could you apply the methods of the self-change project to other aspects of your life (job, children, spouse, mate, and so on).

CRITICAL STATEMENT WORKSHEET

1. Purpose: To develop the habit of encouraging "self" with positive self-talk.
   To apply positive reinforcement to ourselves by using positive statements
   To diminish the habit of discouraging self with negative self-talk.
2. Instructions:
   A. Keep a diary of criticisms. Record each criticism here.
   B. For each critical statement, create three positive believable, realistic statements.
   C. Reinforce yourself positively when you use a positive statement. You will feel good.
3. Example: Criticism   Positive statements
   A. Who is that ugly old lady in my mirror?   A. It is 5 am. I look pretty good for 5 am.
                                                B. It is not an ugly old lady. It is me.
                                                C. I'm not old. I'm 50.

CRITICISMS	POSITIVE STATEMENTS
_____	_____
	_____
	_____
_____	_____
	_____
	_____
_____	_____
	_____
	_____
_____	_____
	_____
	_____
_____	_____
	_____
	_____

LEARNING JOURNAL FOR WHO'S IN CONTROL

Select the statement below that best defines your feelings about the personal value or meaning gained from this chapter and respond below the dotted line.

I LEARNED THAT I   I WAS SURPRISED THAT I

I REALIZED THAT I   I WAS PLEASED THAT I

I DISCOVERED THAT I   I WAS DISPLEASED THAT I

....

Becoming Emotional

The fully human being is aware of the vitality of
his senses, emotions, mind, and will; and he is neither
a stranger to, nor afraid of, the activities of his
body and emotions. He is capable of the whole gamet
of emotions: from grief to tenderness. What I mean,
is that the fully human being experiences the fullness
of his emotional life; he is in "touch with", attuned
to his emotions, aware of what they are saying to him
about his needs and his relationships with others.

Carl Rogers
(On Becoming a Person, 1961)

How would you feel in these situations?

- *It has finally happened! You have found that special person, and the two of you are discussing marriage. You are "soo—" in love.*
- *Once again, your boss said some critical, unfair things to you today. You are "really" angry.*
- *The telephone rings, and you learn that one of your best friends has been killed in an accident. You are "filled" with sadness and grief.*
- *Your spouse has just come in and told you, quite unexpectedly, that he or she wants a divorce. You are "very, very" hurt. No! maybe you're angry.*

Would your feelings and emotions be similar to the feelings and emotions that other people have when they are having the same experiences? How do you feel when you are in love? Can you easily verbalize the words: "I love you?" Do you verbally express your anger, or do you save your "bad" feelings and explode at a later date? Could you talk about your feelings if your best friend or someone very close to you died? How would you deal with your feelings if your spouse walked out?

We know that our emotions play an important part in making our relations with other people pleasant and joyful, or sad and painful. We also know that what we respond to emotionally is learned. For example, we learn what situations or people stimulate our feelings of anger; we learn what situations produce stress or anxiety for us; we learn which kinds of situations leave us with a sense of guilt; and we learn which experiences help us to feel joyful and pleasant.

Because emotional responses and expressions are learned, we can learn how to change emotional patterns that are self-defeating or harmful to our growth towards self-actualization. We can also learn how to develop ways to become more emotionally expressive.

In our society, people often experience alienation or lack of ability to express emotions. And it sometimes appears that many of us have almost forgotten how to cry or laugh or express genuine feelings for ourselves and others. Therefore, we hope this chapter will help you become a more emotionally mature person and help you better understand the reasons behind some of your emotional reactions to certain people or situations. And we hope that you will be able to get ideas about ways you can manage emotional patterns that are giving you trouble in living with yourself and others.

WHAT ARE EMOTIONS?

If someone asked you to explain *emotions,* what would you say? In all probability, you would say, "They are the different feelings I have." You might even give these feelings a label, such as anger, love, hate, and so on. Now, suppose someone asked you to explain the term *feelings.* Would you be likely to say? "They are the different emotions I have." And, you might even give these emotions a label, such as anger, love, or hate. The point is, it is quite difficult to separate the two; therefore, we will use the two interchangeably.

For our purposes, we are going to think of emotions as feelings that are experienced. Actually, our feelings are our reaction to the world around us. For example, our feelings tell us whether what we experience is threatening, painful, regretful, sad or joyous, and so on.

Without emotions, we would be little more than drab, colorless machines that run the same way day after day. We would not know the happiness of success or the pangs of disappointment. We would not experience joy from the companionship of others and would feel no grief at their loss. We would neither love nor hate. Pride, envy, and anger would be unknown to us. We wouldn't even be able to understand the joys and sorrows of others.

Fortunately, we are not machines; we are humans. Therefore, each of us, young or old, male or female, is capable of having and expressing many different emotions. Although it is true that individuals experience and express their emotions in many different ways, psychologists generally agree that emotions are very complex experiences, with at least four common characteristics: physiological or internal changes, cognitive interpretations, behavioral expressions, and motivational tendencies (Arnold, 1870). We will now look more closely at these characteristics, as well as briefly discuss the effect our moods have on our emotional reactions.

The feelings or emotional aspects of life lie pretty close to the value and significance of life itself.

J. B. Watson

CHARACTERISTICS OF EMOTIONS

Physiological or Internal Changes. Let us assume that you are walking alone at night when suddenly a large object jumps in front of you. Would your neck muscles tighten? Would your stomach possibly feel "funny?" Would you be able to hear the sound of your heartbeat, even when you later discovered that the "large object" was just a box blowing in the wind? Would you still be breathing faster? What would be happening inside of you? How do you feel inside when you are nervous, frightened, or angry?

As the question suggests, a main characteristic of emotional states is that they involve physiological changes.

When our emotions are aroused, there are physiological changes over which we have no control. In strong fear and anger, you do not tell your adrenal glands to pump adrenalin into the bloodstream so that you will have extra energy. These physiological changes in the nervous system are nature's way of preparing you to react faster, harder, and for longer periods of time. In essence, your whole body is immobilized for action—you are physiologically ready to run or fight.

When you experience strong feelings, the internal changes in your body contribute to your feelings. For example, in grief or depression, there is a reduction of pulse rate, breathing, and muscular strength. Consequently, you feel tired.

Behavioral Expressions. Even though emotions are felt internally, they often lead to observable expressions. These expressions may come in the form of a blush, trembling hands, sweating palms, or a tremor in the voice. Behavioral expressions can also include crying, laughing, cursing, kicking a chair, or even hitting another person. Sometimes people will deny they're feeling anything, even though their external and behavioral expressions indicate something else. We will discuss some suggestions for verbally expressing feelings later in the chapter.

Cognitive Interpretation. While it is true that there is some connection between physical behavior and emotional states, in most situations, the mind plays an important role in determining how we feel. The *Cognitive Theory of Emotion* emphasizes that the emotion we feel will be determined by the explanation we place on the physiological arousal. (Schachler and Singer 1962). The process of combining the arousal and cognition is called *attribution.* Worchel and Goethals, (1989) explain this idea through a Multiplication Equation:

$$\text{Emotion} = \text{Arousal} \times \text{Cognition}$$

The multiplication sign in this equation means that if either the arousal or the cognition is zero, $A \times C$ (Arousal times Cognition) will equal zero, and the individual will not experience an emotion. The key point here is that our emotions are the result of our attributing a meaning to our arousal.

Cognitive therapists Albert Ellis and Robert Harper (1977) believe our thoughts, beliefs, and prior experiences will color the way we view an event and, thus, profoundly influence our emotional reaction to that event. Two people confronted with the same situation may interpret it in different ways and therefore respond with different feelings.

Actually, we go through life describing the world to ourselves, giving each event or experience some label. We make interpretations of what we see and hear; we predict whether they will bring danger or relative safety. Sometimes, these thoughts are very powerful, and as you will discover in Chapter 8, they can create most of the major stresses we experience in life.

Motivational Tendencies. Emotions themselves may function as motives, directing you toward pleasant situations and away from those that are emotionally unsatisfying, anxiety provoking, or painful. In essence, when you are feeling a particular way, you are going to do certain things because of that feeling, in spite of that feeling, or to avoid or change that feeling. Another way of saying this would be: You do what makes you feel good, and you avoid what makes you feel bad. UCLA Psychologist Gary Emery and Dr. James Campbell (1986) explain this further:

Pleasure motivates you to move toward something. Your pleasure feelings, for example, motivate you to move toward a certain crowd of people ("They think my jokes are funny!"); you continue to interact with these people until it no longer feels good ("They made fun of me because I don't drink").

Anxiety motivates you to run or escape from a possible loss ("I had to run for my life").

Anger motivates you to fight against a perceived loss ("I had to fight for my life"). You yell or you attack someone to get rid of your angry feelings, even though you know your outburst will make matters worse.

Sadness motivates you to shut down and withdraw after a loss. If you lose money in the stock market, your sad feelings motivate you to stop playing the market and protect the money you have left.

Moods. Before we leave our discussion of the characteristics of emotions, we need to briefly discuss the effect our moods have on how we respond emotionally. Your moods are a general feelingtone, and they have a definite influence on your emotions. Stated another way, Morris (1987) says, *"Our mood generally informs about the general state of our being."* Even though we don't like to admit it, our moods are often evident to others: For example, "Don't ask Mr. Jones for a day off—he's really grouchy" or "Mrs. Smith is in such a good mood today, I bet we can talk her out of the test today."

Think for a moment and try to recall how your moods affect your emotions. Are you ever grouchy for no reason at all? Do you know what puts you in a bad mood? Often, we don't know what event or events put us in a particular mood; hence the old saying, "I just woke up on the wrong side of the bed."

There is nothing good or bad but thinking makes it so.

Shakespeare,
Hamlet

Do You Ever Wake Up In A "Bad" Mood?

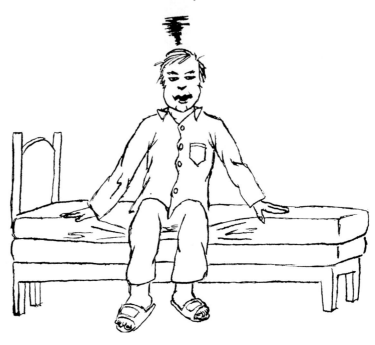

What kind of day do you have?

Now that we have a better idea of what emotions are and how they affect us, we will now discuss some of the emotions which cause us the most difficulty.

ON HUMAN RELATIONS

The greatest comfort is . . . kindness.
The greatest handicap . . . fear.
The nicest feeling . . . appreciation.
The worst mistake . . . bitterness.
The best help . . . clear thinking.
The greatest power . . . love.
The sorriest pain . . . anxiety.
The most needless burden . . . false guilt.
The most pleasant attitude . . . cheerfulness.
The highest barrier . . . false pride.
The most wasteful action . . . self-pity.
The deepest need . . . understanding.
The brightest hope . . . personal maturity.
The most pressing ache . . . loneliness.
The greatest problem . . . the self.
The most constant need . . . self-assurance.
The saddest feeling . . . rejection.
The greatest yearning . . . tenderness.
The sweetest joy . . . romance.
The swiftest resolution . . . self-knowledge.

Anonymous

```
┌─────────────────────────────────────────────────────────┐
│                      Table 4.1                          │
│                    Some Emotions                        │
├─────────────────────────────────────────────────────────┤
```

accepted	guilt-free	powerful
afraid	guilty	powerless
aggravated	happy	puzzled
angry	helpful	regretful
annoyed	hopeless	relieved
anxious	hostile	resentful
ashamed	humiliated	restless
bitter	hurried	sad
calm	hurt	sentimental
cautious	impatient	self-reliant
cheerful	inadequate	shy
comfortable	incompetent	sincere
confident	inferior	sorry
confused	insecure	supported
contented	intimidated	surprised
defeated	isolated	tense
defensive	jealous	terrified
depressed	joyful	tired
embarrassed	lazy	trusting
energetic	lonely	uneasy
envious	loved	unsure
exhilarated	loving	uptight
fearful	optimistic	vulnerable
friendly	out-of-control	wanted
frightened	overcontrolled	weak
glad	pessimistic	worried
grieving		

TYPES OF EMOTIONS

At this point, you may be asking, "Just how many emotions are there?" We really don't know the answer to this question, because our emotions include many subjective factors and individual differences. Our language is rich with words to describe our emotions. Table 4.1 gives a partial list of some common emotions we experience.

In a way, this list only represents labels we give to our feelings. Perhaps we need to explain these labels further. One way we can do this is to identify emotions or feelings as either primary, mixed, mild or intense.

Primary and Mixed Emotions. Psychologists who study emotions have made up lists of certain basic emotions. R. Plutchick (1980) has identified eight *primary emotions:* joy, acceptance, fear, surprise, sadness, disgust, anger, and anticipation. He suggests that these primary feelings can combine to form other *mixed emotions,* such as love, submission, awe, disappointment, remorse, contempt, aggressiveness, optimism, etc.

However, Emery and Campbell, (1986) indicate that there are only four basic emotions: *mad, sad, glad,* and *scared.* They go on to suggest that all the other emotions we experience are just derivatives of these basic four. For example, too much sadness becomes depression, too much gladness becomes mania, too much fear becomes panic, and too much anger becomes rage.

Although you may not agree with the specific primary and secondary emotions just identified, you would probably agree that it is possible to experience several different emotions at the same time. For example, consider the following example.

You are going to have some friends over for hamburgers. Your date is going to help you get ready for your guests and also act as a host for the evening. An hour before your date is due at your house, you get a call that he has an unexpected guest from out-of-town arriving and will be unable to join you and your friends. Your date tells you that this is just an "old friend" he used to date, and she is only going to be in town for the evening.

Our perceptions about the causes of anger can be affected just by talking about them and deciding on an interpretation.

Carol Tavris

Now, would you just be angry? No, you would probably be hurt, jealous, and even embarrassed that you are the only one without a date. The point is, an emotional event can create a wide range of feelings. However, we generally communicate only one feeling—usually the most negative one. In this case, it would probably be your anger. Could your anger become a problem for you? Let's see!

Intense and Mild Emotions. We have discussed that it is human to have and express emotions and that our emotions have a lot to do with how much pleasure and enjoyment we get out of life. However, our emotions can have negative effects and cause problems for us. For example, strong emotions such as fear, depression, anger, and hate can disrupt our functioning and relating with other people.

Generally, our emotions begin to have negative effects when they are viewed as being excessive in *intensity* and *duration.* For example, if intense emotions linger, your ability to get enjoyment from life may be increasingly decreased. It is perfectly normal to be sad when someone close to you dies. However, if you are still depressed about this three years later, this sustained, intense emotion may be a problem for you. For example, other people may want to avoid being with you, because you are so sad and probably feeling really sorry for yourself!

How about another example? Have you ever had to get up in front of a group and give a speech? How did you feel? A "little bit" of anxiety before a speech can help you prepare and do a more effective job in delivery. However, total fear will probably cause you to be unable to concentrate on preparing adequately for the speech. In some cases, intense anxiety can cause you to stammer and forget important aspects of your speech.

Now, let's answer the question concerning your date who did not show for dinner: When could your anger become a problem for you? It would be normal for you to be angry if you were left in this situation. However, if this anger becomes so bad that you awoke for "nights on end" and "stewed" about your anger or even tried to harm your date and his "guest," then your intense anger or rage would be a problem for you.

Consequently, we say that when mild, emotions can be *facilitative*—they assist us in preparing for the future, solving problems, and in doing what is best for us. However, intense, sustained emotions can be *debilitative*—they disrupt our overall functioning. For example, we may experience difficulty in performing certain tasks, such as passing a test or giving a speech, and in solving problems—"stewing" over that date who didn't show up for dinner.

What are we trying to say? Essentially, emotions can serve a purpose in one situation and in other situations may serve as a hindrance. Specifically, what emotions cause us the most difficulty?

LIVING WITH PROBLEM EMOTIONS

Some emotions cause more difficulties than others: fear, anxiety, anger, guilt, grief, and love are such emotions which are experienced often and with mixed reactions.

FEAR

We all experience the emotion of fear. It can take many forms, serve many purposes, and create many different responses. It is important to distinguish *fear* from *anxiety*. Wilbert McKeachie and Charlotte Doyle (1970) offer this distinction:

Fear is the feeling associated with expectancies of unpleasantness. This may solve an expectancy of actual pain or it may involve an expectancy of distress or another, like a fear of failure or a fear of loneliness. Sometimes the basis of a fear is not understood by the person. Then, we call the fear an anxiety.

You may feel the emotion of fear as a type of warning that danger is near. This warning may take the form of an external "cue," or it may reflect your learning. For example, if you walked into your house and a burglar carrying a gun met you in the hallway, you would feel frightened. This feeling of fear was caused by an external force. Sometimes fear reactions are learned through past associations. You

Where fear is, happiness is not.

Seneca

might be afraid of thunderstorms because your father had a tendency to believe that lightening could result in a tornado. After all, his mother had been killed in a tornado when he was quite young.

Although most of the above examples reflect physical dangers, we also have fears of being left out of the crowd, of being ridiculed, of being a failure, or of being rejected. For example, if you have ever been rejected in a relationship, you may be afraid of getting involved in another relationship again. Actually, this is a good example of where you are really experiencing mixed emotions. Is it fear you are feeling, or is it hurt? Could it be that you want to protect yourself from getting hurt again? This type of fear/hurt is one that takes time to work through. After all, do you really want your "bad feelings" from one relationship to "rob" you of the opportunity to have a healthy and satisfying relationship with someone else?

How do you handle your fears? Because fear and anxiety are closely related, some suggestions for dealing with these emotions have been combined in Table 4.2. First of all, let's get a clearer picture of the sometimes troublesome emotion of anxiety.

ANXIETY

As we mentioned earlier, when the basis for our fear is not understood, we are experiencing anxiety. Actually, *anxiety* is an unpleasant, threatening feeling that something bad is about to happen. Rollo May, (1967) in his book, "Man's Search for Himself, states:

Anxiety is the feeling of "gnawing" within, of being "trapped and over-whelmed." Anxiety may take all forms and intensities, for it is the human being's reaction to a danger to his existence, or to some value he identifies with existence. . . . It is the quality of an experience which makes it anxiety rather than the quantity.

I believe that courage is all too often mistakenly seen as the absence of fear: If you descend by rope from a cliff and are not fearful to some degree, you are either crazy or unaware. Courage is seeing your fear in a realistic perspective, defining it, considering the alternatives and choosing to function in spite of risk.

Leonard Zunin

Many times the basis of our anxiety is so vague it is very difficult to explain what we are really feeling. As Rollo May suggests above, anxiety may occur in slight or great intensity. It may be mild tension before going for an important job interview; or it may be mild apprehension before taking an examination in your educational endeavors. These are common examples of *preparation anxiety, which help us get energized to deliver our best.*

The emotional tension that we commonly refer to as anxiety also functions as a signal of potential danger. For example, "I better study for that test, or I will flunk!" However, when the quality of the threatening experience is blown way out of proportion to the actual danger

---

Table 4.2
Facing Your Fears and Anxieties

1. **Admit your fears.** It is one thing to mask your anxieties with physical and creative activities; but if these activities become **avoidance** techniques, anxiety eventually increases.

2. **Take risks.** Fear doesn't go away unless you take chances to make your dreams come true. You will gain new strength and improved self-esteem with each accomplishment.

3. **Acknowledge the positive.** Anxious people tend to overlook their own strengths. When you're scared, make a conscious effort to remember some past positive experiences instead of focusing on your failures.

4. **Avoid catastrophic thinking.** Ask yourself what the worst possible outcome of the situation could be. Having faced the worst possibility makes it easier to deal with what does come.

5. **Stay in the present.** Much anxiety is the result of projecting yourself into future situations. Stay focused in the present—here and now—because that's all you can control anyway.

6. **Have patience.** If you are overwhelmed at the thought of confronting an anxiety triggering situation, take it one step at a time. Don't get in a hurry.

---

posed, and to the point that our anxiety hinders daily functioning, it becomes *"neurotic" anxiety.* A common example of this is when a student loses his "cool" over a test: "I can't do it—I just know I am going to flunk." and "goes totally blank." Is this normal anxiety or neurotic anxiety?

Worry is also a form of anxiety. For example, it is normal for people to worry about future events they are going to be involved in and whose outcome they are uncertain about. However, some people worry and lose sleep, lose sleep and worry even more, over "things" that never happen. Does this ever happen to you?

The difference in normal and "neurotic anxiety" may be in one's ability to handle or cope with the anxiety-producing situation. Just ask yourself, "Am I in control of this situation, or is the anxiety controlling how I react to this situation?"

ANGER

Anger is a signal that tells us that we don't like what's going on. *Anger* refers to a feeling of extreme displeasure, usually brought about by interference with our needs or desires. *Rage* is uncontrolled anger. Hostility, hate, and aggression may include varying degrees of the feeling of anger, but also imply some harmful intent or action as well. Anger doesn't go away if we ignore it, deny it exists, or fail to resolve it. Instead, it goes "underground" where it makes "sneak attacks" on our health and interpersonal relationships. Buried anger can also surface the next time an emotional crisis comes along, intensifying the impact of that crisis on us.

Anger most often begins with a loss or the threat of one, such as: (Lerner, 1985)

Loss of self-esteem. We get angry when we think we've failed or "let ourselves" down.

Loss of face. Public exposure of one's failures or inadequacies can be both humiliating and infuriating.

Threat of physical harm or violence. Anger helps activate our instinct for self-preservation.

Loss of valued possessions, skills, or abilities. Regardless of who's to blame, losing something we're proud of can cause both hurt and anger.

Loss of a valued role. If we lose a part of our life, such as a job, that is important to our identity, we may feel angry at having the role removed.

Loss of valued relationships. Anger is often a response to the loss of an important relationship.

Now stop and think for a moment about the times you have experienced genuine anger. Do you agree that your anger began with some loss or even the threat of a loss you incurred? Which type of loss just described were you dealing with?

From these losses then, there are four *psychological reactions* to anger. They are:

1. seeing yourself as a victim
2. feeling discounted or ignored
3. feeling powerless
4. looking for justice and revenge

In dealing with these psychological reactions to anger, it is important to remember *three characteristics of anger.*
Anger is neither right nor wrong. Everybody gets angry. Haim Ginott (1972) confirms this but provides some limits, too:

You have the right to get angry, but you do not have the right to attack other people or their character traits.

Anger can be released in a right or wrong way. It is important to remember that anger released in inappropriate ways destroys relationships. This most often occurs when we *displace* our anger toward important people onto other relationships. In this way, anger at a boss gets deflected onto our spouse; anger at a spouse onto our child, and so on. Because we trust them to accept us as we are, we often unconsciously choose our strongest relationships as a "dumping ground" for our anger.

Anger is a signal, and one worth listening to.

Harriet Lerner

You are vulnerable when angry. You may say or act in ways that are totally uncharacteristic of you. Sometimes anger causes more anger. Uncontrolled anger leads to bitterness, hatred, and even violence. If your local newspaper carries a brief synopsis of the daily police reports, we encourage you to take notice of the assaults and even murders that occur because people are angry and lose control of their emotions.

The question now might be: How do I express my anger? Carol Tavris (1989) suggests that we have been told if we ventilate our anger, we will experience (1) improved communication and closeness with the target of our anger, (2) have physiological relief and catharsis, (3) solve problems instead of brooding about them, and (4) we will just feel better because we got "rid" of the anger. Tavris goes on further to say that sometimes we get the benefits of this list, but most frequently, we get exactly the opposite: (1) decreased communication and feelings of closeness with the target of our anger, (2) physiological arousal and even higher blood pressure, (3) the problem becomes worse, and (4) we frequently just rehearse the anger and get angrier.

The question then is, how can I ensure the benefits and avoid the "exact opposites?" Psychologist Harriet Lerner (1985) feels that the expression of anger provides maximum results when the *Do's and Don'ts* provided in Table 4.3 are followed. Also, you will find the discussion dealing with resolving interpersonal conflict through the use of "I" messages in Chapter 7 helpful in dealing with your anger.

Table 4.3
Anger Do's and Don'ts

Do speak up when an issue is important to you.

Don't strike while the iron is hot.

Do take time out to think about the problem and clarify your position.

Don't use "below-the-belt" tactics.

Do speak in "I" language.

Don't make vague requests.

Do try to appreciate the fact that people are different.

Don't tell another person what she or he thinks or feels or "should" think or feel.

Do recognize that each person is responsible for his or her own behavior.

Don't participate in intellectual arguments that go nowhere.

Do try to avoid speaking through a third party.

Don't expect change to come about from hit-and-run confrontations.

Anger is a very powerful emotion and one that requires a balance between spontaneous expression and rational control. It is helpful to remember that when you are angry at someone, you are the one with the problem; therefore, you must be the one to correct the problem.

GUILT

Another powerful emotion that can rule our lives is that of *guilt.* We feel a sense of guilt when we have violated our conscience, our internalized standards of good and bad (Atwater, 1983). *Guilt,* in its simplest form, is the realization of sorrow over having done something morally, socially, or ethically wrong. Experts in human behavior report that unjustified, excessive guilt can sour our enjoyment of living, disrupt our social and business lives, worry, dishearten, and even humiliate us. It can cause fears and anxieties and even torment a person to the point of suicide. As you can see, tragedy and much human suffering has been triggered by needless feelings of guilt.

Consider the following example given by a strikingly beautiful 32-year-old mother and student of one of the authors.

The marriage of this student and her lawyer-husband ended in divorce after ten years. The legal papers said "mental cruelty" but they both knew the real reason was her sexual coldness. Yet, there was another, deeper layer. Two years before their marriage, during a relationship with another man, she had become pregnant and undergone an abortion—but she never told her husband about it. Guilt over an act she considered deeply shameful, worsened by harboring a secret she felt he should know, made her feel unworthy of him. She was unable to respond freely and joyously to his lovemaking. Quarrels erupted that in time eroded the foundation of their union.

Without question, that guilt can literally paralyze us, making us totally unable to function as human beings. However, is guilt *all* bad? Sidney Jourard (1973) has an answer for us:

Guilt itself is a desirable human emotion in the sense that it enables us to recognize what we have done wrong, when we have violated our own consciences and the mores of our society. Most of us have been brought up to believe that all guilt is harmful, unnecessary, and should be eradicated. That's as wrong as saying all germs are bad. If we never felt guilt, we would not learn in school, do our jobs properly, obey traffic rules, feed and clothe our children, work for our families, have good relationships with loved ones, or live in harmony within our communities or with one another. In short, guilt is our society's regulator.

Nobody is born with a conscience. It does not come as standard equipment, like the survival instinct or sex drive. Sigmund Freud (1936) states: "Babies are 'notoriously amoral' . . . they have no inhibitions against their pleasure-seeking impulses."

We learn about guilt in several ways. For example, we first learn about guilt through the internalized voice of parental authority—what is right, what is wrong, and what the rules are. Also, the demands of the society in which a child is reared also play an important role. So, too, do the traditions of race and nationality.

Some people feel guilt more strongly than others and for less reasons. Some children grow up being accused frequently and inappropriately by parents and family members of "bad" actions. Shame is drilled into them continually for behavior that is not truly shameful. In some instances, children grow up loaded with a heavy burden of guilt, deeply convinced that he or she is an undeserving person. The result may then be finding a refuge in drugs, delinquency, other forms of antisocial behavior, or even the choice of suicide. Karl Menninger (1980), one of the founders of the famed psychiatric clinic in Topeka, Kansas, and a noted authority on the reasons why people take their lives, provides a thought-provoking view on the results of excessive guilt:

Suicide is a combination of hate, rage, revenge, a sense of guilt, and a feeling of unbearable frustration. In other words, intense feelings of guilt can often make life literally unbearable.

A clear understanding of the significance of our misdeeds is emotionally healthier than hopeless misery afterward.

Dr. Theodor Reik

Table 4.4
Suggestions for Dealing with Guilt

Examine why you feel guilty.   Take a long inward look, seeking the reason for your feelings. It is important to remember that powerful guilt feelings are sometimes pushed far beneath the layers of our conscious thinking. In such cases, professional help may be needed to help bring them to the surface. The point is to find out exactly why you feel guilty.

Determine whether you really need to feel guilty.
Reappraise all the rules that have been set down for you during your lifetime. Take a whole new look at the principles, not created by yourself, but prescribed by parents, friends, society, and others. Are these principles realistic and valid for you at your stage of life and relevant in the society in which you now live and work?

Do what is right for you.   Make decisions that sound "good" to you. No one can tell you how you should live your life. You must make your own decisions about what is right and what is wrong. Don't live your life by listening to what other people say you should or should not do. Obviously, you will have to accept the consequences of your choices, but be your own person.

Forgive yourself.   Learn to accept the fact that perfection is an unattainable ideal. Mistakes happen. If you've done something morally or ethically wrong, accept it and forget it. Apologize if you can or correct the misdeed in whatever way is proper. Say nothing if you will hurt someone else grievously, recognizing that "telling all" is actually asking for punishment to ease your sense of guilt. It is possible to feel sorry about something without feeling guilty. The point is that you will need to tell yourself and also internalize, that you have done something wrong, that it was wrong, and that it is now behind you.

It would be fair to note here that the influence of parents and other circles in which the child moves is only part of the story. Some experts believe that the tendency to absorb large doses of guilt may be inherited. Then, there are some studies that indicate that the sterner your conscience, and the more vigilantly it monitors your thoughts and actions, the worse you'll feel if you do something you think is wrong.

How can you handle excessive and inappropriate guilt? Table 4.4 lists some suggestions for dealing with this powerful emotion. However, we leave you with a reminder: Although excessive guilt can be a truly destructive, troublesome emotion, it is equally as destructive and troublesome to have no guilt at all.

GRIEF AND BEREAVEMENT

Everyone goes through grief and bereavement. All of us make attachments to people, places, and things, and then as we are separated from them we go through a grief reaction. *Grief* and *bereavement,* sometimes even referred to as *mourning,* can be defined as "to be deprived."

The grief process consists of freeing ourselves emotionally from the "loss," readjusting to life without this loss, resuming ordinary activities, and forming new relationships. Elisabeth Kübler-Ross (1975), and R. Kavanaugh (1972) have written extensively on the grief process and have suggested that there are some fairly common stages that people go through in coping with a loss. They are as follows:

Denial is the first step in a grief reaction. When we pick up a phone and hear that our best friend has died, our first response is denial, sometimes also referred to as *shock* and *disbelief.* Denial serves to protect us from the pain of that loss. In other words, it allows us to regroup and to handle the loss setting in. Some people get stuck in denial and never move past this first step of the grief reaction. For example, the wife who waits at home for her divorced husband who is now remarried to come back to her is in a state of unrealistic denial.

Replacement or searching activity is the second step in a grief reaction. Nature abhors a vacuum and when someone dies, divorces us, or moves away, a vacuum is created. When this occurs, we attempt to fill that emotional vacuum with other people in our environment. We also attempt to get them to meet our emotional needs that were met by the person who has left. This will work temporarily, but it is not a permanent solution for dealing with a loss. Obviously, replacement is a defense mechanism to keep us from feeling the pain of loss. Some people get stuck in a permanent replacement phenomenon, such as the lady who gets married over and over again in attempt to fill the vacuum created by the death of her father.

Anger is the third step in a grief reaction. It is natural and normal to be angry at the person who has abandoned us by death, divorce, or just simply moving away. Many people feel cheated and angry over the apparent injustice of what is happening to them. It's hard for us as adults to be angry at a family member who died, because he obviously didn't do it on purpose. However, our unconscious mind doesn't accept the logic of this, and it still gets angry at the person who died. This frequently happens during the tenacious process of settling legal matters. The person may say, or think, "why did you leave me with this 'mess' to get straight?"

People can get stuck in this phase of a grief reaction and be angry and bitter all their life. If this anger is kept bottled up inside, rather than expressed in appropriate ways, it is likely to be turned against themselves and may take the form of depression—*a kind of self-punishment.*

It hurts to lose something important. It hurts worse to pretend otherwise. To expect more than reality can offer only sets you up to hurt badly and needlessly.

David Viscott

Depression is an overwhelming feeling—but remember: It is just a feeling, something you can affect by how you think and act.

Gary Emery and James Campbell

Whatever things make your life most meaningful, plan to do them before it's too late. The greatest lesson we may learn from the dying is simply LIVE, so you do not have to look back and say, "God, how I wasted my life."

Elisabeth Kübler-Ross

Depression is the fourth step of a grief reaction. In the aftermath of death or divorce, a sense of hopelessness may set in. In essence, there is a feeling of emptiness. It is during this stage that people may spend considerable hours thinking of the future they had planned, and now no longer have. In fact, they may avoid people and social encounters and just retreat inside themselves.

It is not uncommon for people who divorce to turn their anger away from their spouse and toward themselves. Thus, they may experience much self-blame and self-doubt. They may say to themselves: "Maybe I didn't give our relationship a fair chance." "Where did I really go wrong?"

A person can get stuck in this stage of the grief reaction too and never resolve the grief. Consequently, the individual may be chronically depressed for an extended period of time. If grief isn't worked through, it may be extremely difficult for a person to form new relationships, because in some ways he or she is still holding on to the past relationship. Obviously, this just creates more depression.

Acceptance is the fifth and last step in a grief reaction. This stage is marked by a gradual acceptance of the reality that life must go on without this person. Then, the resumption of ordinary activities usually takes place. This may occur from a few months to a year or more after the loss, depending on the person and the circumstances surrounding the loss.

The more fully we express our feelings and work through our grief, the more likely we will be to get on with our lives. Refusing to allow tears, suffering in silence, and "being strong" are thought to be admirable behaviors. Yet, the most healthful approach to grief is to approach it head-on.

The four previous steps in a grief reaction do not always fall in quite that order, and a person may skip back and forth between these stages. However, the final step of *acceptance* must be reached to eventually get through a grief reaction.

Grief-work, the process of freeing ourselves emotionally from the deceased and readjusting to life without that person, takes time. However, you will need a strong support system of family and friends to aide you in your progress. People who are fortunate to work out that grief may eventually find it becomes a positive growth experience— sometimes called *good grief.* Sometimes we have to experience grief to really appreciate others. In the process of reaching this awareness, we may tend to value those friends and loved ones who are still living. Furthermore, grief helps us to put our own lives into perspective. We may realize how short life really is and how important it is to do what is meaningful to us before it's too late.

LOVE

Countless volumes have been written about the subject love. Yet do we really understand the true meaning of love? You will have the opportunity to explore love as it relates to more intimate relationships in Chapter 7. Therefore, our discussion in this chapter will be limited to the learned attitudes that interfere with our ability to give and receive love, as well as the use and misuse of love.

Certainly, our ideas about love are shaped by childhood experiences. If your parents hug you and tell you how great you are, hugs and praises become a part of your vocabulary of love. However, if they slap you and tell you you are stupid, you may conclude that in some odd way, abuse is part of a loving relationship. Why would you do this? From a child's perspective: "these are my parents; parents love their children; therefore, the way my parents love me is loving behavior."

We also grow up assuming that others will find the same things lovable that our parents did. For example, if we're lucky, our parents love us unconditionally and continue to love us even when they don't love our behavior or when we disagree with them. Consequently, we grew up believing that we deserved to be loved just because we are who we are.

If, however, our parents loved us only when we were compliant and undemanding, we may have mistakenly learned that compliance was loving behavior. Therefore, we assume that we should not make demands on those we love. In essence, our parents loving us only when we pleased them taught us that we must always be pleasing or risk losing love.

There are also problems we encounter through the misuse of the emotion, love. Because love is such a powerful and yet complicated emotion, we may even have a tendency to "smother" other people because we "love" them. However, do we love them in the appropriate manner?

Psychologist Dr. Foster Cline (1982) makes an interesting comment about the misuse of love: "Love becomes a problem when it gets in the way of our allowing individuals the right to experience the consequences of their choices." For example, what about the countless hours spent in enabling a child or spouse who has a drug or alcohol problem? Why do we find it difficult for those we love to suffer the consequences of their choices? The answer is simple: We love them, and we don't like to see those we love suffer—we want to spare them their pain.

LETTING GO

To **let go** does not mean to stop caring, it means I can't do it for someone else.
To **let go** is not to cut myself off, it's the realization I can't control another.
To **let go** is not to enable, but to allow learning from natural consequences.
To **let go** is not to care for, but to care about.
To **let go** is not to fix, but to be supportive.
To **let go** is not to judge, but to allow another to be a human being.
To **let go** is not to be in the middle arranging all the outcomes, but to allow others to affect their own destinies.
To **let go** is not to be protective, it's to permit another to face reality.
To **let go** is not to deny, but to accept.
To **let go** is not to regret the past, but to grow and live for the future.
To **let go** is to fear less and love more.

Anonymous

To be loved because of one's merit, because one deserves it, always leaves doubt; maybe I did not please the person whom I want to love me, maybe this or that—there is always a fear that love could disappear. Furthermore, "deserved" love easily leaves a bitter feeling that one is loved for oneself, that one is loved only because one pleases, that one is, in the last analysis, not loved but used.

Erich Fromm

The reality is that love can mean letting go of the responsibility we sometimes impose on ourselves to "take care" of those we love. It is in the best interest of those we love to let them assume the responsibility for making their choices and the consequences of those choices. When we jump in and smother them, we take away their choices and their freedom to be self-sufficient human beings. In essence, we have done them a major injustice, quite the opposite of what we really believe we are doing. This is extremely difficult for people to accept, and it takes a great deal of time to work through this emotional understanding of the true meaning of love.

Another misuse of love is when we find ourselves or others using love as a control agent—"If you loved me, you would do this . . . , or you wouldn't do this." Do we really understand what we are saying? This is obviously a strong form of manipulation and can totally destroy whatever love and caring there may be in a relationship.

Although there are many definitions of love, in the final analysis, love may truly be the desire to see another individual become all he or she can be as a person—with room to breathe and grow; and it may be caring as much about another person's well being as we do our own. This is true whether our love be for a spouse, friend, child, or co-worker.

Table 4.5
Expanding Your Ability to Love

Express yourself.   You have positive feelings, so put them into words: "Our relationship means a lot to me," "I like being with you." "I love you."

Love yourself.   Self-love is the opposite of selfishness, not the same thing. If you don't love yourself, you can't love someone else.

Be tolerant.   You can love and be loved without sharing exactly the same opinions, values, and personality traits. Don't make constant agreement your main criterion for love. This is unrealistic.

Hang in there.   You are vulnerable and there is always the risk of hurt, but don't give up at the first sign of trouble. Relationships can be difficult but rewarding.

Learn to be alone.   You cannot be happy until you can be happy being alone. Don't ask another person to be your "security blanket." If you love someone, give the person room to breathe and grow while you keep your distance.

Grow up.   Immature love says, "I love you because I need you"; or "I love because I am loved." Mature loves says, "I need you because I love you"; or "I am loved because I love."

Practice.   The more you practice developing a loving attitude, the more love you will attract. The more frequently you say, "I really care about you," "I love you," the more comfortable you'll become in expressing these loving words.

Certainly, there are many types of love relationships. Depending upon the relationship involved, the true meaning of love will be expressed in various ways, Some people have trouble saying the words, "I love you!" Instead, they show their love by buying presents or doing nice things for those they love. Obviously, for one who says, "I love you" frequently, it is difficult to understand why another person can't "spit" the words out. However, people express their emotions in different ways. Although it is true that adults who did not know love as a child have a greater difficulty learning how to express love, it is never too late to develop or expand our ability to love. Table 4.5 represents some suggestions from *The Art of Loving* (Fromm, 1956) and *Living, Loving and Learning* (Buscaglia, 1982) that may be of benefit to you.

Now that we have a better idea of how some of our more common emotions affect us, we will discuss how we got to be feeling persons. The chapter concludes with a discussion on learning how to express emotions, as well as the benefits to be derived in achieving a balance between emotional expression and emotional control.

DEVELOPMENT OF EMOTIONS

From early infancy, human beings display tendencies toward responding emotionally. Most authorities agree that heredity does predispose us towards fairly specific emotional tendencies (Jung, 1923). For example, one child develops a natural tendency to react calmly to most emotional stimuli, whereas another shows a tendency to react quickly and intensely to all emotional stimuli.

An infant's first emotional expression is crying. For several months, babies will continue to show their excitement by crying when they feel like doing so. After a few weeks, they have learned to distinguish and respond to two basic emotions—*distress and delight.* Bodily discomfort (a wet diaper or hunger) brings forth the earliest unpleasant reaction, known as *distress. Delight,* the earliest pleasant reaction, appears several weeks after distress, in the form of smiling, gurgling, and other babyish sounds of joy.

Soon, we become more aware of the world within us and the world outside us. Consequently, we learn from others and our own experiences other emotional responses such as love, anger, frustration, fear, jealousy, and so on. We learn which emotions will bring us rewards and those that will bring us punishment.

Through our family, school, and social experiences, we learn various ways of dealing with our emotions. We also receive messages on how to express and deal with some of our emotions. For example, we may hear: "Don't make a scene by crying"; "there is nothing to be afraid of"; "don't let everybody see how angry you are"; "cheer up, there is no reason to feel bad"; "be strong, endure your pain"; or even, "control yourself, don't let others know how excited you are." It is even possible that you heard the statement, "big boys don't cry." Consequently, we may grow up thinking that girls and women can cry, but boys and men must not do so. This is an example of how sexist behavior is learned and can be unlearned in the same manner.

The main thing in life is not to be afraid to be human.

Pablo Casals

With modeling and messages from our parents, society, and our peers, is it any wonder that we grow up confused about *what to do with our feelings?*

THE COSTS OF DENYING EMOTIONS

What kinds of messages did you get about expressing or controlling your emotions? Were you taught to express your emotions openly, or did you grow up believing that you should "stop showing" your emotions—even though you continued to experience them. That's right! As long as you live, you continue to experience emotions. Why? You already know the answer: you are a human, not a robot or a machine. You will be given several opportunities in the activities at the end of this chapter to review how you express your emotions.

How, then, do people deal with the emotional aspects of their life? There are only two choices: deny them or express them. Because overcontrol poses our biggest problem in expressing emotions, we'll begin by looking at two common ways we deny our emotions.

Repression. The most common form of overcontrol is repression. In *repression,* the self automatically excludes threatening or painful thoughts and feelings from awareness. By pushing them into the subconscious, we are able to manage the anxiety that grows out of uncomfortable situations.

Perhaps the most destructive aspect of repression is that although we realize we are hurting when we have repressed our true feelings, we do not know why. We have hidden the source of pain in the "dungeon" of the subconscious. However, repressed emotions unfortunately do not die. They refuse to be silenced and continue to influence our whole personality and behavior. For example, when we repress guilt feelings we are forever, though subconsciously, trying to punish ourselves. We will not allow ourselves success or enjoyment because we are so unworthy. For example, rather than accepting compliments, we "qualify" them or quickly give all the credit to someone more deserving than us!

Repressed fears and angers may be acted out physically as insomnia, headaches, ulcers, and so on. However, if such fears and angers had been consciously accepted and expressed, there would be no necessity for the sleeplessness, the tension headaches, or ulcers. David Viscott (1976) indicates that feelings always follow a predictable pattern when you suffer one of three major kinds of loss: (1) *the loss of someone who loves you or the loss of their love* or *your sense of lovability;* (2) *the loss of control;* (3) *the loss of self-esteem.* The predictable pattern then becomes

When a loss threatens, you feel anxious.
When a loss occurs, you feel hurt.
When hurt is held back, it becomes anger.
When anger is held back, it creates guilt.
When guilt is unrelieved, depression occurs.

Viscott goes on to say that if you take care of your fear, hurt and anger, the guilt and depression will take care of themselves. In other words, they will be nonexistent, just like the sleeplessness, the tension headaches, or ulcers. However, when a person is especially sensitive to one type of loss, he or she tends to bury the unpleasant feelings associated with the loss.

What is the result of these buried feelings? John Powell (1969) makes a profound statement about the costs of repressing feelings:

Buried emotions are like rejected people; they make us pay a high price for having rejected them. Hell hath no fury like that of a scorned emotion.

When you deny what is real,
When you hide from life's pains,
When you shut out the world,
Only fantasy remains.

David Viscott

Suppression. Sometimes people suppress rather than repress their emotions. In *suppression* people are usually conscious of their emotions, but deliberately control rather than express them. For example, you might say, "I'll never let her know that I'm jealous." Why would you say this? You might be afraid that your emotional admissions could be used against you; maybe she would bring it up later; and then you would probably always wonder if she might distance herself from you because of the feelings you confided. Obviously, these are all threats to your self-esteem, so why take the risk? After all, what you don't say can't be used against you.

Although suppression of emotions is a healthier way of handling feelings than is repression, habitual suppression may lead to many of the undesirable effects of repression. Furthermore, chronic suppression of feelings interferes with rational, problem-solving behavior. When people have unexpressed feelings that are "smoldering" within, they cannot think clearly. Consequently, they may have difficulty studying, working, or even socializing with others. More importantly, when you consistently suppress your emotions, you may eventually explode and do things or say things totally uncharacteristic of you. Obviously, this makes the problem/s much, much worse. As you can see, chronic suppression can be just as unhealthy as repression (Atwater, 1983).

Now, we are left with the other choice of dealing with our feelings—expressing them. But, isn't this difficult when we've been holding them back for so long? Let's see.

When feelings are avoided, their painful effects are often prolonged, and it becomes increasingly difficult to deal with them.

Andrew Salter

THE CRITERIA OF EMOTIONAL MATURITY*

HAVING the ability to deal constructively with reality
HAVING the capacity to adapt to change
HAVING a relative freedom from symptoms that are produced by tensions and anxieties
HAVING the capacity to find more satisfaction in giving than receiving
HAVING the capacity to relate to other people in a consistent manner with mutual satisfaction and helpfulness
HAVING the capacity to sublimate, to direct one's instinctive hostile energy into creative and constructive outlets
HAVING the capacity to love

William C. Menninger, M.D. 1899–1966

*Courtesy of William C. Menninger, M.D. Copyright 1966, © The Menninger Foundation, Topeka, Kansas.

GETTING OUT OF EMOTIONAL DEBT

Everybody gets into emotional debt from time to time. Gary Emery and James Campbell (1986) define *emotional debt* as a condition of imbalance in which feelings are trapped instead of expressed. As we have already stated, keeping feelings from being expressed naturally employs defenses and drains energy. The more feelings are held in, the less energy you have to be yourself. Obviously, this interferes with your ability to interact with others.

Accepting and learning to handle and express emotions is the mark of maturity. You are a feeling being. If you are to have the joy of positive emotions, you also must accept the reality of your negative emotions without guilt, self-condemnation, or repression of the emotion. Do you want to begin to learn how to express your emotions? Before we discuss the steps involved, we ask you to internalize the words of John Powell (1969):

When you are ready to stop telling your emotions what they should be, they will tell you what they really are.

Now, are you ready to uncover your lost emotions?

GUIDELINES FOR DEALING WITH YOUR EMOTIONS

Emotions are a fact of life, and communicating them certainly isn't a simple matter. It's obvious that showing every feeling of anger, frustration, and even love and affection could get you in trouble. However, withholding emotions can be personally frustrating and certainly affect your relationships. Therefore, the following suggestions can help you to decide when and how to express your emotions (Adler and Towne, 1987).

Listen to Your Body. What is happening inside of you? What are those butterflies in your stomach telling you? Why is your heart pounding? Remember, physiological changes are a part of your emotions and what you are feeling. Those internal changes speak to you very clearly; don't ignore them.

Identify Your Feelings. Just ask yourself, "What am I really feeling?" Is it fear, anger, frustration, etc? Give your feelings a label if you can. If you have difficulty with an exact label, use the techniques in the next suggestion to help you express your feelings. Remember to name all the feelings you are having. Try to identify your primary feeling and then your secondary feeling. Above all, do not deny or suppress your feelings.

Personalize Your Feelings. There are times when you can *name* the feeling: "I'm feeling hurt," "I love you," "I'm angry." However, there are times when it is easier to describe the *impact* the feelings are having on you: "I feel like I'm being dumped on," "I feel used," "I feel he cares for me." Metaphors with a col*orful description* such as "I'm sitting on top of the world," I feel like my world has caved in," "I'm down in the dumps," can be used. Feelings can also be expressed by describing what *action* you feel like taking: "I feel like giving up," "I feel like telling him off," "I just want to jump for you."

The greatest lesson I ever learned was to accept complete responsibility for what I was feeling.

George B. Shaw

Own Your Feelings. Your feelings are yours; no other person can cause or be responsible for your emotions. Of course, we feel better assigning our emotions to other people: "You made me angry," "You frightened me," "You made me jealous." The fact is that another person can't make you *anything.* Another person can only stimulate the emotions that are already in you, waiting to be activated. The distinction between *causing* and *stimulating* emotions is not just a play on words. The acceptance of the truth involved is critical. If you think other people can make you angry, when you become angry you simply lay the blame and pin the problem on them. You can then walk away from your emotional encounter learning nothing, concluding only that the other people were at fault because he or she made you angry. Then, you do not have to examine your own feelings because you gave all the responsibility for your feelings to the other people.

Decide What You Will Do with Your Feelings. This is oftentimes very difficult, because there are many factors to consider. However, careful consideration of the following suggestions may be of assistance to you:

Timing and appropriateness of place We are all familiar with the thought: there is a time and a place for all things. This is particularly true when, expressing emotions because you want to get your message across. You also want your message to be heard, and you hope your message is understood. As we will discuss in Chapter 5, your receiver will probably be more receptive to your message if he or she is not distracted by outside stimuli and if the receiver has the energy and time to listen.

How much emotion to express Young children may squeal with delight or cry with anguish in the grocery store, at church, or wherever they so please. However, adults are expected to exert control over their emotional expressions. This doesn't mean that adults shouldn't express emotion spontaneously. Instead, it means that adults feel an emotion, understand it, and decide how intensely to express it. For example, regardless of how intensely an adult feels he or she wants to laugh and get excited in church, this is just considered taboo, if you are the only one laughing. Also, regardless of how sad you feel that your daughter is marrying this "certain" boy, it might not be a good idea to cry loudly and profusely through the entire wedding. A quiet sob would be much more appropriate.

Significance of relationship There is some risk involved in expressing feelings. In an encounter with a store clerk, an acquaintance, or a distant relative, expressing your feelings may do nothing more than relieve tension. In other words, you might be able to get away with "telling this person off." However, if you value another person's friendship, you may want to carefully consider just "telling this person off." You may find that this relationship means so much to you, you need to be very careful in expressing your feelings. Maybe, you can soften your approach. After all, you want the net effect to be a closer, more meaningful relationship. It is important to realize you are going to be interacting with this person in the future; you can avoid the store clerk if you so choose.

Words and mannerisms You already know some ways to personalize your feelings. You will also want to consider the appropriate verbal and nonverbal techniques to use in getting your message across. This will be discussed in more detail in Chapter 5. However, careful selection of words means that you use tact and deal with facts instead of interpretations, judgments, or accusations.

Recognize the difference between feeling and acting At times you may be so angry that you feel like "punching someone in the nose." In this instance, it would be more constructive to talk about your feelings, rather than act upon your feelings. One point should be made clear: Allowing ourselves the freedom to feel and observe our emotions does not necessarily mean that we should act on those emotions. As a small child, you might punch someone in the nose when you get angry. Although this is not necessarily appropriate, you might just get a spanking or a "time out" period. However, as an adult, if you "punch" someone in the nose, you might get a ticket to jail or even get killed in extreme cases. To live effectively in our world requires that we be sensitive to situations and adjust our emotional expression accordingly. Remember, we used the term *adjust,* not *deny.*

Although it is true that people express their emotions differently and respond to situations differently, the truth is that sometimes, as we have stated above, it is just not possible to openly express what you really feel. In these instances, you need to choose some indirect ways to express your feelings. As you already know, feelings do not just go away. Here are some suggestions for these times:

1. *Ventilate or share your feelings with someone you trust.*
2. *Choose some type of physical or creative activity to help release your "pent-up" emotions.*
3. *Work to maintain a positive or realistic perspective of the situation.*
4. *As much as possible, keep a sense of humor.*

An emotion without social rules of containment and expression is like an egg without a shell: a gooey mess.

Carol Tavris

Feel—the Shorthand Technique

F	Focus on your feelings.
E	Express them constructively.
E	Experience them.
L	Let them go.

Table 4.6.

You are probably thinking or saying to yourself, "I'll never remember all these guidelines." If this is true for you, perhaps the "shorthand technique" developed by Gary Emery and James Campbell (1986) and illustrated in Table 4.6 will be a quick way for you to remember the key concepts in expressing your feelings.

We are emotional human beings. Understanding our emotions, how they affect us, and developing ways of handling them can be beneficial for all of us. And learning to constructively express and to utilize our emotions is a life-long process; we learn by doing.

BENEFITS OF EXPRESSING YOUR FEELINGS

Many emotional responses feel good to us. Feelings of love, tenderness, and warmth toward other people give us a sense of well-being. Emotions involved in our anticipation of some good news we are momentarily expecting feel good. Emotional responses involved in happy or joyful experiences in life are also enhancing to us, as are emotional responses found in humor or laughter that tend to help us feel good about being alive.

However, the real benefit of having the good feelings can only be found if one chooses to truly experience the emotions and share them with others.

As we have stated several times in this chapter, strong feelings that are not expressed or dealt with rarely go away. Instead, you may begin to collect your feelings and cash them in at a later date for a *free* mad, temper tantrum, or an angry outburst at someone else. Also, bottled-up anger may "leak out" in the form of a lack of cooperation, silence, coldness, cynicism, or even sarcasm. Obviously, none of us would really want these types of behaviors to occur.

Do you collect emotional trading stamps—that is, collecting feelings, rather than dealing with them?

Ann Ellenson

Do You Carefully Save Your Feelings . . .

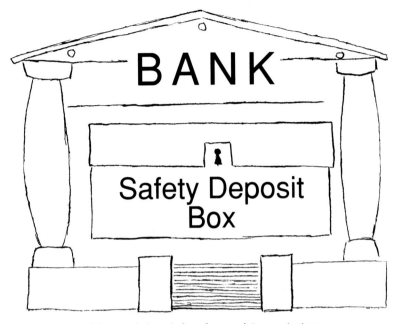

and then cash them in for a free mad, temper tantrum,
or an angry outburst at someone else?

The authors believe after you have carefully considered your options and the consequences involved in expressing your feelings, and *choose to take the risk,* you are likely to derive several long-term, positive benefits. We will name three, although there are many others.

1. You Will Develop Positive Feelings About Yourself. You can't possibly understand that part of yourself which you deny or repress. Furthermore, you can't possibly appreciate yourself when you know you are not being honest with yourself and others. Once you begin to openly and honestly deal with your feelings in a constructive way, you will automatically experience increased feelings of self-esteem. People who feel good about themselves are not afraid of their emotional responses. That is, they trust themselves and their emotions. Obviously, this type of dual trust, leads to a sense of inner harmony and freedom—you don't have to *pretend* any longer.

2. Your Relationships Will Grow Stronger. The expression of feelings is vital to effectively building meaningful relationships. How can others know what you are feeling if you never tell them? How can another person really get to know you if you only talk about the "weather" or "surface" type issues.

The things that most clearly differentiate and individuate me from others are my feelings and emotions.

Anonymous

Other people may have dark hair as you do or drive a Ford as you do, but others will not experience fears, frustrations, love, and joy in the same way as you do. So, you must tell others how you feel, what your "gut" is saying, if you really want to establish and maintain meaningful relationships.

Often, when you begin expressing your feelings, others will be more likely to express some of their own. Consequently, you each know more about each other. When two people can share their feelings in an open, honest, and caring way, their relationship will deepen, even if these feelings are sometimes negative. John Powell (1969) believes relationships deepen through a successive, descending process involving six levels:

Level six. Small talk When you engage in this level of conversation, you use clichés such as "How are things going?" or "What have you been doing?" or "Is it hot enough for you?" This level is just casual, passing communicating that means nothing except it is better than embarrassing silence. There is no sharing of persons at all.

Level five: Talk about things and people This is the usual luncheon or cup of coffee "gossip" conversation. Events, people, and happenings are related, but you tell little about yourself. You might go as far to talk about what you have been doing: "I went to the ballgame." However, you say very little about yourself and invite nothing from others in return.

Level four: You reveal your opinions, thoughts and ideas At this level, you are willing to expose some of the inner you, risking criticism or disagreement. However, at the first indication of rejection, you may go back to the first two levels or say what you think will be what the other person wants you to say. If you become emotionally aroused, you might go to the next level.

Level three: Your emotions talk You may have been wounded, hurt, or threatened. So, your emotions take over and do the talking. You may express anger, jealousy, or hostility by saying things you regret later. Or, in some instances, you may get carried away by positive emotions—excitement, attraction, or enthusiasm.

Level two: You talk about the way you feel and who you are There is a difference between your emotions talking and talking about your emotions. At this level, you talk honestly and courageously about how you feel—your doubts, fears, angers, hopes, joys, your feelings about yourself, and who you think you are inside. You begin to know yourself and others. You grow. You help others know themselves because you let them know you.

Level one: Peak communication These are rare moments when you are perfectly in tune with another, communicating with understanding, depth, and emotional satisfaction. There is complete honesty and openness. You know your reactions are shared and felt completely by the other person.

Although it is true that peak or "gut-level" communication is sometimes difficult, it is also true that there are times when it is most necessary. Among close friends or between marriage partners, there will come, from time to time, a complete emotional and personal communion. Although this is difficult to define, you probably know when you have had such an experience. In fact, this type of complete emotional and personal communion has sometimes been referred to as *emotional intimacy*.

3. Pressure Is Relieved. Experts in psychosomatic medicine believe that the most common cause of fatigue and actual sickness is the repression of emotions. We all experience frustrations and anxieties in our daily lives. For example, our goals may be thwarted, our self-esteem and integrity may be threatened, and our abilities to handle situations may seem overwhelmed. As we have seen, our health and our relationships are negatively affected when we deny "what we are really feeling." However, when we are able to express what we have kept "bottled up" inside us, we normally feel better. Consequently, we naturally reduce some of the stress we are feeling. We will discuss stress and its effects more fully in Chapter 8.

A LAST THOUGHT

We all would agree that emotions are a crucial part of being human. Although we have developed robots and various electronic equipment that can store information and perform a variety of activities, we have not developed a machine that can love, feel angry, or experience sadness.

As René Descartes said, "I think, therefore I am." To that we would add, "I also feel, sense, and intuit." If we were only emotional, we would simply react, as the computer does when a certain key is pushed. However, by combining the feeling side (emotions) of our nature with the thinking side (intellect), we can make judgments about the desirability to act or not act upon certain emotions. And, we then can use our will to carry out the decisions we have made. In other words, *we get to push our own key; no one else does this for us.*

Emotions frighten many people. It's often easier to be just a brain, a Thinker, a human computer than to combine those aspects with emotional responsiveness. However, to the extent that we do not experience our feelings, we do not experience the real world. Reality simply can't be comprehended without taking into account feelings.

As we go through adulthood, we have the opportunity to experiment with a full range of behaviors and full range of emotions. And, as we have discussed, we may overcontrol or undercontrol our emotional expressions, neither of which is desirable. Ideally, we learn to live with our emotions. That is, we learn to achieve a balance between emotional expression and control. There is no magic key to push, but there is a process we all have to learn. Hopefully, we learn to express our emotions in constructive ways and to control those emotions and expressions that might be destructive to ourselves and others.

When you open to me a part of yourself, a reaction, a hurt, a tenderness or a fear that I have never before experienced in you, I am made more aware of your depth and your mystery. I no longer take you for granted, or foolishly believe that I know you so completely.

John Powell

DISCUSSION QUESTIONS

1. Why do our emotions often *color* our point of view and affect our opinions?
2. What are the four characteristics of emotions? Which characteristic is the strongest for you?
3. Describe how your moods affect your emotional reactions.
4. How were you taught to express and deal with your emotions?
5. Do you believe that feelings follow a predictable pattern when we suffer a loss? If so, explain the process for you.
6. Of the problem emotions discussed, which one/s present the greatest problem for you?
7. What are the four psychological reactions to anger? Do you feel that you experience at least one of these reactions when you are angry? Which one is the most difficult for you to deal with?
8. Explain how you handle feelings of "guilt."
9. What are the basic guidelines for learning to deal with your emotions?
10. What are the benefits of expressing your feelings? Do you agree that your relationships are stronger when you express, rather than repress, your emotions? Why do you feel this way?

KEY TERMS

Emotions
Attribution
Cognitive Theory of Emotion
Moods
Primary emotions
Mixed emotions
Mild emotions
Intense emotions
Facilitative emotions

Debilitative emotions
Fear
Anxiety
Preparation anxiety

Neurotic anxiety
Anger
Rage
Guilt
Grief and bereavement
Stages of grief work
Grief work
Good grief
Love
Distress
Delight
Repression
Suppression
Emotional debt
Peak communication
Emotional intimacy

REFERENCES

Adler, Ronald and Towne, Neil. (1987) *Looking Out Looking In.* New York: Holt, Rinehart and Winston.

Arnold, M. B. (ed.) (1970) *Feelings and Emotions.* New York: Academic Press.

Atwater, Eastwood. (1983) *Psychology of Adjustment.* Englewood Cliffs, New Jersey: Prentice Hall, Inc.

Buscaglia, Leo. (1982) *Living, Loving and Learning.* New York: Holt, Rinehart and Winston.

Cline, Foster W. (1982) *Parent Education Text.* Evergreen, Colorado: Evergreen Consultants in Human Behavior.

Ellis, Albert and Harper, Robert. (1977) *A New Guide to Rational Living.* California: Wilshire Books.

Emery, Gary and Campbell, James. (1986) *Rapid Relief from Emotional Distress.* New York: Ballantine Books.

Freud, Sigmund. (1936) *The Problems of Anxiety.* New York: Norton and Norton, Inc.

Fromm, Erich. (1956) *The Art of Loving.* New York: Harper and Row Publishers, Inc.

Ginott, Haim. (1972) *Between Parent and Child.* New York: The MacMillan Company.

Jourard, Sidney. (1973) *Personal Adjustment.* New York: The Macmillan Company.

Jung, Carl G. (1923) *Psychological Types.* New York: Harcourt Brace.

Kavanaugh, R. (1972) *Facing Death.* New York: Nash.

Kübler-Ross, E. (1975) *Death: The Final Stage of Growth.* Englewood Cliffs, New Jersey: Prentice Hall, Inc.

Lerner, Harriet Goldhor. (1985) *The Dance of Anger.* New York: Harper & Row.

May, Rollo. (1967) *Man's Search for Himself.* New York: W. W. Norton & Co.

McKeachie, Wilbert and Doyle, Charlotte. (1970) *Psychology (2nd ed.).* Reading, Massachusetts: Addison-Wesley Publishing Co., Inc.

Menninger, Karl. (1978) "Feelings of Guilt," *DHEW Publication* No. (ADM) 78–580.

Morris, W. N. (1987) *Mood.* New York: Springer Verlag.

Plutchik, R. (1980) *Emotion: A Psychoevolutionary Synthesis.* New York: Harper & Row.

Powell, John. (1969) *Why Am I Afraid to Tell You Who I Am?* Chicago, Illinois: Argus Communications, Co.

Rogers, Carl. (1961) *On Becoming a Person.* Boston, Massachusetts: Houghton-Mifflin Company.

Schachter, S. and Singer, J. (1962) "Cognitive, Social and Psychological Determinants of Emotional States." *Psychological Review,* 69: 379–399.

Tavris, Carol. (1989) *Anger: The Misunderstood Emotion.* New York: Simon & Schuster, Inc.

Viscott, David. (1976) *The Language of Feelings.* New York: Pocket Books.

Worchel, Stephen and Goethals, George R. (1989) *Adjustment.* Englewood Cliffs, New Jersey: Prentice Hall, Inc.

HOW I LEARNED TO EXPRESS MY FEELINGS

Purpose: To review the different messages received during childhood on how to express emotions.

Instructions:

I. Below is a list of common feelings/emotions. Remember and record what you learned/were told as a young person about how you were to express (what were you supposed to do) with these emotions. For example, Resentfulness: "I was told to grin and bear it." "I learned to keep my feelings to myself."

II. Next, indicate whether this early message is still the way you express these emotions or indicate how you currently express and deal with this emotion.

Feelings	What I Learned/ Was Told as a Child	How I Express This Emotion Today
Love		
Anger		
Grief/Crying		
Loneliness		
Resentfulness		
Guilt		
Anxiety/Fear		
Jealousy		

DISCUSSION

1. In general, how does/did your father express his emotions?

2. In general, how does/did your mother express her emotions?

3. What one emotion would you like to learn to express in a different way? How can you learn to do this?

4. What do you plan to tell your children about expressing their emotions?

HOW I EXPRESS MY FEELINGS

Purpose: To identify how you personally express a variety of emotions/feelings.

Instructions: Being as spontaneous as possible, complete the following sentences:

1. When I'm angry, I express it by

2. When I'm worried, I express it by

3. When I'm sad, I express it by

4. When I'm defensive, I express it by

5. When I'm depressed, I express it by

6. When I'm confident, I express it by

7. When I feel like a failure, I express it by

8. When I'm afraid, I express it by

9. When I feel successful, I express it by

10. When I feel anxious, I express it by

11. When I feel affectionate, I express it by

12. When I feel jealous, I express it by

13. When I feel impatient, I express it by

14. When I feel hurt, I express it by

15. When I feel rejected, I express it by

16. When I feel intimate, I express it by

17. When I feel enthusiastic, I express it by

18. When I feel guilty, I express it by

19. When I feel the most happy, loved, successful, and glad to be alive, I express it by

20. When I feel the most unhappy, unloved, depressed, and disgusted, I express it by

DISCUSSION

1. Which of these feelings would you like to be able to express in a different manner?

2. What steps do you need to take to learn how to express the feelings identified in the question #1?

3. Which of these feelings are the most difficult for you to express?

4. Which of these feelings are the easiest for you to express?

EXPRESSING FEELINGS AND EMOTIONS

Purpose: To understand how you react when you express your feelings and emotions.

Instructions:

I. Think about the last time you experienced the following feelings and emotions. Then, using the outline, write down your reactions.

   1. JOY

      A. What were your thoughts?

      B. What physiological reaction did you have?

      C. How did you react in that situation?

      D. What would you do differently the next time you have this experience?

   2. ANGER

      A. What were your thoughts?

      B. What physiological reaction did you have?

      C. How did you react in that situation?

      D. What would you do differently the next time you have this experience?

3. ANXIETY
   A. What were your thoughts?

   B. What physiological reaction did you have?

   C. How did you react in that situation?

   D. What would you do differently the next time you have this experience?

4. DEPRESSION
   A. What were your thoughts?

   B. What physiological reaction did you have?

   C. How did you react in that situation?

   D. What would you do differently the next time you have this experience?

5. LOVE
   A. What were your thoughts?

   B. What physiological reaction did you have?

   C. How did you react in that situation?

   D. What would you do differently the next time you have this experience?

6. REJECTION
   A. What were your thoughts?

   B. What physiological reaction did you have?

   C. How did you react in that situation?

   D. What would you do differently the next time you have this experience?

II. Next, from the list of emotions on page 107, make a list of the emotions most difficult for you to express.

III. Because emotions that are hard to express directly are most often expressed indirectly, select one of the five emotions above that is difficult for you to express and identify the ways you express this emotion. For example, if you cannot express love verbally or physically, what do you indirectly do to express love; if you cannot tell someone you are hurt, what do you do that lets the individual know *something* is bothering you?

DISCUSSION

1. Do you think the significant people in your life understand that you indirectly express some feelings? Would it help your relationship if you shared your difficulty and methods of expressing these feelings?

2. Think about three feelings that are easiest for you to express and describe how you directly express them.

COMMUNICATING EMOTIONS

Purpose: To practice communicating at level two (You talk about the way you feel and who you are).

Instructions:

    I. Divide into small groups of four or five.
    II. Pick out an emotion from list 1 and list 2 below and describe to the other members of the group a recent experience that caused you to feel the emotion.
    III. Tell about the situation and how you felt.

List 1		*List 2*	
SUSPICION	JEALOUSY	PEACE	TRUST
FRUSTRATION	LONELINESS	CONFIDENCE	AFFECTION
DISCOURAGEMENT	INFERIORITY	EXHILARATION	CONTENTMENT
FEAR	REJECTION	HOPE	CURIOSITY
DISAPPOINTMENT	INADEQUACY	FRIENDLINESS	SATISFACTION
ANGER	ENVY	JOY	PRIDE
GUILT	IMPATIENCE	ENTHUSIASM	EXCITEMENT
HOSTILITY	BOREDOM	RELIEF	ACCEPTANCE

DISCUSSION

1. Keep this list handy. The next time you have an emotional encounter with another, positive or negative, pick out the emotions you feel and talk about them. How would this help the relationship? In the family? On the job? With close friends?

2. Would there be hazards or risks in communicating at level two? If so, how?

3. Do you have emotions you don't want others to know about? If so, in what ways might you benefit by sharing them with others? What risks would you take?

4. In what ways could affirmations help you handle your emotions?

IDENTIFYING THE CHARACTERISTICS OF EMOTIONS

Purpose: To learn to identify your feelings and to recognize the characteristics of emotions.

Instructions:

I. Write out the details of the most recent emotional situation that caused you to be upset or have debilitative emotions:

II. What kinds of thoughts did you have about the situation?

III. Describe what you were feeling. It is often difficult to describe feelings. From the list below, circle those feelings you were having. If one is not listed, go ahead and add it to the list:

afraid	happy	worried	anxious
sad	miserable	guilty	angry
concerned	bored	irritated	frustrated
tired	annoyed	depressed	disappointed
apathetic	alienated	despair	resentful
regretful	sorry	remorseful	hurt
jealous	grief-stricken	disgusted	upset
mad	discouraged	ashamed	unhappy

IV. Note the intensity and duration of the emotion. Sometimes we ascribe an inaccurate intensity to our feelings. We may say that we are depressed when we are really just sad; we may say that we are annoyed when we really mean that we are angry. Most emotions can be described along a continuum of intensity. Now, using a scale of 1–10, with 10 being the highest intensity and 1 being the least, describe the intensity of your feelings in the emotional situation you described earlier. Here are some examples of how emotions rank along a continuum:

Low Intensity	1	2	3	4	5	6	7	8	9	10	High Intensity
concerned											anxious
sad											depressed
regretful											guilty
disappointed											depressed
annoyed, irritated											angry, rageful
disappointed											hurt
bored											apathetic

The intensity of your emotion would be _____

Now, put the intensity of the emotion on a SUD (Subjective Unit of Distress) scale:

10 Extreme
5 Moderate
1 Mild

V.   What is the duration of this emotion? How long did it last when it occurred?

VI.   How frequently does this emotion occur? (How many times a day, week, or month?)

VII.   Note the internal or physiological changes: Describe the physiological changes that occurred in your body. Did you have irregular breathing, stomach problems, a fast heart beat, tense muscles?

VIII.   Note the external or behavioral changes: Did you blush, have trembling hands, sweating palms, a tremor in your voice?

IX.   Note the motivational aspects: What were you motivated to do as a result of the feelings you were having? Describe it below:

DISCUSSION

1. Did you have trouble deciding what you were feeling after you described your emotional situation?

2. Was it more difficult for you to identify what you were feeling, your thoughts, physiological changes, overt, behavioral changes, or your motivational aspects about the situation? Which one was the easiest for you to describe?

3. Did you ever express your feelings verbally? Would this have helped you feel better?

4. How do you feel now about the emotional situation?

LEARNING JOURNAL FOR BECOMING EMOTIONAL

Select the statement below that best defines your feelings about the personal value or meaning gained from this chapter and respond below the dotted lines:

I LEARNED THAT I. . . .	I WAS SURPRISED THAT I. . . .
I REALIZED THAT I. . . .	I WAS PLEASED THAT I. . . .
I DISCOVERED THAT I. . . .	I WAS DISPLEASED THAT I. . . .

....

Interpersonal Communication

Communication, the art of talking with each other,
saying it clearly, listening to what the other
says and making sure that we're hearing accurately,
is by all indication the skill most essential
for creating and maintaining meaningful, loving
relationships.

Leo Buscaglia
(Loving Each Other, 1984)

We have developed communication systems to permit man on earth to talk with man on the moon. Yet, mother often cannot talk with daughter, father to son, black to white, labor with management, or democracy with communism.

Hadley Read

Friends say, "We can't communicate anymore. We aren't even on the same wavelength."

Kids say, "I can't talk to my parents. They just don't understand me."

Parents say, "I can't talk to my kids. They won't even listen to me."

Marriage partners say, "We can't talk to each other. We just don't have anything meaningful to talk about."

Students say, "We can't discuss our lack of understanding with Mr. Jones. He thinks he has explained the chapter perfectly well. There is no use in us trying to talk to him."

An employer learns that his secretary is leaving and just can't believe she didn't tell him she was so unhappy. She replies, "I've tried so many times in the past, but we just can't communicate."

Have you ever said to another person? "We just can't communicate." "Has another person ever said that to you?" Actually, you were both communicating at some level, but you weren't *connecting*. What, then, is communication?

Miller and Wackman (1981) indicate that to *communicate* means to make known, to give to another; to interchange thoughts, feelings, and information; to participate, to share; to form a connecting link. How important is this?

The foundation of all relationships is based on communication. Because communication underlies all relationships and the process of communication is such a complex topic, we want to begin by providing some organizational structure for our discussion. The first half of the chapter deals with the communication process, including the verbal and nonverbal aspects of communication. The remaining part of the chapter is devoted to learning how to improve our listening and responding skills.

WHY DO WE NEED TO COMMUNICATE?

Without communication, we, as humans, would not be able to survive. We need to find out about the world we live in; we need to know how to interpret the experiences we have; we need to release tension; we need to find out about other people; we need to know how to get information from others; we need to know how to let others know what is going inside of us.

Communication has been described as the process of conveying feelings, attitudes, facts, beliefs, and ideas between individuals, either verbally or nonverbally. On the surface, then, communication appears to be such a simple act. After all, our daily lives are filled with one communicaton experience after another.

We have all heard the statement that a relationship is only as good as its communication. When we are with other people who are aware of our presence, *it is impossible not to communicate.* No matter what we do, we send out messages that say something about ourselves.

This points to the fact that communication is perhaps the most important factor in determining the kinds of relationships we have with others. Furthermore, communication is the way relationships are created, maintained, and destroyed. The ability to send clear messages and to be heard is central to any ongoing relationship—husband and wife, parent and child, employer and employee, friends, siblings. Robert Bolton (1979) confirms this:

Communication is the lifeblood of every relationship. When open, clear, sensitive communication takes place, the relationship is nurtured. When communication is guarded, hostile, or ineffective, the relationship falters. When the communication flow is largely obstructed, the relationship quickly deteriorates and ultimately dies. Where communication skills are lacking, there is so much lost love—between spouses, lovers, friends, parents, and children. For satisfying relationships, it is essential to discover methods that will help us to at least partially bridge the interpersonal gaps that separate us from others.

However, as much communicating as we do, most of us are not all that efficient in performing this simple act. Perhaps, the trite, but true statement—*keep the communication channels open*—indicates the complexity, rather than simplicity of communication.

Whether clear or garbled, tumultuous or silent, deliberate or fatally inadvertent, communication is the ground of meeting and the foundation of community. It is, in short, the essential human connection.

Ashley Montagu

WHY IS COMMUNICATION DIFFICULT?

Do you generally communicate what you mean or intend? Do you generally interpret messages in the same way the sender intended? Think about the following statement: When two people talk six possible messages can get through:

1. What you mean to say.
2. What you actually say.
3. What the other person hears.
4. What the other person thinks he hears.
5. What the other person says about what you said.
6. What you think the other person said about what you said.

We are all concerned with the ability to communicate real meaning and understanding. Some people think that communication is really the sending and receiving of messages, because both elements must be present for communication to take place. They think that communication originates with the sender, and they believe that the message sent is the one that is received. They expect their listeners to act in accordance with the intentions of their message, and they are often bewildered, hurt, or angry when their listeners do not do so.

As we can see, the fundamental transaction of the message sent and received does not presuppose that communication has occurred. In essence, if I speak and you listen, I may be transmitting information, but that is all. However, if I speak, and you listen, and we understand, then we are communicating effectively.

Effective communication is not just an event, but a *process*—a process that requires the cooperation and understanding of both parties. What kind of cooperation are we talking about?

WHAT'S INVOLVED IN THE COMMUNICATION PROCESS?

In any given situation, there are three commonly accepted parts to the communication process. There is always (1) a sender of the message, (2) a receiver of the message and (3) the content of the material. The message can be either verbal or nonverbal. Could it be possible that there are really more than three parts to the communication process?

Let's look at a simple diagram (See Figure 5.1) of what is involved in a communication transaction. Assume that Jill wants to inform John, her husband, that she would like to remodel the house.

Step One: The Idea. Here the sender creates an idea or chooses a fact to communicate. Jill says to herself, "I think I'll ask John if we can remodel the house."

Some people talk to a person, at a person, or with a person. Which one do you do?

Anonymous

Step Two: Encoding. The sender, in attempting to get his or her message across, forms a mental picture of that message and then organizes and translates this picture into symbols that will make the sender's idea receivable. *Symbols* involve such things as the selection of words, tone and pitch of voice, nonverbal method, or even types of supportive materials. Jill says, "John, there is something I would like to talk to you about after dinner and when the children are in bed." Later, Jill says, "I would like for us to remodel the house this summer."

Step Three: Transmission. This refers to the means by which the encoded communication is to be made, or the channel through which the message must pass from the sender to the receiver. *Communication channels* can be a face-to-face discussion, something in writing, the telephone, or even radio or television. In this instance, Jill chose to talk to John face-to-face.

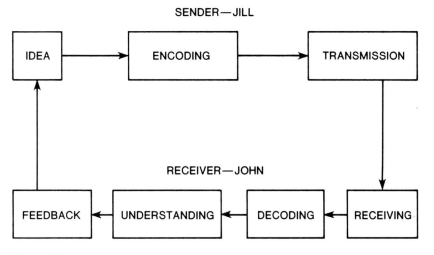

Figure 5.1

Step Four: Receiving. John can only receive the message if he is attentive to Jill. He must not be reading the newspaper or watching the news.

Step Five: Decoding. This is done by the receiver. The message that has been transmitted by the sender must be interpreted and translated into meaning. By decoding, the listener has now formed his or her own mental picture of what the sender said. In our example, decoding is not complete until John hears the whole message. The opening comment, "John, there is something I would like to talk to you about," is a good way to get John's attention and help him listen for the whole message. John hears the complete message from Jill.

Step Six: Understanding. If the receiver has decoded accurately, the mental picture he or she has formed of what the sender said will match. Consequently, the message has been understood correctly. In our example, John doesn't have any trouble understanding that Jill wants to remodel the house this summer.

However, there is always the possibility that the listener may have misinterpreted the speaker's words, thus forming a totally different mental picture. This would mean that communication did not properly take place. This type of communication breakdown occurs much too often, resulting in all sorts of problems, ranging from not knowing what to study for an exam to painful relationship situations.

There is a means of preventing, or at least reducing this type of communication problem, by checking a decoding for accuracy and thus improving the quality of your communication. This method is called *feedback*.

Step Seven: Feedback. *Feedback,* the process by which the sender clarifies how his or her message is being received and interpreted, is really the only means for determining whether there is mutual understanding between the sender and receiver.

In our example, John understands Jill's request, but he does not agree. He acts, or gives feedback, by telling Jill that she will have to wait six more months until his promotion and salary increase will become effective. Jill understands John's position and tells him, "Okay, but I am counting on us starting November 1."

Because there are so many sources of error or distortions in a message, it is wise for both the sender and receiver to provide adequate feedback to one another in an effort to gain understanding and rapport. This completes the process of *two-way communication,* with the key element being feedback. One-way communication frequently results in our making inaccurate inferences or assumptions.

One-way communication is sometimes referred to as *passive listening,* because there is an absence of active verbal feedback. Examples of one-way communication might be a class you may be taking which is strictly lecture oriented, or a certain person you know who tends to dominate conversations. Without a doubt, many of the difficulties that arise in communication stem from the fact that we fail to remember that communication is really a *two-way process.*

After having reviewed the complete communication process, it becomes apparent that "breakdowns" can occur at any step. Sometimes these "breakdowns" are caused by *barriers*—something that stops, blocks, prevents, or hinders. In communication, we may be hindered by a number of barriers that seem to arise from natural human differences and others that are the result of personal habits or attitudes. All or most can be eliminated, changed, or minimized. Review Table 5.1 for a partial listing of barriers to interpersonal communication. Which ones sometimes prevent you from achieving clear, open communication?

The remaining sections of this chapter will discuss ways to minimize these barriers and reduce communication "breakdowns". We will begin with a discussion of nonverbal communication.

It takes two to make communication.

Irving Lee

NONVERBAL COMMUNICATION

The science or study of nonverbal communication, called *kinesis,* composes a great deal of the meanings between people. Most experts on the subject of nonverbal communication agree that more than 60 percent of our communication is by nonverbal means. Randall Harrison (1970), a prominent authority on nonverbal behavior, claims that a mere 35 percent of the meaning of communication derives from words; the remainder comes from body language. Albert Mehrabian, (1968), a psychologist who has studied nonverbal communication, claims that in situations he examined, only 7 percent of the impact was verbal—the remaining 93 percent was nonverbal.

```
┌─────────────────────────────────────────────────────┐
│                    Table 5.1                        │
│        Barriers to Interpersonal Communication       │
├─────────────────────────────────────────────────────┤
│                                                      │
│  Background and experience    Hidden agendas         │
│  Health and physical condition Stereotyping          │
│  Feelings and emotions         Physical environment   │
│  Word meaning and usage        Preoccupation          │
│  Listening only for words      Closed mind            │
│  Jumping to conclusions        Being self-centered    │
│  Making snap judgments         Failure to listen      │
│  Failure to seek clarification Unclear messages       │
│  Disregarding feedback         Highly charged, emotion-│
│                                laden words            │
│  Status of relationships       Talking too fast       │
│  Incongruent verbal and        Generalizations        │
│  nonverbal behavior                                  │
│  Lack of eye contact           Language level         │
│                                                      │
└─────────────────────────────────────────────────────┘
```

The authors may not go to that extreme, but we do agree that it is an extremely important medium of communication. Actually, nonverbal communication relates to verbal communication in three ways.

1. *Nonverbal communication can reinforce the verbal message.*
2. *Nonverbal communication can replace the verbal message.*
3. *Nonverbal communication can contradict the verbal message.*

When the nonverbal message contradicts the verbal message, a *double bind* exists. Usually, however, the nonverbal message is more accurate and is believed over the verbal message.

Do you know how you communicate nonverbally? Let's look at some possible ways:

Facial Expressions and Eye Contact. More than any other nonverbal factor, facial expressions can communicate more emotional meaning more accurately. For example, the face:

• Communicates evaluative judgment.
• Reveals the level of interest or lack of it.
• Can exhibit the level of intensity of the emotions.
• Reveals the amount of control we have over our expressions.
• Shows whether we understand or not.

Through our facial expressions, we reveal a great deal about our feelings and responses to other people as we nonverbally convey shock, sadness, anger, happiness, worry, and so on. This is confirmed by researchers, Paul Eckman and Wallace Friesen (1975):

The rapid facial signals are the primary system for expression of emotion. It is the face you search to know whether someone is angry, disgusted, afraid, sad, etc. Words cannot always describe the feelings people have; often words are not adequate to express what you see in the look on someone's face at an emotional moment.

What you are speaks so loudly, I cannot hear what you say.

Ralph Waldo Emerson

What is the quickest test to find out if you can communicate? The quickest test, a simple smile, is often also the beginning.

Leonard Andrews

The eyes are the most expressive part of the face and have considerable effect on communication. We may use eye contact in a positive way to:

- Invite interaction with another by looking directly at them.
- Show friendship and positive regard by extended mutual eye contact.
- Demonstrate believeability or honesty.
- Demonstrate interest by extended eye contact.
- Signal turn-taking in normal conversation.

Many times we avoid eye contact when we want to hide feelings, when we are tense, when we are interacting with someone we dislike, or when attempting to end social contact. However, it is important to note here that nonverbal expressions have different meanings in various cultures. Therefore, it is wise to be careful about assigning *your* culture's meanings for eye behavior to *all* people. For example, in the United States, maintaining eye contact for any length of time for blacks and chicanos can signal disrespect. To whites, it can mean just the opposite.

Vocal Clues. *Paralinguistics* is the study of vocal cues such as pitch, rate, tone, fluency, etc. Almost everyone distinguishes meanings by noting differences in vocal qualities. For example, the statement "What a vacation I had" can have at least two different meanings, depending on the tone of voice of the speaker. The ambiguous phrase might mean that it was a most enjoyable weekend. With different qualities, however, the listener would assume that it was quite unpleasant.

Dr. Len Sperry (1975) suggests that the voice characteristics described in Table 5.2 are likely to have the meanings described in the right-hand column.

Table 5.2	
Paralanguage	**Probable Feeling/Meaning**
Monotone voice	Boredom
Slow speed, low pitch	Depression
High voice, emphatic pitch	Enthusiasm
Ascending tone	Astonishment
Abrupt speech	Defensiveness
Terse speed, loud tone	Anger
High pitch, drawn-out speech	Disbelief

With practice, we can all learn to notice the pitch and timbre of a person's voice, the rhythm of speech, and the rapidity of expression. These vocal qualities help us to tune into the mood of the speaker.

Gestures and Other Body Movements. Because movements and gestures of other parts of the body are also closely tied to culture, it is extremely misleading to isolate a single body movement (such as crossing the arms) and give it a precise meaning. However, regardless of your intentions, your gestures and body movements may be given specific meanings by others.

For example, the way a person stands may indicate self-confidence, status, friendliness, or enthusiasm. Various types of gestures may be used to indicate feelings of restlessness, nervousness, or perhaps the need to emphasize a meaning. Frequent hand movements, for example, often communicate a positive, enthusiastic attitude. However, movements such as the constant pencil tapper or the doodler may indicate nervousness and boredom. Even weak or overly strong handshakes will be given some significance by many people. They can communicate enthusiasm, or they can communicate uneasiness.

You will be given an opportunity in one of the exercises in this chapter to evaluate your gestures and body movements. Pay very close attention to what you learn about yourself.

Touching. Some people use the language of touch more easily and readily than others. Actually, *one of the most meaningful methods* of nonverbal communication can be that of touching. There are times in our lives when it is difficult to express our feelings through words. We may use a hug, a pat on the shoulder, or a clasp of the hand to communicate meaning without words. However, touching is risky, because this form of nonverbal communication may violate the personal space of others. Because there is indeed a complex language of touch, researchers Heslin and Alper (1983) have suggested a number of factors to consider:

What part of the body does the touching
What part of the body is touched
How long the touch lasts
How much pressure is used
Whether there is movement after contact is made
Whether anyone else is present
The situation in which the touch occurs
The relationship between the persons involved

Think for just a moment and respond to these questions. How do you feel when a friend touches you on the shoulder? How do you feel when your boss touches you on the shoulder? How do you feel when a family member touches you on the shoulder? How do you feel when a stranger touches you on the shoulder?

We would guess that you will have many different answers to these questions, which just illustrates that we feel differently and interpret differently the language of touch.

Personal Space and Distance. Our own personal space is an invisible bubble around us that allows us to feel safe. As we said earlier, if this bubble is violated, we're uncomfortable and may become defensive. Usually, only intimates can violate the space without making us uncomfortable. Sometimes, violation of this space by another can demonstrate that person's dominance of the situation.

Many times you can tell how people feel toward one another by observing the distance between them. Anthropologist Edward T. Hall (1959) defined four distances that we use in our everyday lives. These are:

Intimate distance, which begins with skin contact and ranges out to about 18 inches. This is reserved for close friends and loved ones, or other people you feel affectionate to.

Personal distance, from 18 inches to 4 feet. This is where you may carry on a friendly conversation or sometimes even a heated argument.

Social distance, from 4 to 12 feet. This is reserved for social interactions that are businesslike or impersonal.

Public distance, ranging out from 12 feet. This is reserved for speaking to a large audience.

Hall feels that we choose a particular distance, according to the way we feel toward the other person at a given time, and that by *reading* the selected distance, we can get insight into the other person's feelings.

Physical Environment and Territory. What characteristics in a physical environment make you feel comfortable or uncomfortable? What do you think your room, house, or car communicate to others? Do you prefer a neat and "tidy" room, house, or car, or do you prefer the more "lived-in" look? What meaning do you give to a spotless house or to a friend's constantly clean car? How about your desk at home or work?

When you come closer than an arm's length to me, I may feel uncomfortable. When I'm comfortable with you and want to be closer to you, I will invite you to invade my personal space.

M. Hankins

Is it free of papers, or does it look like someone "works there every minute of the day and night"? Interestingly enough, physical environments not only reveal characteristics of the owner of the territory but also actually affect how a person communicates. Psychologist Mehrabian (1976), found that each person reacts emotionally to the environment with "approach" (positive) or "avoidance" (negative) behaviors.

Clothing and Personal Appearance. What we wear and how we groom ourselves are also important means of nonverbal communication. We send messages about our economic level, level of success, social position, educational background, moral character, and sometimes just our personal preferences. We also may send messages that suggest, "notice me." For example, there is a tremendous amount of pressure in schools to wear the "in" brand of jeans, shoes, dress and so on.

Although it is natural to make assumptions about clothing and personal appearances, it is equally important to note that this area of nonverbal communication is filled with ambiguity. A stranger, wearing worn, ill-fitting clothes might normally be a stylish person or even a millionaire. Maybe, today he or she is on vacation, going to do some "dirty" work, or just wants to be comfortable. This points to the fact that as we get to know others better, the importance of clothing and personal appearance decreases.

What kind of messages do you think you send about the clothing you wear and the manner in which you groom yourself?

Silence. Silence *is communication.* Silence may convey relaxation, contentment, fatigue, anxiety, frustration, uncertainty, shyness, avoidance, or thoughtful analyses. Sometimes, what we do not say has more impact than what we do say. For example, silence can be used to convey negative messages such as "I'm angry with you," "I'm not OK," or positive messages of, "It is nice just to be alone," "I understand."

Nonverbal communication, everything in the communication context except the actual words being uttered, is sometimes very clear and unambiguous. At times it can be difficult to decipher. As we become aware of nonverbal messages in our everyday lives, we need to think of them not as facts, but as clues that need to be checked out. Furthermore, we can be more effective in communicating messages if we support words with appropriate forms of nonverbal communication. Review Table 5.3 for some suggestions for improving your nonverbal communication.

Now, it is time to discuss how meanings go astray in verbal communication.

Beginning with the verbal initiation of hello, language nourishes or starves whatever grows between two people.

S. Miller

WORD POWER*

Words can comfort
  or they can hurt.

Words can compliment
  and they can also insult.

Words can motivate
  just as they can hinder.

They can inspire
  and they can reject.

Words can express feelings
  or they can verbalize reactions.

Words, carelessly or angrily spoken
  can be as destructive a force as the fiercest storm.

And once the damage has been done.
  it takes much more than words to mend or rebuild that
  which in the moment of thoughtlessness received the·
  crashing blow. . . .
                    of piercing, crushing Words.

Delyn Dendy Harrison

Table 5.3
Techniques for Improving Nonverbal Communication

Have a video tape made of you conversing with another person. There is a great deal you can learn from *seeing yourself as others see you.* Are your gestures, facial expressions, and eye contact effective or distracting as you converse with others? Do you have any annoying mannerisms?

Role-play with a friend. Select a topic you feel comfortable with and practice various forms of nonverbal communication. Experiment with various forms of posture, tone and voice inflection, gestures, and so forth. Then, ask the other person to comment on the effectiveness of your nonverbal behavior.

Decide what changes you want to make. After reviewing your total body language, you can begin to make a conscious effort to eliminate the gestures and mannerisms that distract from the effectiveness of your communication endeavors. Don't forget to practice the gestures and mannerisms that will make your verbal communication come alive.

---

*Delyn Dendy Harrison, *Some Things Are Better Said in Black and White* (Fort Worth, Texas: Branch Smith, Inc., 1978) p. 13. Used with permission.

VERBAL COMMUNICATION

Verbal communication—words and language—is generally considered the primary means of communication. We gather, share, give, and receive information through words, and establish, continue, or terminate relationships through words. Words can make us feel good or miserable; they can make us lose our tempers or keep our cool; they can persuade us to take action or convince us not to move; they can be clear and concise or ambiguous and confusing; more importantly, *they cannot be unsaid once they are said.*

Actually, the way we use words may communicate much more than the actual words used. As we have already discussed, our tone of voice and the emphasis placed on our words may reveal far more than our choice of words. As we can see, it is the meaning and understanding behind words that is the essence of communication. And, *meanings are in people—not words.* Let's look at some barriers or ways that meanings can go astray.

Semantics. *Semantics* is the study of meaning and changes of meanings in words. It is virtually impossible to communicate effectively if the people conversing do not understand the same terminology, or if they hold different meanings for the same word. For example, consider the common expressions:

I'll be back in little while.
I'll be back in a few minutes.
I'll be back about 5:00 P.M.

What or when is "a little while" or "a few minutes?" Do we mean a little late, or do we mean 5, 10, or 30 minutes? Does about 5:00 P.M. mean exactly 5:00 P.M., or does the expression mean between 5:00 and 6:00 P.M.? What do you mean when you use these expressions?

Also, certain occupations have their "jargon" too: Realtors talk about going after "listings"; computer programmers talk about "Pascal" language; individuals working in finance and credit talk about a "class 2-A credit rating." Do you know what all of these statements mean? Any profession, avocation, or field of specialization will develop such word usages. This often splits persons inside the group from those outside the group in that they will use the same language terminology to mean different things.

Certain age groups have a language all their own. Teenagers talk about a "cool" party or a "awesome" date. What are they really saying?

Even countries have different meanings for the same word. For example, in the United States, "Let's *table* that motion," means "Let's put it aside." In England, the same phrase means, "Let's bring it up for discussion."

Maybe the meaning only rests in the "eyes of the beholder." The beholder leaves the listener to guess what he or she means, while the beholder operates on assumptions that he or she is, in fact, communicating. The listener, in turn, proceeds on the basis of what he or she guesses. Mutual misunderstanding is an obvious result.

Assumptions. Too often, we make the mistake of assuming that others will understand more than we actually say to them. "If it is clear to me, it must be clear to you also." This assumption is one of the most difficult barriers to successful human communication. In personal relationships, for example, we may expect our intimates to be able to read our minds because they know us so well. "She ought to know how I feel," you may say to yourself, even though you have said nothing about your feelings.

A story is told of a family ruckus that occurred when the father sent his son to the lumber yard for a *longer* board. The young man thought he knew what his father wanted—but the *longer* board he brought back was still three feet too short. His father became angry and accused the boy of being stupid and not listening. The father had simply assumed that since he knew what he meant by *longer,* his son would also know. Could it be possible that Dad had not bothered to make himself clear or to check his meaning with his son?

Self-Concept. The most important single factor affecting our communication with others is our self-concept. Chapter 2 showed that a strong self-concept is necessary for healthy and satisfying interactions. On the other hand, if we have a weak self-concept we may feel inadequate and lack the confidence to converse with others. As a result, we feel our ideas are not worth communicating and we become guarded in our communication attempts.

In circumstances where we feel insecure or unsafe, it is extremely easy for us to feel that our self-image is being threatened. As a result, our defenses are immediately aroused. It is so easy to take an innocent remark and reply with, "What did you mean by that?" We may distort questions into accusations. Our replies become immediate justifications.

For example, a husband may ask his wife, "Did you happen to get my blue shirt from the cleaners?" His intention may be informational. If the wife feels insecure, she may respond as if the issue was her inability to meet his needs. She may say, "No, I didn't. I can't think of everything, you know, when I've got the kids with me and time is getting short, and I can't even find a decent roast that we can afford. I suppose you think my getting your shirt is more important than preparing a good meal." The wife assumes an accusation is made. This accusation may be seen as an "intended putdown." Does the husband really mean to cut the wife down, or does the wife have her feelings on her shoulders?

Emotion-Packed Phrases. As we can see, words stated may not be as important as the way in which we *catch* these words. Because it is highly possible for us to operate on different mood levels, an experience we have had during the day may cause us to react with words

I know you believe you understand what you think I said. But I am not sure you realize that what you heard is not what I meant.

Anonymous

I'm sure you overreact to my overreaction. But if you'd cool your reactions, I wouldn't overreact in the first place.

Dr. Foster Cline

that we really do not mean. Sometimes, our mood level, combined with certain emotion-packed phrases, really sets us off. Some of these emotion-packed phrases are as follows (Hoffman and Graiver, 1983):

After all I've done for you. . . .
I wish you would say what you mean. . . .
After you have been here as long as I have. . . .
When I was your age. . . .
Do you know what you are doing? . . . .
You aren't upset, are you? . . . .
Talk to me later. . . .
Do you understand me? . . . .
I wouldn't do that. . . .
You wouldn't understand. . . .
Are you sure that's right? . . . .
Any very opinionated statement. . . .

Have you ever reacted to one of these emotion-packed phrases? It takes a great deal of practice to learn to listen, to not be distracted by emotion-packed phrases. The key here is to *respond* to the statement and not *react* to the statement. After all, when you respond, the rational, thinking, logical part of you is communicated, but when you react, the emotional, feeling, irrational part of you is communicated.

As we can see, there are numerous ways that words can go astray. Have you ever had a discussion with a friend, spouse, or someone about a particular topic and later realized that your communication attempts fell short of your desires? Perhaps the suggestions for improving verbal communication outlined in Table 5.4 will be of some benefit to you.

Sometimes, our communication attempts go astray because we fail to listen. The remainder of this chapter will be devoted to the skills of listening and responding.

Table 5.4
Techniques for Improving Verbal Communication

Speak with enthusiasm

Enunciate

Use inflection

Avoid antagonistic words

Use short simple sentences

Adjust the volume of your voice to the situation

Adjust your speaking rate to the situation

Keep the door open for feedback

> ## LISTEN
>
> When I ask you to listen to me and you start giving advice,
> you have not done what I asked.
> When I ask you to listen to me and you begin to tell me why
> I shouldn't feel that way, you are trampling on my feelings.
> When I ask you to listen to me and you feel you have to do
> something to solve my problems, you have failed me, strange
> as that may seem.
> So please, just listen and hear me. And if you want to talk,
> wait a few minutes for your turn and I promise I'll listen to you.
>
> Anonymous

LISTENING (WHAT DID YOU SAY)

How many times have you had a conversation with people and not heard a word they said? How many times have you had a conversation with someone, and you felt they were not paying attention to you? Actually, listening is a form of *paying attention,* which is an active process involving much more than hearing and seeing.

We have been given two ears but a single mouth, in order that we may hear more and talk less.

Zeno of Citium

Communication experts describe listening as our primary communication activity. A study of persons of varied occupational backgrounds showed that 70 percent of their waking moments were spent in communication. And of that time, writing took 9 percent, reading absorbed 16 percent, talking accounted for 30 percent, and listening occupied 45 percent (Nichols and Stevens, 1957).

Do you talk twice as much as you listen?

Unfortunately, few people are good listeners. Researchers claim that *75 percent of oral communication* is ignored, misunderstood, or quickly forgotten (Bolton, 1979). Ralph G. Nichols and Leonard Stevens (1957) who developed innovative classes on listening at the University of Minnesota, writes:

For several years, we have been testing the ability of people to understand and remember what they hear. These extensive tests led to this general conclusion: immediately after the average person has listened to someone talk, he remembers only about one-half of what he has heard—no matter how carefully he thought he was listening. What happens as time passes? Our own testing shows that we tend to forget from one-half to one-third (more) within eight hours.

It just seems that the speaker's words go "in one ear and out the other." Yet, the quality of your friendships, the closeness of your family relationships, and your effectiveness at work depend to a great extent on your ability to listen.

Is there really a difference in hearing and listening? *Hearing* says John Drakeford (1967) is a word used to describe the physiological sensory process by which auditory sensations are received by the ears and transmitted to the brain. *Listening,* on the other hand, is an intellectual and emotional process that integrates physical, emotional, and intellectual inputs in a search for meaning and understanding.

In short, you can hear what another person is saying without really listening to him. How can this be possible?

BARRIERS TO LISTENING

Do you have any habits, attitudes, or desires that may screen out what is really said? Are you ever too busy to really listen? What kinds of things prevent you from really listening? Let's examine some possible barriers to listening.

Internal Psychological Filter. Each of us has an internal psychological filter through which we process all the information we receive. This filter consists of prejudices, past experiences, hopes, and anxieties. Everything that we hear, see or read is interpreted through this filter. For example, the style of a speaker's clothing, facial expressions, posture, accent, color of skin, mannerisms, or age can cause you to make prejudgments and tune him or her out—all because of what is in your filter.

The further we go through life, the more clogged that filter can get. Regardless of what we intend to say, what is ultimately heard depends on what is in the filter of the listener. If your filter contains memories of many painful past experiences, then you may perceive hurt where none is intended. If your filter contains a reservoir of unexpressed anger from the past, then you may hear anger in what others say, regardless of their intent.

Our frame of reference is the filter through which we integrate, evaluate, and interpret new persons, events, and ideas.

John Powell

Hidden Agenda. Sometimes we enter a conversation or situation with a special interest in mind, a grudge which we are wanting to bring into the open, or even a "chip on our shoulder. . . ." Consequently, we may hear the message in accordance with our own needs. Either consciously or unconsciously, we may sabotage a meeting or direct a conversation in such a way as to further our own needs and motives.

Preoccupation. The communication failures arising from the gap between what the sender meant doesn't usually arise from word usage or lack of verbal ability. Many times we are so preoccupied that we just do not listen to what others are saying. We may allow our mind to wander while we are waiting for the speaker to make his or her next thought. Perhaps, we need to remember, that the rate of *speech* is about 100–150 words per minute and the rate of *thought* is about 400–500 words per minute. Also, we may be so preoccupied with what we have to say that we listen to others only to find an opening to get the floor to say what we want to say. Sometimes, our fast-paced lifestyle contributes to our not taking the time to really listen to others.

A story is told of a very busy business executive who every morning rushed through the office and asked his secretary, "How are you?" She always said, "Fine, thank you." After all, isn't that what we expect others to say to such a question? Rushing through the office, the executive replied, "That is great." One day, the secretary decided to really "test" the executive's ear. When the usual question came the next morning, the secretary said, "Terrible, terrible, thank you." The executive, still rushing into his office replied, "That is great." The executive's ear had really been tested.

Noise. Noise includes anything that interferes with communication and distorts the impact of the message. *External noise* includes such elements in the physical environment as temperature, a show on television, music on a stereo, loud traffic, or any other external event or distracting influences. *Internal noise* includes such things as a headache, lack of sleep, daydreaming, preoccupation with other problems, or even a preconceived idea that the message is going to be unimportant or uninteresting.

It seems as though the capacity to listen effectively is a "natural gift" for some people. This "natural gift" has been referred to as *sensitivity*. However, the ability to listen can be cultivated by anyone who wants to develop this capacity. It requires a conscious alertness that can become a *habit* with practice. Several principles, outlined in Table 5.5 can aid in developing the *habit of listening* with sensitivity.

One of the best ways to persuade others is with your ears—by listening to them.

Dean Rusk

Table 5.5
Techniques for Improving Listening Skills

Be receptive and attentive
Allow the speaker to speak freely
Listen to the speaker and ignore distractions
Avoid preoccupation with your own thoughts
Use verbal following or minimal encourages
Avoid all judgments, initially
Try to listen for more than just the spoken words
Use feedback and reflect on what the speaker said

ERNEST ROY'S SHORT COURSE
IN HUMAN RELATIONS

The six most important words:

"I admit I made a mistake"

The five most important words:

"You did a good job"

The four most important words:

"What is your opinion"

The three most important words:

"If you please"

The two most important words:

"Thank you"

The one most important word:

"We"

The least most important word:

"I"

STYLES OF RESPONDING

How do you respond when others want to discuss their problems or innermost feelings with you? Do you ask a lot of questions? Are you judgmental, or supportive? Do you ever criticize?

Noted psychologist, Carl Rogers (1961) indicates that a major barrier to building close relationships is the very natural tendency we have to *judge and evaluate the statements made by others.*

There are several ways of responding to others. Thomas Gordon (1970) devised a comprehensive list that he calls the "dirty dozen" communication spoilers. Review Table 5.6 for an expanded list of these communication response patterns. Which style gives you the most difficulty in responding to others?

Table 5.6
21 Communication Spoilers

"I'm sick and tired of being hassled." How would you respond? Some typical responses are listed below:

Threatening	"Feeling like that will get you in trouble."
Lecturing	"You should be glad it's not worse."
Moralizing	"You ought to be trying harder."
Blaming	"Maybe you're just getting what you deserve."
Advising	"If I were you, I'd do something about it."
Sympathizing	"It's too bad you're always getting picked on."
Questioning	"Who's hassling you?"
Kidding	"You don't look like you're being hassled."
Sarcastic	"Why would anyone want to hassle a nice person like you?"
Praising	"They're just hassling you because they're jealous."
Name-calling	"Don't be such a baby."
Ordering or Commanding	"Don't give me any of that garbage."
Criticizing	"Feeling like that isn't going to get you anywhere."
Analyzing	"You just have a persecution complex."
Diverting	"Oh, why don't you just have a cold drink and forget it?"
Rejecting	"I can't do anything about it."
Counterattacking	"Well, how many people have you hassled?"
Placating	"Well, everybody gets hassled at some time in their life."
Overidentifying	"I know what you mean, I get hassled all the time too."
Shifting Focus	"What does your teacher think about what?"
Ignoring	(No response is a response.)

Sometimes we overuse one style, rely on the style too early in the conversation, or fail to know when and how to use a style that will be of most benefit to the sender and thereby create a better relationship. Let's discuss six of the more common styles of responding:

Evaluative or Judging. *This type of response shows that the receiver is making a judgment about the motive, personality, or reasoning of the sender.* The evaluation indicates the sender's statement is either "right" or "wrong." The response may be positive, "You're right on target," or unfavorable, "You shouldn't feel that way." In both cases, the receiver appears to be qualified to suggest to the sender what he or she might or ought to do.

Since evaluative or judgmental responses often lead to defensiveness, it is best to begin your responses with "I feel . . .", rather than "You are . . ." Evaluative or judgmental responses are best accepted when you have been specifically asked to make a value judgment and when you want to disclose your own values and attitudes. In the early stages of relationships, it is generally best to avoid evaluative or judgmental responses.

Criticizing. Even though criticizing is often a part of the evaluative or judging response, it is also a commonly used and even misunderstood response pattern. Therefore, we have decided to discuss it separately. Sometimes, you may want to give someone some constructive feedback, but you are afraid they will perceive it as criticism. After all, haven't you perceived feedback as really just criticism? Criticism often has a negative connotation and may not be pleasant, but it can be helpful when it leads to productive changes. If you want to give constructive criticism or feedback, rather than destructive criticism or feedback, it is wise to remember these points:

Emphasize behavior rather than personalities. Concentrate on what a person does or says rather than who you think the person is. The use of choice adjectives oftentimes leads to labeling the person rather than the behavior. This causes defensiveness. There is a big difference between saying, "John is lazy" and in "John works slowly."

Refrain from using "You" messages. The use of "You" messages creates a feeling of blame and accusation. It is more appropriate to say, "I felt hurt today when . . ." rather than use, "You were cruel today when . . ."

Focus on actual observations rather than judgments. Reporting what actually occurred is giving objective feedback. However, reporting on what you think about what actually occurred is giving subjective, value-laden feedback. It is one thing to say, "I really liked the house better the way it was decorated," and quite another to say, "The house looks terrible now."

Don't criticize when you're angry or upset. Other people will hear only your anger and not your message. "Cool down" until you can express yourself with facts. It is acceptable to say, "I need to think this through and get back with you later."

It hurts to feel small; it helps so to feel big; words to others do either of these.

David Goodman

You have the right to get angry, but you do not have the right or the license to attack another person or their character traits.

Haim Ginott

How Much Criticism Do You Give?

Criticism is like fertilizer—the right amount
does wonders, but too much is fatal.

Concentrate on sharing ideas rather than on giving advice. It is less threatening to say, "Here are some ideas for you to think about . . ." rather than, "Well, you would be wise to do. . . ." Sharing ideas gives options to others; advising implies, "My solution is the best way."

When others respond to you with criticism, it is easier to handle if you can learn to deal with it *intellectually* and not *emotionally*. *Remember,* to respond *and not to react.* Rather than hearing criticism as a personal attack, focus on how it might be helpful to you by learning to:

Listen. Don't panic and get defensive when someone criticizes you. Calm listening helps you think clearly.

Analyze. Is the criticism factually correct or is the critic mostly venting anger? If the critic is really just ventilating, you can sympathize with his or her feelings without accepting the content of what they say.

Decide what to do. If the criticism is accurate, what can you do to remedy the situation and prevent reoccurrences? If you decide to change your behavior as a result of the criticism, let your critic know.

Practice. Make an honest effort to consistently practice the new routine or behavior until it feels natural or becomes a habit.

Interpretative. *In this response, the receiver tries to tell the sender what his or her problem really is and how the sender really feels about the situation.* The receiver implies what the sender might or ought to think. Consider these statements:

I don't think you really mean to say that.
Maybe you are really feeling. . . .
It sounds to me that what is actually bothering you is. . . .

Giving an interpretative response can often offer a person another way of looking at his or her situation. It can produce great insight. Interpretative responses are best received when they are made as suggestions rather than as absolutes and when they are offered with integrity and empathy.

Advising. *This is responding to others by offering a solution.* Sometimes this type of response is helpful and sometimes it is not. For example, we may have the tendency to tell others how we would behave in their place. They may not want to hear what we would do; they may just want us to listen to their thoughts. Giving advice also means that you may get blamed if the advice is followed and *doesn't work. In giving advice, it is helpful* to remember to be sure: (1) your advice is correct, (2) the other person really wants your advice, (3) the other person is willing to accept the responsibility for choosing to follow your advice.

At its worst, advice represents an "interfere-iority" complex.

Robert Bolton

Foster Cline (1982) a nationally known psychologist, frequently suggests two magic sentences that will help you from appearing dogmatic when offering advice:

I wonder if it would be helpful to . . . rather than If I were you, I would. . . .
Do you think it would be beneficial to . . . rather than, You really should. . . .

Supportive. *This response shows the receiver's intent is to reassure, comfort or minimize the intense feelings of the sender.* There is an implication that the sender not feel as he or she does. Statements such as, "Now, it is okay. It is all going to be better," or "Mary, you don't have anything to worry about. I know you can pass your test," are examples of supportive responses. Consider this exchange:

Sender: I could die here, and no one would even notice.
Receiver: Now, now, it's okay. It's all going to be better. I will help you.

This reply may not have acknowledged the content or emotion of the original statement and may get you involved in a situation you wished you had avoided. It might be more helpful to simply say, "Let's talk about why you feel this way."

Supportive statements are best received when they are sincere and help others to feel accepted and motivated to try and solve their problems. Sometimes, supportive statements can be made in a joking manner and result in the sender feeling "put down" and "worse off" than before.

Questioning. *This response indicates that the receiver wants to probe the sender for additional information and to discuss the issue further.* The receiver often implies that the sender might benefit from discussing the issue in more detail. Typical statements might be:

What is your understanding of why your husband lost his job?
How do you feel about that?

There comes a time in some relationships when no matter how sincere the attempt to reconcile the differences or how strong the wish to recreate a part of the past once shared, the struggle becomes so painful that nothing else is felt and the world and all its beauty only add to the discomfort by providing cruel contrast.

David Viscott

Questioning is a way to get additional information so that you can understand the situation in more detail. Actually, if you do not understand the situation, it is extremely important that you try to ask questions for clarification before you respond to the situation. We have a tendency to ask questions that often fail to give us adequate information. Let's distinguish between two types of questions: *closed questions and open questions. Closed questions* often result in yes, no, or a very short response. *Open questions,* on the other hand, provide space for the speaker to explore his or her thoughts.

Let's look at a typical example between a boss and an employee who has been having conflict with a valued customer. The employee enters the boss's office, and the boss replies:

Closed question:	Do you want to see me about the Smith account?
Open question:	What's on your mind, Linda?

In short, closed questions are like multiple choice or true/false test questions, whereas open questions are like essay questions.

It is also important that you ask questions about the issue raised, rather than asking questions about irrelevant issues. You don't want to lead the sender to possibly more problems and forget the original issue.

Another important aspect of questioning is to remember to avoid *interrogating and manipulating* the other person. Too many questions do precisely that.

If you have reviewed Figure 5.6 and given some thought to the styles of responding discussed above, you may be thinking to yourself, "I am confused, it seems that all these responses can spoil my attempts at listening and communicating. Is there another type of response that will be more effective for me?"

ACTIVE LISTENING

In *active listening* you see the expressed idea, attitude, or problem from the other person's point of view, to sense how it feels to the sender, and to achieve the sender's frame of reference in regard to the thing he or she is talking about. This really means that you are listening with the whole body and that you are paying careful attention to the person who is talking. How is this achieved?

As a vehicle of communication, listening must focus on the other person, not just on what the other person is saying. This has been referred to as *listening with the third ear*. The third ear hears what is said between the lines and without words, what is expressed soundlessly, and what the speaker feels and thinks. It is listening in such a way that creates an atmosphere of communication; others will be able to hear us because they feel we have heard them, that we are in touch with them and not just what they are saying. How can you learn to listen with the third ear?

Robert Bolton (1979) and Thomas Gordan (1970) have written extensively about the requirements of active listening. We will now discuss some of these.

The reality of the other person is not in what he reveals to you, but in what he cannot reveal to you. Therefore, if you would understand him, listen not to what he says but rather to what he does not say.

Kahlil Gibran

Develop a Posture of Involvement. This means you practice the habit of inclining your body toward the speaker rather than leaning back in the chair or slouching around on the floor or on the sofa. It also means you position yourself at a comfortable distance from the speaker so that you can have close eye contact. Usually, about three feet is a comfortable distance in our society. Effective eye contact expresses interest and a desire to listen. You will also need to turn the TV or stereo off and remove any environmental distractions. Remember to actively listen means to *move with the speaker.*

Make Use of Door Openers. This is really just an invitation for the other person to say more. These responses do not communicate any of the listener's own ideas or judgments or feelings; they merely invite the other person to share his own ideas, judgments, or feelings. Some examples might be:

Tell me more about that . . .
Let's talk about it . . .
Go ahead, I'm listening . . .
Sounds like you have a lot of feelings about that . . .
This seems like something that is important to you . . .
I'd like to hear some more about that . . .
Can you tell me what's going on . . .
Sounds like this is difficult for you to talk about . . .

Most people feel encouraged to talk with the use of door openers. More importantly, people feel worthy, respected, significant, and accepted when we invite them to share their feelings and ideas.

Keep the Other Person Talking with Minimal Encourages. *Minimal encourages* are brief indicators to the other person that you are still listening. Some examples you can use are:

"Mm-hmmm."	"I see."
"Really."	"Oh."
"You did, huh."	"And."
"How about that."	"Interesting."
"Go on."	"I hear you."

Another way to use minimal encourages is to repeat the last word or two of the speaker's comment. When the speaker says, "I just don't know what to do; I guess I'm confused," the listener may respond, "Confused?" Generally, the speaker will then express more about his or her confusion.

I can never tell you what you said, but only what I heard. I will have to rephrase what you have said, and check it out with you to make sure that what left your mind and heart arrived in my mind and heart intact and without distortion.

John Powell

Respond Reflectively. Thomas Gordon (1970) explains responding reflectively in this way:

In active listening, the receiver tries to understand what it is the sender is feeling or what his message means. Then, he puts his understanding into his own words and feeds it back for the sender's verification. The receiver does not send a message of his own—such as an evaluation, opinion, advice, logic, analysis, or question. He feeds back only what he feels the sender's message meant—nothing more, nothing less.

As you can probably see, when you use active listening, you really respond reflectively in two ways. First, you paraphrase or state the essence of the other's content in your own words, focusing on facts and ideas rather than the emotions the sender is expressing.

Paraphrasing responses usually begin with phrases such as:

What I hear you saying is . . .
Correct me if I'm wrong . . .
Do I understand you correctly that . . .

Let's look at this exchange:

Sender: "My psychology professor is really piling the assignments on, and I'll never get caught up. Does she think psychology is the only course I am taking?"

Receiver: "Do I understand you correctly that she is giving you too much work and doesn't realize you have three other college courses?"

Sender: "Oh she knows I have other courses, but it is just the end of the semester, and she is shoving it all in at the last minute."

Receiver: "It doesn't seem fair, is that it?"

Sender: "It really isn't, but I'll just have to buckle down and get the work done. I need this course on my degree plan."

Sometimes people confuse paraphrasing with parroting. However, *parroting* means to repeat exactly the speaker's words.

Secondly, when possible, mirror back to the speaker, the emotions which he or she is communicating. The most difficult part of learning to respond reflectively is to *listen for the feeling of the other person.* The format is simple when you learn to listen for feeling words. For example:

You sound	----------------- about	------------------ ."
angry		this
frustrated		that
worried		the other thing
upset		. . . .
excited		. . . .

Let's look at some examples:

Sender: "I could die here, and no one would even notice."
Receiver: "You sound really frustrated."
Sender: "Oh, I just get to thinking that no one really cares about me."
Receiver: "So, maybe you aren't frustrated, but just a little angry."
Sender: "Yea, I suppose I am a little angry. I just wish I knew how my family really cares about me."

You will note that in both of these examples, the receiver actively demonstrates that he or she genuinely wants to understand the sender and to hear more of the problem. The receiver does not make evaluative or judgmental responses regarding either the sender or the content. Instead, the receiver just paraphrases or mirrors back what the sender has said. By maintaining an objective stance, the active listener encourages a sharing of ideas and paves the way for a freer exchange of other points of view.

Active listening is an excellent tool to use in "heated discussions." The next time you get into an argument with your wife, husband, friend, or a small group of friends, just stop the discussion for a moment and, for an experiment, generate this rule: *Each person can speak up only after he or she has restated the ideas and feelings of the previous speaker accurately and to that speaker's satisfaction.* This is the heart of active listening.

Do you see what this would mean? It would simply mean that before presenting your own point of view, it would be necessary for you to achieve the other speaker's frame of reference—to understand his or her feelings so well that you could summarize them for him or her. Sounds simple, doesn't it? However, if you try it, you will discover that it is one of the most difficult things you have ever tried to do. Nevertheless, once you have been able to see the other person's point

I wish that you would take the time to try and understand why I think the way I think, and why I feel the way I feel.

David Augsburger

of view, your own comments will have to be drastically revised. You will also find that with this type of listening and response, there is an attitude of open, two-way communication.

Of the styles of responding we have discussed in this chapter, Carl Rogers (1961) has found that *active listening,* sometimes referred to as the *understanding response,* is the least used style in human communication.

A LAST THOUGHT

We all share the common problem of trying to combat communication breakdowns. When we stop to think of how many ways we can misunderstand each other, it seems at times a wonder that any effective communication can take place.

Researchers and theorists in the behavioral sciences have identified three key qualities essential in closing the gap between what you mean to say, what you said, and what you heard: *genuineness, acceptance and respect of others, and empathy* (Rogers, 1957).

Genuineness means being honest and open about one's feelings, needs, and ideas. This also involves the search and constant improvement directed toward self-awareness, self-acceptance, and self-expression.

Acceptance and respect of others refers to the decision to offer an atmosphere largely uncontaminated by evaluations of the other's thoughts, feelings, or behaviors. It also means that we respect the other person's capacity and right to self-direction, rather than believing that his or her life would be best guided by us.

Empathy refers to the ability to understand how another person feels and how he or she perceives the situation. It involves experiencing the feelings of another and at the same time being able to separate our own feelings from the feelings of the other person.

Identity and meaning as a person probably only are possible for us in direct proportion to our ability to communicate and to relate to our fellow human beings.

L. Davis

We need to become aware of the conditions that are interfering with the communication process and make an attempt to modify our behavior in such a way that real meaning and understanding are communicated. This can lead to establishing and maintaining more satisfying relationships with others, which is the basic goal of communication. Virginia Satir (1976) shares this thought:

I believe the greatest gift I can conceive of having from anyone is to be seen by them, heard by them, to be understood and touched by them. The greatest gift I can give is to see, hear, understand and to touch another person. When this is done, I feel contact has been made.

KEY TERMS

Communication

Encoding

Decoding

Feedback

Symbols in communication

Communication channels

One-way communication

Two-way communication

Communication barriers

Nonverbal communication

Verbal communication

Semantics

Double bind

Kinesis

Paralinguistics

Reacting to others

Intimate distance

Responding to others

Personal distance

Hearing

Social distance

Minimal encourages

Public distance

Hidden agenda

Listening

External noise

Internal psychological filter

Judging response

Internal noise

Advising response

Questioning response

Supportive response

Closed questions

Open questions

Listening with the third ear

Active listening

Paraphrase

Passive listening

Empathy

Parroting

Interpretative response

CHAPTER DISCUSSION QUESTIONS

1. Discuss the causes for communication breakdown. In your opinion, what presents the biggest problem?
2. Many times nonverbal messages are more honest and revealing than what is verbally expressed. Why? Give examples of nonverbal communication to support your answer.
3. Discuss how a person's self-concept influences communication with others.
4. Why is "feedback" so important to mutual understanding in communication?
5. A relationship is only as good as its communication. Discuss the implications of this statement.
6. Is it possible to give constructive criticism without causing the other person to become defensive? How?
7. Which style of responding do you use most frequently? Which style of responding is the most difficult for you to use?
8. Discuss the techniques for improving our listening skills. Which one will be the most difficult for you to use?
9. Do you think it will be possible for you to develop the techniques of active listening? With whom will it be most difficult for you to use these skills and techniques?

REFERENCES

Bolton, Robert. (1979) *People Skills*. New York: Simon and Schuster, Inc.

Buscaglia, Leo. (1984) *Loving Each Other: The Challenge of Human Relationships*. New York: Holt, Rinehart and Winston.

Cline, Foster W. (1982) *Parent Education Text*. Evergreen, Colorado: Evergreen Consultants in Human Behavior.

Drakeford, John. (1967) *The Awesome Power of the Listening Ear*. Waco, Texas: Word Publishing.

Eckman, Paul and Friesen, Wallace. (1975) *Unmasking the Face: A Guide to Recognizing Emotions from Facial Clues*. Englewood Cliffs, N.J.: Prentice Hall, Inc.

Gordon, Thomas. (1970) *Parent Effectiveness Training*. New York: New American Library.

Hall, Edward T. (1969) *The Hidden Dimension*. Garden City, New York: Anchor Books.

Harrison, Delyn Dendy. (1978) "Word Power," *Some Things Are Better Said in Black and White*. Fort Worth, Texas: Branch Smith, Inc.

Harrison, Randall. (1970) "Nonverbal Communication: Exploration into Time, Space, Action, and Object," *Dimensions in Communication: Readings,* edited by James Campbell and Hall Harper. Belmont, California: Wadsworth Publishing Co.

Heslin, R. and Alper, T. (1983) "Touch: A Bonding Gesture," *Nonverbal Interaction,* ed. J. M. Wiemann and R. P. Harrison. Beverly Hills, California: Sage Publishing Co.

Hoffman, Gloria and Graiver, Pauline. (1983) *Speak the Language of Success*. New York: G. P. Putnam's Sons.

Mehrabian, Albert. (1968) "Communication Without Words," *Psychology Today,* 9: 53.

———. (1976) *Public Places and Private Spaces*. New York: Basic Books.

Miller, Sherod; Wackman, Daniel; Nunnally, Elam; and Saline, Carol. (1981) *Straight Talk*. New York: Rawson Wade Publishing Co.

Nichols, Ralph and Stevens, Leonard. (1957) *Are You Listening?* New York: McGraw-Hill.

———. (1957) "Listening to People," *Harvard Business Review,* 9: 28–30.

Rogers, Carl. (1961) *On Becoming a Person*. Boston: Houghton Mifflin.

———. (1957) "The Necessary and Sufficient Conditions of Personality Change," *Journal of Counseling Psychology,* 22: 95–110.

Satir, Virginia. (1976). *Making Contact*. Millbrae, California: Celestial Arts.

Sperry, Len. (1975) *Skills in Contact Counseling*. Reading, Massachusetts: Addison Wesley.

ONE WAY/TWO WAY

Purpose: To demonstrate how descriptive communication can be interpreted differently by other people and also to show the superior functioning of two-way communication.

Instructions:

I. A sender is selected to give information to the class.

II. The sender is given a drawing, made up of designs of geometric figures. The participants are given a blank sheet of paper; they are instructed to label one side Diagram I and the other side Diagram II.

III. The sender turns his or her back to the rest of the group and tries to describe verbally how to reproduce the geometric model. This is Diagram I.

IV. Participants may neither ask questions nor give audible responses; participants may not talk or compare sketches with the other group members.

V. After 10 or 15 minutes, repeat the exercise with the sender facing his group, and giving directions for Diagram II. Participants should use the other side of their paper designated as Diagram II.

VI. Participants may ask any questions they desire. Senders may respond verbally, but no gestures, please.

VII. When Diagram II has been completed, the sender shows the participants the two diagrams, and they are to tell him or her how many figures they drew correctly.

NOTE: Instead of selecting one sender for the entire group, dyads may be formed and then follow the same instructions as just outlined.

DISCUSSION

1. What assumptions might you make about one and two-way communications? Which takes longer? Which is more accurate?

2. Which is more frustrating for the sender? For the receiver?

3. What parallels does this exercise have in your everyday life? Does this exercise tell you anything about the way you listen?

WHAT DO YOU COMMUNICATE NONVERBALLY?

Purpose: To evaluate your nonverbal communication behavior and gain insight into how you can improve your silent language.

Instructions:

I. Briefly in one or two sentences, evaluate what you perceive your nonverbal behavior reveals or says about you.

II. THE NONVERBAL CATEGORIES:
   a. **Facial expressions—**
   b. **Eyes—**
   c. **Vocal Clues** (rate of speech, pitch of voice, loud or soft tone of voice, and so on)—
   d. **Gestures and other body movements—**
   e. **Touching** (how much or how little)—
   f. **Personal space and distance** (how close you get to people when you are talking)—
   g. **The physical environment you create** (your home, room, office, inside of car, and so on)—
   h. **Clothing and personal appearance—**
   i. **Silence—**(whether you pause and think before you speak; how much or how little you talk)—
   j. **Any other nonverbal behavior you wish to comment on—**

III. Then, have someone who knows you well complete an evaluation of what they perceive your nonverbal behavior reveals about you. The form is on the next page.

IV. After your friend has completed his or her evaluation, compare the two evaluations of your nonverbal behavior. Then, list the areas where the greatest discrepancy occurs.

DISCUSSION

1. Why is it that we oftentimes do not see ourselves as others see us?

2. What surprised you most about what you learned about yourself?

3. Do you feel there is a need to improve your nonverbal communication? In what areas?

_____ **EVALUATION OF** _____ **NONVERBAL BEHAVIOR**
    (Friend)   (Student)

a. **Facial expressions**—

b. **Eyes**—

c. **Vocal Clues** (rate of speech, pitch of voice, loud or soft tone of voice, and so on)—

d. **Gestures and other body movements**—

e. **Touching** (How much, how little)—

f. **Personal space and distance** (how close does this person get to people when talking)—

g. **The physical environment this person creates** (his or her home, room, office, inside of car, and so on)—

h. **Clothing and personal appearance**—

i. **Silence** (does this person pause and think before he or she speaks; how much or how little does this person talk)—

j. **Any other nonverbal behavior you wish to comment on**—

REALLY LISTENING

Purpose: To develop an understanding of the importance of active listening.

Instructions:

I. In groups of three, select one of the following issues and conduct a small-group discussion.
   A. Abortion
   B. Capital Punishment
   C. Single Parenting
   D. Teenage Pregnancy
   E. Homosexuality
   F. Euthanasia
   G. Drug/Alcohol abuse—
      How to prevent their use

II. Before beginning the discussion you will generate this rule: Each person can speak for himself or herself only after he or she has restated the ideas and feelings of the previous speaker accurately and to that speaker's satisfaction.

III. Someone must first initiate his or her feelings about the chosen issue. The following speakers will use phrases such as: What I hear you saying is . . . or Do I understand you correctly that. . . .

IV. Remember you must restate the feelings of the previous speaker to his or her complete satisfaction.

DISCUSSION

1. As a listener how accurate was your first understanding of the speaker's statements?

2. How did the listening you did here compare with the kind you do everyday? Did it take more effort?

3. Did this method of really listening help you to see the other person's point of view? Why?

4. How can you personally use this method of really listening to "clear up cloudy issues" in your communication endeavors?

STYLES OF RESPONDING

Purpose: To identify different styles of responding and to give feedback accordingly.

Instructions:

I. Divide into groups of two and think of a problem that you would feel comfortable in discussing with your partner. This can be a problem at work, school, or home, where some objective advice would be helpful to you. Repeat with other dyads if time permits.

II. Try to talk five to ten minutes about your problem, and after you have finished, take your partner's workbook and identify his or her style of responding to your problem. The different styles of responding as outlined in this chapter were: Evaluative or Judging, Criticizing, Interpretative, Advising, Supportive, Questioning, Active Listening, or Understanding.

III. After you have identified your partner's style of responding, give your partner some feedback on why you think he or she used the particular style.

IV. Reverse the roles and follow the same procedure.

1. When you listened to my problem on _____

_____ ,

you appeared to respond in a _____ way.

2. Here are the reasons why I felt you responded in this way.

DISCUSSION

1. How do you feel about the feedback you received?

2. Why did you respond in the way you did?

3. Is there anything you would like to change about the way you responded to the problem?

4. What have you learned about your styles of responding?

ARE YOU AN ACTIVE LISTENER?

Purpose: To assess your active listening skills and establish goals for improvement.

Instructions:

I. Before responding to the statements below, make a copy and have a person with whom you talk regularly answer these questions about you.

II. Select the response that best describes the frequency of your actual behavior. Place the letters A, U, F, O, or S on the line before each of the 15 statements.

Almost Always	Usually	Frequently	Occasionally	Seldom
A	U	F	O	S

_____ 1. I like to listen to people talk. I encourage them to talk by showing interest, by smiling and nodding, and so on.

_____ 2. I pay closer attention to speakers who are more interesting or similar to me.

_____ 3. I evaluate the speaker's words and nonverbal communication ability as they talk.

_____ 4. I avoid distractions; if it's noisy, I suggest moving to a quiet spot, turning off the TV, and so on.

_____ 5. When people interrupt me to talk, I put what I was doing out of sight and mind and give them my complete attention.

_____ 6. When people are talking I allow them time to finish. I do not interrupt, anticipate what they are going to say, or jump to conclusions.

_____ 7. I tune people out who do not agree with my views.

_____ 8. While the other person is talking or the professor is lecturing, my mind wanders to personal topics.

_____ 9. While the other person is talking, I pay close attention to the nonverbal communications to help me fully understand what the sender is trying to get across.

_____ 10. I tune out and pretend I understand when the topic is difficult.

_____ 11. When the other person is talking, I think about what I am going to say in reply.

_____ 12. When I feel there is something missing or contradictory, I ask direct questions to get the person to explain the idea more fully.

_____ 13. When I don't understand something, I let the sender know.

_____ 14. When listening to other people, I try to put myself in their position and see things from their perspective.

_____ 15. During conversations I repeat back to the sender what has been said in my own words (paraphrase) to be sure I understand correctly what has been said.

Key for Scoring: To determine your score, give yourself: 5 points for each A, 4 for each U, 3 for each F, 2 for each O, and 1 for each A statement. Place the numbers on the line to your response letter. For items, 2, 3, 7, 8, 10, and 11 the score reverses: 5 points for each S, 4 for each O, 3 for each F, 2 for each U and 1 for each A. Place these score numbers on the lines next to the response letters. Now add your total number of points. Your score should be between 15 and 75. Place your score here _____ and on the continuum below.

Poor Listener 15 _25 _35 _45 _55 _65 _75 _ Good Listener

Generally, the higher your score, the better your listening skills.

Note: To improve active listening, items 1, 4, 5, 6, 9, 12, 13, 14, and 15 should be implemented, whereas items 2, 3, 7, 8, 10, and 11 should be avoided.

Discussion

1. How did you do on the items to be implemented for improved active listening?

2. How did you do on the items to be avoided for improved active listening?

3. How did your perception of your listening skills compare to those of the individual who rated you? Do you agree or disagree?

4. After comparing your perception of your listening skills with those of the individual who rated you, in what areas do you feel you could improve to become a more effective active listener?

LEARNING JOURNAL FOR INTERPERSONAL COMMUNICATION

Select the statement below that best defines your feelings about the personal value or meaning gained from this chapter and respond below the dotted line:

I LEARNED THAT I. . . .   I WAS SURPRISED THAT I. . . .

I REALIZED THAT I. . . .   I WAS PLEASED THAT I. . . .

I DISCOVERED THAT I. . . .   I WAS DISPLEASED THAT I. . . .

....

6

Becoming Intimate

FRIENDSHIP

There is nothing in this whole world, Lord, like having one true,
enjoyable, understanding friend. No one is ever so lonely that he
doesn't have a friend. To find one, all you have to do is go out and
help somebody. Now and then say to a friend, "I love you." Those
words weren't meant only for sweethearts. They are just as
significant, beautiful and life-enhancing when said to a dear friend.
A true test of friendship: If you died, which of your friends would
you trust to clean out your drawers? When I talk, my friend listens.
When my friend talks, I listen. That's one of the reasons we're
friends. Friends are like bracelet charms. If you truly love and
enjoy your friends, they are part of the golden circle that makes life
good. If you want more friends, smile more! I've never known
anyone who smiled a lot who didn't have a lot of friends. Friends
are too precious to lose—even when they disappoint us. Lord, help
me to forgive this friend—it is only because I need and love her.
(And because I'd want her to forgive me!) Friends are worth
forgiving. The heart has many doors, of which friendship is but one.
Don't be too quick to bolt them.

Anonymous

Walt is a junior in college. He has had a lot of dates, but has never had a "real serious" intimate relationship with a member of the opposite sex. Walt has many close friends and is very active in school activities. He likes to ski, play tennis, watch Woody Allen movies, and listen to jazz. Walt would like to become a lawyer and is majoring in political science.

Sarah is a sophomore in college and has dated the same person since her junior year in high school. Sarah was a cheerleader and her boyfriend was captain of his football team. They seem to be "made" for each other. They had the same friends, went to dances together, and studied together. Sarah doesn't seem to have any other friends, because she was always with her boyfriend. Sarah seems to be depressed. There seems to be something missing in her life, but she's not sure what it is. Presently, Sarah's boyfriend is attending college in another state. She misses him, so she writes and calls him often.

Sarah would like to become a judge, so she is in a prelaw program with emphasis in history. She likes to play tennis and racquetball, water ski, and listen to jazz. Her boyfriend likes to play and watch football. Sarah only watches football if her boyfriend is playing. He likes ice hockey and plays basketball with the boys. He enjoys going to rock concerts. Her boyfriend is majoring in computer science. When Sarah and her boyfriend get together they are very active and busy, but they don't seem to really talk.

It's the first day of a new term and classes are just beginning. Walt walks into his European History class and sits down and notices an attractive female sitting three chairs away. It so happens that the attractive female is Sarah. Walt says to himself, "I would like to get to know her. Just looking at her makes my heart beat faster." Now the dilemma, how does he get to know her and what are the chances of him developing a close intimate relationship with her, especially since she already has a boyfriend?

We will continue following the development of this relationship throughout this chapter.

THE DEVELOPMENT OF A RELATIONSHIP

Relationships evolve, they don't just happen. They take time and effort. The first step in a relationship is *becoming aware* of the other person—*first impressions*. At this time we evaluate the person, using our past experience, prejudices, and stereotyping to make a judgement whether or not to take the next step. Walt is impressed with Sarah's physical appearance—he perceives her as being attractive. Remember beauty is in the eye of the beholder, not all people would perceive her as beautiful. Now that Walt has *become aware* of Sarah he needs to decide how he is going to take the next step, that is *making contact,* or getting acquainted with her. This is a difficult step for many individuals.

Be slow in choosing a friend, slower in changing.

Benjamin Franklin

What would you recommend for Walt to do in order to get to know Sarah? The *mere exposure phenomenon* may work in this situation (Moreland & Zajonc, 1982; Nuttin, 1987). The more familiar we are with people or things, the greater the chance of us liking them.

The more Sarah sees Walt, the greater the chance of her interacting with him and liking him. Walt could improve his odds of *making contact* with Sarah by sitting in the chair next to her (*proximity*) or make sure he stands near the doors everyday so she has to pass by him to enter the classroom (*exposure*). Don't be too aggressive in this process or you may threaten the other person. During the first week or so, Walt may not even want to say anything—he doesn't want to make it too obvious.

The third step is *disclosure*. As we become friends, we are more willing to disclose more about our personal lives—our hopes, dreams and fears. As we begin to disclose information about ourselves, we are demonstrating to our partner that we trust them and they in turn will disclose to us. Thus the relationship will become stronger and more intimate. As Walt begins to slowly open up to Sarah and Sarah to Walt, the relationship will begin to develop. Walt could begin by asking Sarah questions about European History, then talk about school related subjects, ask about her hobbies and interest, and tell her about his interests. As they continue disclosing information about themselves to each other, their interest in one another will continue to grow.

Do all the terms and concepts mentioned so far sound familiar? They should, we discussed all of them thoroughly in chapter one. This was a review of how a relationship develops over a period of time and now we will discover how the relationship will continue to evolve into a more intimate relationship.

BECOMING FRIENDS

If I don't have friends, then I ain't got nothing.

Billie Holiday

Friends play a very significant role in our lives. Throughout our life they are important to us. They may provide help in a time of need, praise in times of achievement, sympathy in a time of sorrow, support in a time of failure, and advice in a time of confusion. Without friends we are lonely. Friends provide us with the *emotional support* and *social ties* that is vital to our well being. A good friend will always be there when they are needed. We can rely on their support no matter what happens to us. They also provide us with a feeling of belonging, a feeling that we are part of a group. We need an identity and our friends help us in the development of finding who we are. Good friends satisfy these needs.

Who do you consider your good friends? A good friend could be a family member, a boyfriend or girlfriend, a spouse, a work colleague, a teacher, a clergyman, a fellow member of a religious, social, recreational, or political group or any other person. Remember, the more "good" friends you have the more secure you will be. Research continues to suggest that having close relationships helps people adjust to stressful situations (Mitchell, Billings, & Moos, 1983; Turner, 1983) and buffer people from the ill effects of negative life events, like accidents, divorce, loss of a loved one, family problems etc. (Cohen & McKay, 1985).

What is your definition of a good friend? A recent student poll at Tarrant County Junior College asked, "What values do you think are important in a friendship?" Here are a few of their responses:

- Trust, someone you can share a problem with. Someone who will be there for you and will know you're going to be there for them
- Honesty
- Loyalty
- Acceptance, humor, sense of fun, honesty, mainly acceptance of each other
- Trust, keeping your word, loyalness, love, understanding, be able to trust him around your woman
- Trust is most important, reliability, acceptance, honesty
- You can accept their faults as well as their good traits
- Trust.

Friendship needs feeding.

John Garner

The responses from the 1991 survey in Texas are very similar to the 1979 survey of 40,000 readers of *Psychology Today* magazine. The readers were to indicate what qualities they valued in a friend. Table 6.1 lists the ten most frequently mentioned qualities. The results suggest that keeping confidences and loyalty were the most important factors in a good friend. If you review the responses given by the Tarrant County Junior College students, you will note that trust and loyalty were also mentioned most. The next most important ingredients of friendships are warmth/affection and supportiveness. The respondents also indicated the importance of frankness and a sense of humor in a relationship. In another survey (Block, 1980) the respondents emphasized, as Carl Rogers did in Chapter 2, the importance of unconditional acceptance from a friend—accept me as I am not how you want me to be.

**Table 6.1
Ten Qualities of a Friend
(In Order of Importance)**

1. KEEPS CONFIDENCE
2. LOYALTY
3. WARMTH AND AFFECTION
4. SUPPORTIVENESS
5. FRANKNESS
6. SENSE OF HUMOR
7. WILLINGNESS TO MAKE TIME FOR ME
8. INDEPENDENCE
9. GOOD CONVERSATIONALIST
10. INTELLIGENCE

Does Sarah trust Walt? Is he loyal? Is Walt being honest with Sarah? Are they friends yet? Only time will tell. They are still *getting acquainted*. It takes time for a relationship to grow and develop. What other factors are important in becoming friends?

Similarity. Is it true that "opposites attract?" Or is it true that "birds of a feather flock together?" Look around; do most of your friends have different interests, beliefs, and political preferences than you or are they similar? Research indicates that *similarities* attract. We tend to select our friends who are similar to us in many different aspects, including income level, occupation, status, educational level, and political preferences (Fisher, 1982). Similarities are also important in the selection of a husband or wife. There is a correlation between length of marriage and the similarities between the two people. The more similarities there are between the two spouses, the longer the marriage tends to last.

Why are we drawn to people who are similar to us? For one thing, people with similar interest and attitudes are likely to enjoy the same hobbies and activities. Even more important, however, is the fact that we are more likely to communicate well with people whose ideas and opinions are similar to ours, and communication is a very important aspect of an enduring relationship. It is also reinforcing to be with similar people, for they confirm our view of the world, support our opinions and beliefs. We in turn, provide mutual reinforcement for each other.

What would it be like if your friends always disagreed with you? You're a Republican and they are Democrats, you're pro-life and they're pro-choice, you're religious and they're not, you're conservative and they're liberal, you smoke and they don't, they like rock music and you like classical music, you like to participate in sports and they'd rather smoke dope. Are you going to have fun together, or is there going to be a lot of conflict? Research studies have found that there are two critical similarities that are important within a relationship; they are similar beliefs and similar attitudes. When considering a long-term commitment between you and another person, ask yourself, what do we have in common? Are our beliefs and attitudes similar? If they are not, you may discover that over a period of time, conflict is more apt to develop between the two of you.

Where do I go to find friends? You need to go to those places where you will find other people who have similar interest and needs. If you're not interested in religion, should you go to church to find your friends? If you don't drink and carouse, is the singles' bar the place to find your friends? If you like to dance, you go to dances. If you like sports, go to places where you will find other people who like sports. If you're interested in politics, go to political events that are of interest to you and you will find that you have something in common with the other people attending. These people will not come to you; you need to ask them.

What about Walt and Sarah? Do they have anything in common? To begin, they are both taking European History; that's a good start. They are both in the prelaw program and enjoy studying history and political science. They both like to ski and participate in individual sports like tennis. They seem to have a lot in common, a lot more in common than Sarah and her present boyfriend. These similarities give Walt and Sarah a lot to talk about. Does Walt have a chance to start dating Sarah? Wait and see.

What about the saying "opposites attract"? They do for a period of time, until the novelty wears off, and then you will discover that these dissimilar beliefs, interests, and attitudes cause more conflict than attraction. Most of us are familiar with couples who seem completely opposite in regards to personality but have been married for many years and seem to be happy. Even though they seem to be opposites, they are very compatible. Why?

Personality Fit. People with complementary needs seem to be drawn to each other (Winch, 1958). You notice that one of your friends is very outgoing and her boyfriend is very shy. This doesn't seem consistent with the idea that similarities attract. Why do they get along so well? *We discover that differences in which one person's strengths compensate for the other person's weaknesses may lead to mutual attraction* (Drescher, 1979). The personalities seem to complement each other. In most relationships each person supplies certain qualities that the partner is lacking. Does your partner supply these missing characteristics?

Reciprocity. Flattery will get you . . . everything or nowhere? Which is true? What have you heard? The evidence on reciprocity indicates that we tend to like those who show that they like us and that we tend to see others as liking us more if we like them (Berscheid & Walster, 1978). Thus, there does seem to be an interactive process in which liking leads to liking and loving leads to loving.

If our self-esteem is low we are more susceptible to flattery, especially if the compliment is from someone of higher status. A person of high self-esteem may not be so easily swayed by positive treatment. Do you like to receive compliments? How do you feel about the person who is giving the compliments? Do they have a positive or negative influence on you? Do you now understand why some people seem to be greatly influenced by people who are nice to them, especially if that person is perceived as important to them?

Walt has been complimenting Sarah a lot the last few weeks. He tells her how nice she looks, that he likes her dress, he likes her hair style, and so on. Will this influence her feelings toward Walt, especially because she has been depressed lately? The story continues.

In his book *How to Win Friends and Influence People,* Dale Carnegie (1936) summarized six rules, that are still relevant today, that will help us win friends and influence people. You will see that Carnegie emphasized the use of praise and flattery.

The man who trusts no others doesn't trust himself.

Napolean Hill

Table 6.2
How to Win Friends and Influence People

Rule 1: Become genuinely interested in people.
Rule 2: Smile.
Rule 3: Remember that a man's name is to him the sweetest and most important sound in any language.
Rule 4: Be a good listener. Encourage others to talk about themselves.
Rule 5: Talk in terms of the other man's interest.
Rule 6: Make the other person feel important—and do it sincerely.
Do you think these rules are still relevant today?

Whether we are drawn to people by familiarity, similarity, beauty, or some other quality, mutual attraction sometimes progresses from friendship to the more intense, complex, and mysterious feeling of love.

Man is but a network of relationships and these alone matter to him.

St. Exupery

BECOMING LOVERS

There is a great similarity between love relationships and good-friend relationships (Davis, 1985). In both there are high levels of trust, mutual respect, and acceptance. Further, the interactions between the people involved are characterized by high levels of understanding, nurturing, and confiding. Nonetheless, the love relationship, with its greater depth of caring and exclusiveness, typically generates greater emotion and power. As a result it can affect individuals more, having the potential to meet a broader sweep of human needs or to cause greater frustration and distress.

"LOVE IS A SPECIAL WAY OF FEELING"

Love is a special way of feeling,
It is the way we feel
When we sit on our mother's lap
With her arms around us tight and close.
It is the good way we feel
When we talk to someone
And they want to listen
And don't tell us to go away and be quiet.
It is the happy way we feel
When we save a bird that has been hurt
Or feed a lost cat
Or calm a frightened colt.
Love is found in unexpected places.
It is there in the quiet moment
When we first discover a beautiful thing
When we watch a bird soar high
Against the pale blue sky
When we see a lovely flower
That no one else has noticed
When we find a place that shelters us
And is all our very own.
Love starts in little ways.
It may begin the day
We first share our thoughts with someone else
Or help someone who needs us
Or sometimes it begins
Because even without words
We understand how someone feels.
Love comes quietly
But you know when it is there
Because suddenly you are not alone any more
And there is no sadness inside you.
Love is a happy feeling
That stays inside your heart
For the rest of your life.

Anonymous

Is It Love or Lust? Have you ever looked at someone for the first time and said to yourself, "I think I'm in love?" Is there such a thing as "love at first sight?" Research has found that we don't fall in love, we grow into love. Then, what is this feeling we are experiencing when we see this person?

Remember when Walt saw Sarah for the first time? It was the first day of class and Walt was fearful of having to take the European History class, because he heard the professor was one of the most difficult at the college. He was nervous and his heart was beating rapidly as he looked up and saw Sarah for the first time. Was it love? Walt thinks so; he attributed his physical arousal to Sarah and not to the fear of taking the class.

Positive or negative experiences that stimulate physical arousal, such as anxiety, nervous tension, excitement, heart palpitations, blushing, and accelerated breathing, may lead to the feeling of love, if the labeling process is strong enough. A frightened person, an angry man, a jealous woman, or a euphoric individual is a potentially romantic person. If this emotionally aroused individual attaches these feelings to someone perceived as desirable, it will increase his or her attraction or feeling of love for that person. Once the person is aroused, all that remains is for the person to identify and label this complex feeling as love.

Many of you have experienced this but did not understand the process that created this feeling. Have you ever attended an event, such as a wedding, a funeral, a championship game, an automobile race, or a horror film, where your body reacted by nervous tension, sweating, increased heart beat, or butterflies in the stomach? While this is all happening your date reaches over to hold your hand, and you look at your partner and feel that terrific rush within your body and attribute that feeling to your partner and not to the situation you're in at the time. *You know it must be love.* The event may be positive or negative and still create a positive feeling. A young attractive person stops you as you are jogging to ask directions. Will you be more attracted to that person or to the person that ask you directions while you're waiting at a stop light on your way to work? While jogging your pulse rate has increased and your body is aroused due to the exercise, but you associate the physiological reaction to the other person and feel attracted to them. Is that feeling, love or lust?

What Is Love? This is a question people have been asking for years. Mass media, romantic novels, soap operas, and songs, have all been attempting to answer this question.

- *Love is a many splendored thing*
- *All the world needs is love*
- *Love makes the world go around*
- *I can't live without love*
- *How do I love thee, let me count the ways*
- *Love means never having to say you're sorry*

The love in your heart wasn't put there to stay; love isn't love until you give it away.

Anonymous

Our lives seem to evolve around this subject. But, does anyone know what love is? People seem to have their own definition of love. When your date says that he or she loves you, what does your date mean? Is it the same as when your mother or father says it to you? What is your definition of love? Before you continue, take a few minutes to write down your definition of love. Share your definition of love with your friends and loved ones. Compare your definition with theirs.

We have found a definition of love that we would like to share with you. When the satisfaction, security and development of another person is as important to you as your own satisfaction, security and development, *love exists* (Harry Stack Sullivan, 1953). Using this definition of love, you'll find that you can measure your love not only for your significant other, but your mother, father, siblings, friends, animals, and even inanimate objects. What do you think?

MYTHS ABOUT LOVE

True or False

T F 1. *True love lasts forever?*
T F 2. *Love can conquer all.*
T F 3. *Love is a purely positive experience.*
T F 4. *When you fall in love, you'll know it.*
T F 5. *When love strikes, you have no control over your behavior.*

What are your answers to the above questions? These are some interesting myths about love that many of us have been agonizing over for years. Let's take a look at these myths and dispel some of the confusion regarding them.

1. *Does true love last forever?* It would be nice if love would last forever, but most of us have found that it doesn't. People who believe this myth may pursue love forever, looking for the ideal one that will bring complete happiness. This person will experience a lifetime of frustration. Would we have divorce if love lasted forever? It would be more realistic to view love as a wonderful experience that might be encountered on several occasions throughout life.

2. *Does love conquer all?* Many people believe that love and marriage will allow them to overcome (conquer) all their frustrations and problems in life. A supportive partner will help you solve many of your problems, but it doesn't guarantee success. Many people jump into relationships for this purpose, only to discover that the relationship creates additional problems.

3. *Is love a purely positive experience?* Mass media, television, romance novels, and so on, create an unrealistic expectation that love is such a positive experience. In reality it can be a peak experience, but in contrast love can also bring intense negative emotions and great pain. As many of you know, a lover is capable of taking us to emotional peaks in either directions.

4. *Do you know when you're in love?* There is no physiological cue to tell us we are in love. So, the emotional feeling and the cognitive interpretation is different for each of us. It is a state of

Expect what is reasonable in others, not what is perfect.

Anonymous

confusion that many of us agonize over. It's normal to question our feelings toward another person. Remember, we grow to love someone gradually and don't usually fall in love.

5. *Do you behave irrationally when you fall in love?* Does love take control of your behavior. Some people stop eating, quit studying, are unable to concentrate on their job, and avoid taking responsibility for their actions because they're in love. If you allow your heart to take control of your behavior, you may become vulnerable to irrational decisions about sexual involvement or long term commitments.

Psychologists are doing research, attempting to discover what love is. Robert Sternberg (1986) has developed a theory of love that includes three distinct components: (1) *passion,* an intense physiological desire for another person; (2) *intimacy,* the feeling that one can share all one's thoughts and actions with another; (3) *commitment,* the willingness to stay with a person through thick and thin, for better or worse, in sickness or health. Ideally, marriage is characterized by a healthy amount of all three components.

The Development of Love. Early in a relationship, passion is usually high, which may be one reason new love relationships and affairs are most intense. Intimacy, however, is not as high, because the partners have not spent enough time together or shared enough experiences and emotions to be able to understand each other completely. Passionate love without intimacy creates a risk of misunderstanding and jealousy about any other person or activity that seems to interfere with the relationship. Early in the relationship, commitment also tends to be on the low side. It is interesting to note that these trends are true for most relationships, including the married and unmarried, heterosexual and homosexual couples (Kurdek & Schmitt, 1986).

Over time passion seems to fade, while intimacy and commitment grows stronger. According to Sternberg, passion is like an addiction: in the beginning a touch of the hand, a smile, even a mere glance will produce excitement. Gradually, however, one needs a greater dose of stimulation to get the same feeling. We habituate to the passion, and thus to continue this intense feeling for one another, *novel and significant stimuli* must be provided by each of the two individuals.

An understanding of the three components of love and the developmental process will help couples in the building of their relationship. A couple may want to schedule specific times each week, away from children and family, for a period of intimate sharings—a time to discuss problems as well as happy times. You may want to keep the passion burning by scheduling a weekend at the beach. What else can you do to maintain the three components of love?

Seven Forms of Love

Liking	Intimacy but no commitment or passion.
Infatuation	Passion, but no commitment or intimacy.
Empty Love	Commitment, but no intimacy or passion.
Romantic Love	Intimacy and passion, but no commitment.
Fatuous Love	Commitment and passion, but no intimacy.
Companionate Love	Commitment and intimacy, but no passion.
Consumate Love	Commitment, intimacy, and passion.

Examine the love relationships that you are involved in presently. What form of love does your love relationships exhibit? What could you do to change to a different form? Which form do you consider the most appropriate form of love? Explain why.

As we look at the relationship of Walt and Sarah, we find that Walt finally had the "guts" to ask Sarah out for coffee after class. They discovered that they have a lot in common (similarities) and have begun to disclose a lot of personal information about themselves to each other. As their personal disclosure increases, their level of trust increases. Their attraction for one another grows. The flame is lit and the passion becomes more intense. But, wait a minute, what happened to Sarah's boyfriend? Even though Sarah and her boyfriend have dated for more than four years, they really didn't have much in common other than school activities. And remember that absence makes the heart grow fonder of someone else (proximity).

Sarah and Walt have similar values, religious beliefs, attitudes about life, and interests. They are beginning to spend more and more time together and the feeling of intimacy and commitment grow stronger. Sarah is no longer depressed; she is excited about life and her new relationship. She is looking to the future and setting goals. How does Walt feel about the relationship? We don't know about Walt, but we do know how most men feel.

Men vs. Women. On the whole, men tend to think they are compatible with their partner before women do. One reason may be that men and women tend to have different attitudes about love (Peplau & Gordon, 1985). Men are more likely to be "romantics:" for example, they are inclined to believe in love at first sight and to regard true love as magical, impossible to explain or understand. Women are more likely to be "pragmatists," believing that financial security is as important as passion in nourishing a close relationship and that there are many possible individuals that a person could learn to love. Women tend to be more cautious than men before deciding to take the final step. What is the next step? Is it marriage or some alternative?

The friendship is a plant of slow growth.

George Washington

BECOMING COMMITTED

It is not entirely clear how and when commitment begins. At some time and in some way, two people in a relationship decide that their satisfaction or happiness with each other is significantly greater than in their relationships with other people. They agree to begin a relatively long-lasting, more intimate relationship that to some extent excludes other close relationships. The couple agrees to depend on each other for the satisfaction of important needs, including, companionship, love and sex. The commitment may or may not include the decision to live together.

TRUE HAPPINESS

Love and Be Loved:

Never allow fear, anger, nor hate to take the space of love. When you discover these feelings, replace them with love.

Teach love to your children by approving of them. Praise them and each other.

Parents give and teach love by listening. The tone of voice, expression on your face, even the motion of your body teaches love.

Love is respect and consideration of others. Treat your children as little people, and they will respect and give love in return.

Guard your mental and physical health; both must be healthy to love.

Do not take each other (each member) for granted; always guard against too many "don't, do, won't" words.

Practice peace of mind with your children. Think of beautiful thoughts. Do not allow the mind to dwell on doubts. Trust the Lord to take care of the doubts. Fill your minds with positive thinking and thank the Lord often.

Teach by example. If you see someone standing alone be certain your children see you act with kindness toward that person. Hold your hands out to others, and your children will do so.

Fill your life with friendship. Reach out to others, gathering them into your family circle.

Appreciate nature. Take time with your family to enjoy the stars, the quiet of the night, the lake, the grass on the lawn—even an ant hill.

Touch and hug each other, and those you meet.

Be sincere. If you fill your heart with love, you will be loved.

Anonymous

When I am with you, I grow or diminish according to how you make me feel. And in my turn, I invite you to live or to die simply by existing in your presence, by walking with you or retreating, by holding my hand to you or not holding it to you, by opening my heart to you or keeping it closed.

Sidney Jourard

Making an agreement with another person to enter into a deeper, more exclusive, and lasting relationship is a crucially important life decision that must be made freely and with careful thought. Many individuals, consciously or unconsciously, feel pressured to enter into a relationship that they aren't sure is good for them. Many people aren't happy in their existing relationship or social situation, be it living in a bad home environment, having an abusive mate, getting too old, being lonely, having an alcoholic or addicted mate, and so on. They feel pressured to commit themselves to a new relationship as a means to escape the bad situation. A person who is pushed or pressured into a relationship will discover that their commitment is weaker and less enduring. If the commitment is made in defiance of pressure from parents or peers, the commitment may be very strong (Darley & Cooper, 1972). As many of you know, if your parents were to tell you that you *cannot* date a specific person, you will do whatever it takes to make sure you will date and be more committed to the person. This phenomenon is known as *psychological reactance*—the tendency to protect or restore one's sense of freedom or social control, often by doing the opposite of what has been demanded. This is also known as the *Romeo and Juliet effect,* because their love was intensified, not weakened, by their families opposition. In summation, a commitment is likely to be strongest when it is arrived at freely and when it is cemented by taking action as a result of the commitment.

Marriage or ????? "Love and marriage go together like a horse and carriage." Are these lyrics from this popular old song true? People in love are eager to share their lives, their dreams, and their goals with each other. How can they do this? What are their options? Today our society provides us with more options than we had in the past. But some of these options may not be acceptable to our friends and family. So what do we do, get married or live together?

Although alternatives to marriage are more viable than ever, experts project that between ninety and ninety-five percent of us will marry at least once. During the past 25 years in the United States, the average age of marriage has risen steadily. The proportion of single women has doubled among 20–24-year-olds and nearly tripled among 25–29-year-olds. During the same period, the number of couples living together outside marriage has quadrupled.

Singlehood. Is this an option? Remaining single is becoming a more viable lifestyle. More and more people are remaining single. Furthermore, the negative stereotype of people who remain single, which pictures them as lonely, frustrated, depressed, odd, and unchosen, is gradually disappearing.

Generally, single people do rate themselves as less happy than married people. However, the reported happiness of married people has declined steadily since 1972. In the meantime, the reported happiness for singles has increased (Glenn & Weaver, 1988). There is still substantial pressure in our society to marry. We are taught to believe that we are not complete until we have found our "other half" and entered into a partnership for life.

Cohabitation. Negative attitudes toward couples "living together" appears to be declining, though many people continue to disapprove of this practice. An estimated 2.6 million American couples now live together outside marriage and account for about 4 percent of all couples. Cohabitation tends to be a relatively unstable way of life. Most cohabiting couples either get married or end their relationship. Very few—about 2 percent—live together longer than 10 years.

If we live together, is our chance of having a successful marriage greater than those who don't? The research is inconclusive on this subject. Most people who live together and find that they are incompatible separate before marriage. People who get married before living together and find that they are incompatible will generally work harder at trying to get the relationship to work before actually getting divorced. Recent evidence indicates that there is no benefit to living together prior to marriage. The cohabiting couples who do get married seem to be as happy (no more, no less) as other couples. A lot depends on the individual couple, especially their values.

Why Should I Marry? More than nine out of ten people eventually marry, most of them during their twenties and thirties. People tend to marry out of mixed motives, many of them unclear even to themselves. Now that marriage is no longer necessary for economic survival or the satisfaction of sexual needs, love has become the major rationale for getting married and staying married. Unfortunately, people sometimes marry for the wrong reasons, that is to become respectable, for money, for a regular sexual outlet, for status, or to make their parents happy. Even cohabiting couples may marry for the wrong reason. Just when the relationship begins to falter, marriage may be sought to save the relationship. It's a temporary "fix," because it doesn't solve the underlying conflicts.

Marriage is a risky proposition. In deciding to get married, people make a long range projection about the future of their relationship. Obviously, it is difficult to predict 30, 40, or even 50 years of commitment on the basis of one or two years of premarital interaction.

What Are The Chances Of This Marriage Lasting?

What do you think this couple needs to do to build
a meaningful long-term marriage relationship?

Will Your Marriage Last? There is no foolproof recipe for lasting,
happy marriages. Recent studies have provided us with some valuable
clues as to what makes a happy and successful marriage (Klagsburn,
1985).

1. Happily married couples spend a lot of focused time together doing
   what they both enjoy, much as they did in their courtship days
   before they married.
2. They share many of the same values, such as the importance of
   physical intimacy, childrearing practices, religious beliefs, and
   morals.
3. These couples exhibited a high degree of flexibility—they have
   the ability to accept change within their partners as well as
   changes in the nature of the married relationship.

Other factors that seem to be important predictors of marital success include:

- *Age at time of marriage*—couples who marry young have a higher divorce rate.
- *Socioeconomic class*—the frequency of divorce is higher in working and lower classes than in upper and middle classes (Raschke, 1987).
- *Length of courtship*—longer periods of courtship are associated with greater probability of marital success.
- *Family background*—people whose parents were unhappily married are more likely than others to have an unsatisfactory marriage (Teachman, Polonko, & Scanzoni, 1987).
- *Personality*—if one or both partners has a serious psychological or emotional disorder, problems will occur (Raschke, 1987).

Psychology Today magazine (June, 1985) took a readers' poll asking readers to list the most important reasons that made marriages last. It was interesting to note that they separated the responses by sex. The top seven out of fifteen choices were identical for the two sexes. The top seven reasons are listed in order of frequency:

> My spouse is my best friend.
> I like my spouse as a person.
> Marriage is a long-term commitment.
> Marriage is sacred.
> We agree on aims and goals.
> My spouse has grown more interesting.
> I want the relationship to succeed.

Jeanette and Robert Lauer (1985) conducted a survey of 351 couples with enduring marriages to see what made their marriage a success. Couples were asked questions about their marriage ranging from interests, hobbies, sex, money, and attitudes toward their spouses, and reasons why their marriages had lasted.

The most frequently given reason for a lasting marriage is *having a positive attitude toward one's partner.* These individuals see their spouse as their best friend and they like each other as people. They are aware that their partner has faults, but their likeable qualities more than offset their shortcomings. Many people stated that people of the present generation takes the marriage vows too lightly and are not willing to work at solving their problems. Marriage is a commitment and takes a lot of work. Both partners have to work at solving their problems. Another key ingredient to a lasting marriage is a mutual agreement about aims and goals of life, such as the desire to make the marriage last. A satisfying sex life is important, but this is not what makes the marriage last. However, there is a strong link

When you love someone, you love him as he is.

Charles Perry

between a couples' marital satisfaction and their perception of the quality of their sexual relationship (Fowers & Olson, 1989). Most of the couples surveyed said they almost always agree about sex and many are happy despite lack of such agreement. Couples need to learn to adjust and compromise.

MARITAL ADJUSTMENT

During courtship, many of us wear "rose-colored glasses." We tend to ignore or not notice our partner's faults. We tend to focus mostly on pleasurable activities and our partner's positive characteristics. But when people marry, they must face reality and the problems that they will encounter within this new relationship. Suddenly, marriage brings duties and obligations. One is no longer responsible for only oneself but now shares responsibility for two people and perhaps more if children arrive.

Furthermore, one's identity is changed with marriage. No longer are you simply you, you are now Sarah's husband or Walt's wife or Jon's mother or father. You become interdependent with others in your family and not independent. For some people this loss of independence may become a crisis, but for others this new identity grants them a new lease on life.

The changing nature of male and female roles creates problems for all types of couples as they settle down to live together. Even the most mundane tasks may become a problem. Who pays the bills? Who takes out the trash? Who cooks? Who will stay home and take care of young children? There is no such thing as a problem-free marriage. Successful marriages depends on the couples' ability to handle their problems.

What Are Your Expectations of Marriage? When you get married what are your expectations of how life will be? Will marriage be a "bed of roses?" Will all your needs be met by your new spouse? Many people enter marriage with unrealistic expectations about how wonderful it's going to be (Sabatelli, 1988). People tend to create unrealistic ideas about what it's going to be like when they are married. We predict our future and have expectations about ourselves, our spouse, our children, and our future. Mass media, magazines, novels, TV, etc. tends to romanticize marriage and mislead us into thinking that marriage is such an exciting and fulfilling institute. Romantic ideals lead us to expect so much from our mate and from our marriage that disappointment is likely. People who marry quickly are more likely to have unrealistic expectations of marriage and their mates and thus, they are more likely to experience more difficulty when reality sets in.

Role Expectations. What is the woman's role in married life? Is it different from a man's role? Should a man's and a woman's role be different? When a couple marry, they assume new roles, that of husband and wife. We all have developed our own expectations of how a wife or husband should behave. These expectations may vary greatly from one person to another. What happens if your expectations are different from your partner's? Serious problems may occur. The more the two partners agree about marital roles, the more likely the marriage will last over a longer period of time (Sussman & Kitson, 1982).

Where did you learn what the role of a husband or a wife should be? Most of us learned this from watching our parents through the process called *modeling*. But times are changing, and other social forces are having an affect on our roles within a relationship. Careers are interfering with the timing of marriage and the caring of the family. The women's movement has given women more options and has changed their perception of what their role is in a relationship. Marriage seems to be in a state of transition and, consequently, most of us are in a state of confusion as to what role we should be playing.

It is imperative that couples discuss role expectations in depth before marriage. If they discover that their views are very different, they need to take seriously the potential for problems. Many people ignore gender-role disagreements, thinking they can "straighten out" their partners later on. But as we have all discovered, it is difficult to change our own behavior and even more difficult to change someone else's behavior, especially their attitude.

While we are dating and during the honeymoon period, which can be anytime from the wedding day to a year or so from that day, many people don't see the people they love as they really are, but rather as they wish (expect) them to be. We see what we expect to see, we hear what we want to hear—this is a psychological phenomenon of perception that can interfere with the way we perceive the world. We tend to only perceive the positive characteristics of our partners and ignore the negative characteristics. In essence, a person is in love with his or her own dreams and ideals and not with the spouse. Living together day in and day out makes it only a matter of time until each partner is forced to compare ideals with reality.

The Honeymoon Is Over. *One morning, after Walt and Sarah have been married for about a year, Sarah awakens and realizes that Walt is not the same man she married. She accuses him of changing for the worse. He's not as considerate and as kind to her as he was before. He doesn't pay as much attention to her. He doesn't enjoy going out all the time like they use to. He just wants to stay at home. Walt insists, of course, that he has not changed; he is the same person that she married and he enjoys quiet evenings at home alone with her.*

Passion is a fragile essence. It provides joy, excitement, delirium, and fulfillment—along with anxiety, suffering, and despair—for a short time. Companionship love is a heartier flavor. It can provide gentle friendship for life.

Walster and Walster

This interaction may be signaling that the "honeymoon" is over for Walt and Sarah. This stage is very important in most marriages. It usually indicates that the unrealistic, overly high expectations about marriage and one's mate created by "love" are being reexamined. No one can live up to perfection. In a successful relationship it means that subjective perceptions are becoming more realistic and more objective. It also means that we are at last coming to know our mate as a real human being rather than as a projection of our expectations. Realizing the humanness of our partner allows us to relax, to be human as well, and not feel that we have to live up to our partner's expectations. If my partner can make mistakes and be less than perfect, so can I, thank goodness.

After the *honeymoon period,* intensity diminishes and satisfaction with marriage generally dips, especially for wives. The most commonly cited reason for this change is the arrival of children. For most couples, the time and effort spent on parenting usually comes out of the marital relationship. Does this mean that marriages without children are more satisfying? This is a complicated question. In general, when both partners agree to postpone or decide not to have children, they tend to be much more pleased with each other than couples who have several young children.

What are some of the other issues and problems that a couple may encounter as they begin to face the reality of being married and functioning as a "twosome" rather than an individual? Now you need to consider your partner's needs as well as your own while you interact and get involved in the world of work and leisure. Peoples' job satisfaction and involvement can affect their own marital satisfaction, their partners' marital satisfaction, and their children's development and satisfaction.

Should a woman work after she gets married? Should she work after she has children? Should her husband stay at home with the children while she pursues a career?

Marriage and/or a Career. Men have been told that their career is of utmost importance in their lives, whereas women are still in a state of confusion about careers and family roles. Should they pursue a career or stay home and be a "mother" or do both? A successful career woman may experience role conflict and guilt over her strong work commitment. Many times finances make the decision for us. A woman may have to work to help provide for the family while still feeling guilty because she is not home taking care of the kids. There is not enough research evidence to draw any conclusions about the effects of wives' work on their marital satisfaction. But we do know that if people are satisfied with their job, they will be happier at home. The reverse is also true: If people are satisfied with their marriage, they are more likely to be more effective on the job. If people are highly committed to a satisfying career, they may have less time and energy to devote to their marriage and family. If people have a high commitment to their marriage and their family, they will find time for both. It really depends on the person's commitment and values. Research indicates that there is no consistent differences in marital adjustment of male breadwinners versus dual career couples (Piotrowski, Rapport, & Rapport, 1987). It appears that marital satisfaction tends to be the highest when partners share similar gender-role expectations and when the wife's employment status matches her own expectations.

Parenthood and Career. What does research on maternal employment indicate? In general, the research indicates that maternal employment is not harmful to children (Etaugh, 1974). In fact, there is evidence that maternal employment can have *positive* effects on children. Some studies have found that children of working mothers seem to be more independent, self-reliant, and responsible than children of nonworking mothers. There seems to be a particular advantage for daughters of working mothers. They tend to perceive women as being very capable and independent individuals and thus perceive themselves as being very competent and successful. They tend to be more successful in their academic endeavors and tend to exhibit higher than average career aspirations (Hoffman, 1987).

One common problem of two-paycheck families is the division of housework and child care. Usually, employed wives do much more of the housework and child care than their employed husbands. As you might expect, men who are better educated or younger tend to be more helpful around the house. Surprisingly, however, the more children a couple has, the less likely they are to share equally in the household labor, even if both are working an equal number of hours outside the home (Haas, 1981). Thus, many employed mothers feel overworked and underappreciated. If a new mother quits her job to care for the children, she gives up an external source of self-esteem, social support, and status. However, most mothers who have left the work force believe that the sacrifices are worth it (O'Donnell, 1985).

Overall, research indicates that adults who combine all three roles—spouse, parent, and employee—are healthier and happier than those who do not (Baruch et al., 1983; Moos, 1986).

What other issues and concerns do married couples encounter as they strive to succeed in marriage?

What Do Most Couples Argue About? Is it sex, money, children, power, roles and responsibilities, jealousy, or extra-marital affairs? Money ranks as the single most common cause of conflict in marriage. Money not only influences a couple's lifestyle but also their feelings of security, self-esteem, confidence, and acceptance by others. Without money, families live in a constant state of stress, fearing the loss of jobs, illness, or household emergencies. Husbands tend to view themselves as poor providers, and their self-esteem may crumble as a result.

The fact that two human beings love each other does not guarantee they will be able to create a joyful and rewarding relationship. Their love does not ensure their maturity or wisdom; yet without these qualities their love is in jeopardy. Their love does not automatically teach communication skills or effective methods of conflict resolution, or the art of integrating their love into the rest of their existence. Their love does not produce self-esteem; it may reinforce it but it cannot create it; still without self-esteem love cannot survive.

Nathaniel Branden

Neither financial stability nor wealth can ensure marital satisfaction. Even when financial resources are plentiful, money can be a source of marital strain. Quarrels about how to spend money are common and potentially damaging at all income levels (Pittman & Lloyd, 1988). Couples that tend to be more satisfied with their marriage engage in more joint decisions regarding their finances in comparison to couples that eventually divorce.

Examine the last sentence and decide what underlies most problems in relationships—be it a marriage, a business relationship, or wherever two or more people interact.

Communication Problems. Successful communication is the cornerstone of any relationship. Such communication must be open, realistic, tactful, caring, and valued. Maintaining this kind of communication is not always easy unless all the people involved are committed to the belief that good communication is important to life and marital satisfaction. This sounds simple, yet couples in marital trouble almost always list failure to communicate as one of their major problems. Basically, communication failures occur because one or perhaps both partners choose not to communicate or because of the lack of communication skills. You may want to refer back to the communication chapter and apply the material discussed in that chapter to improve your communication skills.

Many couples get so involved in the activities of everyday life—their career, their family activities, and their outside interests—that they forget about the needs and interests of their spouse. Even though they spend time with their spouse, they really don't communicate. If this seems to be true of your relationship, you may want to change this by *scheduling a time to communicate*. Tell your mate that you would like to take him or her out to dinner every Thursday night, even if it is to a fast food restaurant, so you have a time to sit down and talk. This is your time, don't take the kids or anyone else. You may want to write down things you want to talk about during the week so you won't forget about them. Many times a person will get to the scheduled session and say, "there's something I want to talk about, but I forgot what it was." You may want to schedule a weekend away from the family every few months so you can talk and plan for the future.

Fighting Fairly. Many couples state that their basic problem is that they fight all the time. Yet rather than a problem, fighting is a normal part of a relationship. The problem is not whether one fights but how one fights. Fighting is simply a matter of communication and all the principles of good communication skills apply here (see chapter 7). If this is true of your relationship, you should learn to fight constructively and not destructively (Bach, 1971). Here are a few tips that might help:

Don't fight when you are emotionally upset:
- Slowly count to ten before saying what you may regret later.
- Take a walk around the block, exercise, or take a shower.

- If you can, you may want to sleep on it. Sleep can help relieve stress and frustration, and when you awaken you can look at the problem more logically. This works only if your mate understands and doesn't become more upset because you don't seem to be concerned and are just sleeping.

Don't call your partner names:
- This makes him or her more upset.

Be specific, state exactly what the problem is that is bothering you:
- Don't *beat around the bush,* the other person may not know what the problem really is—your partner is not a mind reader.

Don't bring up past faults, mistakes, and problems:
- We can't change the past.
- Discuss, only the immediate problem and what you are willing to do to solve the problem.

Fighting fairly and using problem-solving techniques will enhance any relationship and keep it alive and growing. Failure to communicate clearly and fight fairly will usually cause disruption and the ultimate failure of intimate relationships.

Family Violence. Physical violence is most apt to erupt in families lacking communication skills. Such families often can't talk to one another, don't listen to one another, and simply lack enough communication skills to make themselves understood. Children are often physically violent because they haven't learned how to communicate. In a way, adults who cannot communicate are like children and too often express themselves physically rather than verbally.

Family violence is difficult to measure and document, because most of it occurs in the privacy of the home, away from public view. Much of it also goes unreported. Family violence includes child abuse, violence between spouses, sibling abuse, sexual abuse, and parental abuse by children (especially to elderly parents).

It is estimated that one out of every twenty-eight American children under the age of 14 was reported as abused or neglected in 1986. That is more than a million reported cases a year. *Neglect* is actually the most common form of maltreatment as well as the most destructive, causing more deaths, injuries, and long-term problems than abuse (Wolock & Horowitz, 1984). Some instances of neglect are blatant and horrifying: infants who are allowed to starve or freeze to death are examples. Others are less obvious, involving infants whose parents rarely hold, talk, or play with them, or infants who are deliberately undernourished. Also, many childhood accidents (by far the greatest cause of childhood death and serious injury) can be traced to neglect.

The causes of family violence are many, including problems in the society (such as cultural attitudes toward women and children), in parents (such as drug addiction, alcoholism, and financial problems), and in the child (such as being a difficult child or being sickly). The most effective strategies should emphasize prevention and treatment rather than blame. In addition, any measures that help reduce stress and increase an individual's social support will make violence and abuse less likely. Remember, good communication skills underlie all good relationships.

It is actually easier than you think to avoid a violent or abusive relationship. Our problem is that we allow our emotions to take control of our behavior and not our common sense and intellect. Recent research has shown that in most relationships where violence has occurred some form of abuse began during the dating period. If a person is abusive while the couple is dating, what are the chances of the person *not* being abusive after marriage? Not very likely. A person does not change overnight or as soon as he or she signs a marriage license. To the contrary, some people feel that the marriage license is sign of ownership and they can now do whatever they want to their partner. If you are in an abusive relationship before marriage, you may want to think twice before making a serious commitment to that person.

Codependence. But, wait a minute, you know you can help your intended spouse. He or she needs your help and love, and you feel you can help your partner change. If you can get them to marry you it will be easier to help him or her change. This sounds like the beginning of a *codependent relationship*—one person has allowed another person's behavior (abuse, chemical addiction, and so on) to affect him or her and is obsessed with controlling that person's behavior (Beattie, 1987). It is natural to want to protect and help the people we care about. It is also natural to be affected by and react to the problems of people around us. As the problems become more serious and remain unresolved, we become more affected and react more intensely to them. Does this sound like anyone you know?

- Have you become so absorbed in other people's problems that you don't have time to identify or solve your own?
- Do you care so deeply about other people that you've forgotten how to care for yourself?
- Do you need to control events and people around you because you feel everything around and inside you is out of control?
- Do you feel responsible for so much because the people around you feel responsible for so little?

If you or any of your friends answer yes to the above questions, you may be codependent. Whatever problem the other person has, codependency involves a habitual system of thinking, feeling, and behaving toward ourselves and others that can cause us pain. Codependent behaviors or habits are self-destructive, not only to themselves, but also to all their relationships. Most codependents have been so busy responding to other people's problems that they haven't had time to identify, much less take care of, their own problems.

Can a codependent change? Yes, definitely. But as we have already learned, change is not easy, it takes a lot of work and effort on everyone's part. The first step toward change is awareness of the problem and the second step is acceptance. In order to become aware

---

Table 6.3
What is Codependency?

- My good feelings about who I am stem from being liked by you.
- My good feelings about who I am stem from receiving approval from you.
- Your struggles affect my serenity. My mental attitude focuses on solving your problems or relieving your pain.
- My mental attention is focused on pleasing you.
- My mental attention is focused on protecting you.
- My mental attention is focused on manipulating you "to do it my way."
- My self-esteem is bolstered by solving your problems.
- My self-esteem is bolstered by relieving your pain.
- My own hobbies and interests are put aside. My time is spent sharing your interests and hobbies.
- Your clothing and personal appearance is dictated by my desires, because I feel you are a reflection of me.
- Your behavior is dictated by my desires, because I feel you are a reflection of me.
- I am not aware of how I feel. I am aware of how you feel. I am not aware of what I want. I ask you what you want. If I am not aware, I assume.
- The dreams I have for my future are linked to you.
- My fear of rejection determines what I say and do.
- My fear of your anger determines what I say and do.
- I use giving as a way of feeling safe in our relationship.
- My social circle diminishes as I involve myself with you.
- I put my values aside in order to connect with you.
- I value your opinion and way of doing things more than my own.
- The quality of my life is in relation to the quality of yours.

---

of what codependence is we need to know what the characteristics of a codependent are. Table 6.3 will give you a summary of these characteristics.

Codependency is many things. It is a dependency on people—on their moods, behavior, sickness or well-being, and their love. It is a paradoxical dependency (Subby & Friel, 1984). Codependents appear to be depended upon, but they are dependent. They look strong but feel helpless. They appear controlling but in reality are controlled themselves, sometimes by a disorder such as alcoholism. If you find yourself in a codependent relationship, you may want to read some of the self-help books available at your local bookstores or seek professional help through the counseling office or mental health center near you.

During the courtship period and continuing throughout married life, there is an insecure feeling in many individuals when they fear the loss of affection of their partner, especially when they feel threatened by an outside source. That outside source may be a new baby, a new friend, or a new career. Let's take another look at Walt and Sarah.

Love is the only thing which gives value in life; it is the deepest, the greatest, the strongest reason for living.

Solar Frost

Walt has been working for a law firm for two years now and seems to be doing well. But the job is not as exciting as it originally was. Walt is not considering changing jobs, because he still knows that he could be a full partner within five years and that's been his goal for a long time.

On the other hand, Sarah just changed jobs and is extremely excited about the new challenges and the new friends she is getting to know. Sarah is beginning to spend more and more time at work and more time socially with her new friends. Occasionally, she has been working late with a male colleague to complete a major project.

Walt comes home after work and Sarah's still working. He's used to having her companionship in the evenings. Walt's beginning to question Sarah about her late evenings and the fact she seems to be so happy recently and excited about life. He seems to be bored with his job and not too happy with the world around him. Walt's becoming suspicious of Sarah and her friends. What's happening in this relationship?

What's the Green-Eyed Monster? Is Walt *jealous? Jealousy* is an emotion familiar to most of us, if not from direct experience, at least through the experience of friends, from novels, television and movies. *Romantic jealousy* carries the additional stress associated with the threat of losing an important relationship and often involves feelings of having been betrayed and perhaps deceived. Thus, this feeling of romantic jealousy provokes a host of negative feelings focused on the lover, the self, and the perceived rival, and it can be very destructive in a relationship.

Some people are more prone to get jealous than others. It appears that this jealous-prone disposition is primarily a function of poor self-esteem, feelings of insecurity about the one's self-worth, or less commitment from one partner (as when couples cohabitate instead of marry). After experiencing a jealousy-provoking situation, people feel even more insecure, unattractive, and dependent, making future jealous reactions even more likely (Radecki-Bush, Bush, & Jennings, 1988). One study indicated that single and divorced people were more likely than married ones to experience jealousy and to act on that feeling by calling lovers unexpectedly, listening in on their phone calls, and looking through their belongings (Salovey & Rodin, 1985).

Overcoming jealousy is not easy. Anything we can do toward becoming confident, secure individuals will help us cope with our own jealousy. We can try to learn what is making us jealous. What exactly are we feeling and why are we feeling that way? We can try to keep our jealous feelings in perspective. We can also negotiate with our partner to change certain behaviors that seem to trigger our jealousy. Negotiations assume that we too are working to reduce our own unwarranted jealousy. Choosing partners who are reassuring and loving

Jealousy is not a barometer by which the depth of love may be read. It merely records the degree of insecurity. It is a negative, miserable state of feelings, having its origin in a sense of insecurity and inferiority.

Margaret Mead

will also help reduce our irrational jealousies. Unfortunately, it is not as easy as it sounds to follow this advice, because jealousy is so often irrational, emotional, and unreasonable, and, at the moment, all too often uncontrollable. It remains one of the puzzling components of love relationships.

During the last year of Walt's and Sarah's marriage, we find that Walt has been spending a lot of his spare time working on their computer, playing games and learning new programs. Sarah doesn't like to spend her time playing with some "dumb" computer when she could be exercising or interacting with people. When they first got married, Walt and Sarah seem to have a lot in common—tennis, history, same friends and same goals—but now they seem to be growing apart. Sarah has her new job and new friends, and Walt doesn't seem to be interested in either. All he seems to be interested in is his computer and watching sports on television.

GROWING APART

Relationship evolve and people evolve, but not always in the same direction. It is important that spouses allow each other room for personal growth. We need to recognize that it is unrealistic to expect one's partner to remain exactly the same forever. We all need personal time for the activities and hobbies that we enjoy that may not be of interest to our spouse. But at the same time, it is important to strive to maintain joint activities as well. Remember, there is a strong correlation between marital satisfaction and the amount of activities the two people have in common, especially leisure activities.

WHEN WE WERE IN LOVE

Once upon a long ago when we were so in love,
    It seemed we'd never be apart, we're meant like hand in glove.
But years play tricks upon the young, and suddenly we're old,
    And though we love each other still, the fires of youth are cold.
The loving patience that we had is now in short supply,
    And keeping peace between us now is something we don't try.
The secret conversations we would have when night was deep,
    All about our hopes and dreams; and love instead of sleep.
We used to give each other comfort, sweet when we were sad,
    And face the world as man and wife; together things weren't bad.
But now our secret selves are hidden far away inside,
    Our little world of lovers young has withered up and died.
And though I'll love you always dear, it's not the same to me,
    Through all the lonely years ahead, apart we'll have to be.

Anonymous

There comes a time in some relationships when no matter how sincere the attempt to reconcile the differences or how strong the wish to recreate a part of the past once shared, the struggle becomes so painful that nothing else is felt and the world and all its beauty only add to the discomfort by providing cruel contrast.

David Viscott

In Happiness and in Good Health, Till Divorce Do Us Part. Is this how the new marriage vows should read? As most of you know, the number of divorces have increased rapidly over the last twenty years. Married adults are now divorcing two and one-half times as often as adults did twenty years ago, and four times as often as fifty years ago. In fact, for every two American marriages that occurred in 1985, there was approximately one divorce. In the United States half of all divorces occur within the first seven years of marriage (Fisher, 1987). Is this what people are referring to when they say the "seven year itch?"

What accounts for the rise in the divorce rate over the past few years? One major factor, clearly, is that spouses today expect a great deal more from each other than spouses in the past. In earlier decades, earning the money was considered the man's responsibility; and housework and child care, the woman's. In addition, husbands and wives in the past usually did not expect to really understand each other: they generally assumed that masculinity and femininity are opposites, and that the sexes therefore are naturally a mystery to each other.

Today, marriage partners have a much more flexible view of marriage roles and responsibilities and are likely to expect each other to be a friend, lover, and confidant as well as wage-earner and caregiver.

Walt and Sarah have been married for eight years now. Walt believes in the "traditional" type of marriage, where there are male and female roles. Sarah believes in the "equalitarian" type marriage, where the responsibilities are shared equally. As you can see, there is beginning to be a lot of conflict within this relationship. Walt and Sarah no longer seem to have much in common. Sarah has tried to talk to Walt about their problems, but Walt doesn't want to talk about it. He thinks everything is "okay." She's just a complainer.

Sarah decides that it's not worth trying anymore and files for divorce. Walt gets very upset and feels depressed, because he feels that they can save the marriage. He says he will do anything to keep the relationship together, but Sarah says it's too late. Can this marriage be saved?

The Impact of Divorce. The dissolution of a marriage tends to be a very emotional and traumatic event for most people (see Table 6.4). Divorced men suffer primarily from loss of emotional support and disrupted social ties to friends and relatives. In comparison, divorced women suffer most from reduced income. There is evidence that people who are currently divorced are significantly less happy than those who are currently married (Weingarten, 1985). A nationwide survey revealed that divorce can impair an individual's well-being for at least five years after the event, producing a greater variety of long-lasting negative feelings than even the death of a spouse (Nock, 1981).

Table 6.4
Steps in Divorce Grief

---

1. Relief—moment of no more fussing.
2. Shock and surprise—I can't believe this is happening to me.
3. Emotional release—How much should I let people see my feelings and how long will I keep crying?
4. Physical distress and anxiety—Will I lose my friends?
5. Panic—There is something wrong with me; I can't eat or I eat all the time.
6. Guilt—Two basic emotions in divorce:
   a. guilt—what did I do wrong?
   b. rejection—I am not capable of being loved.
7. Hostility and projection—I know we are both angry but we are going to end this divorce in a friendly manner.
8. Lassitude—suffering in silence, hard to get anything done.
9. Healing—gradual overcoming of grief and getting on with reality.

The first emotional impact of divorce is often that the former spouses become even angrier and more bitter with each other than they were in the marriage. This increased hostility is often followed by, or interspersed with, periods of depression and disequilibrium, as patterns of eating and sleeping, drug and alcohol use, and work and residence change (Kelly, 1982). It is most likely to be the wife who first finds fault with the marriage and files for divorce. In fact, many men are surprised and shocked by the break, and in the short term, divorce is more devastating to the man than the woman. Over the long term, however, women are more affected, primarily because they are likely to have less money and fewer marriage prospects than divorced men. If they are mothers with custody rights, the impact of divorce is particularly strong.

Divorce may have more of an impact on the children than anyone else. The children have no control in this relationship; they are helpless in this situation. Whatever the kids say or do will not benefit the situation; generally, no one will listen anyway. Evidence suggest that in the long run it is less damaging to the children if unhappy parents divorce than if the children grow up intact but in a dissension-ridden home (Demo & Acock, 1988). The children's recovery and subsequent adjustment seem to depend primarily on the quality of their relationship with the custodial parent and how well the custodial parent is adjusting to the divorce (Stolberg, Camplair, Currier, & Wells, 1987). What about remarriage? Generally, the adjustment is easier if both ex-spouses either remarry or stay single than if one does.

Relationships seldom die because they suddenly have no life left in them; they wither slowly, either because people do not understand how much or what kind of upkeep, time, work, love, and caring they require or because people are too lazy or afraid to try. A relationship is a living thing. It needs and benefits from the same attention to detail that an artist lavishes on his art.

David Viscott

Remarriage. Almost 80 percent of divorced people remarry, on the average within three years of being divorced. Remarriage is more likely to occur if the divorced person is relatively young, because there seem to be more potential partners still available. There is no guarantee that marriage will be better the second time around: The divorce rate for remarriages is higher than for first marriages. It may be that some lonely divorced people marry too quickly, as they say, "on the rebound." Stepchildren can also be a disruptive factor. The divorce rate for remarriages involving stepchildren is 7 percent higher than for childless remarriages within the first three years after marriage (White & Booth, 1985).

Stepfamilies. An increasing number of remarriages now involve children. Remarriages involving children pose special demands on both the adults as well as the children. In addition to learning how to live with one new person, which can be difficult enough for most people, one or both partners must also become accustomed to a ready made family. When the children are young, the stepparent has more opportunity to develop rapport and trust with the children. But when there are adolescents involved, it's more difficult for everyone involved. If the father too quickly assumes the authority as a parent, especially in matters of discipline, the stepchildren may resent it. Both parents must make allowances for their stepchildren's initial suspiciousness, jealousy, and resistance. One of the problems is that there are no rules or guidelines to assist stepparents in the process of building a happy blended family. When both parents develop a good working relationship, talk things out, and cooperate on discipline and household chores, the blended family may do at least as well as intact families.

As we have previously noted, the traditional model of marriage has been undermined by many different changes within our culture. More and more people are selecting alternatives to marriage. Earlier in the chapter we discussed two alternatives, single life and cohabitation. Another alternative exists.

Gay Relationships. Statistics indicate that there may be as many as 25 million gay people in the United States. Roughly 2 percent of the women and 4–5 percent of the men are exclusively homosexual (Van Wyk & Geist, 1984).

The dynamics of a gay relationship don't seem to be any different than those in a heterosexual relationship. They are similar in terms of the forces that bring couples together, the factors that predict satisfaction with the relationship, and the problems couples face. Most of the material already discussed is relevant to gay couples.

The major problem that most gays encounter is the negative attitude about homosexuality in our society, especially now with people's attitude about AIDS. Most homosexual men and nearly all homosexual women prefer stable, long-term relationships. Promiscuity among gay men is clearly on the decline. Lesbian relationships are generally sexually exclusive. Gay relationships are characterized by great diversity. It is not true that gays usually assume traditional masculine and feminine roles. Both gays and heterosexual cohabitants may face opposition to their relationship from their families and from society in general, and neither enjoys the legal and social sanctions of marriage.

The traditional model of marriage is being challenged by the increasing acceptability of additional alternatives. There are many more alternatives available to us now than we have had in the past. Some are considered acceptable to society, and others are considered nontraditional or even unacceptable. Society and cultures change and evolve over time, not always for the best, but who are we to judge others before we look into ourselves and accept ourselves as we really are.

A LAST THOUGHT

We are all social beings and seek social relationships. We all have a need for other people. Relationships satisfy needs. We are motivated not only to seek the company of others but to form close and lasting relationships. The relationships you have are your greatest assets. We all need to find ways to preserve the relationships we have and develop new ones. Friendships grow into intimate relationships, and the will to please and the willingness to learn go a long way toward building a close, intimate feeling among people.

"I do" will get you into marriage, but "I will" may keep you there. *Willingness* is the key to a happy union, no matter what type of relationship you are involved in. The experts say: a willingness to commit, to appreciate, to allow for each other's differences, and to work at the relationship.

Intimacy doesn't exist if you can't *talk* about what's important to you with your partner. Intimacy means being vulnerable, knowing that your dreams and your fears will be heard and supported rather than used against you. Interpret all conflict as growth trying to happen.

"Real love" is loving what is real in your partner rather than what is desired. "Mature love" is being committed to the emotional and spiritual welfare of your partner as you are your own. Self-knowledge and self-esteem are vital to a satisfying relationship. A relationship is only as healthy as the people involved.

CHAPTER DISCUSSION QUESTIONS

1. Why do we need friends?
2. What is your definition of a good friend? Explain what a good friend is.
3. If you knew someone who was new to town, what would you recommend they do to find new friends?
4. Friendships satisfy needs. Study three relationships (friendships) that you currently have. What needs are they satisfying for you? Explain.
5. What is your definition of love? How do you know you're in love?
6. What are the pro's and con's of cohabitation vs. marriage? Explain.
7. What are your experiences with jealousy? How should a person deal with a jealous lover?
8. Explain the role (job) of the male and the role (job) of the female in a married relationship. Are these roles different from how your parents viewed the role of within their marriage? Explain.
9. What direct or indirect impact has divorce had on your life?

KEY TERMS

friend
similarity
personality fit
love
commitment
marriage
role expectation
parenthood
codependent
divorce
stepfamilies
gay relationship

singlehood
opposites attract
reciprocity
lust
intimacy
cohabitation
honeymoon period
communication
jealousy
remarriage
blended families
psychological reactance

REFERENCES

Block, J. D. (1980). *Friendship: How to Give It; How to Get It.* New York: Macmillan.

Demo, D. H., and Acock, A. C. (1988). "The Impact of Divorce on Children." *Journal of Marriage and the Family,* 50, 619–648.

Etaugh, C. F. (1974). "Effects of Maternal Employment on Children: A Review of Recent Research." *Merrill-Palmer Quarterly,* 20, 71–98.

Fowers, B. J., and Olson, D. H. (1989). "ENRICH Marital Inventory: A Discriminant Validity and Cross-Validation Assessment." *Journal of Marital and Family Therapy,* 15(1), 65–79.

Glenn, Norval D., and Weaver, Charles N. (1978). "The Marital Happiness of Remarried Divorced Persons." *Journal of Marriage and the Family,* 48, 737–748.

Haas, Linda. (1981). "Domestic Role Sharing in Sweden." *Journal jMarriage and the Family,* 43, 957–976.

Hoffman, L. (1987). "The Effects on Children of Maternal and Paternal Employment," in N. Gerstel and H. Gross (Eds.), *Families and Work.* Philadelphia: Temple University Press.

Kelly, Joan Berlin. (1982). "Divorce: The Adult Perspective," in Benjamin B. Wolman (Ed.), *Handbook of Developmental Psychology.* Englewood Cliffs, NJ: Prentice-Hall.

Nock, Steven L. (1981). "Family Life Transitions: Longitudinal Effects on Family Members." *Journal of Marriage and the Family,* 43, 703–714.

O'Donnell, Lydia N. (1985). *The Unheralded Majority: Contemporary Women as Mothers.* Lexington, MA: Heath.

Peplau, Letitia, and Gordon, S. L. (1985). "Women and Men in Love: Sex Differences in Close Heterosexual Relationships, in Virginia O'Leary, Rhosa K. Unger, and Barbara S. Wallston (Eds.), *Women, Gender, and Social Psychology.* Hillsdale, NJ: Erlbaum.

Piotrkowski, C. S., Rapoport, R. N., and Rapoport, R. (1987). "Families and Work." In M. B. Sussman and S. K. Steinmetz (Eds.) *Handbook of Marriage and the Family.* New York: Plenum Press.

Pittman, J. F., and Lloyd, S. A. (1988). Quality of Family Life, Social Support, and Stress. *Journal of Marriage and the Family,* 50, 53–67.

Radecki-Bush, C., Bush, J. P., and Jennings, J. (1988). "Effects of Jealousy Threats on Relationship Perceptions and Emotions. *Journal of Social and Personal Relationships,* 5, 285–303.

Raschke, H. J. (1987). Divorce. In M. B. Sussman and S. K. Steinmetz (Eds.), *Handbook of Marriage and the Family.* New York: Plenum Press.

Salovey, P., and Rodin, J. (1986). "The Differentiation of Social-Comparison Jealousy and Romantic Jealousy." *Journal of Personality and Social Psychology,* 50, 1100–1112.

Sabatelli, R. M. (1988). "Exploring Relationship Satisfaction: A Social Exchange Perspective on the Interdependence Between Theory, Research, and Practice. *Family Relations,* 37, 217–222.

Sternberg, Robert J. (1986). "A Triangular Theory of Love." *Psychological Review,* 93, 119–135.

Stolberg, A. L.; Camplair, C.; Currier, K.; and Wells, M. J. (1987). "Individual, Familial and Environmental Determinants of Children's Post-Divorce Adjustment and Maladjustment." *Journal of Divorce,* 11, 51–70.

Teachman, J. D.; Polonko, K. A.; and Scanzoni, J. (1987). "Demography of the Family," in M. B. Sussman and S. K. Steinmetz (Eds.), *Handbook of Marriage and the Family.* New York: Plenum Press.

Weingarten, H. R. (1985). "Marital Status and Well-Being: A National Study Comparing First-Married, Currently Divorced, and Remarried Adults." *Journal of Marriage and the Family,* 47, 653–662.

Wolock, Isabel, and Horowitz, Bernard. (1984). "Child Maltreatment as a Social Problem: The Neglect of Neglect." *American Journal of Orthopsychiatry,* 54, 530–543.

ROLES AND EXPECTATIONS

Purpose: To discover the roles and expectations people have of themselves and other people in specific categories such as a spouse, parent, student, breadwinner, male, and female.

Instructions:

   I. Divide into groups of approximately six individuals (three females and three males would be ideal).
  II. Discuss the following:
     1. What career have each of you chosen for yourself?
       a. What type of career is selected by the females; by the males?
       b. Are the careers sex-role oriented?
     2. What roles do you expect to play at home? Specify the tasks you are willing or not willing to do.
     3. What role will you take as a parent (full-time parent, half-time, change diapers, and so on)
     4. What role will you take as a breadwinner?
 III. After about twenty minutes, return to a large class setting to discuss the following.

DISCUSSION

1. Do you see evidence that today's college students subscribe to traditional sex roles or that they are free of such barriers to independent choice? Give examples.

2. What messages did you receive as you were growing up regarding specific expectations or behaviors appropriate to your gender?

3. How do you feel that your life would be different, if at all, if you were a member of the opposite sex?

4. How will you relate to your son regarding sex-role development? What about your daughter?

5. How can we change people's attitudes about role expectations?

6. How does the self-fulfilling prophecy affect role expectations?

PERSONAL ADS

Purpose: To gain a better understanding of yourself through introspection; to get a better understanding of what you want in a date; to perceive yourself as others view you.

Instructions: This could be a fun and interesting project. Personal ads are no longer relegated to underground newspapers and sex magazines. Today they are a booming business and run in over 100 newspapers and magazines. Personal ads have become a popular and reputable way of meeting people in our mobile and urban society.

Composing an ad with one's self as the product is in itself an interesting exercise, requiring a blend of self-confidence and humor.

1. Describe yourself—write down your physical characteristics, hobbies, interests, and beliefs.
2. Describe the characteristics you would like your date to have—physical characteristics, interests, beliefs, and hobbies.

   For example: Divorced black female (DBF) in her thirties; interested in hiking, skiing, reading, dancing, the beach and just having a good time; seeks a black male (BM) 28–35 for companionship; attractive, not too heavy, not too tall, interested in outdoor activities and country western music. Must be sincere.

This project may be done in small groups, or with the total class. Individually, the student may write the ad. Make sure all the students use the same type of paper. Form a small group, mix the ads up, have someone select an ad and read it and discuss. The students may want to see whether they can identify which person wrote the ad. This may be a good way to discover if the other students perceive you the way you perceive yourself.

DISCUSSION

1. How did most people describe themselves: by physical characteristics, interests, or attitudes?

2. What were most people looking for in a date: attractiveness, similar interests, or satisfaction of needs?

3. Why do you think most people advertise? Is it because they're lonely, because it's a quicker way of screening your dates, or because they're weird?

4. Can you believe what most people are saying about themselves?

5. Should a person advertise? What are the advantages and disadvantages?

6. Have you or anyone you know advertised? What were the results?

RELATIONSHIP SURVEY

Purpose: To develop an understanding of people's perception of different aspects of a relationship.

Instructions: This activity may be done in groups or as an individual project. The class should decide on the questions to be asked. As a group activity—divide the class into groups of no more than four per group. Each member of the group is assigned a different question, such as What is a friend? What is love? Should a couple live together before marriage? What are the advantages and disadvantages of cohabiting? (one member in each group should have similar questions). If there are four members in each group, you need at least four different questions. If your class has five groups of four people each, five members from the class will be asking the same question. Each group member will ask at least five different people the questions to be answered. The questions should be related to material in this chapter. You may want to publish your results or send them to the school newspaper.

After the survey is completed, each group should discuss the answers to each of the questions. Afterward have the total class discuss each question.

DISCUSSION

1. Were the general survey results similar to the responses you received? How were they similar and different?

2. Write down your answer to the question/s here prior to doing the survey.

3. What questions would you like to ask next time?

4. Were your answers similar or different? Explain.

5. What did you learn from this activity?

MATE SELECTION

Purpose: To identify the characteristics that are most important to you in selecting the person you wish to marry.

Instructions:

I. Rate each of the following factors according to their importance to you in selecting the person you would wish to marry (#1 = most important characteristic, #18 = least important characteristic).

Intelligence
Emotional stability and maturity
Good financial prospects
Similar educational background
Social ability (friendly)
Similar religious background
Desire for children
Refinement
Mutual love and attraction

Good looks
Ambition and industriousness
Dependable character
Good health
Similar political backgrounds
Pleasing disposition
Neatness
Chastity
Favorable social status or rating

II. List characteristics according to importance to you.

1. _____
2. _____
3. _____
4. _____
5. _____
6. _____
7. _____
8. _____
9. _____

10. _____
11. _____
12. _____
13. _____
14. _____
15. _____
16. _____
17. _____
18. _____

III. Divide into groups of three to four people. Discuss the following questions.

DISCUSSION

1. How do the top four characteristics on your list differ from the other members of your group?

2. Discuss why you think your top four characteristics are important to you.

3. After discussing these characteristics with the group, would you change the order of your list? Why?

WHY PEOPLE GET DIVORCED—WHY PEOPLE STAY MARRIED

Purpose: To better understand why people divorce and what it requires to choose to remain married.
To get a better understanding of why people stay married.
To discover if unmarried individuals perceive the reasons for divorce differently than divorced individuals.
To discover whether unmarried, married, and divorced individuals have similar perceptions of why people stay married.

Instructions:

   I. Interview four to six people who have been divorced, four to six people who have never been married, and four to six people who are married to find out why they feel divorce generally occurs.
  II. Ask them what they would consider the major reason (in order of importance) for the high divorce rate in this country. (Ask the divorced individuals to make this judgment based on their own experiences.)
 III. Ask them what they would consider the major reasons (in order of importance) for staying married.
  IV. Divide into small groups or have large class discussion.

DISCUSSION

1. Do any people consider unrealistic romantic expectations to be a contributing factor for getting divorced? If so, what are they?

2. Do the divorced and the never-married people respond differently? If so, how would you characterize these differences? If not, why do you think people agree on the basic causes even when they have had very different experiences?

3. What seems to be the major reasons for divorce?

4. What seems to be the major reasons for staying married?

5. What could we do to prevent the high number of divorces in our society?

DISCUSSION

1. Did the exercise stimulate your thinking about yourself, your interpersonal style, and your relationships to your fellow group members? Why or why not?

2. Instructors might want to ask each group member to use the questions in the categories above and write a two-page description of their present interpersonal style. This could be shared with the members of the group.

LEARNING JOURNAL FOR BECOMING INTIMATE

Select the statement below that best defines your feelings about the personal value or meaning gained from this chapter and respond below the dotted line.

I LEARNED THAT I

I REALIZED THAT I

I DISCOVERED THAT I

I WAS SURPRISED THAT I

I WAS PLEASED THAT I

I WAS DISPLEASED THAT I

....

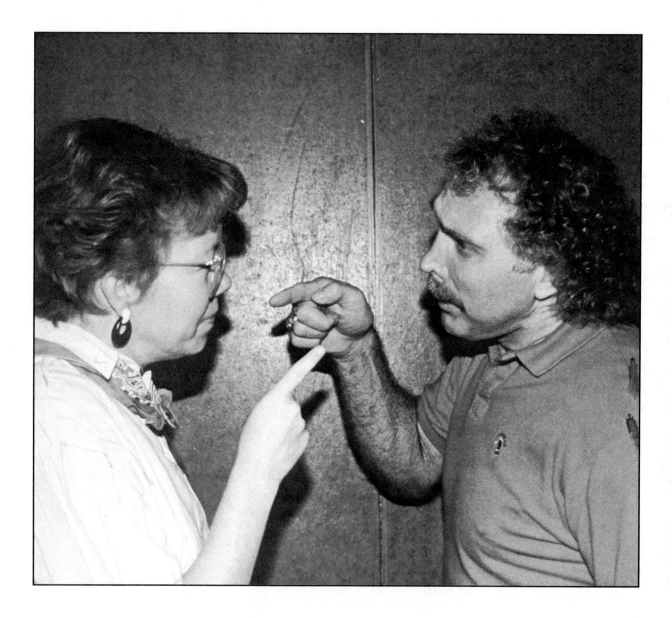

Resolving Interpersonal Conflict

Arguments
Remind me
Of hot grease
In a skillet.

I can't
Control
Where it
Will pop next;

And if I don't
Stand back
Or turn the
Fire down.

I'll get
All splattered
And
Burned.

Delyn Dendy Harrison
Some Things Are Better Said in Black and White.
(Fort Worth, TX : Branch Smith, Inc., 1978)
*Used with permission.

Have you ever found yourself in one of the following situations?

- *You and your spouse seem to be in constant disagreement. Can this marriage be saved?*
- *Your parents have really been yelling at you. They don't understand you, and you don't understand them.*
- *You and your roommate can't seem to divide the chores equally. Is there any hope for this living arrangement?*
- *You and your best friend had a major argument. You left mad and hurt.*
- *You and your co-workers have been squabbling and productivity is down. The boss is really angry.*

Actually, the list could go on and on, but the fact is clear: when two or more people live or work closely together, for any length of time, a degree of conflict will be generated. Furthermore, the greater the emotional involvement and day-to-day sharing, the greater the potential for conflict. Although it is impossible to eliminate conflict, there are ways to manage it effectively. There is *hope* for healthier, stronger, and more satisfying relationships.

WHAT IS CONFLICT?

Little things often become the major irritants of life.

Robert Bolton

The word *conflict* comes from the Latin roots *com* meaning "together," and *figere* meaning to "strike." Common synonyms of conflict emphasize words like "struggle," "fight," "clash," and "sharp disagreements." Using these thoughts, Joyce Frost and William Wilmot (1985) provide an interesting definition of conflict. Their idea is that conflict is an expressed struggle between at least two people who perceive the situation differently and are experiencing interference from the other person in achieving their goals. Ross Stagner (1967) adds some different insights: Conflict is a situation in which two or more humans desire goals which they perceive as being attainable by one or the other, but not by both.

What causes these struggles, interferences, and perceptions?

WHAT CAUSES CONFLICT?

Conflicts occur between people because people are different, think differently, and have different needs and wants. In fact, Deutsch (1973) believes that conflicts usually involve any of six basic types of issues: *(1) control over resources, (2) preferences and nuisances, (3) values, (4) beliefs, (5) goals, and (6) the nature of the relationship between the partners.*

Perhaps the key word is *differentness,* because this is what causes conflict in human relationships. Differentness is a reality to reckon with, and the reality is that people enter relationships with differences in socioeconomic and cultural backgrounds, sex-role expectations, levels of self-esteem, ability to tolerate stress, tastes and preferences, beliefs and values, interests, social and family networks, and capacity to change and grow (Deutsch, 1973). Add to these differences that many people are deficient in communication and interpersonal skills, really may not want to cooperate, and have a lack of basic conflict resolution skills. Therefore, it is easy to understand why *differentness* leads to disagreement and conflict.

THE REALITIES OF CONFLICT

Even though conflict is inevitable, it can have positive as well as negative effects. Thomas Gordan (1975), noted author and psychologist, explains this clearly:

A conflict is the moment of truth in a relationship—a test of its health, a crisis that can weaken or strengthen it, a critical event that may bring lasting resentment, smoldering hostility, psychological scars. Conflicts can push people away from each other or pull them into a closer and more intimate union; they contain the seeds of destruction and the seeds of greater unity; they may bring about armed warfare or deeper mutual understanding.

However, in our society conflict is viewed negatively: it is "bad" to show anger, to disagree or to fight. Some people look at conflict as something to avoid at all costs; but conflict is not necessarily bad—it exists as a reality of any relationship.

It would be a rare relationship if over a period of time one person's needs did not conflict with the other's needs. As a matter of fact, a relationship with no apparent conflict may be unhealthier than one with frequent conflict. A good example is a marriage in which the wife is always passive and submissive to a dominating husband. The couple might boast that they never have any serious disagreements, but does this really mean the relationship is healthy? How about a work environment where the message from the boss is, "Do as I say or get out." Are the workers happy in this environment? Is productivity what it could be? Is this a healthy work relationship? What about a parent-child relationship in which the child is so frightened of his parent that he does not feel he can cross him in any way? This frequently exists in families where the message is clear: Children are to be seen and not heard. Is this relationship healthy, and does it teach children how to deal with conflicts in the *real world?*

Positive outcomes can be achieved from constructive resolution of conflicts. We will discuss three common benefits of constructive conflict resolution.

Most families today need more honest conflict and less suppression of feeling.

Gibson Winter

POSITIVE EFFECTS OF CONFLICT

Promotes Growth in a Relationship. People who work through their conflicts can develop a stronger and more intimate relationship. They take the time to learn about each other's needs and how they can be satisfied. They take the time to clarify their feelings. They take the time to share, and in so doing, realize that dealing with problems can be an opportunity to know each other better.

Allows for Healthy Release of Feelings. When conflicts are resolved in constructive ways, both parties are able to air their feelings and leave the situation free of anger and hostility. For example, in a family conflict, unresolved anger and hostility can affect a person's performance at work or school. Likewise, unresolved anger and hostility in a work-related conflict is frequently brought home and may interfere with family and even social relationships. Talking things out and sharing what is going on are marvelous ways to relieve tension and anxiety.

Increases Motivation and Self-Esteem. When you have been able to resolve a personal conflict or make a difficult decision, you naturally feel stronger and more motivated to tackle other struggles and difficult times. There is a real sense of pride and freedom when you join others and show respect for your rights and the rights of others. As a result, self-esteem is enhanced, and you are more motivated to take other interpersonal risks.

We have seen that constructive conflict resolution can result in positive outcomes. However, conflict can be destructive and result in negative outcomes, too.

A quarrel between friends, when made up, adds a new tie to friendship, as experience shows that the callosity formed round a broken bone makes it stronger than before.

St. Francis De Salis

NEGATIVE EFFECTS OF CONFLICT

How we view conflicts and how we manage them can cause destructive outcomes. Two negative effects are:

The Manner in Which We Approach Interpersonal Conflict. People generally view conflict with a belief that there must be a winner and a loser. It is human nature to want to win, just like it is human nature to not want to lose. However, when people approach a conflict situation with attitudes of winning and losing, a "tug of war" is often proclaimed. The net result is often one of disaster.

Larger Problems and Deeper Personal Resentments May Occur. Just because you avoid a conflict or fail to resolve a conflict doesn't mean the conflict is forever gone. It is likely to return again with much greater intensity. You may be less willing to cooperate if you have leftover anger or "bad" feelings from a previous confrontation. Failure to deal with conflict constructively can even "rob" you of a potentially satisfying relationship.

So far, we have been discussing the positive and negative realities of conflict. The question now is: How can we manage conflict in such a way as to minimize the risks and maximize the benefits? We will start by examining the make-up of a conflict situation. Perhaps we can then determine why some conflicts don't get resolved.

WHAT'S INVOLVED IN A CONFLICT SITUATION?

In order to resolve conflict, we must recognize that there are three elements to a conflict situation: *self, other,* and the *issue.* (It should be noted here that the terms *self* and *other* also mean individual or groups.) Any interpersonal conflict can be diagrammed like this:

Conflict Situation

Figure 7.1.

Dealing with Self, Other Person, and the Issue. As we discover ourselves in a conflict, *we* are inside the circle of the situation with the *other person* and the *issue.* If the conflict is to be resolved constructively, all of these elements must be dealt with congruently. If any element is removed, the conflict cannot be resolved. According to Virginia Satir (1972), our tendency is to:

1. *Placate or conceal our own feelings* by saying statements like, "Yes, it was all my fault, I am sorry, forgive me." The *placater* tends to talk in an insinuating way, trying to please and apologize

Our marriage used to suffer from arguments that were too short. Now, we argue long enough to find out what the argument is about.

Hugh Prather

at the same time. When we do this, we remove the "*self*" from the conflict, leaving the "*issue*" and the "*other person.*" The situation then looks like this:

Conflict Situation

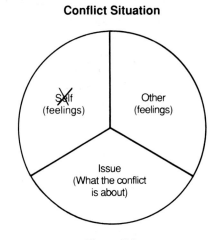

Figure 7.2.

2. ***Blame the other person*** by saying, "This is all your fault—can't you see where you messed up!" "You never do anything right!" The blamer is a fault-finder, a dictator, and a boss. When we do this, we remove the "*other person*" from the conflict, leaving the "*self*" and the "*issue.*" The diagram now changes to this:

Conflict Situation

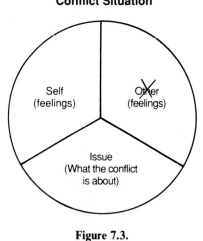

Figure 7.3.

3. ***Hold the issue irrelevant*** by saying, "Oh, you haven't got any problem; I've had worse than this many times." This is frequently referred to as the *distractor,* with the goal being to respond in an irrelevant way to what anyone else is saying or doing. This removes the "*issue*" and "*both persons.*" The conflict situation now looks like this:

Figure 7.4.

4. ***Be ultra reasonable and even appeal to higher authority*** by saying, "Do what you know is right. The Bible says . . . God would have you. . . ." This is referred to as the *computer,* being very correct and logical, with no semblance of any feeling showing. This tends to remove "*both persons*" involved in the conflict, leaving only the "*issue.*" The conflict then looks like this:

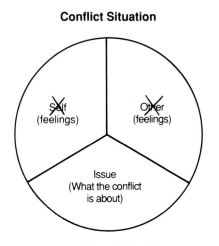

Figure 7.5.

THE DIMENSIONS OF CONFLICT

From our previous discussion, it would be logical to conclude that there are two main dimensions of any conflict situation. We will refer to these as the *emotional* or *feeling* dimension and the *issue* dimension. If conflicts don't get resolved because we sometimes disregard the feelings of the people involved, as well as the issue involved, then there must be three important questions for us to answer.

First, how can we deal with the feelings of anger, distrust, defensiveness, resentment, fear, and rejection, which are often a part of a conflict situation?

Second, how can we deal with the issues of conflicting needs, preferences, values, and beliefs?

Third, do we deal with the issue dimension or the feeling dimension first?

THE EMOTIONS (FEELINGS) HAVE PRIORITY

It is sometimes difficult to separate the feeling dimension from the issue dimension. They frequently interact with each other. Issue conflict often generates emotional conflict—anger, resentment, and so on. Emotional conflicts multiply the issues into additional differences over needs, goals, values, and beliefs.

Although it is vitally important to examine the tangible issues, most authorities agree that rational problem solving should usually be the second step.

While my emotions are throbbing with these fears, angers, and self-defensive urges, I am in no condition to have an open-minded, honest and loving discussion with you or with anyone else. I will need . . . emotional clearance and ventilation . . . before I will be ready for this discussion.

John Powell

Robert Bolton (1979), author and communication's consultant, offers this advice: *When feelings run high, rational problem solving needs to be preceded by a structured exchange of the emotional aspects of the controversy.* George Odiorne (1974), a management consultant, confirms this thought: *When a person is emotionally equipped for a brawl, he's very poorly equipped to get a problem solved.*

Let's look first at how we can deal effectively with the emotional content. Then, we will discuss the different behavior styles and approaches used in conflict resolution. The chapter will be concluded with how to deal with the important tangible issues—referred to as *collaborative problem solving,* or the *win-win* approach to conflict resolution.

DEALING WITH THE EMOTIONAL DIMENSION

In order to deal with the emotional content of any conflict, Bolton (1979) believes it is important to remember the following rules of conflict resolution. You will recall that some of these principles were also discussed in Chapter 5.

Rule 1: Treat the Other Person with Respect. You convey respect or lack of respect by:

1. the way you look at the other person—do you approve or disapprove with various facial gestures?
2. the way you listen to the other person—do you maintain eye contact? do you appear bored with the conversation?
3. tone of voice used—do you speak in a harsh, loud tone?
4. selection of words—do you "put down" the other person?

Rule 2: Listen Until You Experience the Other Side. This can best be achieved by remembering Carl Rogers' (1961) communication rule: *Each person can speak up for himself only after he has first restated the ideas and feelings of the previous speaker accurately and to that speaker's satisfaction.* This means we try to understand the content of what the other person is saying, what the meaning is for him, and the feelings he has about it. It also means we actually try to step into the other person's shoes and look at the situation from his point of view.

We do not understand an opposing idea until we have so exposed ourselves to it that we feel the pull of its persuasion.

Dr. Richard Cabot

Rule 3: State Your Views, Needs, and Feelings. After you have demonstrated respect for the other person and conveyed your understanding of his or her feelings and point of view, it is then time to express your feelings to the other person. This means you: (1) keep your message short, (2) avoid loaded words that may hurt or harm others, and (3) be honest and state the truth as it really is for you.

Do *you* deal with the emotional content as suggested above? When faced with a conflict, how do *you* handle it?

WHAT IS YOUR STYLE OF CONFLICT MANAGEMENT?

You are probably thinking that your style of conflict management depends on the conflict and who is involved. Although that is probably true, most people have developed a characteristic style of managing conflicts. This style has emerged from our unique personality traits, as well as from what we learned growing up.

Think for a moment about how your parents managed conflicts. If your mother cried, sulked, or avoided confrontations, you may find yourself imitating her behavior. If your father yelled, intimidated, and dominated others with his anger, you may see some of these traits in your own pattern of conflict management. The question then is: How is your style of conflict management like and unlike those of your parents?

The test of a man or woman's breeding is how they behave in a quarrel.

George Bernard Shaw

Actually, most of us go through life responding to conflict in a natural way that feels good to us. We may be unaware of our particular style and of even what methods we use to resolve interpersonal conflict. We may continue to use our approach whether it is appropriate or not.

Before we discuss the ways of responding to conflict, it might be beneficial to identify some interpersonal rights that each person has in interpersonal interactions, whether conflictual or not. According to Grasha (1978), these rights are to:

1. say no to a request
2. not give people reasons for every action we take
3. ask other people to listen to our point of view
4. ask others to correct errors they made that affect us
5. change our minds
6. ask other people to compromise rather than get only what they want
7. ask others to do things for us
8. persist in making a request if people won't respond the first time
9. be alone if we wish
10. maintain our dignity in relationships
11. evaluate our own behaviors and not just listen to evaluations that others offer
12. make mistakes and accept responsibility for them
13. avoid manipulation by other people
14. let other people know how we are feeling

A person's individual rights in any relationship are the same rights he enjoyed before he even knew the other person existed. Rights are not to be bargained for. They simply exist. A relationship's task is to recognize and protect the rights of both parties.

David Viscott

Now that you know some rights that each person has in interpersonal interactions, what would your answers be to these questions: Is it difficult for you to make your wishes known to others? Are you sometimes pushed around by others because of your own inability to stand up for yourself? Do you ever push others around to get what you want? Do you speak your thoughts and feelings in a clear, direct manner, without judging or dictating to others? Do you use clean fighting or dirty fighting techniques in resolving your conflicts? The answers to these questions characterize your behavior style in responding to conflict.

WHY?*

Why is it we always
seem to fight?
Why is it we sleep
apart every night?
Why is it our attempts
at talking, all seem
to escalate quickly
into so many screams?

WHY?

Why is it you turn
a deaf ear to my plea?
Why is it your view
I refuse to see?
Why is it your feelings
I try hard to hurt?
Why is it you retaliate
and treat me like dirt?

WHY?

Why is it you say "always"
and "everytime," too?
Why is it I say
the same things to you?
Why is it my faults
you so readily see,
and yours I point out
so rapidly?

WHY?

Why is it so easy
for me to make you cry?
Why is it that you tell me
"Oh, just eat dirt and die!"
Why is it we can't try again
to start each day anew?
With just four simple little words,
the words I DO LOVE YOU?

WHY?

Bob Crawley, 1988

*Used with permission of Bob Crawley, Fort Worth, Texas, 1988

BEHAVIOR STYLES

Now, we will return to our earlier question: How do you respond to conflict? Dr. George Bach (1968), a leading authority on conflict resolution and communication skills, has indicated that people tend to deal with conflict by using clean fighting or dirty fighting techniques. Dirty fighting techniques can weaken relationships and cause much pain, resentment, and hostility. Table 7.1 shows some of the ways that people engage in dirty fighting behavior to resolve conflicts.

Table 7.1		
THE KITCHEN SINKER—throws in everything that has been a problem instead of dealing with the specific conflict at hand.	THE BACK STABBER—after agreeing to a solution fails to carry out or express different opinions to parties outside the conflict.	THE BLAMER—is concerned with assigning guilt or placing blame for the conflict, rather than resolving it.
THE AVOIDER—pretends the conflict does not exist and refuses to deal with it in an open manner.	THE STAMP COLLECTOR—stores up days or months of hurt feelings and resentment and "cashes" them all in at once.	THE MARTYR—attempts to change the other person's behavior through a guilt-trip, hoping the other person will feel some responsibility for the martyr's pain.
THE ARMCHAIR PSYCHIATRIST—attempts to read the other person's mind, making sure to tell the other person why he or she is doing "whatever" they are doing.	THE JOKER—refuses to take the fight seriously, laughing at the other person, making a joke, or even avoiding the conflict.	THE WITHHOLDER—intentionally denies what the other person wants—sex, affection, approval, or anything else that makes life more pleasant for the other person.
THE IRRITATOR—intentionally expresses resentment by doing something that really annoys the other person: smacking gum loudly, turning up the TV too loud, and so on.	THE TRAITOR—openly encourages attacks from outsiders or refuses to defend the partner when he or she is being put down by others.	THE HUMILIATOR—uses intimate knowledge of the other person to "hit" below the belt. This is usually a sensitive issue the other person is trying to overcome.

There are basically three behavior styles we use in handling opposition and responding to conflict. These have been classified as *passive, aggressive,* and *assertive.* We will now discuss the behaviors, belief systems, advantages, disadvantages, and when it might be appropriate to use each style.

Passive Style. You may respond to conflict situations by *avoidance.* That is, you may remove yourself from the situation by leaving, shutting up, placating, concealing your feelings, or postponing a confrontation until a better time.

Behavior description: When you behave passively, sometimes referred to as *submissively,* you are usually emotionally dishonest, indirect, and self-denying. You are likely to listen to what has been said and respond very little. Because you don't express your honest feelings, needs, values, and concerns, you actually allow others to violate your space, deny your rights, and ignore your needs. More importantly, you actually demonstrate a lack of respect for your own needs and rights.

Belief system: The message of a submissive person is, "I should never make anyone uncomfortable or displeased except myself. I'll put up with just about anything from you; my needs and my feelings don't matter, you can take advantage of me."

Advantage: You usually don't experience direct rejection or get blamed for anything. Others may view you as nice, selfless, and easy to get along with. This approval from others is extremely important to you.

Disadvantage: You're taken advantage of and may store *up a heavy load of resentment and anger.* You don't get your needs met and other people don't know what you want or need. Consequently, passive people lack deep and enduring friendships. They frequently lose the love and respect of the people they were busy making sacrifices for.

When to use: When neither the goal nor the relationship is very important, it may be wiser to just avoid the conflict.

Aggressive Style. You may respond to conflicting situations by *fight.* That is, you *move against* another with the intent to hurt. This style is also referred to as *domination.*

Behavior description: You may literally or verbally attack another person. Typical examples of aggressive behavior are fighting, blaming, accusing, threatening, and generally stepping on people without regard for their feelings, needs, or ideas. You may be loud, abusive, rude and sarcastic. You are in this world to intimidate and to overpower other people.

Belief system: The message of an aggressive person is, "I have to put others down in order to protect myself; I must exert my power and control over others. This is what I want; what you want is of lesser importance or of no importance at all."

Are there genuinely nice, sweet people in the world? Yes, and they get angry as often as you and I. They must—otherwise, they would be full of vindictive feelings, which would prevent genuine sweetness.

Theodore Rubin

Advantage: Other people don't push the aggressive person around, so they *seem* to wind up getting what they want. They tend to be able to protect themselves and their own space. They *appear* to be in control of their own life and even the lives of others.

Cutting comments create hostility.

Haim Ginott

Disadvantage: In the process of gaining control, the other person in the interaction frequently feels humiliated, defensive, resentful, and usually hurt. Others don't want to be around you, and you wind up with an accumulation of enemies. This causes you to become more vulnerable and fearful of losing what you are fighting for: power and control over others. Therefore, you may create your own destruction.

When to use: When your goal is important and the relationship involved is considerably less important, you may want to move against your opposition.

Assertive Style. You may respond to conflicting situations by *moving toward*. That is, you move toward your opposition until you are either closer together or on the same side. This style is used in *compromise, negotiation,* and *cooperative (collaborative) problem solving.*

Behavior description: You behave assertively when you stand up for yourself, express your true feelings, and do not let others take advantage of you. However, you are considerate of others' feelings. Actually, assertion is a manner of acting and reacting in an appropriately honest manner that is direct, self-respecting, self-expressing, and straightforward. You defend your rights and personal space without abusing or dominating other people. Assertive people talk about things in such a way that others will listen and not be offended, and they give others the opportunity to respond in return.

Belief system: The message of the assertive person is, "I respect myself, and I have equal respect for others, too. I am not in this world to conform to others' expectations, and likewise, they are not in this world to conform to my expectations."

Advantage: You generally get more of what you want without making other people mad. You don't have to feel wrong or guilty because you ventilated your feelings—you left the door to communication open. Consequently, effective confrontation is mutually acceptable. From this, you develop more fulfilling relationships. Also, because you exercise the power of choice over your actions, you are in a much better position to feel good about yourself. Therapist Herbert Fensterheim (1975) shares this thought: *The extent to which you assert yourself determines the level of your self-esteem.*

Disadvantage: As you become more open, honest, and direct, you also take some real risks in how others will perceive you. Some people have difficulty with these kinds of exchanges; therefore, you may experience some hurts and disappointments in some of your relationships.

When to use: When both the goal and the relationship are important to you, the most appropriate approach is to *move toward* your opposition.

Now that we have discussed the three behavior styles, it might be helpful to note the characteristics of the assertive and nonassertive person. Table 7.2 lists these characteristics. Then, we will look at the three styles in action. The *passive, aggressive,* and *assertive* styles are illustrated in the following examples of a woman who wants help with the house.

Be fair with others, but then keep after them until they are fair with you.

Alan Alda

Table 7.2

Characteristics of the Nonassertive Person

He confuses the goal of being liked with being respected.
He is conditioned to fears of being disliked or rejected.
He is unable to recognize the difference between being selfish in the bad sense and in the good sense.
He allows others to maneuver him into situations he doesn't want.
He is easily hurt by what others say and do.
He feels inferior because he is inferior. He limits his experiences and doesn't use his potential.

Characteristics of the Assertive Person

He acts in a way that shows he respects himself, is aware that he cannot always win, and accepts his limitations.
He strives, in spite of the odds, to make the good try. Win, lose or draw, he maintains his self-respect.
He feels free to reveal himself: "This is me. This is what I feel, think, and want."
He can communicate with people on all levels—strangers, friends, family. Communication is open, direct, honest, and appropriate.
He has an active orientation to life. He goes after what he wants—in contrast to the passive person who waits for things to happen.

THE STYLES IN ACTION

Passive Style:

MARGRET: Excuse me, but would you be a sweetie and pick up your clothes in the bathroom?

CHARLES: I'm reading the paper.

MARGRET: Oh, well, all right.

ANALYSIS: The statement "Oh, well, all right" only rewards Charles for postponing Margret's request. Margret certainly doesn't get what she wants. She probably feels sorry for herself and may pay him back by giving him the "silent treatment" over dinner.

Aggressive Style:

MARGRET: I've got another thing to tell you. I've had it with picking up after you and trying to keep this house straight. You either pitch in and help me, or I'm quitting this nonsense.

CHARLES: Now, calm down, I'm reading the paper.

MARGRET: Did your mother just "wait" on you and treat you like a king? You don't give a flip about anything around this house, as long as you get to read the daily news whenever you want.

CHARLES: Now, don't start in on me about my mother.

MARGRET: All you do is come home and relax in the easy chair and grab the paper.

CHARLES: Shut up! What's wrong with you?

Sarcasm is dirty fighting.

George Bach

ANALYSIS: The opening statement is an attack, and Margret "relives" hostilities of earlier annoyances. Interactions such as this clearly have no winner, because aggressive behavior hurts another person, creates resentment, and guarantees resistance to change.

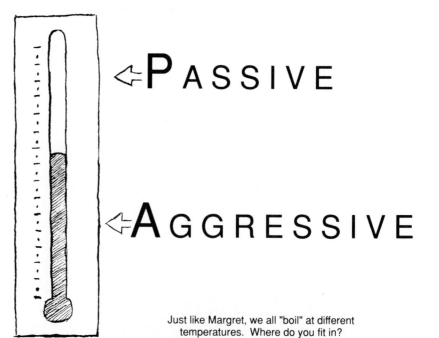

←PASSIVE

←AGGRESSIVE

Just like Margret, we all "boil" at different temperatures. Where do you fit in?

Assertive Style:

MARGRET: I would like for you to pick up your clothes in the bathroom.

CHARLES: I'm reading the paper.

MARGRET: I would feel much better if we shared in keeping the house straight. You can read the paper when we're done straightening the house.

CHARLES: I'm almost finished with the sports section.

MARGRET: Well, I can start the wash. Will you help me when you are through reading the sports section?

CHARLES: Sure!

ANALYSIS: Assertive behavior does not aim to injure but to solve an interpersonal problem. Assertive requests include a specific goal and the willingness to negotiate a mutually agreeable plan to solve the problem.

It would be unreasonable to expect people to use assertive behavior exclusively. There are times when it is wise to be passive and just give in to others; there are times when it is necessary to aggressively defend your rights; there are times when being assertive does not succeed in obtaining its goal. Bolton (1979) views the effects of the three behavior styles in this way:

My observation of others and my personal experience leads me to believe that more of a person's needs will be satisfied by being consistently assertive than by submissive (passive) or aggressive behavior. In most circumstances, assertive behavior is the most appropriate, effective, and constructive way of defending one's space and fulfilling one's needs.

Would you like to be more assertive in dealing with interpersonal conflicts and other difficult situations? We will begin by discussing the different types of assertive expressions you may need to make.

LEARNING TO BE ASSERTIVE

The main goal of assertiveness training is to help people express their thoughts, feelings, and rights in a way that respects those of others. As you learn to do this, it is important that you become aware of the different types of assertive expressions (Atwater, 1986).

Basic assertion is learning to stand up for your rights or express your feelings, such as saying, "Pardon me, I'd like to finish what I was saying."

Another type of assertiveness is *learning to express positive feelings,* such as, "I really liked the way you cleaned the car." Do you have difficulty in giving compliments, as well as receiving them? Some people do.

You may have to use an escalating type of assertion when people fail to respond to your earlier request. An example here would be, "This is the third time I'm going to tell you. I don't want to change insurance companies."

Then, there are times when you need to express *negative feelings.* The *"I" message, frequently referred to as the focal point of learning to be assertive,* is a way of expressing yourself effectively before you become angry and act in self-defeating ways.

The "I" Message. According to Thomas Gordon (1970), an "I" message has four parts: (1) an objective, nonjudgmental description of the person's behavior in specific terms, (2) how I feel about this, (3) the concrete effects on me; and (4) what I'd prefer the person do instead. Let's look at each part.

1. An objective, nonjudgmental description of the person's behavior in specific terms. There are four guidelines to help you deliver an effective behavior description.

First, describe the person's behavior in specific terms, rather than fuzzy, unclear words. For example,

Specific	Fuzzy
When you frequently call after 11 o'clock at night . . .	When you frequently call me late at night . . .

The person you are angry with may have a different idea of what late means. Therefore, if you want your needs to be met, you will need to give the *exact* time you consider *too late* to receive a phone call.

Second, do not add your thoughts and perceptions about the other person's motives, attitudes, character, and so on. It is human nature to describe another person's behavior by stating what you think the other person intended. This causes defensiveness, whereas describing what a person actually did creates an atmosphere for further communication.

Third, make your behavior description an objective statement, rather than a judgment. Assertion messages avoid character assassinations, blame, sarcasm, or profanity.

Fourth, behavioral descriptions should be brief as possible. The longer your message is, the more likely you will not be heard and understood. Also, there is less tendency for others to judge and evaluate when you keep your message simple. One sentence is ample, too.

2. How I feel about this. Once you have identified what your *real* feelings are, you must take the responsibility for your own feelings. This means you say "I feel angry or disappointed," rather than "You made me feel angry or disappointed." Continuing with the late-night calls as an example, we now have the following:

When you call me after 11:00 o'clock at night, *I feel angry.*

Table 7.3
Examples of "I" Messages

Nonjudgmental description of person's behavior	My feelings about it	Concrete effects on me	What I'd prefer the person to do
1. When you call me after 11:00 o'clock at night . . .	I feel angry . . .	because I am awakened by your call at least twice a week.	I'd like you to call before 10:00 o'clock, except in an emergency.
2. When you're late picking me up from school . . .	I feel frustrated . . .	because I waste a lot of time waiting for you.	I'd like to be picked up on time.
3. When you do not put your dirty clothes in the hamper . . .	I feel irritated . . .	because it makes extra work for me when I do the wash.	I'd like you to put your dirty clothes in the hamper each day.
4. When you borrow my car and bring it home on "empty" . . .	I feel annoyed . . .	because I have to get gas before I can even go to work.	I'd like you to refill the tank with as much gas as you use.

3. The concrete effects on me. People may not be aware of how their behavior is affecting you. In most instances, they are not deliberately trying to annoy or frustrate you. Once they become aware of how their behavior affects you, they are usually more considerate. Our example now becomes:

When you call me after 11:00 o'clock at night, I feel angry, *because I am awakened by your calls at least twice a week.*

4. What I'd prefer the person to do instead. Simply stated, this means that you use "I" messages and tell others what behavior you would like for them to substitute the next time a similar exchange occurs. Be sure and express your request in one or two simple sentences. It is important to be firm, specific, and kind. Our example now looks like this:

When you call me after 11:00 o'clock at night, I feel angry, because I am awakened by your call at least twice a week. *I'd like you to call before 10:00 o'clock, except in an emergency.*

To be sure that you understand each part of the "I" message, review the examples in Table 7.3. You will notice that these "I" messages do not attack or blame the other person. Instead, "I" messages are a way of expressing your sincere feelings and requests in a way that encourages others to listen and co-operate.

SUGGESTIONS FOR DELIVERING
AN ASSERTIVE (I) MESSAGE

Robert Alberti (1982), offers three suggestions for improving the success of assertive ("*I*") messages.

Write and practice your message before delivering it. This will give you an opportunity to review two important questions: (1) Is it likely to arouse defensiveness in the other person? (2) Are you likely to get your needs met with this assertion?

Develop assertive body language with your "I" Message. In order to assure that your verbal message is congruent with your nonverbal behavior, you will need to (Review Chapter 5 for more details):

1. maintain direct eye contact
2. maintain an erect body posture
3. speak clearly, firmly, and have sufficient volume to be heard
4. emphasize your message with appropriate gestures and facial expressions
5. do not whine or have an apologetic tone to your voice.

Don't be sidetracked by the defensiveness or manipulation of others. This can be accomplished by using the *broken-record technique—* calmly repeating your point without getting sidetracked by irrelevant issues. Some examples might be:

Yes, but . . . ; Yes, I know, but my point is . . . ; I agree, but . . . ; Yes, but I was saying . . . ; Right, but I'm still not interested.

Remember, persistence is one of the keys to effective assertion. One of the main reasons why people do not get their needs met when they assert is because they give up or give in after the first defensive or manipulative response of the other person.

So far, we have discussed the passive, aggressive, and assertive behavior styles used in interpersonal conflict. These three styles combine to form one of three possible methods of conflict resolution: *Win-Lose, Lose-Lose,* and *Win-Win.* We will now discuss these in detail.

Peace cannot be kept by force. It can only be achieved by understanding.

Albert Einstein

METHODS OF CONFLICT RESOLUTION

When you approach a conflict situation, you can choose to *avoid* the situation, *fight* with the use of power and force, or *move toward,* using negotiation skills.

Win-Lose. One approach to conflict resolution is that one person gets his or her way, and the other does not. For example, Linda and Tom have a conflict-of-needs situation about where to build the swimming pool. Let's look at their interaction:

TOM: I've decided we will build the swimming pool to the right of the patio.

LINDA: What do you mean, you've decided! I want to build it to the left of the patio.

TOM: That's a stupid idea, then, we will have to move all the shrubs.

LINDA: Well, first of all, I'm not stupid, because the contractor can do that for us.

TOM: I make the money around here, and I'm not paying for the shrubs to be moved.

LINDA: Well, okay, if that's what you say.

Analysis: Tom decides what the solution should be and announces it to Linda. Obviously, Tom hopes Linda will accept his idea. When Linda doesn't, Tom uses persuasion to get Linda to "give in." However, this fails, so Tom tries to get compliance by employing his aggressive, power, control, and authoritarian techniques to get his way.

Although Tom and Linda both wanted their way, Tom, the person satisfied, was inconsiderate and disrespectful to the needs of Linda. He was issue oriented. Consequently, Linda felt defeated, angry, and resentful at Tom for not considering her feelings.

Lose-Lose. In the **Win-Lose** type of conflict resolution, Linda was very unhappy with the outcome, but Tom was "happy as a lark." In the **Lose-Lose** type of conflict resolution, neither party is happy with the outcome. Let's listen to Linda and Tom again.

TOM: I've decided we will build the swimming pool to the right of the patio.

LINDA: What do you mean you have decided! You're not the only one who lives here, you selfish jerk!

TOM: You are too stupid to understand we can't put the pool where the shrubs are.

LINDA: I'm not stupid! You are just too stupid to understand the contractor will do it for us.

TOM: I'm the one who makes most of the money here, you fruitcake! I'm not paying the contractor to move 100 shrubs.

LINDA: Then, we won't even build a pool, Mr. Penny Pincher deluxe!

Analysis: Linda decides she will be more aggressive this time. Very quickly, she starts verbally attacking Tom. There is no way that Tom is going to take this, so he reciprocates and verbally attacks Linda. She comes back for more of the same. . . . Tom comes back for more of the same. Linda leaves angry and hostile, with the issue never resolved. Tom is angry and hostile, with the issue never resolved.

Linda and Tom both lose. They both forgot the feelings of each other; they both forgot the issue.

RESOLUTION

Today we had a meeting
like so many other times.
At once we started listing what
we saw as each other's crimes.
But there was one thing different
on this bright and wonderous day.
We'd sworn till all had been resolved
we would not walk away.

The first ground rule that we laid down
was different from before.
We agreed we would not scream and shout
nor storm out of the door.
We then agreed right then and there
that we would "fairly" fight.
We would not call each other names
nor take a "psychic" bite.

The little things we could concede
that we could live without.
We tore them into little bits
and then we threw them out.
Upon our individual slips
of paper we did write,
the concessions each of us would make
to help to end the fight.

And then upon another sheet
we wrote what it would take,
to finally happy once again
each of us to make.
We then exchanged the papers
and to both of our surprise,
we each had written just one thing
for the other's eyes.

And now we are together
but not as before.
For we learned a lesson
to carry us evermore.
The lesson was so simple
that things are easy to solve,
when we sit down *together*
our problems to resolve.

Bob Crawley, 1989

*Used with permission of Bob Crawley, Fort Worth, Texas, 1989.

Win-Win. In this approach to conflict resolution, conflicts are resolved with no one winning and no one losing. Both win because the solution *must be acceptable to both.* Let's see how Tom and Linda handle the swimming pool issue this time.

TOM:	Will tonight after dinner be a convenient time with you for us to talk about where we can build the swimming pool?"
LINDA:	That will be fine!
TOM:	Good, let's both be thinking of some possible locations.
LINDA:	That's a great idea.

AFTER DINNER

TOM:	What are your ideas and how do you feel about this?
LINDA:	I see three possible locations—to the left of the patio, the right of the patio, or in the middle. What are your ideas?
TOM:	Well, I've been thinking of those, too. Let's talk about the pros and cons of all three. Let's hear your ideas first.
LINDA:	Ok, the left side would be a prettier view from the bedroom; the right side would be more convenient for the kids, but we wouldn't have a view from the house; the middle would be a prettier view from the den. What are your ideas?
TOM:	The left side would be more expensive, since we would have to move 100 or more shrubs; the right side would really be more convenient for the kids; the middle would give a nice view from the house, I guess. I really had not thought about the middle as a possibility.
LINDA:	Those shrubs really do look nice from the bedroom, and we can save a lot of money by not having to move all those shrubs. The kids can probably adjust to a few feet of inconvenience.
TOM:	The kids will be gone in a couple of years anyway, and their convenience won't be a factor then. I'm getting to like the middle more and more.
LINDA:	Why don't we tentatively think about building the pool in the middle, and then each of us can think about this for a week.
TOM:	That sounds good. Can we talk about this again next Monday night?
LINDA:	Sure!

Hatred is never ended but by love, and a misunderstanding is never ended by an argument but by tact, diplomacy, conciliation, and a sympathetic desire to see the other person's viewpoint.

Buddha

Analysis: Tom asks Linda to participate with him in a joint search for some solution acceptable to both. Tom and Linda both offer possible solutions. They critically evaluate them and eventually make a decision on a final solution acceptable to both. No selling of the other is

We meet naturally on the basis of our sameness and grow on the basis of our differentness.

Virginia Satir

required after the solution has been selected, because both have already accepted it. No power is required to force compliance, because neither is resisting the decision.

One of the strong advantages to this type of conflict resolution is that Linda is more motivated to carry out a decision that she has participated in making than she is a decision that has been imposed upon her. Also, Tom and Linda feel better about themselves and each other. Neither feel defeated; neither feel hostile. Tom and Linda resolve their conflict by dealing with each other's feelings and the issue, too. From the examples of Tom and Linda, it is easy to see that the *win-win* method of conflict resolution is clearly superior to the win-lose and lose-lose.

STEPS FOR WIN-WIN CONFLICT RESOLUTION

Earlier in this chapter we stated that there were three elements in a conflict situation—*self, other,* and the *issue.* We also stated that if the conflict situation is to be resolved constructively, all of these elements—the *feelings* and *emotions* of both individuals, plus the *tangible issue* involved—must be dealt with congruently.

You've already learned how to deal with the feelings and emotions involved in a conflict situation. You saw how Linda and Tom listened to the feelings of each other and how they dealt with the tangible issue, too.

Let's look more closely at the exact steps used in the win-win approach to interpersonal conflict resolution.

Many authorities have written on the no-lose or win-win approach to conflict resolution. However, win-win problem solving works best when it follows a seven-step approach, based on the writings of Deborah Weider-Hatfield (1981) and Thomas Gordon (1970). The steps are:

1. Define the problem in terms of needs, not solutions. This is the critical point where you need to decide what it is you want or need. We generally define a problem in terms of solutions—what will satisfy our need. This really leads to win/lose results—one person gets what he or she wants, and the other loses what he or she wants. For example, let's consider this exchange between David and John.

DAVID: I need the car to go to the library and study.
JOHN: I need the car to go to the out-of-town basketball game.

David and John have both defined their goal in terms of solutions. They each want to get what they want—the car. Actually, David and John both had a need for transportation, and the family car was the solution.

A useful key to identify a need is to fill in the following blank "I need . . ." (statement of the goal, transportation, not the solution, the car)

Sometimes your needs may not be as clear as the example above. In these cases, either think about your *needs* alone before approaching the other person or talk to a third party who may be able to help you separate your thoughts. Don't forget to explore all the reasons you are dissatisfied as well as the relational issues that may be involved.

2. Share Your Problem and Unmet Needs. Once you've defined your problem and unmet needs, it's time to share them with the other person. Remember, no one can be expected to meet your needs unless they know why you're upset and what you want. There are two guidelines to remember in this step:

First, *be sure to choose a time and place that is suitable.* Frequently, destructive fights often start because the initiator confronts the other person who isn't ready. Unloading on a tired, busy person is likely to result in your concerns not being heard or given much attention. Furthermore, it is important that you are calm and have time to discuss what is bothering you. Bringing up issues of concern when you are angry, overly upset, or in a hurry frequently causes you to say things you really don't mean. Making a date to discuss what is bothering you increases the likelihood of a positive outcome. You might say, "Something's been bothering me. When would be a convenient time for us to talk about it?"

Second, *be sure and use "I" messages and the assertive techniques* you've already learned in this chapter. You will remember that the most important part of the "I" message is to describe how your partner's behavior affects you—not attach blame or labels.

The final part of this step is to confirm your partner's understanding of what he or she heard.

3. Listen to the Other Person's Needs. Once you are sure the other person understands your message, it is now time to find out what he or she needs to feel satisfied about the issue. Remember, if you expect some help in meeting your needs, it is only fair that you be willing to help the other person meet his or her needs. Thinking back about the exchange between David and John, John might say, "Now that I've told you that I need a way to go to the library to study, tell me what you need to feel okay about this situation with the family car." David might say, "I also need a way to the out-of-town basketball game." Be sure to review the listening skills discussed in Chapter 5 and be prepared to listen actively to your partner. It is also important to check your understanding of your partner's needs before going any further. You might say, "Now, do I understand correctly that you need. . . ?"

To discover needs, we try to find out why the person wants the solution he/she initially proposed. Once we understand the advantages that a solution has for them, we have discovered their need.

Robert Bolton

What we need are fewer talks and more listens.

Roger Fisher

You are now ready to arrive at a shared definition of the problem that expresses *both needs*. Try to state both sets of needs in a one-sentence long summary of the problem. For example, David and John might conclude, "We both need a way to go where we want or need to go, and we only have one car."

4. Brainstorm Possible Solutions. Once the problem is adequately defined, the search for possible solutions begins. You might suggest, "What are some things we might do? Let's think of possible solutions."

Here are some important guidelines to assist you in the brainstorming session:

First, *seek quantity rather than quality*. Think of as many solutions as possible. Don't evaluate, judge, or belittle any of the solutions offered. This will come in the next step.

Second, *avoid ownership of a solution*. It is important to not get involved with *your* solution and *my* solution. Build upon each other's solutions by adopting an attitude: These are *our* solutions.

Third, *list every possible solution*. The final result should be a long list of possible ideas and solutions. Since each idea needs to be considered, it is advisable for all solutions to be written down. Otherwise, a good idea may get lost.

5. Evaluate the Possible Solutions and Choose the Best One. Check Possible Consequences. Now it is time to evaluate the solutions in terms of how they best meet the mutually shared goals. You want to evaluate how each solution meets each partner's needs and then arrive at a final understanding of which solution satisfies the most goals. However, sometimes it is easier and less time-consuming to initiate these four guidelines:

First, *ask the other person which solution he or she feels best solves the mutual shared goal*. Be sure his or her needs are met.

Second, *state which solution looks best to you*. Be sure your needs are met.

Third, *see which choices are congruent with yours and the other person*.

Fourth, *together, decide on one or more of the solutions*. If you took the time to carefully examine each other's needs when you began your conflict resolution, several of the same solutions will generally be selected by both people.

It is extremely important that each person is satisfied with the final solution. Remember, people are generally more motivated to work on resolving a problem if they are not manipulated or pressured into deciding on the *best* solution.

The final aspect of this step is to *consider the possible consequences of your final solution or combination of solutions*. Sometimes it is helpful to ask, "What is the worst thing that could happen by choosing this solution?"

6. Implement the Solution. It is extremely important that you agree on exactly how the solution will be implemented. Your solution will only be effective if you mutually agree on *who does what and by when.*

Because people are forgetful, it is usually desirable to write out the agreement that was reached, being sure to include the details of *who will do what by when.* The written agreement should be viewed as a reminder to both parties about exactly how the solution will be implemented.

7. Evaluate the Solution at a Later Date. Just like you made a date to begin talking about your problem and unmet needs, it is also important to make a date and review the progress of your final solution. This is an opportunity to "check back" with each person to see how the solution is working for each person. Is the mutually shared goal being met? If changes need to be made, now is the time to discuss what is on your mind.

When you fail to use your creative problem-solving talent, you strike at the quality of your own life.

George Prince

ISN'T THE WIN-WIN APPROACH JUST A COMPROMISE?

The answer is No! *Compromise really means agreement reached by mutual concessions.* While there are times when compromise may be the best obtainable result, it is important to realize that two people in a dispute can often work together to find more creative solutions.

In compromise, each side gives something up to end the conflict or solve the problem. This solution is often much quicker, but it generally prevents people from communicating their needs and wants and listening to the needs and wants of others. Consequently, the emotions and feelings are frequently not recognized. Compromise then, becomes more issue based. When practiced frequently, this approach to conflict resolution may create distance and generate hostility between the people involved.

The win-win approach to conflict resolution is not a panacea for all of life's problems. There are some occasions when this method will not work or when another approach is more fitting. However, when people join together and take the time to find a solution acceptable to both, most problems that occur between them can be resolved with a high degree of success.

It is important to note here that a modification of the win-win approach to interpersonal conflict resolution can also be used in personal problem solving. The steps would be:

1. *Identify and define the conflict.*
2. *Generate a number of possible solutions.*
3. *Evaluate the alternative solutions.*
4. *Decide on the best solution.*
5. *Evaluate the solution at a later date.*

A LAST THOUGHT

When any two people (groups) live or work closely together, conflict is bound to occur just because people are different, think differently, and have different needs and wants that sometimes do not match. There is really no end to the numbers and kinds of disagreements possible. Likewise, there are a wide range of feelings and emotions that accompany the conflict. These feelings must not be forgotten; the area of disagreement (issue) must not be forgotten.

Even though conflict is part of a meaningful relationship, you can change the way you deal with it. For example, you can *choose* to approach your interpersonal conflicts differently—*there doesn't have to be a winner and a loser*. Second, you can choose to recognize a conflict exists and use communication skills to express your needs and defend your rights without abusing or dominating other people. Third, you can choose to recognize and deal first with the emotions and feelings of your partner/s. Fourth, you can choose to initiate win-win conflict resolution methods.

What are the benefits if you make the choices above? The authors do not make any guarantees, but we believe that *how* you resolve your interpersonal conflicts is the single most important factor in determining whether your relationships will be healthy or unhealthy, mutually satisfying or unsatisfying, friendly or unfriendly, deep or shallow, intimate or cold.

When differences exist, people need to learn how to assert their thoughts, wishes, feelings, and knowledge without destroying, invading, or obliterating the other, and while still coming out with a fitting joint outcome.

Virginia Satir

KEY TERMS

Conflict
Placater
Blamer
Distractor
Feeling Dimension
Issue Dimension
Passive
Aggressive
Avoidance
Submissively
Broken-Record Technique

Move Against
Domination
Moving Toward
Assertive
"I" Message
Win-Lose
Lose-Lose
Win-Win
Collaborative Problem Solving
Compromise

CHAPTER DISCUSSION QUESTIONS

1. What is the most recent conflict you had to settle? What method of conflict resolution did you choose?
2. Which one of the three methods of conflict resolution do you use most often? Which one of the three behavior styles of conflict resolution do you use most often?
3. What kinds of differentness in others causes you the greatest interpersonal conflict?
4. Is the win-win approach to conflict resolution too good to be true?
5. To what situations do you find most difficult to respond with assertive behavior?
6. Generally speaking, have your conflicts made your relationships stronger or weaker? Why?
7. Which one of the parts of the "I" message is most difficult for you to remember to use?
8. Is it really possible to deal with the emotional dimension of a conflict before discussing the tangible issue involved?
9. Which one of the steps of win-win problem solving would be most difficult for you? Why?

REFERENCES

Alberti, Robert E., and Emmons, Michael L. (1991) *Your Perfect Right: A Guide to Assertive Living.* (Sixth Edition) San Luis Obispo, California: Impact Publishers, Inc.

Atwater, Eastwood. (1986) *Human Relations.* Englewood Cliffs, N.J.: Prentice-Hall, Inc.

Bach, George, R. (1971) *Aggression Lab: The Fair Fight Manual.* Dubuque, Iowa: Kendall/Hunt Publishing Co.

Bolton, Robert. (1979) *People Skills.* New York: Simon and Schuster, Inc.

Bower, S. A., and Bower, G. H. (1976) *Asserting Your Self.* Massachusetts: Addison-Wesley.

Deutsch, M. (1973) *The Resolution of Conflict.* New Haven: Yale University Press.

Fensterheim, Herbert and Baer. (1975) *Don't Say Yes When You Want to Say No.* New York: David McKay.

Frost, Joyce Hocker, and Wilmot, William W. (1985) *Interpersonal Conflict.* 2nd. ed. Dubuque, Iowa: Wm. C. Brown.

Grasha, A. (1983) *Practical Applications of Psychology.* Boston, Massachusetts: Little Brown and Co.

Gordon, Thomas. (1970) *Parent Effectiveness Training.* New York: New American Library.

Harrison, Delyn Dendy. (1978) *Some Things Are Said in Black and White.* Fort Worth, Texas: Branch Smith, Inc.

Odiorne, George. (1974) *Objectives-focused Management.* New York: Amacom.

Rogers, Carl. (1961) *On Becoming a Person.* Boston, Massachusetts: Houghton Mifflin.

Satir, Virigina. (1972) *Peoplemaking.* California: Science and Behavior Books.

Stagner, Ross. (1967) *The Dimensions of Human Conflict.* Detroit: Wayne State University Press, 1967.

Weider-Hatfield, Deborah. (1981) "A Unit in Conflict Management Skills." *Communication Education* 30:265–273.

PERSONAL CONFLICT RESOLUTION

Purpose: To review your style of conflict management.

Instructions:

I. Respond to the following questions.
   1. Describe the last "fight" or conflict you had with a friend or family member.

   2. What was your goal in the conflict?

   3. What do you think the other person's goal was in the conflict?

   4. Describe how you responded to the conflict—passively, assertively, or aggressively.

   5. Describe how the other person responded to the conflict—passively, assertively, or aggressively.

   6. Was the conflict resolved by the win-lose, lose-lose, or win-win method? Explain how the method was used.

DISCUSSION

1. What does this event tell you about your style of conflict management?

2. What can you do to improve your approach to conflict resolution?

HOW DID YOUR PARENTS HANDLE CONFLICT?

Purpose: To review your parents' style of conflict management and to determine in what ways you may be presently imitating their behavior.

Instructions:

I. Respond to the following questions:
   1. How did your mother deal with interpersonal conflict?

   2. How did your father deal with interpersonal conflict?

   3. How is your style of conflict management like and unlike those of your parents?

      MOTHER:
      Like:

      Unlike:

FATHER:
Like:

Unlike:

4. What bothered you most about your parents' style of conflict management?
MOTHER:

FATHER:

5. What did you admire most about your parents' style of conflict management?
MOTHER:

FATHER:

II. After you have responded to the previous questions, divide into groups of four and share your answers or have an open class discussion.

DISCUSSION

1. What does this tell you about the power of learning by imitation?

2. Why is it that we continue to imitate behavior we saw in our parents but also disliked?

THE ASSERTIVENESS INVENTORY*

Purpose: To assess your strengths and weaknesses in being assertive and to establish goals for improvement.

Instructions:

I. Respond to the following questions by drawing a circle around the number that describes you best: For some questions, the assertive end of the scale is at 0, for others at 4.

        Key:

0 means **no** or **never**

1 means **somewhat** or **sometimes**

2 means **average**

3 means **usually** or **a good deal**

4 means **practically always** or **entirely**

1. When a person is highly unfair, do you call it to their attention? 0 1 2 3 4
2. Do you find it difficult to make decisions? 0 1 2 3 4
3. Are you openly critical of others' ideas, opinions, behavior? 0 1 2 3 4
4. Do you speak out in protest when someone takes your place in line? 0 1 2 3 4
5. Do you often avoid people or situations for fear of embarrassment? 0 1 2 3 4
6. Do you usually have confidence in your own judgment? 0 1 2 3 4
7. Do you insist that your spouse or roommate take on a fair share of household chores? 0 1 2 3 4
8. Are you prone to "fly off the handle?" 0 1 2 3 4
9. When a salesperson makes an effort, do you find it hard to say "No" even though the merchandise is not really what you want? 0 1 2 3 4
10. When a latecomer is waited on before you are, do you call attention to the situation? 0 1 2 3 4
11. Are you reluctant to speak up in a discussion or debate? 0 1 2 3 4
12. If a person has borrowed money (or a book, garment, thing of value) and is overdue in returning it, do you mention it? 0 1 2 3 4
13. Do you continue to pursue an argument after the other person has had enough? 0 1 2 3 4
14. Do you generally express what you feel? 0 1 2 3 4
15. Are you disturbed if someone watches you at work? 0 1 2 3 4
16. If someone keeps kicking or bumping your chair in a movie or a lecture, do you ask the person to stop? 0 1 2 3 4
17. Do you find it difficult to keep eye contact when you are talking to another person? .. 0 1 2 3 4
18. In a good restaurant, when your meal is improperly prepared or served, do you ask the waiter/waitress to correct the situation? 0 1 2 3 4
19. When you discover merchandise is faulty, do you return it for an adjustment? 0 1 2 3 4
20. Do you show your anger by name-calling or obscenities? 0 1 2 3 4
21. Do you try to be a wallflower or a piece of the furniture in social situations? 0 1 2 3 4

22. Do you insist that your property manager (mechanic, repairman, janitor) make repairs, adjustments or replacements which are his or her responsibility? 0 1 2 3 4
23. Do you often step in and make decisions for others? 0 1 2 3 4
24. Are you able openly to express love and affection? 0 1 2 3 4
25. Are you able to ask your friends for small favors or help? 0 1 2 3 4
26. Do you think you always have the right answer? 0 1 2 3 4
27. When you differ with a person you respect, are you able to speak up for your own viewpoint? 0 1 2 3 4
28. Are you able to refuse unreasonable requests made by friends? 0 1 2 3 4
29. Do you have difficulty complimenting or praising others? 0 1 2 3 4
30. If you are disturbed by someone smoking near you, can you say so? 0 1 2 3 4
31. Do you shout or use bullying tactics to get others to do as you wish? 0 1 2 3 4
33. Do you finish other people's sentences for them? 0 1 2 3 4
33. Do you get into physical fights with others, especially with strangers? 0 1 2 3 4
34. At family meals, do you control the conversation? 0 1 2 3 4
35. When you meet a stranger, are you the first to introduce yourself and begin a conversation? 0 1 2 3 4

II. Analyzing Your Results:

When you complete the Inventory, you'll probably be tempted to add up your total score. Don't! It really has no meaning, since there is no such thing as a *general* quality of assertiveness. The authors of the inventory suggest the following steps for analysis of your responses to the Assertiveness Inventory:

1. Look at individual events in your life, involving particular people or groups, and consider strengths and shortcomings accordingly.

2. Look at your responses to questions 1, 2, 4, 5, 6, 7, 9, 10, 11, 12, 14, 15, 16, 17, 18, 19, 21, 22, 24, 25, 27, 28, 30, and 35. These questions are oriented toward *nonassertive* behavior. Respond to these questions:

   A. Do your answers to these items tell you that you are rarely speaking up for yourself? How do you feel about what you have learned about yourself?

3. Look at your responses to questions 3, 8, 13, 20, 23, 26, 29, 31, 32, 33, and 34. These questions are oriented toward *aggressive* behavior. Respond to these questions:

   A. Do your answers to these questions suggest you are pushing others around more than you realized? How do you feel about what you have learned about yourself?

DISCUSSION QUESTIONS

Most people confirm from completing these three steps that assertiveness is *situational* in their lives. No one is nonassertive *all* the time, aggressive *all* the time, assertive *all* the time! Each person behaves in each of the three ways at various times, depending upon the situation. It is possible that you have a *characteristic style* that leans heavily in one direction. Reread each question on the Inventory and carefully analyze your answers. Look specifically at four aspects of the information and respond to the questions below:

1. What situations give you trouble? Which can you handle easily?

2. What are your attitudes about expressing yourself? For example, do you feel you have a "right" to be assertive? Why or why not?

3. What obstacles are in the way of your assertions? For example, are you frightened of the consequences, or do other people in your life make it especially difficult? Who?

4. Are your behavior skills (eye contact, facial expression, body posture) intact? Can you be expressive when you need to?

5. What specific goals do you need to set for yourself in learning to be more assertive?

LEARNING TO BE ASSERTIVE

Purpose: To learn how to construct an assertive ("I" message) in order to express your feelings and get your needs met.

Instructions:

I. Select an uncomfortable situation that suggests itself from items on the Assertiveness Questionnaire. Be sure and select a situation that has been a source of interpersonal conflict for you.

II. Next, review pages 275–277 on how to construct an "I" message and respond to the following four-parts of the "I" message:

A. An objective, nonjudgmental description of the person's behavior in specific terms:

B. How I feel about this:

C. The concrete effects on me:

D. What I'd prefer the person do instead:

III. Now, divide into groups of four and share your assertive message. Members of the group will give each person feedback on his or her assertive message.

IV. Correct any errors in your assertive message and try to practice it within the next week.

DISCUSSION

1. What errors, if any, did you find in your assertive message?

2. Do you think you will be able to practice this in the next week?

3. What will your biggest problem be in using this assertive message?

4. How do you plan to overcome this problem?

MUTUAL CONFLICT RESOLUTION

Purpose: To mutually engage in interpersonal conflict resolution by first assessing your feelings about the dynamics of the conflict, and then secondly, initiating the seven-step approach to win-win problem solving.

Instructions:

  I. Think of a "special" person with whom you are presently having a conflict. This should be an individual who is as concerned about resolving the conflict as you are.
 II. Make a copy of the questionnaire, Assessing an Interpersonal Conflict, and give to this person. Without discussing the conflict any further, individually complete your feelings about the dynamics involved in the conflict.
III. Then, exchange the questionnaires and carefully read and assess the other person's feelings and ideas about the conflict. There still should be no verbal discussion.
 IV. Finally, initiate the seven-step approach to win-win conflict resolution as discussed on pages 282–285. Be sure to share this discussion with your partner.

DISCUSSION

  I. Evaluate with the other individual the joint participation in the seven-step process and share your results in small groups or with the entire class. How successful were you in each of the steps? What were your problems?

1. Define the problem in terms of needs, not solutions.

2. Share your problem and unmet needs.

3. Listen to the other person's needs.

4. Brainstorm possible solutions.

5. Evaluate the possible solution/s and choose the best one. Check possible consequences.

6. Implement the solution.

7. Evaluate the solution at a later date.

II. Did the conflict get resolved?

III. How do you feel about the conflict now?

IV. How does the other person feel about the conflict now?

ASSESSING AN INTERPERSONAL CONFLICT

1. How do you define the problem between yourself and the other person?

2. How do you think the other person defines the problem?

3. What behavior of yours contributes to or represents the problem?

4. What behavior of the other person contributes to or represents the problem?

5. What is the situation in which the above behavior occurs?

6. What is the smallest way possible to define the problem?

7. What are the areas of difference or disagreement between the two of you?

8. What are the areas of commonality or agreement between the two of you?

9. As explicitly as possible, state the other person's behaviors that you find unacceptable in the conflict situation.

10. As explicitly as possible, state your behaviors that the other person finds unacceptable in the conflict situation.

11. What events triggered the conflict?

12. What are the things you need to do in order to resolve the conflict?

13. What are the things the other person needs to do to resolve the conflict?

14. What are the possible mutually desired goals for which the two of you could cooperate in order to resolve the conflict?

15. What are your strengths you could utilize to resolve the conflict?

16. What are the other person's strengths he or she could utilize to resolve the conflict?

17. How will the two of you know if the conflict has been resolved?

LEARNING JOURNAL FOR INTERPERSONAL CONFLICT

Select the statement below that best defines your feelings about the personal value or meaning gained from this chapter and respond below the dotted line:

I LEARNED THAT I . . .   I WAS SURPRISED THAT I . . .

I REALIZED THAT I . . .   I WAS PLEASED THAT I . . .

I DISCOVERED THAT I . . .   I WAS DISPLEASED THAT I . . .

....

8

Managing Stress

What is the true picture of your life? Imagine that
there is an hourglass on your desk. Connecting the bowl
at the top with the bowl at the bottom is a tube so thin
that only one grain of sand can pass through it at a time.

That is the true picture of your life, even on a super-
busy day. The crowded hours come to you always one
moment at a time. That is the only way they can come.
The day may bring many tasks, many problems, strains,
but invariably they come in single file.

You want to gain emotional poise? Remember the
hourglass, the grains of sand dropping one by one.

James Gordon Gilkey

Have you ever thought or said to yourself, "If I just didn't have all these problems and pressures, life would be so much better." Maybe you have even thought or said, "I just can't handle all these problems—I'm at the end of my rope."

Certainly it is true that fewer health, financial, family, work, or social problems would make life more secure and satisfying. However, not having any problems or any stress would leave you with no choices in life, which would be dull and uninteresting.

We must understand that some stress is good and necessary; the only people who don't have stress are dead. Stress is as necessary as food; however, when it comes to food, do you utilize all you eat or is there some waste? Obviously there is waste, and your body eliminates that. If you didn't eliminate food waste on a regular basis you would have a real physical problem. Similarly, if you do not eliminate excessive stress on a regular basis it can create physical problems and/or behavioral changes.

Did you know that you have the power within yourself to modify both the amount of stress in your life and your reaction to it? Some of you may need to make only a few minor adjustments in your daily life for stress to become more constructive and manageable. Some of you will have to make some radical external (for example, change jobs) or internal changes (such as change some of your social requirements and/or attitudes).

Most people who with courage and support undertake such changes, have only one regret: They didn't do it sooner. We would like to encourage you to begin considering what adjustments you may need to make in your daily life for stress to become more constructive and manageable.

Let's begin by discussing what stress is and what causes it.

Stress is like spice—in the right proportion it enhances the flavor of a dish. Too little produces a bland, dull meal; too much may choke you. The trick is to find the right amount for you.

Donald Tubesing

WHAT IS STRESS?

Hans Selye (1956), a stress expert, defines stress as *the non-specific response of the body to any demand placed on it, whether that demand be real, imagined, pleasant, or unpleasant.* Dan Taylor, a stress management consultant in Arlington, Texas, defines stress as *the mismatch between an individual's coping skills and the demands of his or her environment.* From these definitions, the authors conclude that stress arises when the perceived demands of a situation exceed the perceived capabilities for meeting the demands.

Which of the following would you call stressful?

1. Building a new home
2. Being audited by the IRS
3. Getting a promotion
4. Sitting in a dentist's chair for braces
5. Getting married
6. Taking an exam

All of these six life events are stressful because they require us to adapt and change in response to them, which taxes our mental and physical adaptive mechanisms. Because positive or pleasurable events, such as getting a new home, can require as much adaptation on our part as negative or painful events, like being audited by the IRS, they can be equally stressful.

How much stress we feel depends on the amount of change required to cope with the situation. How can we tell the difference in good stress or bad stress?

TYPES OF STRESS

Hans Selye (1974) has described and labeled four basic types of stress:

1. **Eustress** is defined as good stress or short term stress that strengthens us for immediate physical activity, creativity, and enthusiasm. It's characterized as short-lived, easily identified, externalized, and positive. Two examples would be an individual who experiences short-term stress by psyching up for the hundred yard dash, and an individual who is really excited about beginning a new project at work. The secret of positive stress is a sense of control. When we can make choices and influence the outcome of a situation, we meet the challenge successfully and return to a normal level of functioning relatively quickly. This is the happy feeling of "I did it!"

2. **Distress** is negative or harmful stress that causes us to constantly readjust or adapt. Distress occurs when we feel no control over outcomes; we see few or no choices; the source of stress is not clear; the stress is prolonged over a period of time, or several sources of stress exist simultaneously. Distress is accompanied by feelings of tension, pressure, and anxiety rather than the concerted energy of eustress.

3. **Hyperstress or overload** occurs when stressful events pile up and stretch the limits of our adaptability. An example would be an individual who goes through a divorce, loses a parent, and then has a serious illness, all in the same year. It is when we have to cope with too many changes at once or adapt to radical changes for which we are not prepared that stress can become a serious problem.

4. **Hypostress or underload** occurs when we're bored, lacking stimulation, or unchallenged. This type of stress frustrates our need for variety and new experiences. For example, having a job that does not have new challenges can cause constant frustration. This is considered negative stress. Hans Selye (1974) believes that people who enjoy their work, regardless of how demanding it may be, will be less stress-ridden than people who are bored with a job that makes few demands or is too repetitive. It is not the stress

Successful activity, no matter how intense, leaves you with comparatively few "scars." It causes stress but little distress.

Hans Selye

itself that is enjoyed but instead the excitement or stimulation of the anticipated rewards. If you are involved in something you like, you are much more likely to handle frustration, pressure, or conflict effectively. This kind of stress is just not as "stressful."

We have seen that some stress is necessary to give our lives variety and to challenge us to grow and expand our abilities, but too much stress, or the wrong kind, or at the wrong time, becomes debilitating.

As important as it is to understand what stress is, it is even more important to understand where the stress originates. When you determine what stress means for you, you have a choice of dealing with it more effectively or eliminating it completely.

CAUSES OF STRESS

Is it other people, your job, your financial situation, pressure, illness? Stress consists of an event, called a *stressor,* plus how we feel about it, how we interpret it, and what we do to cope with it.

Common stressors include:

- the setting in which we live
- other people
- places we go
- our daily routine
- family members
- our job
- time—too little, too much
- money
- school
- dating
- our given health condition
- a spoken word
- a certain event
- a simple thought

Have you ever felt that it's the little things in life that get you down? Daily hassles may have a greater effect on our moods and health than do the major misfortunes of life.

Richard Lazarus

· Two words best relate to the actual cause of stress: *change* and *threat.* Either or both can disturb the psyche. When workers lose their job, that is a significant change and usually a threat to their ego, self-esteem, and even the material aspects of their life. Similarly, the loss of a spouse is a major change and may pose many different threats.

These changes and threats would probably fall into three possible categories (Taylor, 1990):

1. Anticipated Life Events. Examples might be graduation from high school and entering college, a job promotion, marriage, birth, and retirement.

2. Unexpected Life Events. Some examples might be a serious accident, separation from a spouse or someone we love, sudden death of a loved one, divorce, and financial problems.

3. Accumulating Life Events. This would include a dead-end job, traffic, deadlines and pressures, and on-going conflict with friends or family members.

Now, we have a question for you. What causes some people to be devastated and others motivated by the same event?

I AM YOUR MASTER!

I can make you rise or fall. I can work for you or against you. I can make you a success or failure.

I control the way that you feel and the way that you act.

I can make you laugh . . . work . . . love. I can make your heart sing with joy . . . achievement . . . elation. . . .

Or I can make you wretched . . . dejected . . . morbid. . . .

I can make you sick . . . listless. . . .

I can be as a shackle . . . heavy . . . attached . . . burdensome. . . .

Or I can be as the prism's hue . . . dancing . . . bright . . . fleeting . . . lost forever unless captured by pen or purpose.

I can be nurtured and grown to be great and beautiful . . . seen by the eyes of others through action in you.

I can never be removed . . . only replaced.

I am a THOUGHT

Why not know me better?

Anonymous

Table 8.1
Internally Created Pressures

- Do you expect problem-free living?
- Are you pessimistic and expect the worst from life?
- Do you compare your achievements, or lack of them, to those of others?
- Do you worry about situations you can't control?
- Are you a perfectionist? Do you expect too much of yourself or others?
- Are you competitive and seem to turn every encounter into a win/lose situation?
- Are you a victim of "hurry sickness" and constantly expect yourself to perform better and faster?
- Are you self-critical? Do you focus on your faults, rather than your strengths?
- Do you expect others, rather than yourself, to provide your emotional security?
- Do you assume you know how others feel and what they want from you, instead of asking them?
- Do you feel powerless and fail to see your available choices?

The Power of Our Thoughts. Dan McGee (1989) teaches his clients that stress is caused by the interaction between the events in a person's environment and how he or she interprets these events. Modern stress theory agrees that what causes us stress is not what happens, but how we perceive what happens.

Now, let's answer our earlier question: What causes some people to be devastated and others motivated by the same event? Think about it like this:

QUESTION: What does a person do when they are coping more effectively than someone else?
ANSWER: They draw different conclusions about the same event.

Often, our greatest source of stress is the tremendous pressure and anxiety that we create internally with our thoughts and feelings. Do you often worry about situations you cannot control? Do you often feel powerless and fail to see your available choices? Review Table 8.1 for more negative thoughts and feelings. Do any of these sound familiar to you?

Because how we interpret and label our experiences can serve either to relax or stress us, you will learn how to deal with stressful thoughts and feelings later in this chapter. However, one helpful technique seems appropriate to discuss at this time.

We can control our thoughts, so we would be wise to practice *thought-stopping* techniques in stressful situations. Thought stopping can help you overcome the nagging worry and doubt which stands in the way of relaxation. Thought stopping involves concentrating on the unwanted thoughts and, after a short time, suddenly stopping and emptying your mind. The command *stop* is generally used to interrupt the unpleasant thoughts. Then, it is time to substitute thoughts that are reassuring and self-accepting. For example, you say, "I know I am going to survive this divorce," rather than, "I will never make it without Joe."

Now, let's see what happens to the body when stressful events and thoughts arise.

Man is not disturbed by events, but by the view he takes of them.

Epictetus

THE EFFECTS OF STRESS

Dr. Hans Seyle (1974), in his years as a stress-researcher, found that the body has a three-stage reaction to stress: Stage 1—Alarm; Stage 2—Resistance; and Stage 3—Exhaustion. He called these stages of chain of reactions to stress the *general adaptation syndrome*. We will discuss each of these reactions.

The Alarm Stage. Your body recognizes the stressor and prepares for fight or flight, which is done by a release of hormones from the endocrine glands. These hormones cause an increase in the heartbeat and respiration, elevation in the blood sugar level, increase in perspiration, dilated pupils, and slowed digestion. According to Dr. Walter B. Cannon of the Harvard Medical School, you then choose whether to share this burst of energy to fight or flee.

The Resistance Stage. This is a period of recovery and stabilization, during which the individual adapts to the stress. Consequently, the individual does what he or she can to meet the threat. Although it is true that the level of bodily arousal is not as high as it was in the alarm stage, it does remain higher than usual. This is nature's way of giving us greater protection against the original stressor. Coping responses are often strongest at this point. Because the individual attempts to do what is necessary to meet the threat, the most effective behavior of which the person is capable of often comes forth. Often, people are so overwhelmed in the alarm stage that they simply can't function. However, if there is effective functioning, it occurs in the resistance stage.

Stress is poison in your body.

Anonymous

The Exhaustion Stage. Stress is a natural and unavoidable part of our lives, but it becomes a problem when it persists and becomes long term. Continuous stress will not enable the important *resistance* step to take place, and you will go from step one, *alarm,* directly to step three, *exhaustion.* When you remain exhausted because of continual exposure to stress, you become more receptive to physiological reactions and behavioral changes. What are these reactions and changes?

PHYSICAL EFFECTS OF STRESS

John Powell (1960) says, *We do not bury our emotions dead—they remain alive in our subconscious minds and intestines to hurt and trouble us.* Below are some examples of the "trouble" that can result:

Headaches	Skin rashes
Dermatitis	Allergies
Asthma	Hyperventilation
Common colds	Vaginal discharges
Dizziness	Fatigue
Muscle spasms	Aching back and limbs
Hypertension	Neck and shoulder tension
Rapid heart rate	Excessive sweating
Impotence	Blurry vision
Indigestion	Burning stomach
Diarrhea	Vomiting
Stomach aches	Delayed menstruation

These physical problems are your body's natural way of telling you that there is too much stress and tension in your life, and most of us have a special physical organ or target area that lets us know when the stress is too great. Do you know what your special target area is? Once you have learned to tune into your own signals, you will be able to recognize stress when it starts, before it takes a toll on your body.

BEHAVIORAL EFFECTS OF STRESS

Another measuring tool for you to help recognize excessive stress in yourself and others is through behavioral changes. Below are some of these changes:

Nervous tics	Frowning
Door slamming	Hair twisting
Fist clenching	Jaw tightening
Insomnia	Nail biting
Tears	Grinding of teeth
Temper tantrums	Acts of violence
Apathy	Impatience
Visible fears	Changed eating habits
Clammy skin	Changed drinking habits
Withdrawal	Changed smoking habits
Depression	Worry
Irritability	Boredom

Evaluate this list in relationship to your own life and add any other behavioral changes you may experience that are not included here. This list can help you recognize imbalance and disharmony within and without, and that recognition is necessary if you are to effect a positive change for yourself.

Now that you know how to recognize physiological and behavioral effects of stress, is there anything else you need to be aware of?

Stress is how the body tells the mind what the mind is telling the body.

Vic Shaw

PERSONALITY TYPES

Are you a stress seeker or a stress-avoider? How do you perform under pressure? Is it possible to respond to the normal pressures and stress of life with vitality, meaning, and joy? What kind of lifestyle do you prefer to live: rushed, relaxed, or somewhere in between?

Research has indicated that there are basically three personality types in relation to stress, with each type differing in their abilities to effectively handle it. These types are *Type A, Type B,* and a combination of Type A and Type B, now referred to as *Type C.* What behavioral characteristics do these types have?

Type A. In recent years, there has been a tremendous amount of research directed toward determining the correlation between heart disease and emotional stress. Among the findings is strong evidence that the major cause of coronary artery and heart disease is a complex of emotional reactions which have been designated *Type A Behavioral Pattern* (Friedman & Rosenman, 1974). These researchers consistently found that almost all of their cardiac patients had in common a competitive, aggressive, ambitious, and stressful lifestyle. They also found that the element of hostility was very prevalent among their patients. Here are some other characteristics of this type:

- A drive to succeed, coupled with impatience, irritability, and aggressiveness
- Trouble relaxing and is restless
- Perfectionist and seeks results *now*
- Feelings of pressure even when relaxed
- A constant clock watcher
- Ignores fatigue while doing strenuous work
- Thrives on stress; his or her work is never done
- Only happy with a vigorous, fast-paced lifestyle
- Time pressures frequently create frustration and sometimes hostility
- May appear nervous, scattered, and hyper
- Eats fast, walks fast, and talks fast

One striking thing we have discovered is that there are two main types of human beings: "racehorses" and "turtles."

Hans Selye

Recent research suggests that Type A behavior begins in childhood with an early emphasis on competition and achievement. Although Type A people tend to be high achievers, they pay a high price for their accomplishments in terms of decreased ability to enjoy life and an increased risk of stress-related diseases.

Type B. This behavior pattern (Friedman & Rosenman, 1974) is the opposite of the Type A. Type B people are seldom harried by the need to be involved in an ever-increasing series of activities in a continually decreasing amount of time. Here are some other characteristics of Type B people:

- Serious but easy going
- Patient and relaxed
- Enjoys leisure and opportunities to experiment and reflect
- Prefers a peaceful, steady, quiet, and generally tranquil lifestyle
- Not easily irritated
- Are less competitive than A's
- Slower paced; feels no need to hurry
- May appear lethargic, sluggish, and bored
- Is a stress avoider; may *avoid* new challenges
- Speaks slow, walks slow, eats slow
- Sometimes lacks the excitement, enthusiasm, and dynamism needed to perform at peak levels under pressure

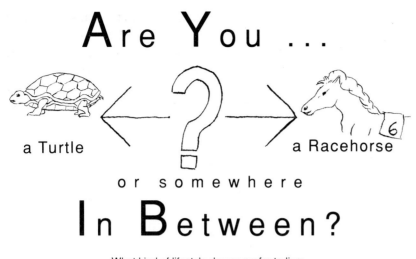

Are You ...

a Turtle

or somewhere

In Between?

a Racehorse

What kind of lifestyle do you prefer to live:
rushed, relaxed, or a balance between the two?

Type B people may have a tremendous drive, but they may not take the risks necessary for big rewards. When they do take the risks, their drive is coupled with time to ponder leisurely and weigh alternatives. It may sound like Type B people do not have a lot of stresses. However, if they are in a Type A environment that requires a great deal of structure, this can be very stressful to them.

Type C (A balance of A and B). This pattern, according to Robert and Marilyn Kriegel (1984), characterizes people who perform at peak levels under pressure and change, without the debilitating effects of stress. These people are ambitious, motivated, and success-oriented. Here are some other characteristics:

- Recognizes a need to respond quickly and appropriately to change and pressure
- Does not respond to pressure by being driven and aggressive Type A's
- Does not respond to pressure by being patient and passive Type B's
- Chooses a balance between the behavior most suited to meet their needs
- Confronts challenges and takes risks
- Approaches life with a balance of confidence, commitment and control
- Remains positive, spontaneous, and focused in their endeavors
- Feels calm but experiences high energy
- Accomplishes tasks without straining or pushing themselves or others

These individuals feel confident and secure and are able to be more relaxed. They know if they push themselves too hard, they will increase their day-to-day anxiety and endanger their health.

Learning to perform as a Type C enables you to uncover and express your innate potential and use it to perform optimally—no matter what the external pressure.

Robert Kriegel

WHICH TYPE ARE YOU?

Most of us are either Type A or Type B, with varying degrees of Type C. It is estimated that Type A's outnumber Type B's by a little over half.

You will be given an opportunity to complete a stress inventory at the end of this chapter. Like most stress inventories, this one is somewhat flawed because it doesn't give enough weight to individual differences. Be sure and take this into consideration when you look at your scores.

Actually, each of us is really the best judge of ourselves, and we can gradually develop an instinctive feeling that tells us whether we are running above or below the stress level that suits us best. Do you know what your normal stress endurance level is? We encourage you to examine your own behavior in relation to stress, because the key to effective stress management is recognizing when stress becomes more debilitating than stimulating.

In the following section, we will discuss some negative and debilitating techniques of coping with stress.

NEGATIVE AND DEFENSIVE COPING

The ability to handle stress comes from inside yourself—not pills, liquor, or overeating.

Anonymous

When we *cope,* we consciously think and make a decision to deal with the problems we face. However, we may cope in negative ways. We may drink too much, eat too much, worry too much, or even abuse medication and drugs. See Table 8.2 for other negative copers.

Sometimes the stress, frustration, and conflict of dealing with these problems interferes with our ability to maintain a healthy self-concept. We become extremely sensitive to threats to our ego. We will do almost anything to avoid, escape, or shield ourselves from the anxieties elicited by these threats.

In order to protect our feelings of self-esteem and self-respect, we may unconsciously resort to various distortions of reality, frequently referred to as *defense mechanisms* (Freud, 1936).

Defense mechanisms do not eliminate the problems that are the cause of anxiety, but they help us to hide or disguise our feelings and temporarily deal with anxiety or stress. Defense mechanisms have two primary characteristics. First, they distort and deny reality. Second, they operate unconsciously, so that we are unaware that we are using them.

Table 8.2
Negative Copers*

ALCOHOL:	Drink to change your mood.
	Use alcohol as your friend.
DENIAL:	Pretend nothing is wrong.
	Lie. Ignore the problem.
DRUGS:	Abuse coffee; aspirin/medications.
	Smoke pot. Pop pills.
EATING:	Keep binging. Go on a diet.
	Use food to console you.
FAULT FINDING:	Have a judgmental attitude.
	Complain. Criticize.
ILLNESS:	Develop headaches/nervous stomach/ major illness.
	Become accident prone.
INDULGING:	Stay up late. Sleep in.
	Buy on impulse. Waste time.
PASSITIVITY:	Hope it gets better. Procrastinate.
	Wait for a lucky break.
REVENGE:	Get even. Be sarcastic. Talk mean.
STUBBORNNESS:	Be rigid. Demand your way.
	Refuse to be wrong.
TANTRUMS:	Yell. Mope. Pout. Swear.
	Drive recklessly.
WITHDRAWAL:	Avoid the situation. Skip school or work.
	Keep your feelings to yourself.
WORRYING:	Fret over things.
	Imagine the worst.

*Reprinted with permission from *Structured Exercises in Stress Management, Volume II*, Nancy Loving Tubesing and Donald A. Tubesing, Editors. (c) 1983 Whole Person Press, P. O. Box 3151, Duluth, MN 55803, (218) 728–6807.

Following is a discussion of some of the more commonly used defense mechanisms:

Rationalization is perhaps the most widely used defense mechanism, because we all feel a need sometimes to explain our behavior. When the explanations offered are reasonable, rational, and convincing—but not real reasons—we say a person is rationalizing. Rationalization unconsciously provides us with reasons for behavior we ourselves find somewhat questionable. We frequently see this defense mechanism used in schools and universities. Every teacher is familiar with a rather amazing phenomenon that occurs whenever a test is scheduled. An incredible number of disasters sweep through the area. An amazing number of grandparents, mothers, fathers, aunts, uncles, relatives, and pets become ill or die. Alarm clocks don't work and cars won't start.

Repression is the exclusion of painful, unwanted, or dangerous thoughts and impulses from the conscious mind. However, these thoughts and impulses continue to influence our behavior. They may be the cause of our "forgetting" an appointment with the doctor, "inadvertently" working so late that we cannot go to the meeting we felt uncomfortable attending.

Projection is when we attribute our own feelings, shortcomings, or unacceptable impulses to others. An individual is suspicious of her boyfriend. She thinks he is dating other women and is overcome with the feeling of jealousy. The young woman's feeling of anxiety comes from her unconscious desire to date others.

Reaction formation is a defense in which impulses are not only repressed, they are also controlled by emphasizing the opposite behavior. A person who has strong sexual desires that are considered immoral joins The Association to Eliminate Pornography. By joining this organization, the individual is able to avoid his or her undesirable feelings by acting out a behavior opposite from the real impulse or feelings.

Sublimation is when we redirect our basic desires toward a socially valued activity. An example is the hostile individual who was beaten by a parent and later finds a productive outlet in establishing an organization for victims of child abuse. Although this is certainly a valued activity and may provide a degree of comfort for the individual, he or she may have been able to accomplish more by directing hostility toward changing and strengthening the laws for child abuse criminals.

Displacement is when the person redirects strong feelings from one person or object to another that seems more acceptable and less threatening. Your boss gets mad at you, but you cannot release your feelings on your boss, so you go home and yell at your spouse. Your spouse gets mad at your child, so your child kicks the dog and the dog bites you. These are all examples of displacement. Substitute objects are rarely as satisfying as the original objects, but they are less anxiety arousing.

Who Pays The Price For Your Stress?

Is it your spouse, friend, child, or your dog?

Defense mechanisms are designed to help us escape the pain of anxiety in stressful situations. Most of us would have difficulty maintaining our mental health without resorting to such defenses. However, the trouble is that these defenses can become common patterns of behavior for reacting to problems and stress.

Do you have a habit of using any of these defense mechanisms? Think of it like this: the more aware you are of the defense mechanisms you use and why you use them, the more likely will be your attempts to face your stressful situations in an open and honest manner. It is important for you to remember that although defense mechanisms offer you short-term relief, your discomfort quickly returns. Why? Your problem has not been solved!

The question then becomes: How can I cope when I have so many problems and so many stressors?

COPING CHOICES

Actually, we have three different options when we are confronted with stressful events and situations. We can (McGee, 1989):

1. Change Environments. We might choose to move to another city, change jobs, separate from our spouse, and so on.

2. Change the Environment. We can often work to improve the situation that is causing us so much stress.

Your response to an event is based on your thought, which is in control, since the quality of your thought is based on your beliefs, prejudices, and attitude.

Dale Rink

3. Change Me (Improve My Coping Skills.) William James once said, *"The greatest discovery of our generation is that men can alter their lives by altering the attitudes of their mind."* This is especially important to remember in relation to stress because, as we stated earlier, *it is not really the event that causes stress, it is our reaction to it— our attitude.*

Our reaction to any event, stressful or not, depends on our thoughts and feelings about what happened or what should have happened. Earlier in this chapter, we stated that most often, the greatest source of stress is the tremendous pressure and anxiety we create internally with our own thoughts and feelings. We also indicated that we would discuss how to deal with stressful thoughts and feelings. We are now ready to do this.

DEALING WITH STRESSFUL THOUGHTS AND FEELINGS

Have you ever said, "I can't help the way I feel!" You want to feel calm when taking tests, but you still get butterflies in your stomach. You want to feel confident when talking to your teacher about a "bad" grade, but you still feel nervous. You don't want to be afraid of heights, but you can't keep yourself from feeling scared. It is almost like you have no control over your feelings. These feelings are just automatic responses to certain stressful events and people in your life.

Consequently, you may say that these events or people *cause* you to feel the way you do. After all, touching your hand to a hot burner causes pain, so why can't people and certain events cause you stress? Let's diagram two events and see what is happening:

Activating Event	Causes	Consequences or Feelings
Touching your hand to a hot burner	**causes**	physical pain
Talking to your teacher	**causes**	stressful, tense feelings

By now, you are still convinced that certain events and other people cause you to feel the way you do. The authors will not argue with you that touching your hand to a hot burner really does cause pain. However, we can't agree that talking to your teacher really causes you to have tense, stressful feelings. Here's why!

THE POWER OF SELF-TALK

Rational emotive therapist Albert Ellis (1980) indicates that the event of talking to your teacher does not cause you to feel tense and stressed. Instead it is your beliefs, or what you say to yourself (self-talk) about talking to your teacher that causes you to feel tense, nervous, and stressed.

Ellis (1980) believes that a great deal of our stress is unnecessary, and that it really comes from faulty conclusions we have made about the world. It is really our interpretations, *what we say to ourselves about our experiences,* that creates the debilitating emotions of anxiety, anger, and depression, as discussed in Chapter 4.

Let's examine the theory of Dr. Ellis by looking at an example he frequently gives at the Institute for Rational-Emotive Therapy in New York:

Assume you walk by your friend's house, and he sticks his head out the window and calls you a bunch of nasty names. You would probably become angry and upset with your friend.

Now let's imagine that you were walking by a mental hospital, rather than your friend's house, and your friend is a patient in the hospital. This time, he yells at you, calling you the same ugly names. What would your feelings be? Would you be as angry and upset now that you know he is not normal and does not live in his house? Probably not!

Actually, the activating event (being called nasty names) was identical in both cases, but your feelings were very different because you were saying something very different to yourself.

In the first example, you were probably saying things like, "He shouldn't call me those nasty names! That's really awful! I'll pay him back!"

However, in the second example, you might be telling yourself something like, "Poor sick John. He can't help what he is doing." Instead of feeling angry, you were probably feeling a degree of sympathy for your friend.

It's easy to see that your *different beliefs (interpretations and thoughts)* about the events determined your feelings. Let's look at the diagram of your two emotional experiences:

> *In a real sense, through our own self-talk, we are either in the construction business or the wrecking business.*
>
> Dorothy Corkville

> *The way one interprets and evaluates reality is the key to one's emotional and mental health.*
>
> Albert Ellis

Activating Event	+	Thoughts or beliefs	=	Consequences or feelings
Being called names		My friend shouldn't do this		angry, upset
Being called names		My friend must be sick		pity, sympathy

Dr. Ellis and cognitive therapist Aaron Beck (1979) stress that our extreme, debilitative emotions are due largely to our irrational beliefs.

Do you have some of the irrational beliefs outlined in Table 8.3? What is the difference between rational and irrational beliefs? Perhaps we need to examine this further.

Table 8.3
Rational and Irrational Beliefs

Albert Ellis (1977) has identified some common irrational beliefs. The rational belief is listed next to the irrational belief.

Irrational Belief	*Rational Belief*
1. It is a dire necessity for me to have love and approval from peers, family, and friends.	1. It is desirable to win the approval of others for practical purposes. It is productive to concentrate on giving rather than receiving love.
2. I must be competent, adequate, achieving, and almost perfect in all that I undertake.	2. It is better to accept oneself as a fallible human being who makes mistakes. It is more important to do your best than to be perfect.
3. When people act badly or unfairly, they should be punished or reprimanded. They are bad people.	3. Individuals may engage in inappropriate acts. It is useful to try to help them change or to just accept them as they are.
4. It is awful, horrible, and catastrophic when people and things are not the way I want them to be.	4. It is too bad that life isn't always the way I'd like it to be. It makes sense to try to change those things that can be changed and to accept those things that can't be altered.
5. Human unhappiness is caused by external events and individuals have little or no ability to control their unhappiness.	5. Emotional disturbance is caused by our attitudes about events, and we can reduce our misery by working hard to change our irrational beliefs.
6. I should be anxious about events or things in the future that are unknown or dangerous.	6. One can neither predict nor prevent unknowns in the future. It is better to change what can be changed and accept the inevitable when it is beyond our control.

	Table 8.3 **Continued**	
7. It is easier to avoid than to face life's difficulties and responsibilities.	7. The easy way out is usually more difficult in the long run.	
8. Human beings must be dependent on others and have someone strong on whom to rely.	8. Although it is helpful to turn to others for advice or feedback, making your own decisions is ultimately the better path toward accomplishing your aims.	
9. My present problems are a result of my past history. Because I have this past, my problems must continue to endure.	9. Just because something affected me in the past, there is no reason that it must continue to affect me in the future. I can learn from past experiences.	
10. There must be a perfect solution to this problem, and it is awful if I can't find it.	10. Some problems are insoluble. Even where solutions exist, it is likely that no solution will be perfect.	
11. The world should be fair.	11. We live in an unfair world. It is more productive to accept what we can't change and to seek happiness despite life's inequities.	
12. I should be comfortable and without pain at all times.	12. Few things can be achieved without pain. Although pain is uncomfortable, it can be tolerated.	

IDENTIFYING RATIONAL AND IRRATIONAL BELIEFS

Sometimes, *self-talk,* what we say to ourselves, is irrational. It doesn't even make sense, but we believe that it is true. The ingredient that makes a belief irrational is that it cannot be scientifically verified. There is no empirical evidence or proof to support the belief.

Irrational beliefs result in inappropriate emotions and behaviors. Inappropriate emotions and behaviors are those that are likely to thwart an individual's desired goals. As we discussed in Chapter 4, when annoyance turns into anger or disappointment turns into depression, an individual is likely to be unsuccessful in achieving his or her goals. Consequently, the individual feels stressed.

On the other hand, *rational beliefs are those beliefs that result in appropriate emotions and behaviors.* Appropriate emotions and behaviors are those that are likely to help an individual attain desired goals. Consequently, the individual feels less stress. It is important to remember that even negative emotions (such as disappointment, concern, etc.) can be appropriate. *The ingredient that makes a belief rational is that it can be scientifically verified. There is empirical evidence to support the belief.*

CHARACTERISTICS OF IRRATIONAL SELF-TALK

As you can see from Table 8.3, almost all irrational self-verbalizations include Should Statements, Awfulizing Statements, and Overgeneralizations. We will now look at these individually.

Should Statements. These are absolutistic demands or moral imperatives that the individual believes *must* occur. Individuals tend to express their shoulds in three areas: *I should, you should,* and the *world should.* Should statements also contain words such as *ought, have to,* and *must.*

Have you ever made statements similar to the ones below?

Helen *should not* be so inconsiderate.
John *should* be a better teacher.
People *ought* to be at meetings on time.
I have *to (must)* make an "A" on the next test.

These statements all imply that other people and things in your world need to be as you want them to be. This is really unreasonable.

True, it would be more pleasant if Helen were more considerate; it would be helpful if John were a better teacher; it would be beneficial if people were at meetings on time; it would be nice to make an "A" on the exam.

It is perfectly rational for us to wish that people would behave differently and that things in our world would be as we want them to be. It is even okay to change what can be changed and accept those things that cannot be altered. However, it is unreasonable for you to expect that other people or the world will ever meet your unrealistic expectations. Reality is reality! Failure to accept this reality can result in your life being filled with disappointments and *more stress.*

Long ago, I made up my mind to let other people have their own peculiarities.

David Grayson

Awfulizing Statements. Generally, when we say that the world, ourselves, or someone *should* be different, we imply that it is *awful* or *terrible* when they are not different. Have you ever made any of the following statements?

What she did to me is just *awful!*
It is just *terrible. . . .*
I just can't *stand it. . . .*
I can't *bear it. . . .*

It is true that things in our world could be improved and that events that happen to us are unfortunate. However, when you consistently talk about how *terrible* or *awful* something is, you will eventually convince yourself that what you are thinking and saying is right. This kind of *self-talk* causes you to feel angry, depressed, and therefore stressed.

In some instances, something is so *terrible* or *awful* that you convince yourself that "*you can't stand it*" or "*you can't bear it.*" As cold and callous as it may sound, if you are alive and conscious, you are "*standing it,*" "*you are bearing it.*"

Overgeneralizations. We often make overgeneralizations based on a single incident or piece of evidence, and we ignore everything else that we know about ourselves and others. Cue words that indicate you may be overgeneralizing are: *all, every, none, never, always, everybody,* and *nobody.* Overgeneralizations frequently lead to human worth statements about ourselves and other people. Think about these statements!

YOU WERE FIRED: I'll never get another job—I'm a complete failure.
YOUR SPOUSE LEFT YOU: No one will ever want to marry me now—
                                    I must be unlovable.

First of all, *never* and *ever* mean a long time. Just because you lost your job, does that prove that no one else will *ever* hire you and that you are a *complete* failure? To be a *complete* failure, you would have to fail 100 percent of the time. This is unrealistic. Oh yes, have you forgotten that you have had other jobs besides the one you just lost? Just because your spouse left you, does that prove that you are unlovable? Think about it: Who else in your life cares about you? Surely, someone else does.

Sometimes we use overgeneralizations when we exaggerate shortcomings of others. For example:

You *never* listen to me.
You *never* do anything for me.

Some people make mountains out of molehills.

Anonymous

Statements such as these lead to anger, resentment, alienation from other people, and *more stress*. Wouldn't it be more accurate to say:

Sometimes you do not listen to me.
You have done some nice things for me.

DISPUTING IRRATIONAL BELIEFS

How do you avoid these irrational beliefs that create feelings of stress? Dr. Ellis (1977) and his colleagues at The Institute of Rational-Emotive Therapy in New York have created a four-step process.

1. Monitor Your Emotional Reactions. Try to describe what you are feeing as accurately as possible. Say, "I feel angry, depressed, fearful, hurt, jealous, sad, worried." Because it is possible to experience more than one negative emotion at the same time, be sure and write down all the unpleasant feelings that you are having.

2. Describe the Activating Event. Write down your perception of the event or whatever seemed to trigger the events that led to your unpleasant feelings and your present stressful condition. It may be something that someone did; it may be something you need to do but are afraid of doing; it may be a series of several small unpleasant happenings, and you have just had too much!

3. Record Your Self-Talk. What are you saying to yourself that is causing you to feel angry, depressed, and so on? What are you thinking or what is going through your head? What are you worried about? When you think about . . . (the activating event) . . . , how do you make yourself depressed or angry? Becoming aware of your self-talk may be difficult at first, but with practice, you can learn to do so.

Remember, the real question for you to answer is: What did you think to feel that?

Dan Taylor

4. Dispute Your Irrational Beliefs. It is now necessary for you to go back to step 3 and do three things: (1) decide whether each statement is a rational or an irrational belief; (2) explain why the belief is rational or why it is irrational; and (3) write some different statements that you can say to yourself in the future to prevent yourself from having such debilitative emotions and experiencing such stress.

Now that you know how to identify and dispute the irrational beliefs that have been causing you stress, we will now discuss some additional ways of managing stress.

> ## AFTERWARD:
> ## IF I COULD LIVE IT OVER
>
> If I had to live my life over again, I'd dare to make
>   more mistakes next time.
> I'd relax.
> I would limber up.
> I would be sillier than I have been this trip.
> I would take more chances.
> I would take more trips. I would climb more
>   mountains, swim more rivers.
> I would eat more ice cream and less beans.
> I would perhaps have more actual troubles, but I'd
>   have fewer imaginary ones.
> You see, I'm one of those people who live seriously
>   and sanely hour after hour, day after day.
> Oh, I've had my moments. And if I had it to do
>   over again, I'd have more of them.
> In fact, I'd try to have nothing else, just moments,
>   each after another, instead of living so many years
>   ahead of each day.
> I've been one of those persons who never goes
>   anywhere without a thermometer, a hot water
>   bottle, a raincoat and a parachute.
> If I had it to do over again, I would travel lighter
>   than I have.
> If I had to live my life over, I would start barefoot
>   earlier in the spring and stay that way later in the
>   fall.
> I would go to more dances.
> I would ride more merry-go rounds.
> I would pick more daisies.
>
> Nadine Stair
> (This delightful perspective of life
> was written at age 85.)

20 TIPS FOR MANAGING STRESS

Following is a list of several suggestions that may help you live with stress, whether it is an occasional mild upset, which most of us experience, or one that is more lasting and severe. Table 8.4 also gives some additional positive coping strategies.

1. **Work off stress.** If you are angry or upset, try to do something physical such as running, gardening, playing tennis, or cleaning out the garage. Working the stress out of your system will leave you much better prepared to handle your problems.

A man is hurt not so much by what happens, as by his opinion of what happens.

Montaigne

2. **Enjoy yourself.** Part of the zest of life that minimizes the adverse effect of stress is enjoyment. That is really what a vacation is all about. Have a little vacation each day. Do something each day that you really enjoy, whether it is reading your favorite book or magazine, gossiping on the phone, having lunch with a friend, watching your favorite TV program, taking a walk, or playing your musical instrument. Reward yourself with some pleasure. It is this type of pleasure that makes life enjoyable and energizes you for other tasks.

3. **Talk it out.** When something is bothering you, talk it out with someone you trust and respect such as a friend, family member, clergyman, teacher, or counselor. Sometimes another person can help you see a new side to your problem and thus, a new solution.

4. **Give in occasionally.** If you find yourself getting into frequent quarrels with people, try giving in once in awhile instead of fighting and insisting that you are always right. You may find others beginning to give in, too.

5. **Do something for others.** If you find that you are worrying about yourself all the time, try doing something for somebody else. This helps get your mind off yourself and can give you a sense of well-being.

6. **Have some real close friends.** Having true friends that you do not need to fear criticism from, and whom you can talk freely to, is important. Friends who are accepting are not a threat to your ego. Without at least one such friend, a person is forced into emotional isolation, which in itself is a stress, and one that usually produces adverse responses.

7. **Eat sensibly.** Try to have balanced meals and pay close attention to the habit of eating "junk foods." Don't starve yourself to lose weight. Watch excessive sugar and caffeine. Think of your body as a car. If you don't put oil, gas, and water, in your car frequently, it will quit running. So will your body if you abuse it with improper eating habits.

8. **Get organized.** Plan, schedule, take notes, and keep good files. Organizing the daily nitty-gritty of life reduces stress. Save your memory for more creative and pleasurable things.

9. **Rehearse.** When you're facing a situation that you know will be stressful to you, rehearse it. Either mentally or with a friend, anticipate what might occur and plan your response. Being prepared reduces stress.

10. **Do it now.** Do your most difficult or most hated task at the beginning of the day when you're fresh; avoid the stress of dreading it all day. Procrastination breeds stress!

11. **Learn to say "No".** Say no when your schedule is full: to activities you don't enjoy; to responsibilities that aren't really yours; to emotional demands that leave you feeling drained; to other people's problems that you can't solve.

12. **Learn to accept what you cannot change.** If the source of stress is beyond your control at the present, try your best to accept it until you can change it or it changes itself. This is much better than spinning your wheels, and getting nowhere.

13. **Avoid self-medication.** There are many chemicals such as alcohol and other drugs that can mask stress symptoms, but they do not help you adjust to stress itself. Also, many are habit-forming and can cause more stress than they solve; consult with your doctor before you decide to use them. It is important too, that the ability to handle stress comes from within you, not from externals.

14. **Live a balanced life.** Make time for what is important to you. Work and school are important, but they are not the only important areas in your life. What about time with your family and friends? What about time for a hobby? Stop and ask yourself, "Am I spending too much time on one important area of my life and forgetting the others?"

15. **Get enough sleep and rest.** Lack of sleep can lessen your ability to deal with stress by making you more irritable. If stress continually prevents you from sleeping, you should inform your doctor.

16. **Make yourself available.** Many of us have the feeling that we are being left out, slighted, neglected, or rejected. Often, we just imagine that others are feeling this way about us, when in reality they are eager for us to make the first move. Instead of withdrawing and feeling sorry for yourself, get involved.

17. **Shun the "Superman" urge.** Some people expect too much from themselves and are in a constant state of worry and anxiety because they think they are not achieving as much as they should. No one can be perfect in everything, so decide which things you do well and put your main effort into these. Next, give the best of your ability to the things you can't do as well, but don't be too hard on yourself if you do not excel at these tasks.

18. **Develop a regular exercise program.** Like most things, including stress, there is an optimal amount. A sensible exercise program can begin with a short daily walk that is gradually increased. To avoid excess physical stress you need to develop your own program gradually and then maintain it constantly. There is increasing evidence that regular, sensible exercise causes a number of important chemical changes in the body. It helps to eliminate depression. It helps to alleviate anxiety. Sensible, enjoyable exercise is nature's anti-stress reaction remedy. Experts consider aerobics to be an excellent release.

19. **Take care of yourself.** If you don't, no one else will. Don't say, "I don't have time." You've got all the time there is—24 hours a day—so begin today by choosing some stress reduction techniques that will divert your attention from whatever is causing you stress.

God grant me the serenity to accept the things I cannot change, courage to change the things I can, and the wisdom to know the difference.

Anonymous

Keeping in good physical shape is an important antidote to stress overload, but it's not the cure.

Michael Cavanagh

20. **Learn to relax.** You can learn to counteract your habitual reaction to stress by learning to relax. Learning to relax all the muscles in your body returns your blood pressure, heartbeat, respiration, and circulation to normal. Relaxation gives you more energy and normalizes your physical, mental, and emotional processes. Consequently, you are more equipped to handle the stresses in your life.

Would you like to try a deep breathing and relaxation exercise now. For those times when you don't have the 10–15 minutes that this normally requires, here's a mini-version of relaxation therapy that requires less than 10 seconds of your time. Do it as often during the day as you can. Charles Stroebel (1982) author of *The Quieting Reflex,* is confident you will soon feel the difference in your stress level.

1. *Shut your eyes and draw your attention and concentration inward.*
2. *Smile inwardly with your mouth and eyes.*
3. *Say to yourself: "Alert mind, calm body."*
4. *Take a deep easy breath all the way down to your abdomen.*
5. *As you exhale, let your jaw, tongue, and shoulders go limp.*
6. *Feel a wave of warmth and heaviness sweep down to your toes.*
7. *Enjoy the feeling of peace and relaxation that this brings.*
8. *Open your eyes and resume normal activity.*

Table 8.4
Positive Copers*

DIVERSIONS

GETAWAYS:	Spend time alone. See a movie. Daydream.
HOBBIES:	Write. Paint. Remodel. Create something.
LEARNING:	Take a class. Read. Join a club.
MUSIC:	Play an instrument. Sing. Listen to the stereo.
PLAY:	Play a game. Go out with friends.
WORK:	Tackle a new project. Keep busy. Volunteer.

FAMILY

BALANCING:	Balance time at work and home. Accept the good with the bad.
CONFLICT RESOLUTION:	Look for win-win solutions. Forgive readily.
ESTEEM BUILDING:	Build good family feelings. Focus on personal strengths.
NETWORKING:	Develop friendships with other families. Make use of community resources.
TOGETHERNESS:	Take time to be together. Build family traditions. Express affection.

	Table 8.4 **Continued**

INTERPERSONAL

AFFIRMATION:	Believe in yourself. Trust others. Give compliments.
ASSERTIVENESS:	State your needs and wants. Say "No" respectfully.
CONTACT:	Make new friends. Touch. Really listen to others.
EXPRESSION:	Show feelings. Share feelings.
LIMITS:	Accept other's boundaries. Drop some involvements.
LINKING:	Share problems with others. Ask for support from family and friends.

MENTAL

IMAGINATION:	Look for the humor. Anticipate the future.
LIFE PLANNING:	Set clear goals. Plan for the future.
ORGANIZING:	Take charge. Make order. Don't let things pile up.
PROBLEM SOLVING:	Solve it yourself. Seek outside help. Tackle problems head-on.
RELABELING:	Change perspectives. Look for good in a bad situation.
TIME MANAGEMENT:	Focus on top priorities. Work smarter, not harder.

PHYSICAL

BIOFEEDBACK:	Listen to your body. Know your physical limitations.
EXERCISE:	Pursue physical fitness. Jog. Swim. Dance. Walk.
RELAXATION:	Tense and relax each muscle. Take a warm bath. Breath deeply.
SELF-CARE:	Energize your work and play. Strive for self-improvement.
STRETCHING:	Take short breaks through your day.

SPIRITUAL

COMMITMENT:	Take up a worthy cause. Say "yes." Invest yourself meaningfully.
FAITH:	Find purpose and meaning. Trust God.
PRAYER:	Confess. Ask forgiveness. Pray for others. Give thanks.
SURRENDER:	Let go of problems. Learn to live with the situation.
VALUING:	Set priorities. Be consistent. Spend time and energy wisely.
WORSHIP:	Share beliefs with others. Put faith into action.

*Reprinted with permission from *Structured Exercises in Stress Management, Volume 2*, Nancy Loving Tubesing and Donald A. Tubesing, Editors (c) 1983 Whole Person Press, P. O. Box 3153, Duluth, MN. 55803 (218) 728–6807.

Was Dr. Stroebel correct? Do you feel more relaxed?

Obviously, not all of these coping strategies and stress-management techniques are applicable to everyone. So take a long, hard look at your own personal life style, and try to make a good evaluation as to what factors are adding stress to your life, particularly negative stress. Perhaps, you will even find yourself falling into the category of Type A behavior. Then, select the specific strategies that fit your personal situation and make a commitment to do whatever is necessary to reduce the negative stress in your life or at least to learn to better cope with it effectively.

Things usually turn out best for people who make the best of the way things turn out.

Art Linkletter

A LAST THOUGHT

On a day-to-day basis we are knowingly and unknowingly bombarded by stimuli from both the real world and our imagination. Our reaction to this stimuli requires a certain amount of adaptive energy. How well we can adapt is determined to a large part by our attitude. Think of your adaptive reservoir as a battery. As the stress level rises, so does the drain on the battery. If there is a continuous drain without recharging, we end up with an empty energy reservoir. It is at this point that our resistance is lowest, and we are susceptible to physiological and behavioral changes.

Even if it were possible to go through life without stress, we really wouldn't want to, because stress is what prepares us to handle things we are unfamiliar with, or things that appear to threaten us. A certain number of problems and stresses are just stimulating. Most of us desire the excitement of trying something new occasionally, the challenge of doing a difficult job, and the strength to face unhappy, frightening or even tragic events that happen in almost all our lives. Without a doubt, some stress challenges us to think creatively and to find innovative solutions to problems.

Handled well, then, stress is a positive force that strengthens us for future situations. But handled poorly, or allowed to get out of hand, stress becomes harmful and can lead to physical, mental, or emotional problems.

Therefore, it is extremely important not only that we recognize stress, but that we learn how to handle it, live with it, and make it work for us.

KEY TERMS

Stress

Distress

Hypostress

Thought-stopping

Resistance stage

Type A

Type B

Type C

Repression

Reaction Formation

Displacement

Rational Belief

Eustress

Hyerstress

Stressor

Alarm stage

Exhaustion stage

General Adaptation Syndrome

Defense Mechanisms

Rationalization

Projection

Sublimation

Self-talk

Irrational Belief

CHAPTER DISCUSSION QUESTIONS

1. What is your personal definition of stress?
2. What types of situations are most stressful to you?
3. What can you do to alleviate some of the stress in your life?
4. Why do you feel some people are devastated and yet others feel motivated by the same event?
5. How does stress affect you physically as well as behaviorally?
6. Which personality type (A, B, or C) best describes the way you prefer to live your life?
7. Which defense mechanism do you tend to use most frequently and in what situations?
8. Name and give examples of the three self-verbalizations frequently found in irrational beliefs.
9. What is the difference in rational and irrational beliefs?
10. Name and discuss the four steps to use in disputing irrational beliefs. Which of these steps would be most difficult for you?
11. How do you personally cope and manage stress?

REFERENCES

Beck, A. T (1979) *Cognitive Therapy and Emotional Disorders.* New York: New American Library.

Ellis, A. (1980) "Overview of the Clinical Theory of Rational-Emotive Therapy," R. Greiger and J. Boyd (Eds.). *Rational Emotive Therapy: A Skills-Based Approach.* New York: Van Nostrand Reinhold.

Ellis, Albert and Harper, Robert. (1977) *A New Guide to Rational Living.* California: Wilshire Books.

Freud, S. *The Problems of Anxiety.* (1936) New York: Norton.

Friedman, M., and Rosenman, R. H. (1981) *Type A Behavior and Your Heart.* New York: Fawcett.

Kriegel, Robert and Kriegel, Marilyn Harris. (1984) *The C Zone, Peak Performance Under Pressure.* New York: Ballantine Books.

Powell, John. (1969) *Why Am I Afraid to Tell You Who I Really Am?* Chicago: Argus Communications.

Seyle, Hans. (1974) *Stress Without Distress.* New York: J. B. Lippincott Co.

———. (1956) *The Stress of Life.* New York: McGraw-Hill.

Stroebel, Charles. (1982) *The Quieting Reflex.* New York: G. P. Putnam's Sons.

Taylor, Dan and McGee, Dan. (1989 & 1990) "Stress Management Workshop Series." Metro-McGee Associates, Inc. Arlington, Texas.

Tubesing, Nancy Loving and Tubesing, Donald A. (1983) *Structured Exercises in Stress Management, Volume II* Duluth, Minnesota: Whole Person Press.

WHERE DOES STRESS COME FROM IN YOUR LIFE?

Purpose: To discover where the sources of stress are in your life.

Instructions:

I. You need to keep track of any stressful event that occurs in your life for a one-week period of time. Each day at approximately 10:00 A.M., 6:00 P.M., and 10:00 P.M. write down each of the stressful events that occurred to you during the previous period of time.

II. Use the following form:

Day	Time	Stressful Event	Type of Stress (Indicate whether the event involves conflict, change, frustration, or some combination.)	Your Reaction

III. Complete the following questions at the end of the week.

  1. Is there a specific type of stress that is most frequent in your life? Explain.

  2. Is there a specific location or set of circumstances that produce a great deal of stress for you? Explain.

  3. What specific reaction to the stressful events did you display? Give examples.

  4. What could you do to reduce the amount of stress in your life?

HOW VULNERABLE ARE YOU TO STRESS?*

Purpose: To assess how vulnerable you are to stress and to make specific lifestyle changes for coping with stress.

Instructions:

I. Score each item from **1 (almost always) to 5 (never),** according to how much of the time each statement applies to you.

_____ 1. I eat at least one hot, balanced meal a day.

_____ 2. I get seven to eight hours sleep at least four nights a week.

_____ 3. I give and receive affection regularly.

_____ 4. I have at least one relative within 30 miles on whom I can rely.

_____ 5. I exercise to the point of perspiration at least twice a week.

_____ 6. I smoke less than half a pack of cigarettes a day.

_____ 7. I take fewer than five alcoholic drinks a week.

_____ 8. I am the appropriate weight for my height.

_____ 9. I have an income adequate to meet basic expenses.

_____ 10. I get strength from my religious beliefs.

_____ 11. I regularly attend club or social activities.

_____ 12. I have a network of friends and acquaintances.

_____ 13. I have one or more friends to confide in about personal matters.

_____ 14. I am in good health (including eyesight, hearing, teeth).

_____ 15. I am able to speak openly about my feelings when angry or worried.

_____ 16. I have regular conversations with the people I live with about domestic problems, chores, money and daily living issues.

_____ 17. I do something for fun at least once a week.

_____ 18. I drink fewer than three cups of coffee (or tea or cola drinks) a day.

_____ 19. I am able to organize my time effectively.

_____ 20. I take quiet time for myself during the day.

_____ TOTAL

II. To Get Your Score:

Add up the figures and subtract 20.

III. Analyzing Your Results:

Any number over 30 indicates vulnerability to stress.

A score between 50 and 75 indicates serious vulnerability to stress.

A score of over 75 indicates extreme vulnerability to stress.

---

*"Vulnerability Scale" from the *Stress Audit,* developed by Lyle H. Miller and Alma Dell Smith. Copyright Biobehavioral Associates, Brookline, MA., reprinted with permission.

DISCUSSION

1. Specifically, what areas are causing you the greatest amount of difficulty?

2. Specifically, what lifestyle changes are you willing to make in order to more effectively cope with stress?

THE SOCIAL READJUSTMENT RATING SCALE*

Purpose: To help you become more aware of stress-producing events in your life, whether negative or positive, and to demonstrate the correlation between cumulative stress and major health changes.

Instructions:

I. Each participant is to individually fill out the Social Readjustment Rating Scale by placing in "Your Event" column the value of each stressful event experienced in the past 12 months.

II. Total "Your Event" column.

III. Become aware of what your chances are of experiencing a major health change in the next two years:

    0–150 points = 1 in 3 chance

    150–300 points = 50–50 chance

    Over 300 points = almost 90 percent chance

IV. Divide into groups of four or five to discuss the results of each individual's scale.

SOCIAL READJUSTMENT RATING SCALE

Rank	Life Event	Value	Your Event
1.	Death of spouse	100	_____
2.	Divorce	73	_____
3.	Marital separation	65	_____
4.	Jail term	63	_____
5.	Death of a close family member	63	_____
6.	Personal injury or illness	53	_____
7.	Marriage	50	_____
8.	Fired from job	47	_____
9.	Marital reconciliation	45	_____
10.	Retirement	45	_____
11.	Change in health of family member	44	_____
12.	Pregnancy	40	_____
13.	Sex difficulties	39	_____
14.	Gain of new family member	39	_____
15.	Business readjustment	39	_____
16.	Change in financial state	38	_____
17.	Death of a close friend	37	_____
18.	Change to different line of work	36	_____
19.	Change in number of arguments with spouse	35	_____
20.	Mortgage or loan for major purchase (home, etc.)	31	_____
21.	Foreclosure of mortgage or loan	30	_____
22.	Change in responsibilities at work	29	_____
23.	Son or daughter leaving home	29	_____
24.	Trouble with in-laws	29	_____
25.	Outstanding personal achievement	28	_____
26.	Wife begins or stops work	26	_____
27.	Begin or end school	26	_____
28.	Change in living conditions	25	_____

*Holmes, T. H. and Rahe, R. H. "The Social Readjustment Rating Scale," from JOURNAL OF PSYCHOSOMATIC RESEARCH, No. 227. Reproduced by permission from Pergamon Press Ltd., Headington Hill, Oxford, England.

29. Revision of personal habits .... 25 _____
30. Trouble with boss .... 23 _____
31. Change in work hours or conditions .... 20 _____
32. Change in residence .... 20 _____
33. Change in schools .... 20 _____
34. Change in recreation .... 19 _____
35. Change in church activities .... 19 _____
36. Change in social activities .... 18 _____
37. Mortgage or loan for lesser purchase (car, TV, etc.) .... 17 _____
38. Change in sleeping habits .... 16 _____
39. Change in number of family get-togethers .... 15 _____
40. Change in eating habits .... 15 _____
41. Vacation .... 13 _____
42. Christmas .... 12 _____
43. Minor violations of the law .... 11 _____

TOTAL _____

DISCUSSION

1. Did you already have an awareness of the amount of stress in your life or were you surprised?

2. What are some things you could do to lessen or control stress-producing events in your life?

3. Why do you think some people are more negatively affected by stress than others?

TYPE A AND TYPE B BEHAVIOR*

Purpose: To help you identify individual personality characteristics that would indicate Type A or Type B behavior.

Instructions:

  I. Rate yourself as to how you typically react in each of the situations listed below by circling one response for each question.
 II. Find your total score by adding together the circled number response of each question.
III. Determine whether your behavior is primarily Type A or Type B according to the following scale:

        1– 47 Extreme Type B
       48– 94 Type B
      95–141 Both Type A and Type B
    142–188 Type A
    189–235 Extreme Type A

    In general: a score greater than 120 is Type A
                  a score less than 120 is Type B

	Always	Frequently	Sometimes	Seldom	Never
1. Are you punctual?	5	4	3	2	1
2. Do you work under constant deadlines?	5	4	3	2	1
3. Do you indulge in competitive hobbies?	5	4	3	2	1
4. Do you like routine household chores?	5	4	3	2	1
5. Do you prefer to do a task yourself because others are too slow or can't do it as well?	5	4	3	2	1
6. Do you work while you are eating, in the bathroom, etc.?	5	4	3	2	1
7. Do you walk fast?	5	4	3	2	1
8. Do you eat hurriedly?	5	4	3	2	1
9. Are you patient and understanding?	5	4	3	2	1
10. Do you carry on several lines of thought at the same time?	5	4	3	2	1
11. Do you interrupt others when they talk about subjects that don't interest you?	5	4	3	2	1
12. Do you pretend to listen to others when they talk about subjects that don't interest you?	5	4	3	2	1
13. How often does time seem to pass rapidly for you?	5	4	3	2	1
14. How often do you look at your watch?	5	4	3	2	1

*Mirabal, Thomas E. "Identifying Individual Personality Characteristics." Reproduced by permission from Synergistic Training Systems, Inc., Dallas, Texas.

	Always	Frequently	Sometimes	Seldom	Never
15. Do you feel vaguely guilty when you relax and do absolutely nothing for several hours/days?	5	4	3	2	1
16. How often do you become exasperated when standing in line at movies, restaurants, etc.?	5	4	3	2	1
17. Do you ever find that you cannot recall details of the surroundings after you left a place?	5	4	3	2	1
18. How often are you preoccupied with getting materialistic things?	5	4	3	2	1
19. Do you use a relaxed, laid back speech pattern?	5	4	3	2	1
20. How often do you attempt to schedule more and more in less and less time?	5	4	3	2	1
21. How often do you feel aggressive, hostile, and compelled to challenge people who make you feel uncomfortable?	5	4	3	2	1
22. Do you accentuate your speech, talk fast?	5	4	3	2	1
23. How often do you gesture by clenching your fists, banging your hand on the table, pounding one fist into the palm of the other hand, clenching your jaw, grinding your teeth, etc.?	5	4	3	2	1
24. Do you prefer respect and admiration to affection?	5	4	3	2	1
25. Do you listen well and attentively?	5	4	3	2	1
26. Do you evaluate the activities of yourself and others in terms of numbers (e.g., minutes, hours, days, dollars, age)?	5	4	3	2	1
27. How often do you play to win?	5	4	3	2	1
28. How often do you stay up late to socialize?	5	4	3	2	1
29. How often are you angry?	5	4	3	2	1
30. Do you go out of your way to conceal your anger?	5	4	3	2	1
31. How often are you dissatisfied with your present position or promotional progress?	5	4	3	2	1
32. Do you daydream a lot?	5	4	3	2	1
33. Do you participate in numerous organizations?	5	4	3	2	1

	Always	Frequently	Sometimes	Seldom	Never
34. Did you ever attend night school?	5	4	3	2	1
35. How often do you go to a doctor?	5	4	3	2	1
36. Do you ever "sigh" faintly between words?	5	4	3	2	1
37. How often do you come to work even when you are sick?	5	4	3	2	1
38. How often is your laughter a grim, forced chuckle?	5	4	3	2	1
39. Do/would you avoid firing people?	5	4	3	2	1
40. How often are you genuinely open and responsive to people?	5	4	3	2	1
41. How often do you go to bed early?	5	4	3	2	1
42. If you smoke, do you prefer cigarettes as opposed to a pipe or cigar?	5	4	3	2	1
43. How often do you salt your meal before tasting it?	5	4	3	2	1
44. How often do you exercise?	5	4	3	2	1
45. Do you ever combine vacations with business?	5	4	3	2	1
46. How often do you work late?	5	4	3	2	1
47. How often do you hum, fidget, or drum your fingers while not involved in an activity?	5	4	3	2	1

DISCUSSION

1. Did the results of this exercise make you aware of any Type A behavior pattern in your own personality? Were you surprised?

2. What are some of the dangers of Type A behavior?

3. Is it possible to change from Type A to Type B? How?

4. Would you want to change your behavior patterns if you could?

IDENTIFYING AND DISPUTING SELF-TALK AND BELIEFS

Purpose: To identify irrational beliefs, consequences of those beliefs, and then dispute and challenge those beliefs, to improve emotional functioning.

Instructions:

I. Think of a recent situation in which you had negative feelings that caused you to be emotionally upset.

II. Next, review the examples below and write your responses to each category.

1. Write down the facts of what happened—the *activating event.* Be sure to write down only the objective facts; do not include your subjective, personal value judgments.

EXAMPLE:

My husband came in and told me he wanted a divorce because he wanted to marry a woman at the office where he works.

YOUR EVENT:

2. Write down and number your self-talk about the event. This includes your subjective value judgments, assumptions, beliefs, and predictions that you said to yourself.

EXAMPLE:

1. If he marries her, I won't be able to stand it.
2. He should not have done this to me and the children. He is a sick person.
3. I trusted him so much.
4. Everybody will think I am a complete fool.
5. Why didn't he tell me before now. I just wish he would have done this.

YOUR BELIEFS:

1.

2.

3.

4.

5.

3. Identify the consequences of your self-talk and beliefs. Label your feelings with words such as depressed, angry, hurt, afraid, jealous, and insecure.
   EXAMPLE:
   I felt hurt and angry.
   YOUR CONSEQUENCES:

4. Dispute your beliefs and self-talk. For each sentence in Number Two of this exercise, decide whether what you have written is a rational or irrational belief. Explain why it is rational or irrational and write some alternative rational self-talk.

   EXAMPLE:
   1. I am being irrational. I won't like it one bit if he marries her, but I am sure I can stand it. After all, I do want to keep on living. I am just telling myself I can't stand it.
   2. This is irrational. He really can do whatever he wants—he can get away with this. I cannot control what he or anyone else does. I wish this had not happened, but I will try to concentrate on loving the children and being an effective parent.
   3. I chose to trust him. This is rational. After all, I loved him and trusted him. I cannot imagine loving John and not trusting him. It is only natural that I would feel some hurt, but I will be okay. I just need some time.

4. I am overgeneralizing. This is irrational. I am not a complete fool. I'm not even sure what a complete fool really is. Who is everybody, anyway? It is best that I not concern myself with what other people think. I really have more important things to be concerned with.

5. Of course I wish he had told me before now. It is very rational for me to desire this. He chose not to do so, what else can I say?

YOUR DISPUTES:

1.

2.

3.

4.

5.

DISCUSSION

1. Was it difficult for you to decide which of your beliefs were rational or irrational?

2. Was it difficult for you to write some alternative self-talk to your irrational statements?

3. Do you believe that your self-talk about your emotional situation caused you to have emotional pain?

4. How do you feel about the situation now?

LEARNING JOURNAL FOR MANAGING STRESS

Select the statement below that best defines your feelings about the personal value or meaning gained from this chapter and respond below the dotted line:

I LEARNED THAT I . . .   I WAS SURPRISED THAT I . . .

I REALIZED THAT I . . .   I WAS PLEASED THAT I . . .

I DISCOVERED THAT I . . .   I WAS DISPLEASED THAT I . . .

....

9

What Is Important to Me

I have been able to function as a catalyst,
trying to bring to our awareness that we can
only truly live and enjoy and appreciate life
if we realize at all times that we are finite.
Needless to say I have learned these lessons
from my dying patients—who in their suffering
and dying realized that we have only NOW—"so
have it fully and find what turns you on,
because no one can do this for you!"

Elisabeth Kübler-Ross

What is life all about?
Where do I fit in?
How can I find meaning?

Have you ever asked yourself any of these questions? These and similar questions are being heard with increasing frequency in modern society.

Today, people are confronted by many more choices than in previous generations. It is no longer uncommon for people to change careers (or even spouses) two or three times in a lifetime; the choice of pursuing a college education or vocational training is now the norm, rather than the exception; and the "dual career marriage/family" is increasing in numbers each year. Then, there are choices concerning premarital sex, the fear of AIDS, and even the experimentation with drugs.

There was a time when children grew up knowing to a far greater extent than we, what roles they would play in adult life, where they would live, and what they would believe in. They didn't have to choose who and what they would be. Actually, these issues were decided before they were born.

Today, though, we must make decisions about issues that were never before even called into question. We must not only make these decisions for ourselves, we must often reevaluate our choices every couple of years. And, it is for this reason that people are asking more value questions. In order to begin to find answers to these questions, we need first of all to be able to identify what values are (Smith, 1977).

Things have the value that we ourselves have the capacity to give them.

Nikos Kazantazakis

WHAT ARE VALUES?

If you were going to build a new home, one of the first considerations would be to decide upon your house plan. After having carefully studied your house plan and having made the necessary adjustments, you would have your house plan converted into a blueprint. This blueprint would serve as a guide for the construction of your new home. For example, the choices and decisions concerning the layout of the kitchen, the placement of doors and windows, the design of electrical outlets, and so on, would be in accordance with this blueprint—the plan or guide for your new home.

Could it be possible that we also have a *blueprint* or *guide* concerning the choices and decisions we make in our way of living?

A *value* is the personal worth that we place on an object, thought, or idea. This object, thought or idea is held to be desirable and worthwhile because it is of particular importance to us. Review Table 9.1 for a partial listing of some typical values. Which ones are important to you?

Because we have many values, it is, therefore, appropriate to speak of our set of values or our value system. A set of values is more than just a set of rules and regulations. Instead, it is the underlying system of beliefs about what is important in life to a person. Therefore, our value system represents the blueprint or guideline for the choices and decisions we make throughout our life. Table 9.1 gives an example of a value system. Kluckhohn (1956) explains these choices and decisions:

Every individual operates according to a system of values, whether it is verbalized and consistently worked out or not. In selecting goals, in choosing modes of behavior, in resolving conflicts, he is influenced at every turn by his conception of what is good and desirable for him. Although everyone's value system is in some degree unique, an individual's values are usually grounded in the core values of his culture. . . . Depending on his conception of what is desirable and good in human life, he selects certain goals over others and patterns his behavior according to standards of what he believes to be right and worthwhile. The way a man carries on his business activity, the kind of relationships he has with his wife and children and with his friends, the degree of respect he has for other individuals (and for himself), his political and religious activity—all these reflect the individual's values, though he may scarcely have thought them through.

Table 9.1
Twenty-one Typical Values

- Being honest and trustworthy
- Having a family and staying close to them
- Being financially and materially successful
- Being independent
- Feeling safe and secure
- Having plenty of leisure time
- Looking in style
- Having friends
- Having a religious or moral code
- Being in good health
- Having a special love relationship
- Having a fulfilling career
- Being approved of and liked by others
- Having self-respect and pride
- Being of service to others
- Learning and getting an education
- Being productive and achieving
- Loving others and being loved
- Living a long, healthy life
- Belonging to a chosen group
- Living in a World of Peace

Actually, everything we do, every decision we make and course of action we take is based on our consciously or unconsciously held beliefs, attitudes, and values.

An excellent test to determine the intensity of your conscious or unconscious values is to notice how strongly you feel about an idea or thought. For example, how would you react to these issues: abortion, drug abuse, and euthanasia? If you have a strong conviction on any of these issues, it is highly likely that aspects of your value system are being revealed.

TYPES OF VALUES

Milton (1985) classifies values into two broad categories: *moral values and nonmoral values*. In this book, the terms *moral* and *nonmoral* are used without any religious connotations.

It is a law of human life, as certain as gravity: To live fully we must learn to use things and love people. . . not love things and use people.

John Powell

Moral Values. These values have to do with right and wrong, good and evil. They form the basis for judgments or moral responsibility and guide such ethical behavior as telling the truth, keeping agreements, and not injuring others. Character traits such as honesty, loyalty, and fairness are often associated with moral values. Moral statements often contain words such as *must, ought, should, never,* and *always*.

Nonmoral Values. These values have to do with tastes, preferences, and styles. They relate to what is desirable and undesirable, as opposed to what is right and wrong or good and evil. Nonmoral values carry no sense of obligation. There is no moral responsibility connected with accepting or rejecting a nonmoral value.

The traits associated with nonmoral values tend to be personality traits like charm, shyness, or cheerfulness, as opposed to character traits like honesty or fairness. The activities that come out of nonmoral values are merely preferred, not dictated: going to the ballgame instead of to a movie, reading a book instead of watching television.

Nonmoral values are a lot more plentiful than moral values, because they are expressions of your attitudes toward all sorts of objects, concepts, and experiences: cars, paintings, art, knowledge, pleasure, democracy, history, sports, hobbies, and so on. Statements of nonmoral values often contain the same words as statements of moral values, but examination shows that the words are not meant in an absolute, normative sense.

Without a doubt, values are highly operative in our life. Have these values *just always been there,* or do we gradually acquire them, as if through familial and cultural osmosis?

HOW DO VALUES DEVELOP?

Throughout your life, you have, in all probability, heard many *life messages:* "Life is . . .", "Success is . . .", "The most important thing is . . ." transmitted to you by parents, peers, and society in general. Some possible messages about the nature and purposes of life you may have heard are listed in Table 9.2.

We are not born with values, but we are born into cultures and societies that promote, teach, and impart their values to us (Smith, 1977). We learn to be what we are. Basically, the years of adolescence are extremely important for the learning and development of values. We first gain our value orientation from the "significant others" in our lives—parents and siblings. Actually, our first goals and ambitions will be drawn from this frame of reference. During the first few years of our life, we lacked the knowledge and maturity to evaluate our value orientation.

However, as we entered school, parental influence was combined with the influence of peers, teachers, and public media. We had one set of *shoulds* and *should nots* from our parents. The church often suggested a second. Our friends and "peer group" offered a third view of values. And then, the chaos of value conflicts: values from opposing political groups; the influence of television, advertising claims, Hollywood, and popular magazines; militancy of left or right; and the values of different cultures and social classes (Kerschenbaum, 1977).

Table 9.2
Possible Life Messages

- "Life is to have things: your own home, enough money for an emergency, security for old age."
- "Life is to get ahead, to prove yourself, to make people respect you."
- "Success in life is judged by how popular you are—by how many people love you."
- "You are worth only what you are worth in God's eyes."
- "Success in life is spelled: M-O-N-E-Y."
- "Life is for having good times."
- "If you've got your health, you'll be all right."
- "Education is what is important. They can take everything away from you except your mind."
- "Life is for loving and sharing with others."

What messages did you hear about the nature and purposes of life? Have you had any conflicts between what you heard and in what you now actually believe?

Shoulds And Should Nots ...

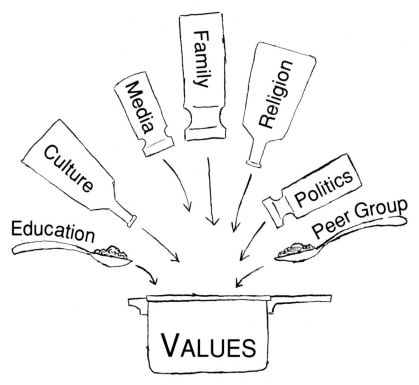

come from many different sources. What source has had the greatest influence in the development of your value system?

Life can only be understood backwards; but it must be lived forwards.

Soren Kierkegaard

With all of this additional information we began to question and reevaluate our original value orientation. Much of this questioning was revealed through testing the *shoulds* and *should nots*. Therefore, actual experience became very real in the forming of our value system. For some people, this reevaluation period occurred during the adolescence period, early adulthood, or maybe even later.

How old were you when you reevaluated your original value system? Were you 18, 20, 25, or . . . ? Regardless of the exact time, examining and acquiring your personal set of values was, or is, the birth of your own individuality. In fact, Carl Jung (1923) one of the early psychoanalysts, called the process of becoming an individual individuation.

Individuation refers to the separation from our family system and the establishing of our identity based on our own experiences, rather than merely following our parents' dreams. Although individuals may accept many of their parents' values, to genuinely individuate they must choose these values freely rather than automatically incorporating them into their personality (Okun, 1984).

The values we place upon different aspects of our environment have an effect upon how we view things and how we function. In other words, an act viewed as right or wrong, moral or immoral will depend upon the frame of reference of the perceiver. As a result, something that one person considers worthwhile and desirable may appear exactly the opposite to another person. Do we, therefore, tend to judge other people's actions by our own standards—our values?

What else influences the development of our values?

THE INFLUENCE OF OTHER FACTORS

Other important factors are influential in the formation of our value system. Some of these are religious beliefs, attitudes, and prejudices and stereotypes (Ellenson, 1982).

Religious Beliefs. What is a belief? A *belief* is the acceptance of some thought, supposition, or idea. This belief may be in a God, or in Gods, or even in the supernatural. Nevertheless, in some form or another, religion and established moral codes are found in all cultures and societies. Regardless of the exact nature of people's beliefs, they view their convictions as an important foundation for their entire value system. A commitment toward a chosen moral code helps to define our purpose in life, gives meaning and direction in life, and thus, becomes an integral part in shaping our value system.

Prejudice is being down on what we are not up on.

John Stevens

Attitudes. *Attitudes* are positive or negative orientations toward a certain target. For example, you have attitudes toward specific persons (parents, children, teachers), as well as toward groups of people (Blacks, Whites, male ministers, female ministers). You also have attitudes toward things or targets such as food, movies, holidays, or marriage.

The attitudes you have today have been acquired throughout your life. How did you acquire them? More than likely, your positive attitudes are a result of positive experiences, and your negative attitudes are a result of negative experiences. Whatever you learned in these experiences is likely to take the form of *expectations* later in life. It is just natural to expect the same or similar results from similar situations. Consider these statements:

I'm not going to get married again; if I did, it would just probably end in another divorce.
Tom's mother is so different from Frank's mother—certainly not what I expected from a mother-in-law.
I'm sure I can work for Mrs. Jones; I've worked for another female, and we got along just great.

As you can see in these examples, the attitudes were formed from prior *experiences* and *expectations*. Is it possible that your prior experiences and expectations are shaping the attitudes and values you presently hold? If so, do you need to reevaluate these attitudes and values? Remember, the stronger an attitude is, the more difficult it is to change. Why? Because your emotions are involved.

Prejudices and Stereotypes. A *prejudice* is a preconceived opinion, feeling, or attitude, either positive or negative, that is formed without adequate information. For example, you may have a negative prejudice towards the Black English teacher who is going to teach your class next semester. Although you have not had this teacher before, you have heard statements made by other students, and you have already formed your opinion. It is only when you are actually in this teacher's class that you can make a justified opinion. Why? Prejudices are often unjustified attitudes.

Sometimes we allow our prejudiced attitudes to make *generalizations* by categorizing an object, person, or situation. When we do this, we are guilty of stereotyping. Do any of these statements sound familiar to you?

Career women often neglect their family.
Latin Americans are a hot-headed race.
Mothers-in-law are bossy and interfering people.
There are just a bunch of hypocrites at *that* church.

According to these examples, if you are a career woman, a Latin American, a mother-in-law, or if you go to *that* church, you have now been given a label. You are not thought of as an individual—you are a member of the group of career woman and so on; and, of course, you have *their* similar characteristics.

It is so easy for us to engage in stereotyping and then permit these attitudes to shape our value system. Pause for a minute and just ask yourself these questions: What prejudices and stereotypes do I have? What are they based on? How do they affect my present value system? Do I really want to have these values?

WHAT ARE MY VALUES?

At the present time, what things are most important to you in your life? Is your career of primary importance? How about your school work and/or the training for your future career? How about the time you spend with your family? Do you have outside leisure interests, community activities, or volunteer work?

There are always many factors in your life that compete for your time and attention. Actually, what you value most often determines how you will spend your time. When you decide to work late on a repeated basis rather than go home to dinner, this is a value decision. When you decide to go to a movie rather than attend your son's baseball game, this is another value decision. You are always making value decisions, and an awareness of what values are most important to you can help you to live a more harmonious and less stressful life. When you know which values have a higher priority, you can more easily make life's major and minor decisions. We'll have more to say about prioritizing values a little later.

DESIDERATA*

Go placidly amid the noise and haste, and remember what peace there may be in silence. As far as possible without surrender be on good terms with all persons. Speak your truth quietly and clearly; listen to others, even the dull and ignorant; they too have their story.

Avoid loud and aggressive persons, they are vexations to the spirit. If you compare yourself with others, you may become vain and bitter; for always there will be greater and lesser persons than yourself. Enjoy your achievements as well as your plans.

Keep interested in your own career, however humble; it is a real possession in the changing fortunes of time. Exercise caution in your business affairs; for the world is full of trickery. But let this not blind you to what virtue there is; many persons strive for high ideals; and everywhere life is full of heroism.

Be yourself. Especially, do not feign affection. Neither be cynical about love; for in the face of all aridity and disenchantment it is perennial as the grass.

Take kindly the counselor of the years, gracefully surrendering the things of youth. Nurture strength of spirit to shield you in sudden misfortune. But do not stress yourself with imaginings. Many fears are born of fatigue and loneliness. Beyond a wholesome discipline, be gentle with yourself.

You are a child of the universe, no less than the trees and the stars; you have a right to be here. We are all children of God. We are made in His image and likeness. This being the case, we must treat everyone with the respect and dignity and thoughtfulness and considerateness that this situation commands. And whether or not it is clear to you, no doubt the universe is unfolding as it should.

Therefore be at peace with God, whatever you conceive Him to be, and whatever your labors and aspirations, in the noisy confusion of life keep peace with your soul. With all its sham, drudgery, and broken dreams, it is still a beautiful world. Be careful. Strive to be happy.

Your values do change as you go through the various life stages. As children, your highest value might have been play and having fun; as adolescents, perhaps it was peer relationships; as young adults, it may be relationships with the opposite sex, and as adults your highest value may be your family and the work you do. For many older people, service to others and enjoying leisure time is often the highest value (Smith, 1977).

If you are currently seeking some change in your career or lifestyle, it may be due in part to the fact that some of your values may have changed. What was important to you in the past may be less important now. You may want to devote greater attention in your life to new things or to some of the things you did not have as much time for in the past.

The cost of a thing is the amount of what I call life which is required to pay for it, immediately or in the long run.

Henry David Thoreau

*The above was found in Old Saint Paul's Church, Baltimore; dated 1692.

Do you see any changes in your personal set of values over the past five or ten years? Has there been any change in the kinds of values you consider to be important in your life? You will be given several opportunities in the activities at the end of this chapter to review your values, past and present. For now, though, consider the questions in Table 9.3.

We have already stated that because we are unique individuals, something that one person considers a value might not be a value to another person. For example, we all want a feeling of security. However, your idea of what makes you feel secure may differ remarkably from that of other people. Some people may equate security primarily with money; others may equate security with education, religion, or close family relationships. Sometimes a combination of all these types of security are desired. However, the order of importance then becomes a matter of value.

CLASSIFYING YOUR PERSONAL VALUES

Your values may be *abstract (intangible)* or *specific (tangible)*. For example, one may value such entities as a car, helping others, knowledge, career, security, close relationships with family and friends, an education, religious or spiritual growth, social interactions, material possessions, money, being an honest person, freedom, creativity, and so on. What are some of your intangible and tangible values?

Table 9.3
Your Values—Some Hard Questions

You probably do not have the answers to these questions on the tip of your tongue. They require some thought and discussion. They will lead you to a better understanding of your values.

1. If you were independently wealthy, what would you do with your life?
2. What issues are of deep concern to you regarding your home, campus, community, church, state, country, or world?
3. If you were independently wealthy, to what causes would you contribute?
4. After your death, what would you like people to say about you? How would you like to be remembered?

Value Orientations. Value systems may be divided into three categories: *thing-oriented, idea-oriented,* or *people-oriented.* A person who is willing to work hard and save to obtain material objects or even a large bank account may be *thing-oriented.* On the other hand, some people have a zest for knowledge; they like to think, imagine, and intellectualize. We might say their value system is *idea-oriented.* However, if you truly enjoy working and being with other people, your value system may be *people-oriented.*

It is highly possible that a combination of these three value orientations may be desired. However, one of these value orientations is probably at the core of your value system, even though you may not be aware of how your behavior is reflected in this particular value orientation. Where do your values fit in? Perhaps the real question is—what do you direct your life toward acquiring?

CLARIFYING YOUR PERSONAL VALUES

Sometimes important choices in life are made on the basis of peer pressure, unthinking submission to authority, or the power of propaganda. We may even guide our lives by what others expect of us, instead of what we truly believe is right. Many times, oughts and expectations of society and others largely influence our value system. Thus, our value orientation becomes other-directed rather than self-directed. The obvious result is a feeling of being very insecure and easily threatened in our valuing process.

When we become conscious of our own personal value system and how it functions, we can begin to manage our own value system rather than allowing others to manage it. How do we discover what our true values are?

Values clarification is a process that helps people arrive at an answer. Simon (1975) shares this thought:

It is not concerned with an ultimate set of values (that is for you to decide), but it does stress a method to help you determine the content and power of your own set of values. It is a self-audit, and an inventory of soul and spirit. It is a tool to help you freely decide between alternatives or among varied choices. It is a methodology to help you make a decision, to act, to determine what has meaning for you.

According to Raths, Harmin, and Simon (1966), the process of clarifying values involves:

CHOOSING: (1) freely;
(2) from alternatives;
(3) after thoughtful consideration of the consequences of each alternative.

Establishing your value system involves a weighing of "what is" with "what should be."

Ann Ellenson

PRIZING:	(4) cherishing, prizing, and being happy with the choice;
	(5) willing to affirm the choice publicly;
ACTING:	(6) doing something with the choice, taking action;
	(7) acting repeatedly, in some pattern of life.

Before something can be a *full,* true value, it must meet all seven of the above criteria. Ellenson (1982) suggests that there are three levels involved in the criteria: *choosing* relies mainly on the cognitive or thinking area: *prizing* relies on the affective or feeling area; and *acting* relies on the behavioral areas. When we have a *full value,* our thoughts, feelings, and actions are in agreement; what we think, say, feel, and do are in agreement and are evident in our lives.

Let us look at the seven criteria a little more closely.

Choosing freely means we consciously and deliberately make the choice ourselves. There is no pressure to believe what our parents taught us. An example of choosing freely would be when you have been raised and taught that there is only one religion worthy of your belief, and you later decide that your beliefs are more in line with another religious faith. Even if you end up choosing the same religious faith which your parents hold, that becomes a full value for your because you make the personal choice to follow that faith.

Choosing from alternatives means there are options. If there are no alternatives, there is no freedom of choice. For example, you really cannot value breathing, of itself, because there is no choice involved; a person must breath to live. However, you can value mountain air, or a special breathing technique, such as Yoga.

Choosing after considering the consequences means you ask yourself, "What would be the result of the alternatives of my choice?" This gives you the opportunity to choose with thoughtful consideration, and not on impulse. Many of the problems which we have are the result of impulsive, poorly thought-out decisions, or action taken without regard for ourselves or others. For example, sometimes people impulsively decide to get a divorce and then later realize they are not happy with their "quick" decision.

Cherishing and feeling happy about the choice means that it influences your behavior in some way, and you don't mind spending your time on this value. For example, if you value being thrifty and you need to buy a new VCR, you will spend a considerable amount of time researching and comparing prices. When you finally get your VCR, you will be satisfied and content that you "got the best buy."

Publicly affirming a value means you are willing to tell others about it. Some people even crusade for their values. For example, if you value a particular political ideology, you may be seen campaigning for the politician who holds the same value. Remember, you

Life is an endless process of self-discovery.

Dave Gardner

have the right to publicly affirm your values, but you don't have the right to impose your values on others. This interferes with their freedom of choice.

Doing something about a value means taking action. Full values are those things which we work for, do something about, and take action on. Thus, what a person does reflects his or her values. For example, you will read literature that supports your values; you will join clubs or organizations whose members share your values and whose goals correspond to your values.

Acting repeatedly means there is a life pattern that is evident, and the stronger the value, the more it influences your life. There is a consistency of action which manifests itself in all aspects of your life: in dress; in friends selected, in the place you live, in leisure time, in what you read, in your career, in the selection of your spouse, and how you spend your time and money.

In summary, a value that is freely chosen from alternatives whose consequences have been thoughtfully considered,of which we are proud and happy to the point that we publicly take a stand, and that we act upon with repetition and consistency is a full value. (Ellenson, 1982).

Maury Smith (1977) adds an eighth criterion as the natural outgrowth of the other seven: A *value* enhances the person's total growth. If a value has been affirmed as a full value by having met the seven preceding criteria, it follows as a matter of course that that value will contribute to and enhance the person's total growth toward the goals and ideals that he has chosen for himself. We are more likely to continue choosing, prizing, and acting upon those values that help us to grow in our lives and that help us to achieve the goals which we have set for ourselves.

What about those values we simply say are important to us?

Do what you value; value what you do.

Sidney Simon

VALUE INDICATORS

Most of us have partial values that are in the process of being formed. Partial values, or *value indicators,* include desires, thoughts not acted on, opinions, interests, aspirations, goals, beliefs, attitudes, feelings, convictions, activities, day-dreams (Rokeach, 1973). For example, we may say that we have a certain goal, but we are not working toward it. Also, we may say that we have an interest in learning to play bridge, but we have never taken the time to act on that interest.

We've already stated that the way we use our money and time is a strong value indicator. For example, John may say he values very highly the importance of reading and keeping up in "his thinking." However, if you asked him how much time he spends reading each week or when he last bought a good book, you may be surprised to discover that he doesn't even remember. It has been said before that a simple process in determining the strength of a value is to ask a person or family to describe how they spend their money. Generally speaking, the more money they spend on something, the greater the value is to people.

From the preceding, it is easy to see that we can find out what our real values are by examining our actual behaviors—the way in which we invest our time, money, energies, and resources. Consequently, in order to better understand your real values, you might want to apply the following four tests to your value orientation (Rokeach, 1973):

1. The Choice Test. What do I do in situations involving a choice?

2. The Time Test. How much time and energy am I willing to spend on the value?

3. The Sacrificial Test. What satisfaction am I willing to forego on behalf of the value?

4. The Emotion Test. How much satisfaction or guilt do I experience when I am true to my value or when I violate it?

The most important thing to remember is that to claim a value, you must *act* in accordance to what you say you believe. Otherwise, you will be on a seesaw, going up and down and back and forth between "what is" and "what should be" in your life.

If you can bring your actions and the time you spend in your life more into harmony with your values, you will feel more in control of your life and more satisfied with the decisions you make.

Fred Hecklinger

Life Is A Series Of Choices!

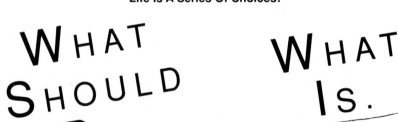

Establishing your real values involves balancing "what is" with "what should be" in your life.

VALUES TESTING THROUGH GOAL SETTING

From the discussion above, we might conclude that values may either be *conceived* (stated) or *operative* (real). Many individuals have conceived values but do not bother to implement them. *Operative* values are the ones we work on (Kluckhohn, 1956). You will be given several opportunities in the activities at the end of this chapter to evaluate your stated or real values. We would encourage you to give special attention to the results of the activity: What Do You Value?

A direct relationship exists between our value structure and our motivation. That is, what we value we will be motivated to work toward achieving. This is not to say that what we say we value will necessarily motivate us. Many students say, "I value a college education." Yet, they do not get it, because on the emotional level of valuing, it is less important than other values. Their behavior indicates that something else is more valuable to them right now.

One way of clarifying our stated or real values is by testing our values through *priority ranking.* This is a process whereby an individual takes inventory of his or her values, examines them, and puts them in order of their importance. Next, the individual is asked to set a goal in relation to his or her stated top values. For example, let's look at the following illustration.

Mrs. Smith, a community college counselor, described her top values as follows:

1. my professional career
2. my personal growth and awareness
3. my family
4. my friends

Using her top values, Mrs. Smith decided to set a goal to write all the local high schools and see whether they needed any of her college's catalogues, brochures, and so on. The following week came, and Mrs. Smith had not written any letters. When Mrs. Smith was asked what she had really done in the past week, she said "I took my little boy to the zoo and museum." The next week Mrs. Smith decided she would really get those letters written. Once again, she had not completed her goal. Instead, she had made clothes for the other family members. After talking with Mrs. Smith in a group discussion, it soon became evident that her family was really of more value than her profession. She admitted that she really had wanted to quit her job and have another child. However, she felt her husband needed her to work. Finally, she was able to admit her priority to her husband. It wasn't too long before Mrs. Smith made plans to terminate her job; she was pregnant. Mrs. Smith admitted that her "professional career" was not one of her top four values.

We write our own destiny . . . we become what we do.

Madame Chiang Kai-Shek

By testing her values through goal setting, Mrs. Smith's behavior demonstrated that something else (her family) was more valuable to her and more motivating to her than her stated top value.

Mrs. Smith had actually listed a *should* value in her priority list rather than an *actual* or *want* value. Her priority ranking didn't really change her values as much as it helped them to become clearer. Actually, Mrs. Smith's *should* value was not motivating enough to be valuable to her. Setting a goal in relation to one's values and achieving that goal, simply indicates the importance of that value to the individual.

WE LEARN TO LOVE WHAT WE SUFFER FOR

Why does a child who has to work to earn money value his or her bicycle more than the child who is given a bicycle? Why are members of cults so dedicated to their organizations? These questions and many others may be answered through cognitive dissonance.

Cognitive Dissonance. What is *cognitive dissonance,* and how does it affect our values, beliefs, and attitudes? We are all motivated to maintain consistency within ourselves. We do not normally hold values, beliefs, or attitudes that are mutually incompatible or dissonant with each other, nor do we behave in ways contradictory to our values or attitudes. Although people differ in the amount of inconsistency they can tolerate, a basic assumption of cognitive dissonance theory is that inconsistency is intolerable to an individual.

The concept of cognitive dissonance was introduced by Leon Festinger (1957) to account for reactions to inconsistencies in attitudes and beliefs. According to this theory, when two or more cognitions such as beliefs, opinions, and the things we know about various types of behavior, people, objects, or circumstances are in disagreement (dissonance), a state of tension results. This inconsistency (dissonance) motivates the individual to adjust these cognitions so as to reduce the dissonance and thereby reduce the tension. When there is dissonance between attitudes and behavior, the individual may modify attitudes rather than behavior.

To illustrate these points, suppose that a cigarette smoker is aware of the dangers of smoking to his or her health but continues to smoke. The individual is faced with two dissonant cognitions: "I enjoy smoking, or smoking is harmful." The *dissonance theory* predicts that such an inconsistency would produce an uncomfortable state that would motivate the individual either to give up smoking or change his or her ideas about the risks involved in continuing to smoke. In cases such as this, we typically find the individual expressing one of the following ideas: (1) I enjoy smoking and it is worth it; (2) the chances of ill-health from smoking are not as serious as most people say; (3) a person can't always avoid every possible dangerous situation and still continue to live an enjoyable life; or (4) perhaps even if I stopped smoking I would put on weight, which is equally as bad for one's health. Thus, Festinger suggests that continuing to smoke is, after all, consistent with the person's ideas about smoking.

Although the individual may have stated that he or she would like to give up smoking, the person's inability to do so resulted in rationalizing some facts to support his or her belief system and to match the person's behavior. Now the tension is somewhat relieved. However, it has been suggested by some authorities that the individual may have to deal with his or her true feelings and behavior again.

Can you think of ways cognitive dissonance might apply to difficulties in losing weight or in breaking a substance abuse habit?

To answer the questions asked earlier, as we have observed through cognitive dissonance, an individual is motivated to justify his or her behavior. A child who has to work to earn money to buy a bicycle will value it more because he or she put more effort into getting it. Cult members, just as other members of groups and organizations, will generally experience some type of initiation process that will take a lot of effort on the individual's part. After putting in all this effort, the individual has to justify why he or she suffered or worked so hard in order to be a member of the cult or organization. As a result of all this, the individual will generally become a very dedicated member of this group as a means of justifying why he or she went through this process. As a student, most of you would admit that you value a class you succeed in that takes more effort than a class you succeeded in that was considered "easy." As you can see from these examples, *we learn to love what we suffer for.*

If you do not live the life you believe—you will believe the life you live.

Anonymous

LIVING WITH YOUR VALUES

This is a confusing world to live in. At every turn, we are forced to make choices about how to live our lives. Ideally, our choices will be made on the basis of the values we hold, but sometimes we may experience confusion and conflict. There are several value-oriented conflicts listed in Table 9.4. Which ones present a problem for you?

Perhaps one of the most difficult things to do is to establish for ourselves a consistent set of values. If we go against a value, we feel bad. Inconsistencies in our values makes us unhappy; they make us feel guilty. If we allow inconsistencies to become a habit, we become hypocrites. Hypocrites are people who do not act on the values they claim to hold. If we usually live up to our values, we are happy, satisfied people with consistent value systems.

Table 9.4
Value-Oriented Conflicts

- Maybe John and I should live together before marriage. Wouldn't this help us know if we're really compatible?
- Does religion have some meaning in my life, or is it nothing more than a series of outmoded traditions and customs?
- What will my family and friends think and say if Jane and I get a divorce? We've *always* been the model couple.
- Should I go back to work or college when the kids all get in school, or should I be a full-time Mom and homemaker?
- How can I really enjoy working and living and avoid getting into the rat race for the convertible and the house in the suburbs?
- Do I really need to take that career promotion and be gone from home most of the time, or would it be better to stay with my current job and be home with the family?
- Should I quit school and get a job? I'm tired of living in poverty. I can always get an education later.
- Should I buy a new car or save my money?
- What occupation shall I choose, so that I don't spend my life like so many others who dislike the jobs they go to every morning?
- Do I want children? Being a parent is kind of frightening to me.

It's important for people to know what you stand for. It's equally important that they know what you won't stand for. Above all, you better not compromise yourself; it is all you got.

Janis Joplin

However, values are useless unless we live by them or implement them. Implementation simply means carrying out, or making an honest effort to satisfy, a value. We can honestly implement only those values we have consciously chosen. It is only when we have consciously chosen a value and affirmed a way of acting toward it that the value has meaning for our own life. Obviously, this is the only way we can or will take responsibility for our actions. Assuming responsibility for our actions helps us to learn from our mistakes. Thus, the most effective way we learn to clarify our values is by experiencing things and evaluating our behavior during these experiences.

It is true that we can't always satisfy our values; many compromises must be made, because value conflicts are likely to appear when two or more people get together. Therefore, we need to learn when we can afford to give up and compromise values and when we cannot. It is best not to compromise values of high priority. Values that are not so important may be compromised without destroying our self-concept. Actually, satisfied, happy people are people who do not compromise their most important values but are willing to compromise their less important values.

Perhaps the question is really—*What is most important to me?* In making value compromises, therefore, it is very important that we understand our *priorities*. It is this understanding that helps us define our purpose and give meaning to our life.

JUST FOR TODAY

Just for today I will think about what is important to me. Then, I will try to live this day accordingly.

Just for today I will be happy. This assumes to be true what Abraham Lincoln said: "Most folks are about as happy as they make up their minds to be."

Just for today I will try to strengthen my mind. I will learn something useful. I will read something that requires effort, thought, and concentration.

Just for today I will adjust myself to what is, and I will not keep trying to adjust everything else to my own desires.

Just for today I will look as well as I can, dress becomingly, talk less, act courteously, criticize no one, and not try to improve or regulate anybody except myself.

Just for today I will have a goal and a plan of action. I may not follow it exactly, but I will have it; I will save myself from indecision on this day.

Just for today I will volunteer some of my time, even if it is only thirty minutes, helping someone else. This will help me keep my mind off myself.

Just for today I will have a quiet half-hour all by myself for meditation and relaxation. During this half-hour I will try to get a better perspective of my life.

Just for today I will be unafraid. Especially I will not be afraid to enjoy what is beautiful, and to believe that, as I give to the world, so the world will give to me.

Anonymous

THE IMPORTANCE OF MEANING AND PURPOSE

Viktor Frankl, a European psychiatrist, dedicated much of his professional life to the study of meaning in life. According to Frankl (1978), what distinguishes us as humans is our *search for purpose*. The striving to find meaning in our lives is a primary motivational force. Humans are able to live and even die for the sake of their ideals and values. Frankl (1963) is fond of pointing out the wisdom of Nietzsche's words: *"He who has a why to live for can bear with almost any how."* Drawing on his experiences in the death camp at Auschwitz, Frankl asserts that inmates who had purpose or a meaningful task in life had a much greater chance of surviving than those who had no sense of mission (Corey, 1989).

As human beings, it is our challenge and our task to create our own meaning. No one can do this for us. We encourage you to take some of the hints from *Just For Today* and begin to practice them each day.

Yalom (1980) reviewed a number of studies of the role of meaning in people's life and described the following results.

1. A person's lack of a sense of meaning in life is related to the existence of emotional and behavioral disorders; the less the sense of meaning, the greater the degree of personal disturbances.
2. A positive sense of meaning in life is associated with having a set of religious beliefs.
3. A positive sense of meaning is associated with possessing values relating to the betterment of humanity and an interest in the welfare of others.
4. A positive sense of meaning is associated with a dedication to some cause and with having a clear set of life goals.
5. Meaning in life is not to be seen as a static entity but should be viewed in a developmental perspective. The sources of meaning differ at various stages in life, and other developmental tasks must precede the development of meaning.

Something to do, someone to love, and something to hope for, are the true essentials of a happy and meaningful life. No matter how rich you are, if you lack one of these essentials, life's true fulfillment will not be yours. No matter how poor you are, if you possess all three of these, you can build a satisfying existence for yourself.

David Goodman

Along with Frankl, Yalom concludes that humans require meaning to survive: To live without meaning and values provokes considerable distress, and in its severe form it may lead to the decision for suicide. Jourard (1971) confirms this by making the following point:

People decide to live as long as they experience meaning and value in life, but they may decide to die when meaning and value vanishes from life.

Corey (1989) summarizes the importance of meaning and purpose:

Humans apparently have a need for some absolutes in the form of clear ideals to which they can aspire and guidelines by which they can direct their actions.

Do you have clear ideals to which you can aspire and guidelines by which you can direct your actions?

A LAST THOUGHT

We each have our own unique philosophy of life and system of personal ethics. It is true that we may not be exactly sure of what they are. However, can you answer the following questions? What is the good life for me? What is really important to me? The answers to these questions is highly determined by the values and attitudes that you practice in your daily living.

Therefore, your system of personal ethics becomes an attempt to reconcile what *ought to be* with *what is*. Each of us, relying on our set of personal ethics, must decide what is *right* or *wrong* for us. There are many alternatives, but each of us can *choose* our direction in life. However, we are responsible for the consequences of the choices we make.

A well-defined value system is basic to personal motivation, self-determination, and a lifestyle with meaning. Actually, our value system should be the control point of our life, helping us to choose the direction and course we will take. When we can control the direction of our life, rather than allowing it to be controlled by forces and values outside ourselves, a feeling of self-affirmation is created.

The real values in life are those we have actually experienced. Thus, what we say we believe in is sometimes insignificant; *what we really do is where the significance lies.*

To describe a man's philosophy is to say how he orients himself to the world of his experiences, what meanings he finds in events, what values he aspires to, what standards guide his choices in all that he does.

Abraham Kaplan

CHAPTER DISCUSSION QUESTIONS

1. What have been some of the factors that have influenced the development of your value system? Which factor has been of the greatest significance?
2. What are some differences between your value system of today and that of five or ten years ago?
3. How would you describe your personal ethics?
4. Explain any prejudice you may have.
5. What does a person's behavior reveal about his or her values?
6. What is the "good life" to you?
7. Have you ever applied the cognitive dissonance theory to one of your stated values? If so, explain how you changed your belief system to "match" your behavior.
8. Describe your value orientation as being either thing-oriented, idea-oriented, or people-oriented.
9. What are some of your partial values which are in the process of being formed?

KEY TERMS

Value
Value System
Moral Values
Non-Moral Values
Individuation
Belief
Attitudes
Prejudices
Stereotypes
Intangible Values
Tangible Values
Thing-Oriented Value System

Idea-Oriented Value Syestem
People-Oriented Value System
Values Clarification
Full Value
Choosing
Prizing
Acting
Value Indicators
Conceived Values
Operative Values
Cognitive Dissonance

REFERENCES

Corey, Gerald and Corey, Marianne. (1990) *I Never Knew I Had a Choice.* Pacific Grove, California: Brooks Cole Publishing Co.

Ellenson, Ann. (1982) *Human Relations.* Englewood Cliffs, New Jersey: Prentice-Hall, Inc.

Festinger, L. (1957) *A Theory of Cognitive Dissonance.* Stanford, California: Stanford University Press.

Frankl, V. E. (1963) *Man's Search for Meaning.* New York: Washington Square Press.

Frankl, V. E. (1972) *The Unheard Cry for Meaning.* New York: Bantam.

Jourard, Sidney. (1971) *The Transparent Self: Self-Disclosure and Well-Being* (rev. ed.). New York: Van Nostrand Reinhold.

Jung, Carl (1923) *Psychological Types.* New York: Harcourt Brace.

Kerschenbaum, Howard. (1977) *Advanced Value Clarification.* California: University Associates.

Kluckhohn, Florence. (1956) "Value Orientations," in *Toward a Unified Theory of Human Behavior: An Introduction to General Systems Theory,* ed. Roy R. Grinker, Sr. New York: Basic Books, Inc., Publishers.

Milton, Walter. Ph.D. (1985) "Values Clarification Workshop." Dallas Texas.

Okun, B. F. (1984) *Working with Adults: Individual, Family and Career Development.* Pacific Grove, California: Brooks/Cole Publishers.

Raths, Louis; Harmin, Merrill; and Simon, Sidney. (1966) *Values and Teaching.* Ohio: Charles E. Merrill.

Rokeach, M. (1973) *The Nature of Human Values.* New York: The Free Press.

Simon, Sidney and Clark, Jay. (1975) *Beginning Values Clarification.* La Mesa, California: Pennant Press.

Smith, Maury. (1977) *A Practical Guide to Value Clarification.* LaJolla, California: University Associates, Inc.

Yalom, I. D. (1980) *Existential Psychotherapy.* New York: Basic Books.

SELF-INVENTORY

Purpose: To understand and evaluate your value system for personal goal setting.

Instructions:

I. For each statement below, indicate the response that most closely identifies your beliefs and attitudes. Use this code:

5 = Strongly agree
4 = Agree in most respects
3 = Undecided
2 = Disagree in most respects
1 = Strongly disagree

_____ 1. Because of the demands and expectations of others, it is difficult for me to maintain a true grasp of my own identity.

_____ 2. At this particular time, I have a sense of purpose and meaning that gives me direction.

_____ 3. I have evaluated and questioned most of the values I now hold.

_____ 4. Religion gives a source of meaning and purpose to my life.

_____ 5. I generally live by and proclaim the values I hold.

_____ 6. I have a close idea of who I am and what I want to become.

_____ 7. I let others influence my values more than I'd like to admit.

_____ 8. The majority of my values are similar to those of my parents.

_____ 9. Generally, I feel clear about what I value.

_____ 10. My values and my views about the meaning of life have changed a great deal during my lifetime.

_____ 11. The way I use my time right now reflects my personal values.

_____ 12. I have a clear picture of "my philosophy of life."

_____ 13. I must admit that I have some prejudices and stereotypes that are currently part of my value system.

_____ 14. The way I spend my money right now reflects my personal values.

_____ 15. The values that I presently believe in are the ones I want to continue to live by.

II. Responses may be shared in small groups or just viewed as a personal inventory.

DISCUSSION

1. Would you like to change your responses to any of the questions? Which ones, and to what numerical degree?

2. What goals would you like to set to ensure that the desired responses occurs?

TRACING VALUES THROUGH MY LIFE

Purpose: To review the importance of early learning on your value system.

Instructions:

I. Below is a list of common value areas. Remember and record what you learned/were told as a young person and what was important about each of these values, for example, money: I was told to save my money and not be a "spendthrift." I learned to manage money well so I would be able to have things I wanted or needed.

II. Next, indicate whether this early value is still important (I) or not important (NI).

III. Lastly, look through the list as a whole and rank the areas 1–12 in how important they are to you today.

Value Area	What I Learned/ Was Told as a Child	Current Importance	Ranking
Education/ new knowledge			
Health— emotional and physical well-being			
Money/ Possessions			
Love/Affection			
Religion/Morals			
Achievement/ Recognition			
Helping Others			

Value Area	What I Learned/ Was Told as a Child	Current Importance	Ranking
Marriage/Family			
Friendships			
Security			
Work/Career			
Leisure Time			

IV. Have your values changed over the past 5–10 years? Are things that were important then not as important now? Have other things taken on greater importance? In what ways have your values changed? List those things that have become more important and those that have become less important to you. (Feel free to use value areas other than the ones listed in this activity.)

More Important   **Less Important**

_____   _____

_____   _____

_____   _____

_____   _____

DISCUSSION QUESTIONS

1. Are you surprised at the changes you see or don't see? What insights did you get from this exercise?

2. How do you think your parents would have ranked the 12 values?

3. How are you living your life today to reflect your four most important values?
   1.

   2.

   3.

   4.

WHAT DO YOU VALUE?

Purpose: To identify what you "really" value in everyday life.

Instructions:

  I. Write down the three things that you most value in life, such as your family, education, religion, money, boyfriend or girlfriend, and so on.
  1.
  2.
  3.
 II. Identify at least two days within a week, a normal work or school day and a day that you have more freedom to choose what you like to do, such as a weekend day. During each of those two days, write down what you do every two hours within a 24-hour day, including sleep.
  Day One _____

  Day Two _____

III. Review your daily diary. How much time did you spend doing those things you stated that you value in Instruction I?

DISCUSSION

What you do in your everyday life demonstrates what you really value in life. Did you spend only ten minutes with family and five hours watching television? What does that tell you about your values?

1. Based on your diary, time-wise, what do you value most (list 1, 2, 3, and 4)?
   1.
   2.
   3.
   4.
2. How does your daily diary compare to what you stated your values to be?

3. What can you do in order to allow your behavior to follow your values (change your values or your behavior)?

4. What did you learn from this activity?

PERSONAL VALUES ASSESSMENT*

Purpose: To identify your values through priority ranking.

Instructions:

I. The following is a list of personal values. Go through this list and rate the personal values in terms of their importance to you. Place a check (✓) mark in the category that best represents your feelings about how important the personal value is to you.

Personal Value	Very Important	Moderately Important	Somewhat Important	Not Important
Good Health Many close friendships Having a large family A fulfilling career A long life				
A stable marriage A financially comfortable life Independence Being creative Participating in an organized religion Intimacy with another				
Having children A variety of interests and activities Freedom to create my own lifestyle Having a house A happy love relationship				
Fulfilling careers for me and my spouse Contributing to my community Abundance of leisure time Happiness Ability to move from place to place				
A life without stress Strong religious values A chance to make social changes To be remembered for my accomplishments Helping those in distress				

*Fred Hecklinger and Bernadette Curtin, *Training for Life* (Dubuque, Iowa: Kendall/Hunt Publishing Co., 1982), pp 27-29. Used with permission.

Personal Value	Very Important	Moderately Important	Somewhat Important	Not Important
Freedom to live where I wish A stable life Time to myself Enjoyment of arts, entertainment and cultural activities A life without children A life with many challenges				
Opportunity to be a leader Opportunity to fight for my country A chance to make a major discovery that would save lives A good physical appearance Opportunity to establish roots in one place				
Opportunity for physical activities An exciting life A chance to get into politics To live according to strong moral values Opportunity to teach others				
To write something memorable A chance to become famous To help others solve problems To make lots of money Others:				

II. In the space below, list at least ten of your most important personal values from your personal values assessment.

1. _____   6. _____

2. _____   7. _____

3. _____   8. _____

4. _____   9. _____

5. _____   10. _____

III. In the space below, list your top *five* personal values in *order of priority,* with number one as the most important.

1. _____ first priority

2. _____ second priority

3. _____ third priority

4. _____ fourth priority

5. _____ fifth priority

DISCUSSION QUESTIONS

1. Does your life right now reflect your values? Is the time you spend consistent with your priorities?

2. If the time you spend in your life right now does not reflect your personal values, how can you change your life so that the time you spend is more in keeping with your values?

3. Are there some parts of your life that you would like to change but that you cannot right now? If so, what is your timetable for bringing your lifestyle more into harmony with your values?

WHAT WOULD YOU CHANGE IN THE WORLD?

Purpose: To allow your creative insights to uncover and reveal your values.

Instructions:

I. Think for a few minutes about some concerns/issues in the following areas: social, moral, political, family, work, or current news stories that really get you "steamed up," or get your energy flowing because of your strong negative feelings. In your opinion, aspects of these issues or concerns need to be changed.

II. Now, try to list at least three issues that you feel strongly about and include what changes you would make.

  1.

  2.

  3.

III. Now, divide into groups of three and take turns sharing your issues and changes.

IV. After each group member shares his/her issues and changes, the group will generate feedback as to what values are reflected.

MY ISSUES AND CONCERNS REFLECTS THE FOLLOWING VALUES:

_____

_____

_____

DISCUSSION QUESTIONS

1. Do you agree or disagree with the feedback given by your group members? Why or Why not?

2. Did you realize that your attitude/feelings toward these issues was really a value for you?

LEARNING JOURNAL—WHAT'S IMPORTANT TO ME

Select the statement below that best defines your feelings about the personal value or meaning gained from this chapter and respond below the dotted line:

I LEARNED THAT I . . . .   I WAS SURPRISED THAT I . . . .

I REALIZED THAT I . . . .   I WAS PLEASED THAT I . . . .

I DISCOVERED THAT I . . . .   I WAS DISPLEASED THAT I . . . .

....

Life Planning

I bargained with Life for a penny,
And Life would pay no more,
However, I begged at evening
When I counted my scanty store.

For Life is a just employer,
He gives you what you ask,
But once you have set the wages,
Why, you must bear the task.

I worked for a menial's hire,
Only to learn, dismayed,
That any wage I had asked of Life,
Life would have willingly paid.

Anonymous

For just a few minutes, we are going to share an analogy with you we recently heard at a Life Planning workshop, based on the work of author Fred Hecklinger (1984).

Compare your journey through life to a train trip. You are constantly moving ahead, with stops along the way. With every mile and every new passenger, the train changes just a small amount. For every new person you meet or new experience you have, you change a bit. Just as the train will take on new passengers, employees, and supplies and will eventually let them go, so will you take on new interests, friends, and skills. Some of them you will choose to keep and others you will let go. But just as the train keeps going, remaining basically the same, so do you keep going. You are changed by your experiences, but you always come back to you and you must make the decisions that significantly alter your journey through life.

Just as a train goes through tunnels, around curves, and encounters bumpy tracks, slowdowns and detours, your journey through life will be marked by both smooth and rough travel. At times the direction in which you are headed may not seem very clear. But a course is there, just as the train tracks are there. You may end up going in circles at times, but you still keep kmoving.Whenever you come to a junction and have to decide which track to take, you must make a decision. Some of these decisions can significantly alter the direction of your life. You run your life, just as an engineer runs a train. You will be responsible for making many decisions. You must invest time and energy on this journey, but the rewards should be well worth your investment.

You are now on your journey and have already been through many stations or experiences, on the way. Do you like the direction that your life is taking? Do you feel that you have control over where you are going? You must decide whether to take charge of your trip and be the engineer or simply be a passenger on your train, letting others make the critical decisions for you.

The authors believe you have the right and power to make choices about your life. Furthermore, we believe that *your* long-range happiness is guaranteed when you decide to *direct* and *plan* your own life. "But, isn't this all just a little bit frightening, you might ask."

LEARNING TO TAKE RISKS

If you are ever going to get serious about life planning, you'll have to take risks. There is simply no way you can grow without taking chances, because everything you really want in life involves taking a risk.

David Viscott (1977) defines *risk* in this way:

To risk is to loosen your grip on the known and the certain and to reach for something you are not entirely sure of but believe is better than what you now have, or is at least necessary to survive.

Security is mostly a superstition. It does not exist in nature, nor do the children of men as a whole experience it. Avoiding danger is no safer in the long run than outright exposure. Life is either a daring adventure or nothing.

Helen Keller

Howard Figler (1979), a life-planning specialist at the University of Texas at Austin, gives the following advice to his students: *One-half of knowing what you want in life is knowing what you are willing to give up to have what you want.* This translates into a basic law of life: *For everything you get in life, you also have to give up something.*

Think about the truth of this. For example, if you go to college to further your education and career opportunities, you have to give up some time for study and going to class; if you take a job promotion in another state, you have to give up the security of your friends and familiar places; if you get married, you have to give up some of your independence; if you decide to have children, you have to give up some of your personal time; if you decide to lose some weight, you have to give up some of your high-calorie snack foods; and if you decide to retire from the world of work, you have to give up a higher paycheck.

As you can see, in every risk, there is some unavoidable loss, something that has to be given up to move ahead. Sometimes this can be overwhelming. How do you really know what you are getting is going to be all that much better? Will the new job really be all that great? Will my marriage work out? Will retirement be as wonderful as everyone says it is?

Many people are terrified by any possible loss and try to avoid all risks. However, this is really the surest way of losing. Why would you lose if you didn't take risks?

David Viscott (1977) gives us the answer:

If you do not risk, risk eventually comes to you. If a person postpones taking risks, the time eventually comes when he will either be forced to accept a situation that he doesn't like or to take a risk unprepared. . . . If you continually shun any risk, you become comfortable with fewer and fewer experiences. . . . Your world shrinks and you become rigid. . . . Your life has no direction but is only a reaction to what the world presents to you.

Therefore, the purpose of life planning is not to eliminate risks but to be certain that the risks you take are the right ones, based on careful thought (Boles, 1981). The question then becomes, how can I find direction for my life?

WHAT MOTIVATES YOU?

What is it that causes a person to consider life planning? Let's look at the definition of two words: (1) *Need*—a lack of something desirable or useful; to be in want. (2) *Motive*—something (a need or desire) that causes a person to act. Actually, the two words are very closely related. When we find ourselves in *need* of something, we begin to search for it. Therefore, the *need* gives us a reason to act—a *motive*.

Happiness is a man's greatest achievement: it is the response of his total personality to a productive orientation toward himself and the world outside.

Eric Fromm

Psychologists have said that there is a reason for everything a person does. Therefore, what are some of these wants and needs that lead people to different types of action?

Murray Banks (1959), a psychologist in New York, has said that human beings have four basic wants. They are:

1. *To be happy*
2. *To have a feeling of importance*
3. *To be loved*
4. *To have a little variety*

Dr. John Schindler (1973), a former physician at the Monroe Clinic in Monroe, Wisconsin, has stated that human beings have six basic needs. They are:

1. *Love and affection*
2. *Security*
3. *Creative expression*
4. *New experience*
5. *Recognition*
6. *Self-esteem*

MASLOW'S HIERARCHY OF NEEDS

Perhaps the most widely accepted category of human needs was presented by Abraham Maslow (1970). It might help us to understand Maslow's theory of human motivation by referring to how we reach the top of a ladder—*one step at a time.* Maslow feels that before we can "blossom" and grow toward self-actualization, the top of the ladder, we progress through certain steps. His theory of the step-ladder, better known as, *Maslow's Hierarchy of Needs,* might look something like this:

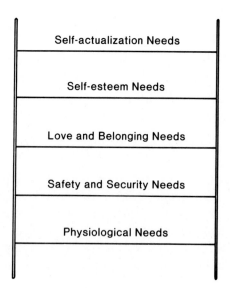

Basically, Maslow believes that there are certain survival needs that must be met before we can become concerned with the satisfaction of other needs. We will now examine Maslow's Hierarchy of Needs.

Physiological Needs. These biological needs include food, water, and air, which are essential to our physical well-being. Hence, they are often referred to as our *primary needs* because they keep us alive. Some people will live and die on this first step of the ladder, because they have barely enough food to keep themselves and their families alive.

Safety and Security Needs. When our physiological needs have been satisfied, the safety needs are the next most important step on the ladder. Safety and security needs include a reasonably orderly and predictable way of life, a savings account, shelter, insurance policies, etc. Actually, there is an endless series of things that can be acquired to protect ourselves. People who live in countries where their safety is constantly threatened by a dictator never get past this second step on the ladder.

Love and Belonging Needs. If our physiological needs are satisfied and our safety needs have been reasonably fulfilled, needs for love, affection, and belonging are the next step on the ladder. Love and belonging needs drive us to seek meaningful relationships with others. We seek acceptance, approval, and a feeling of belonging in our social relationships. Companionship and friendship are very important in satisfying this need to love and be loved. Unfortunately, some people spend their entire lives searching for love, acceptance, and a desire to belong, which they felt they never received from their parents.

Esteem Needs. Maslow believes that if people have their survival, safety, and affection needs met, they will develop a sense of appreciation for themselves. This sense of appreciation may be nothing more than the development of self-confidence, which strengthens our self-esteem—our self-worth. We need to experience some degree of success to feel that we have achieved something worthwhile. Unless we fulfill our need for self-worth, we feel inferior, weak, and worthless; we die on the fourth step of the ladder. However, we may become "hung" on the fourth step of the ladder if we allow status, prestige, titles, and material possessions to dominate our lives.

Self-Actualization Needs. The last step on the ladder represents the fullest development of our potentialities. Some writers believe that *self-actualization* is the need for self-fulfillment—to fulfill oneself as a creative, unique individual according to his or her own innate potentialities. It has been said that we develop and use only about *10 to 15 percent* of our potential mental ability. Therefore, only a small percentage of people achieve what they are really capable of doing. There are degrees of achievement of self-actualization, however. One person might feel complete fulfillment is being the ideal mother. Another person might satisfy this need by setting an occupational goal and reaching it. Actually, self-actualization is a matter of interpretation, and we have the right to decide what constitutes our satisfaction of this top step on the ladder.

Maslow's last book (1971) contains some specific suggestions for increasing our self-actualization. Those suggestions are listed in Table 10.1.

Where are you on the ladder? It is important that we realize that this stepladder of needs is somewhat flexible. All people do not fulfill their needs in the order that Maslow gives; there are some exceptions. For example, some people may feel that self-esteem is more important than belonging and love. Furthermore, many of us move around on the ladder, as we strive to satisfy several needs together.

How do you go about satisfying the needs and wants in your life?

If we are not doing what we are best equipped to do, or doing well what we have undertaken as our personal contribution to the world, there will be a core of unhappiness in our lives which will be more and more difficult to ignore as the years pass.

Anonymous

PLAN YOUR LIFE LIKE YOU WOULD A VACATION

Richard Boles (1976), in his workshops on Life Planning, frequently refers to our lives being divided into three periods. The first period is that of *getting an education;* the second period is that of *going to work and earning a living or working in the home and community;* and the third and last period is that of *living in retirement.*

Table 10.1
Suggestions for Increasing our Self-Actualization

1. Experience life fully, be alive and absorbed with what you are doing at the moment.
2. Learn to trust your own judgment and feelings in making life choices, such as marriage and career.
3. Be honest with yourself and take responsibility for what you do.
4. Whenever possible choose growth, rather than safety or security.
5. Recognize your defenses and illusions, and then work to give them up.
6. Even though peak experiences are transient, keep the inspiration of these moments of self-actualization alive in your everyday thoughts and actions.
7. Remember that self-actualization is a continual process; it is never fully achieved.
8. Commit yourself to concerns and causes outside yourself, because self-actualization comes more as a by-product of developing your full capacities than the egocentric pursuit of growth itself.

One of Boles concerns is that these periods have become more and more isolated from each other. He makes a statement you may find somewhat surprising:

Life in each period seems to be conducted by those in charge without much consciousness of . . . never mind, preparation for . . . life in the next period.

Why Plan? If you really want to take an active part in satisfying the needs and wants of your life, you need a plan or an outline that will direct you toward your ultimate goal. The dictionary says a *goal is an aim or purpose—a plan.* You wouldn't think of going on a vacation without some plans or goals for your trip. After all, you might get lost. Are you trying to play the game of life without goals by moving from different periods of your life without any plans or any direction?

If this describes the picture of your life right now, read the following words of Maxwell Maltz (1970) carefully:

We are engineered as goal-seeking mechanisms. We are built that way. When we have no personal goal which we are interested in and means something to us, we have to go around in circles, feel lost, and find life itself aimless and purposeless. We are built to conquer our environment, solve problems, achieve goals, and we find no real satisfaction or happiness in life without obstacles to conquer and goals to achieve. People who say that life is not worthwhile are really saying that they themselves have no personal goals that are worthwhile. Get yourself a goal worth working for. Better still, get yourself a project. Decide what you want out of a situation. Always have something ahead to look forward to.

In short, we might say that goals give purpose and meaning to our lives; they give us something to aim for, something to achieve. Remember, the reason you make plans for your vacation is so you will reach your destination and have a good time in the process. Achieving what we want out of life is much like climbing to the top of a ladder. We do not leap to the top of the ladder; we have to take a few steps at a time. As the steps on a ladder lead to the top—the goal—our plan for achieving what we want out of life must have steps, too. Otherwise, we will be unable to climb.

After you reach the top, can you quit? No! Goals become self-extending. We do not achieve a goal and suddenly feel comfortable and just quit. You don't get to your vacation destination and quit either. There are things you want to do, and then you have to get back home, too. Rather, we achieve one goal and then find that another fills its place. This is the way we continue to grow and get what we want out of life.

Who is running you? Who should be running you? What is your life worth if you don't take responsibility for it.

David Viscott

The Responsibility Is Yours. It is your responsibility to build the road to your own enrichment; you must lay the foundation. David Campbell (1974), in his thought-provoking book, *If You Don't Know Where You're Going, You'll Probably End Up Somewhere Else,* likens life to a never-ending pathway, which has many side roads or paths in the form of options which confront us along that road; these side roads or paths have gates which are open or closed to us. When we come to each new option, there are two factors that determine whether we continue on the same path, or take a new direction: one is *credentials,* and the second is *motivation.*

If you have the credentials (such as education, training, skills), you have an option available to you and may choose or not choose to take a new path. If you do not have the credentials, the gate remains closed at that point even if you are extremely motivated. In other words, no matter how much you may *want* that option, if you have not prepared for it, it is not going to be available to you.

Where will you be in five/ten/twenty years? You may not know, but you probably have some dreams and ideas. Planning today will help you to go where you want to go, just like you want to get to your vacation destination, rather than drift along relying on luck or fate. Remember, don't forget to keep your options open.

Because we live in a world of change, the fulfillment of our needs may vary from the experiences we encounter. A death of a spouse, for example, may threaten our security needs. Furthermore, as we grow and understand ourselves more clearly, our needs and wants probably change, too. We may have to ask ourselves once more, "Where am I on the stepladder? What are my goals?" "What are my plans for reaching these goals?"

SETTING YOUR GOALS: WHAT DO YOU WANT?

What do you want to achieve? It is important that you get to the "heart of yourself" and answer this question. Whatever is satisfying and worthy can be a goal for you to accomplish. Therefore, no goal is *too insignificant* if it contributes to your sense of achievement. It cannot be small; only you can make it small. Living each day fully is just as important as writing a book. At any rate, you, not anyone else, must be impressed with the goals you set for your life. Richard Boles (1984) confirms this statement:

You have got to know what it is you want, or someone is going to sell you a bill of goods somewhere along the line that can do irreparable damage to your self-esteem, your sense of worth, and your stewardship of the talents that God gave you.

Zig Ziglar (1970), author of *See You At The Top,* says that there are seven different kinds of goals:

1. physical
2. financial
3. spiritual
4. career
5. family
6. mental
7. social

Do you have any needs, wants, or desires that could be worked on in any of these areas? Think about some of these possibilities:

- Would you like to lose some weight or improve your appearance in some way? Would you like to start a personal physical fitness program?
- Would you like to meet some new people? Would you like to do some volunteer work for not-for-profit organizations or become more involved in your community?
- Are you satisfied with your spiritual life? If not, what could you do to improve that element in your life?
- Have you been thinking of further developing your skills and capacities? What would you like to accomplish while you are in college?
- Do you need to spend more time with your family? Do you need to reestablish a relationship with a distant family member?
- Is your financial management what it needs to be to provide for necessities and some of your wants? How can you save to buy that new car next year?
- Would you like an enjoyable, satisfying job? Have you thought of planning to make an appointment with a counselor at your school and begin some serious career counseling?

As you can see, the list of possibilities is just endless. You know what some of your wants and needs are. Are you ready to select one or more of the seven goal areas and begin to establish some serious goals? When? What is wrong with today? Don't procrastinate. There will never be a completely convenient time.

Our aspirations are our possibilities.

Robert Browning

Life Is Like A Piano ...

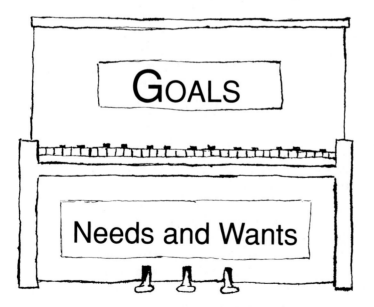

What you get out of it depends on how you play it!

CRITERIA FOR GOAL SETTING

Some guidelines or criteria for identifying personal goals and making them work are listed here. These guidelines will make the task of personal goal setting more useful and satisfying.

Live all you can; it is a mistake not to. It doesn't so much matter what you do in particular, so long as you have had your life. If you haven't had that, what have you had?

William James

Your Goals Must Be Your Own. You are more likely to accomplish personal and internal goals that you set for yourself than if you strive to achieve goals others want you to accomplish. Unless you really own your goals, you will lack the proper motivation to "climb to the top of the ladder." Without a doubt, the most constructive goals for you are those you have decided on for yourself. After all, you are the one that is going to have to do all the work on your goal.

The Goal Must Not Be in Conflict with One's Personal Value System. Before committing yourself to a goal, ask yourself: Is this goal legal in my society and does it fit with my moral and ethical beliefs? If the answer is no, remember you and you alone will have to deal with the consequences of your decision. How important is this? John Crystal and Richard Boles (1974), well-known authorities in the field of life planning, have this to say:

Whole life planning is incomplete without your values and ethical system being explored and counted as an important element in whatever decisions you make.

Goals Need to be Specific and Written Down. If you are not making the progress you would like to and are capable of making, it is probably because your goals are not clearly defined. You need to be focused in on exactly what you will be doing. Be careful of either/or goals; they only divide your energy and attention.

The purpose of writing goals is to clarify and make them concrete for yourself. Once a goal is written, you have more invested than before it was written, and this definitely develops commitment. Also, writing your goals will help you to identify conflicting goals. As you write your goals, be sure to list them in order of priority and identify all the obstacles you must overcome to reach your goals.

Start with Short-Range Goals. Learning involves making mistakes as well as achieving success. Start your goal setting by working on some short-range goals that are easily attainable. As these are accomplished, you will gain more and more confidence to tackle more challenging long-range goals. Because short-range goals are more likely to be within your control, start with goals covering days, weeks, or months, rather than years. Short-range goals will better ensure success, and success is the greatest motivator of all. For example, a goal of losing 10 pounds in one or two months is more motivating than having a goal of losing 50 pounds in a year.

The reward of a thing well done is to have done it.

Ralph Waldo Emerson

Goals Must Be Realistic and Attainable. If a goal is unrealistic and not attainable, it is not a goal, but purely fantasy and daydreaming. We are not suggesting that goals should be low, but they must represent a reasonable objective toward which you are willing and able to work. Obviously, the higher the goal, the stronger is your motivation. However, if you do not believe accomplishment is possible, there is probably no motivation. In other words, do you believe you can achieve the goal? Self-confidence or mental attitude is crucial in achieving goals. Be careful about becoming overambitious by setting too many goals for too short a period of time. A good guide is to cut your first list in half; then, if you have more than six, keep prioritizing the list until you have only three to six new goals to work on at one time. Achievement is what you want, not excess frustration.

Goals Should Contain Specific Time Deadlines. Arriving at target dates for completing each step of a plan provides constant reinforcement and a sense of accomplishment that helps sustain your motivation. Be realistic, but challenge yourself, as you arrive at your completion date. Obviously, dates can and should be adjusted with changed conditions to be reasonable. However, be careful not to use "changed conditions" as a handy excuse.

To summarize our guidelines, the most effective goals are freely chosen, written down, have time deadlines, are within your control, have their consequences thought through, and are based on your personal values.

Do these guidelines guarantee success? Let's look further!

DON'T QUIT

When things go wrong, as they sometimes will,
When the road you're trudging seems all uphill,
When the funds are low and the debts are high,
And you want to smile, but you have to sigh,
When care is pressing you down a bit—
Rest if you must, but don't you quit.

Life is queer with its twists and turns,
As everyone of us sometimes learns,
And many a fellow turns about
When he might have won had he stuck it out.
Don't give up though the pace seems slow—
You may succeed with another blow.

Often the goal is nearer than
it seems to a faint and faltering man;
Often the struggler has given up
When he might have captured the victor's cup;
And he learned too late when the night came down,
How close he was to the golden crown.

Success is failure turned inside out—
The silver tint of the clouds of doubt,
And you never can tell how close you are,
It may be near when it seems afar;
So stick to the fight when you're hardest hit,—
It's when things seem worst than you mustn't quit.

Anonymous

In order to succeed, you must know what you are doing, like what you are doing, and believe in what you are doing.

Will Rogers

CONTRIBUTORS TO SUCCESS

There are countless definitions of what success really is. Success has often been referred to as the *progressive realization of a worthwhile, predetermined personal goal* (McCullough, 1987). For example, some people define success in terms of money and material possessions. Others may feel success is found in personal relationships. Then, there are some people who believe that developing their potential in work or some particular interest defines success. We might conclude that *success is setting a goal and achieving that goal, whatever that goal may be.*

What actually contributes to success?

A Sense of Direction. If we don't know where we are going, we will certainly end up elsewhere. There will, no doubt, be conflicting wants and needs. However, we need to establish priorities and make choices. A *philosophy of life*—or rules for living and values in life—is basic to the direction we choose. Successful people know the direction in which they are moving, and why they are going there. A unified purpose, whatever that may be, gives meaning to our existence, and you already know from Chapter 9 how important this is.

A Feeling of Self-Confidence. If we desire to be successful, a belief in our abilities and our worth as a human being is extremely essential. Most of our actions, feelings, behavior, and even our abilities are consistent with the degree of self-confidence we have. Surely, we have all experienced failures, as well as successes in life. However, if we allow our failures to rule our life, we will never be able to realize our full potential. We are all imperfect. To be successful, we must learn to accept that our blunders, as well as our successes, are a part of us. Our blunders should only be remembered as guides to learning.

Certainly, feelings of successful achievement are the greatest motivation for continued success. We have all heard the statement that *we can do whatever we think we can.* Thus, we will never experience success unless we have confidence in ourselves. Because your performance is directly tied to the way you see yourself, real confidence in yourself is always demonstrated by action.

Happiness is not dependent upon circumstances but upon attitudes; it is not so much environmental as mental.

William Ward

A Healthy Mental Attitude. The one word that influences our life more than any other is *attitude.* This word actually controls our environment and our entire world. Actually, our life is what our thoughts make it. If we think happy thoughts, we will be happy. If we think miserable thoughts, we will be miserable. If we think sickly thoughts, we will be ill. If we think failure, we will certainly fail. Successful people succeed because they think they can attain their goal.

Table 10.2 **The Two Frogs**
Once upon a time, two frogs fell into a bucket of cream. The first frog, seeing that there was no way to get any footing in the white liquid, accepted his fate and drowned. The second frog didn't like that approach. He started thrashing around in the cream and doing whatever he could to stay afloat. After a while, all of his churning turned the cream into butter, and he was able to hop out. Which frog are you more like? Do you have a tendency to "give up" easily at the first sign of defeat, or do you generally "hang in there" and turn your set backs into a success?

Certainly, a healthy mental attitude doesn't imply a pollyanna attitude toward all our problems. It simply means that we approach our problems and goals with a positive attitude. A negative attitude defeats us before we even start to work on our goals. On the other hand, a positive attitude enables us to take action toward facing our problems and obtaining our goals. (See Table 10.2.) Mamie Mc-Cullough (1987), author and motivational speaker, defines a positive and a negative attitude in this way: A positive attitude says, "*I can*"; a negative attitude says, "*I can't*" or "*I won't.*"

A Belief in Perseverance. In the game of life, you have to put something in before you can take anything out. After all, isn't this what you also have to do with your checking account? Successful people *itch* for a lot in life, but they are willing to *scratch* for what they want. Therefore, we must determine how much time we are willing to give and what sacrifices we are willing to make towards the attainment of our goals. The magic word to success has been referred to as work—working hard and long to accomplish goals.

We need to remember that to give up is to invite complete defeat. Some people, just like the first frog, *quit* before they have given themselves a chance to succeed. People with a true belief in perseverance work toward their goals when encouraged and work harder when discouraged. It is very easy to give up, but much harder to continue, especially when "the going gets rough." However, nothing worthwhile has ever been accomplished the easy way.

Success is the sum of small efforts, repeated day in and day out.

Robert Collier

An Understanding of Others. More than likely our goals will involve other people. As a matter of fact, it is dangerous to make goals without carefully considering the effects they could have on your family. Remember, *you do have to work around and with these folks.* Furthermore, you want to take them with you down the road to your successes.

It is important, therefore, that we learn to understand what their needs are, how they feel, and how to interact with them. Learning the art of human communication is vitally important to achieving success. Successful people rarely make it completely on their own; they have generally been encouraged by others.

In essence, people who are successful in reaching their goals have *direction, dedication, discipline, and a super positive attitude.*

But, will you have enough *time* to develop these qualities of success?

THOUGHTS ON TIME

Time is the inexplicable raw material of everything. With it, all is possible, without it, nothing. The supply of time is truly a daily miracle, an affair genuinely astonishing when one examines it.

You wake up in the morning, and lo! your purse is magically filled with twenty-four hours of the unmanufactured tissue of the universe of your life! It is yours. It is the most precious of possessions. . . . No one can take it from you. And no one receives either more or less than you receive.

You have to live on this twenty-four hours of daily time. Out of it you have to spin health, pleasure, money, content, respect, and the evolution of your immortal soul. Its right use, its most effective use, is a matter of the highest urgency and of the most thrilling actuality. All depends on that. Your happiness—the elusive prize that you are all clutching for, my friends—depends on that.

If one cannot arrange that an income of twenty-four hours a day shall exactly cover all proper items of expenditure, one does muddle one's whole life indefinitely. . . .

We never shall have any more time. We have, and we have always had, all the time there is.

Anonymous

THE TIME IN YOUR LIFE

Time presents a problem to all of us. Alec McKenzie (1981), a time-management expert, offers some interesting insights:

You can't save it and use it later.
You can't elect not to spend it.
You can't borrow it.
You can't leave it. Nor can you retrieve it.
You can't take it with you, either.

But . . .

Time is always with you—and you can lose it or use it—the choice is up to you. However, sometimes we get up-tight about "time." These frustrations of time are largely due to your attitudes toward time. Many of these attitudes are based on false assumption (Douglas, 1980).

For example, you have been told that to be successful you must learn to manage your time. This is impossible. You cannot "manage time." It is frustrating to think you can manage something over which you have absolutely no control. But you can learn to manage *yourself*.

Another false assumption is saying, "I don't have time to do that." Probably not so. You have the time. You just do not choose to spend it in that manner. It is probably an unpleasant task that you would rather not do. That's okay. But why blame time?

Or how about, "She has more time than I do." Everybody has the same amount of time. But everybody spends it doing different things by choice or habit.

Time Management is Really Self-Management. There are several ways of looking at exactly how much time we have. For example, each of us has twenty-four hours—1440 minutes a day, 10,080 minutes a week, or 8,760 hours a year to spend, invest, or fritter away. We spend time doing the maintenance tasks of life—working, eating, sleeping, and so on. We invest time in learning, creating or loving. These time "investments" continue to pay dividends in personal satisfaction, career advancement, or fond memories. Sometimes we fritter away valuable time in activities we don't really enjoy and soon forget. Often, this is caused by our inability to say No!

Remember, you should be the master of time and not let it master you. Discovering your *timewasters* is the key to managing yourself in relation to time. The word *timewaster* can be defined to mean anything preventing you from achieving your objectives most effectively.

What, of all things in the world, is the longest and the shortest, the swiftest and the slowest, the most neglected, and the most regretted, without which nothing can be done: TIME.

Voltaire

Most timewasters are self-generated. For example, do you ever procrastinate—put things off until it's too late or no longer matters? You might be surprised to learn that *procrastination* is one of the most common time management problems, or timewasters.

Table 10.3 lists other timewasters. Which of these create a problem for you? Which of these do you have control over?

The people who accomplish the most do so not because they have more time, but because they *use* it more wisely. Planning and goal-setting are the keys to successful time management. Using time effectively is dependent on just one thing—*your daily identification of priorities of the things you have to do or want to do.* You must decide what the important objectives are in your life and then establish priorities every day in relation to these objectives. Victor Hugo confirms this:

One who every morning plans the priorities of the day and follows out that plan carries a thread that will guide one through the most busy life. But, where no plan is laid, where the disposal of time is surrendered merely to the chance of incidents, chaos soon reigns.

**Table 10.3
Common Timewasters**

- Procrastination
- Personal disorganization
- Lack of planning
- Poor communication
- Commuting and/or traffic delays
- Lack of self-discipline
- Not setting deadlines
- Inability to say No!
- Watching TV
- Talking on the telephone
- Meetings
- Excessive errands
- Attempting too much at once
- Leaving tasks unfinished
- Drop-in visitors

Which of these timewasters create a problem for you?

CREATING HARMONY IN YOUR LIFE

Think about the last time you heard a symphony orchestra play and then answer these questions: Just by chance, was there one instrument that was given so much emphasis the others simply weren't heard? Was there one instrument that seemed "out-of-synch?" Or, were all the instruments playing in a harmonious melody?

What does a symphony orchestra have to do with your life? The important areas in your life, to which you devote your time and energy, do not exist in isolation but are very much like a symphony orchestra playing. Individual instruments (like work) sound fine, but when combined into a symphony (your life), the effect on your whole life is then multiplied. Could it be possible that you have not found a harmonious melody to play with all of the important areas in your life? Could it be possible that you might have one important "instrument" that has been given so much emphasis, there is not any way for the others to be heard? Balance is important with our lives, as with a symphony orchestra (Anstin, 1980).

Your Chair of Life. Someone once said that each individual has a *chair of life*. This chair contains four legs, each representing an extremely valuable part of our life. For example, the four legs might be: (1) Vocation, (2) Family and friends, (3) Avocation—interests and hobbies, and (4) Spirituality.

If we are experiencing contentment in each of these areas, we must be contributing some quality time to each of these areas. In short, our chair of life is in balance—there is a harmonious melody in your life. However, if one of the legs becomes longer or shorter than the others because of too much time or too little time, we feel uncomfortable, stressed, and oftentimes dissatisfied. In short, our chair of life is out of balance—a harmonious melody does not exist in our life.

If it is difficult for you to relate to a symphony orchestra, then find a chair with four legs and sit down for just a moment. Label each leg of the chair with the important areas of your life. For example, (1) Work, (2) Family, (3) School, (4) Playing tennis with friends. Let's assume that by the time you go to school and work and spend some time with your family, you are finding little time for your favorite stress-relieving hobby—playing tennis with your friends. As a result, you are beginning to feel a little cheated. Get several books and place them under the leg of the chair representing this very important leisure activity. Now, sit down in the chair. How do you feel? Off-balance, right! Are you afraid you are going to fall over?

Where I was born and where and how I have lived is unimportant. It is what I have done with where I have been that should be of interest.

George O'Keeffe

What Would Your Chair Of Life Look Like ...

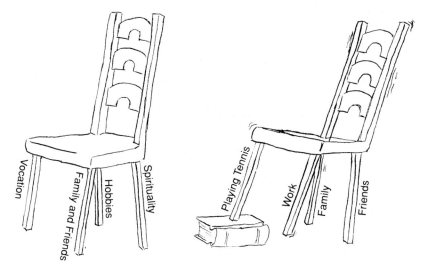

Would it be in balance or out of balance?

This is the true picture of what goes on in our life when we either direct too little or too much time to the important areas in our life. Something is "out of synch." You notice yourself getting really irritated or even depressed.

This illustration can even be used to describe a person who is so committed to the World of Work that there is little time for family life or anything else. Is the pursuit of a career worth losing the respect and admiration of your family? You'll have to decide that, but here is a view from Mary Kay Ash (1981), the founder of Mary Kay Cosmetics:

It's most fulfilling to build a successful career, but if you lose your spouse and family in the process, then, I think you have failed. Success is so much more wonderful when you have someone to share it with. It's no fun to come home and count your money by yourself.

The important thing is to learn to recognize when your chair of life is getting out of balance and take immediate action to balance your time and energy on all the important aspects of your life. Otherwise, you may lose a major portion of one or more legs of your chair of life. When this happens, you whole life is out of balance. M. Scott Peck (1978) makes a thought-provoking statement:

Mature mental health demands an extraordinary capacity to flexibly strike and continually restrike a delicate balance between conflicting needs, goals, duties, responsibilities, etc. The essence of this discipline of balancing is "giving up." . . . As we negotiate the curves and corners of our lives, we must continually give up parts of ourselves since the loss of balance is ultimately more painful than the giving up required to maintain balance.

In essence, in life there are trade-offs. There is a price to pay for what is important to you. You and you alone must decide what your trade-offs will be.

EFFECTIVE LIFE .PLANNING: IT'S ALL UP TO YOU!

The key to successful life planning is the *willingness to take responsibility for ourselves.* It is indeed possible for us to take control of our lives in the midst of the forces around us. In a life situation, we have three choices: *change it, enjoy it and tolerate it,* or *leave it.* To *change it,* we must change our behavior, goals, or circumstances. If we choose to *enjoy it,* we must recognize that it is our choice to stay with it, for whatever set of reasons. Then, if we choose to *leave our life situation,* we must find another environment for our energies. We must remember that feeling forced to stay with our life situation and hating it is not a viable and productive alternative.

There are many opportunities for us to grow, to find interesting work, and to vary our lives. Actually, the freedom and opportunity to realize our potential are relatively rich and available to a relatively large proportion of people. However, we must choose to actively pursue the possibilities we do have. We cannot wait for "good things" to happen to us; we have to make them happen.

Because goals give direction and purpose to our life, goal setting should be a continuous activity throughout our lifetime. What happens in life planning is that we pause frequently to reevaluate ourselves, our goals, and our performances. As we improve in the understanding of ourselves, our wants, our needs, and our goals may change. If we are careful in assessing our potentials, needs, and wants, we will be able to set more realistic goals and keep our chair of life in balance.

With this thought in mind, there are some questions you can ask yourself about the arena of life and work planning.

Who Am I? This seems like such a simple question. However, this is a very complex and difficult question to answer cogently. Knowledge of yourself must be organized and properly focused in order to contribute to practical progress.

What Am I Up To? This question implies what is really going on with you *right now,* what are you trying to get done *right now,* and what are your needs and motives *right now.*

Where Am I Going? Obviously, this question relates directly to effective goal setting. At this point, you may have to take an inventory of your priorities—what means the most to you *right now.* Also, you might want to take a look at where you have been versus what you want to be doing in the near future.

What Difference Does It Make Anyhow? The difference lies in the degree of happiness and fulfillment you are experiencing in your life. You can be happy and fulfilled, or miserable and stifled. You choose who you become.

If we, from time to time, apply these questions to our personal objectives, our lives will be more effective, satisfying, and of course, more in balance.

Others can stop you temporarily—you are the only one who can do it permanently.

Zig Ziglar

A LAST THOUGHT

We must be aware of the needs and wants that exist in each of us and look at the ways in which we meet them. The drive for growth and expression will not be denied, and if it cannot be channeled in a positive and healthy direction, it will take an undesirable course. The better we understand ourselves, our motives, and our abilities, the more readily we will react to opportunities for personal development. However, regardless of our past experiences, our future growth and development is placed squarely on our own shoulders.

We must remember that our rewards in life are in exact proportion to our contribution—our service. Thus, adopting a healthy attitude toward life determines how much we will reap of what we have sown. How much are we willing to sow? How much do we want to reap? In essence, if we want a rich, full, and satisfying life, we must make a significant number of contributions.

We leave you with this short recipe for successful life planning:

1. *Know what you want*
2. *Know what you are willing to give up to have what you want*
3. *Have a game plan*
4. *Go to work consistently each day on your game plan.*

Life can't give me joy and peace, it's up to me to will it. Life just gives me time and space, it's up to me to fill it.

Anonymous

Now that you know that you can be in control of where you want to go and how you are going to go about getting there, will you choose to exercise that control? Remember, you are in charge of the steering wheel of *your* life. You are the engineer of *your* train. Where will you go?

KEY TERMS

Risk
Need
Motive
Maslow's Hierarchy of Needs
Physiological Needs
Safety and Security Needs
Love and Belonging Needs

Esteem Needs
Self-Actualization Needs
Goals
Success
Timewaster
Chair of Life

CHAPTER DISCUSSION QUESTIONS

1. What risks are you afraid of taking right now in your life?
2. What are you going to have to give up to have what you want?
3. What do you think are the basic needs and wants of human beings?
4. Identify some of the needs and wants you have established right now in your life. What are you now doing to satisfy them?
5. Of Maslow's five basic needs, which one seems most important for you to satisfy right now?
6. What does success mean to you?
7. What determines success in our society?
8. Discuss this statement—Each of us becomes what we think about.
9. What is your greatest timewaster? How much of your time do you spend in this activity?
10. Diagram and discuss your chair of life. Is it in balance? If not, why?

REFERENCES

Anstin, Margaret. (1980) *Voyage.* Dubuque, Iowa: Kendall/Hunt Publishing Co.

Ash, Mary Kay. (1981) *Mary Kay.* New York: Harper & Row.

Banks, Murray. (1959) *How to Live with Yourself.* New York: Murmil Associates, Inc.

Boles, R. N. (1978) *The Three Boxes of Life.* Berkeley, California: Ten Speed Press.

————. (1984) *What Color is Your Parachute?* Berkeley, California: Ten Speed Press.

Campbell, David. (1974) *If You Don't Know Where You're Going, You'll Probably End Up Somewhere Else.* Niles, Illinois: Argus Communications.

Douglas, Merrill and Douglas, Donna. (1980) *Manage Your Time, Manage Your Work, Manage Yourself.* New York: AMACOM.

Hecklinger, Fred and Curtin, Bernadette M. (1984) *Training for Life.* Dubuque, Iowa: Kendall/Hunt Publishing Co.

Figler, Howard. (1979) *The Complete Job Search Handbook.* New York: Holt, Rinehart and Winston.

Mackenzie, Alec and Waldo, Kay. (1981) *About Time.* New York: McGraw-Hill Book Co.

Maltz, Maxwell. (1960) *Psychocybernetics.* Englewood Cliffs, New Jersey: Prentice Hall, Inc.

Maslow, Abraham. (1970) *Motivation and Personality* (2nd. ed.). New York: Harper and Row.

————. (1971) *The Further Reaches of Human Nature.* New York: Viking.

McCullough, Mamie. (1987) *I Can. You Can Too!* Nashville, Tennessee: Thomas Nelson Publishers.

Peck, M. Scott. (1978) *The Road Less Traveled.* New York: Simon & Schuster, Inc.

Schindler, John. (1970) *How to Live 365 Days A Year.* Englewood Cliffs, New Jersey: Prentice Hall, Inc.

Viscott, David. (1977) *Risking.* New York: Pocket Books.

Ziglar, Zig. (1977) *See You At The Top.* Gretna, Louisiana: Pelican Publishing Co.

YOUR LIFE'S ACTIVITIES

Purpose: To demonstrate how your activities make up your life.

Instructions:

I. Divide the circle on the left, as a pie, into parts that represent your current life. Label each part: for example, home life, work, personal, education, leisure, and whatever else represents your current life.

II. Divide the circle on the right into parts that represent your life three years ago. Use the same labeling as in the first circle or add others as needed.

III. For the third circle, divide it in a way that represents the ideal way you'd like your life to be. Label each part as in previous circles.

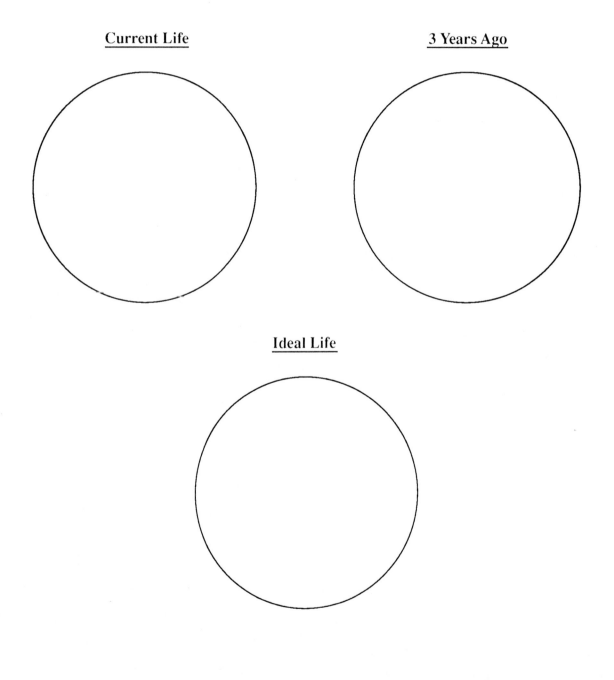

Current Life

3 Years Ago

Ideal Life

IV. Complete the answers to the questions below and be prepared to discuss them in small groups.

Discussion: Let's compare and contrast the three circles.

1. What's keeping your present circle of activities from being like the ideal circle?

2. What can you do within the next six months to make the ideal circle like your real life?

3. What did you learn about yourself from this activity?

WHAT DO YOU WANT?

Purpose: To establish three sets of goals and to examine what you are really working toward accomplishing.

Instructions:

I. Write down what goals you would like to accomplish in the following areas. If you do not have a goal in a particular area, that is okay. You decide.

FAMILY:

1.

2.

PHYSICAL:

1.

2.

MENTAL:

1.

2.

SOCIAL:

1.

2.

RELIGIOUS:

1.

2.

FINANCIAL:

1.

2.

CAREER:

1.

2.

II. Next, select the three things you want most to accomplish within the next six months.

1.

2.

3.

III. Now, select from your goals the three things you want most to accomplish in the next year.

1.

2.

3.

IV. Now, select your three most important life goals.

1.

2.

3.

V. Now, write down anything, large or small, you have done within the past month to accomplish any of these goals.

DISCUSSION

1. Are you presently working toward what you say is important to you?

2. Why are you not doing anything about what you say you want?

3. Do you really want these things?

4. Review the seven areas of possible goals and write down what goals you really want to start working on *now*.

LIFELINE

Purpose: To take a look at where you've been, where you are, and where you want to go.

Instructions:

   I. On a piece of heavy poster board or construction paper, start with the year in which you were born and depict the significant experiences and people who have helped shape your life.
  II. Your lifeline will be dated in terms of the years these significant experiences or people appeared in your life.
 III. Make notations above or below each year to remind you of exactly what occurred.
  IV. When completed, your lifeline will appear like a graph: "highs and lows," "hills and valleys," and "steady" periods of your life. You may use pictures, words, or whatever you wish to depict these significant time periods in your life.
   V. The last dot on your lifeline should be on a "hill," a high point in the future. Fantasize and jot some words down to describe what you would like to have happening in your life in the next five or ten years. What will you be doing, where will you be, and who will be with you?
  VI. After you have completed your life line, you will divide into small groups and explain your lifeline. Be prepared to give a ten-minute presentation.

DISCUSSION

1. How do you feel about the quality of your life at the present time?

2. What experiences are primarily responsible for where you are today?

3. What experiences are primarily responsible for what you want to accomplish in the future?

4. What goals are implied as you picture yourself five to ten years in the future?

MY FUTURE AUTOBIOGRAPHY

Purpose: To think about the quality of your life and to demonstrate that you still have a life ahead with which to do whatever you choose.

Instructions:

I. In the space below, write at least a two or three paragraph autobiography for yourself. Include things that you would like to have said or written about you near the end of your life. Write about things that you would like to accomplish and things that are possible for you to accomplish.

II. Have someone else read your autobiography and complete the first discussion question.

DISCUSSION

1. What long-range goals are implied in this autobiography? Write them below, even if they are vague.

2. Do you see any similarity in the goals implied here and in the goals you listed in the previous activity?

GOAL DEVELOPMENT

Purpose: To further understand yourself and to define your goals.

Instructions:

I. List your strengths, based on questionnaires, personal assessments, assignments, and personal experiences gained in or out of class this term.

II. List your weaknesses, based on questionnaires, personal assessments, assignments, and personal experiences gained in or out of class this term.

III. Re-evaluate your responses to the exercises in this chapter and what you now know about yourself. List the five most important things in your life at the present time.

1.

2.

3.

4.

5.

IV. Review your lifeline and what you know about yourself and list at least three peak experiences that have been meaningful to you.

1.

2.

3.

V. What other peak experiences would you like to have in the future?

VI. Review your autobiography and your lifeline and list the tentative goals implied in each activity.

VII. Review your responses to the activity "What Do I Want" and your responses to the previous questions in this activity and write down at least three goals that you want to start working on *now*.

Consider the following questions before listing your goals.

Is this a goal I really want to achieve?

Is it realistic; that is can it be achieved?

Does this goal contradict any of my basic values?

Do I have the personal strengths to achieve this goal?

Do I need and have the support of my family?

MY GOALS:

1.

2.

3.

GOAL PROJECT

Purpose: To develop a plan of action for what you want to accomplish.

Instructions:

I. From the previous exercise, select two goals and develop a plan of what you can do this next year to achieve this goal.

GOAL NUMBER ONE

1. I want to _____

_____

2. What obstacle must I overcome?

3. How do I plan to overcome these obstacles? Be specific.

4. What behaviors must I change?

5. How do I plan to change these behaviors? Be specific.

6. When will I achieve this goal? Be specific.

GOAL NUMBER TWO

1. I want to _____

_____

2. What obstacles must I overcome?

3. How do I plan to overcome these obstacles? Be specific.

4. What behaviors must I change?

5. How do I plan to change these behaviors? Be specific.

6. When will I achieve this goal? Be specific.

DISCUSSION

1. How do you feel about the goal project you have just completed?

LEARNING JOURNAL FOR LIFE PLANNING

Select the statement below that best defines your feelings about the personal value or meaning gained from this chapter and respond below the dotted line:

I LEARNED THAT I . . .   I WAS SURPRISED THAT I . . .

I REALIZED THAT I . . .   I WAS PLEASED THAT I . . .

I DISCOVERED THAT I . . .   I WAS DISPLEASED THAT I . . .

....

BECOMING THE PERSON YOU WANT TO BE

Now that you know that a meaningful relationship between two people develops as the two become more open and honest about themselves . . .

Will you make the choice to present the "real you" to those with whom you desire to form a special, close relationship?

Now that you know that personal growth and self-awareness involves accepting yourself and enjoying relationships with others . . .

Will you make the choice to embark upon this exciting, lifelong journey?

Now that you know you have the option of controlling your behavior, as well as what you want to achieve in life . . .

Will you make the choice to accept personal responsibility for who you become?

Now that you know that you are capable of expressing any type of human emotion or feeling . . .

Will you make the choice to try to understand, describe, and deal with your feelings in a healthy, rational manner?

Now that you know that effective communication is important to every aspect of your life . . .

Will you make the choice to evaluate your own communication skills and work to make them the very best possible?

Now that you understand that love consists of attachment, caring, and intimacy for another person . . .

Will you carefully evaluate your love for that "special person" before making a long-term commitment to him or her.

Now that you know that conflict is a natural part of *all* relationships . . .

Will you make the choice to recognize when conflict exists and then take the time to initiate a win-win approach to your interpersonal conflicts?

Now that you know that stress is very much a part of your life . . .

Will you make the choice to recognize stress, live with it, and make it work for you.

Now that you know that the real values in life are those you have actually experienced . . .

Will you make the choice to open yourself to each experience life has for you and live each experience to the fullest?

Now that you know that your long-range happiness is guaranteed when you decide to plan and direct your own life . . .

Will you choose to exercise that option?

The time to begin is now; the place to begin is here; the person who is capable of taking the knowledge and skills presented herein and directing them toward developing a more meaningful life is you. The choice is yours. We hope your decision marks the beginning of your becoming the person you want to be. It is to this "end" that we conclude with the words of an anonymous writer.

YOU CAN BE WHATEVER YOU WANT TO BE

There is inside you all of the potential to be whatever you want to be—all of the energy to do whatever you want to do.

Imagine yourself as you would like to be, doing what you want to do, and each day, take one step . . . toward your dream.

And though at times it may seem too difficult to continue, hold on to your dream.

One morning you will awake to find that you are the person you dreamed of—doing what you wanted to do—simply because you had the courage to believe in your potential and to hold on to your dream.

READINGS AND REFERENCES

Alder, Alfred. *What Life Should Mean to You.* New York: G. P. Putnam's 1958.

Adler, Ronald, and Towne, Neil. *Looking In/Looking Out.* New York: Holt, Rinehart and Winston, Inc., 1981.

———. *Looking Out/Looking In.* New York: Holt, Rinehart and Winston, Inc., 1987.

Alberti, Robert E. and Emmons, Michael L. *Your Perfect Right: A Guide to Assertive Living.* (Sixth Edition) San Luis Obispo, California: Impact Publishers, Inc., 1991.

Allport, Gordon. *Becoming.* Boston, Massachusetts: The Colonial Press, Inc., 1973.

Amick, Robert, and Brennecke, John. *Psychology and Human Experience.* California: Glencoe Press, 1974.

Anstin, Margaret. *Voyage.* Dubuque, Iowa: Kendall/Hunt Publishing Co., 1980.

Arkoff, Abe. *Psychology and Personal Growth.* Boston, Massachusetts: Allyn and Bacon, Inc., 1975.

Arnold, M. B. (ed.). *Feelings and Emotions.* New York: Academic Press, 1970.

Ash, Mary Kay. *Mary Kay.* New York: Harper & Row, 1981.

Atwater, Eastwood. *Psychology of Adjustment.* Englewood Cliffs, New Jersey: Prentice Hall, Inc.

———. *Human Relations.* Englewood Cliffs, New Jersey: Prentice-Hall, Inc., 1986.

Axline, Virginia. *DIBS in Search of Self.* New York: Ballantine Books, 1971.

Bach, George R. *Aggression Lab: The Fair Fight Manual.* Dubuque, Iowa: Kendall/Hunt Publishing Co., 1971.

Bach, Richard. *Jonathan Livingston Seagull.* New York: The MacMillan Company, 1973.

Banks, Murray. *How to Live with Yourself.* New York: Murmil Associates, Inc., 1959.

———. *Just In Case You Think You're Normal.* New York: Murmil Associates, Inc., 1961.

Barwick, Dee Danner. *Great Words of Our Time.* Missouri: Hallmark Cards, Inc., 1970.

Beck, A. T. *Cognitive Therapy and Emotional Disorders.* New York: New American Library, 1979.

Berne, Eric. *The Games People Play.* New York: Grove Press, Inc., 1967.

———. *What Do You Say After You Say Hello?* New York: Grove Press, Inc., 1964.

Berscheid, E., and Graziano, W. *The Initiation of Social Relationships and Interpersonal Attraction.* In R. L. Burgess and T. L. Huston (eds.), *Social Exchange in Developing Relationships.* New York: Academic Press, 1979.

——— and Walster, E. *A Little Bit About of Love.* In T. L. Huston (ed.), Foundation of Interpersonal Attraction. New York: Academic Press, 1974.

———. *Physical Attractiveness.* In L. Berkowits (ed.), Advances in Experimental Social Psychology, vol. 7. New York: Academic Press, 1974.

Block, J. D. Friendship: *How to Give It; How to Get It.* New York: Macmillan, 1980.

Boles, R. N. *The Three Boxes of Life.* Berkeley, California: Ten Speed Press, 1978.

———. *What Color is Your Parachute?* Berkeley, California: Ten Speed Press, 1984.

Bolton, Robert. *People Skills.* New York: Simon and Schuster, Inc., 1979.

Bower, S. A. and Bower, G. H. *Asserting Yourself.* Reading, Massachusetts: Addison Wesley, 1976.

Bry, Adelaide. *The T A Primer.* New York: Harper and Row Publishers,1973.

Burgess, R. L. and Huston, T. L. (eds.) *Social Exchange in Developing Relationships.* New York: Academic Press, 1979.

Buscaglia, Leo. *Living, Loving and Learning.* New York: Holt, Rinehart and Winston, 1982.

———. *Loving Each Other: The Challenge of Human Relationships.* New York: Holt, Rinehart and Winston, 1984.

Campbell, David. *If You Don't Know Where You're Going, You'll Probably End Up Somewhere Else.* Niles, Illinois: Argus Communications, 1974.

Carkuff, Robert. *The Art of Problem Solving.* Boston, Massachusetts: Human Resource Development Press, Inc., 1973.

Carnegie, Dale. *How to Win Friends and Influence People.* New York: Pocket Books, 1970.

Clark, Tony; Bock, Doug; and Cornett, Mike. *Is That You Out There?* Columbus, Ohio: Charles E. Merrill Publishing Co., 1973.

Cline, Foster W. *Parent Education Text.* Evergreen, Colorado: Evergreen Consultants in Human Behavior, 1982.

Coleman, J. *Intimate Relationships, Marriage, and Family.* Indianapolis, Indiana: Bobbs-Merrill Co., 1984.

Corey, Gerald and Corey, Marianne. *I Never Knew I Had a Choice.* Pacific Grove, California: Brooks Cole Publishing Co., 1990.

Davis, M., Eshelman, Elizabeth Robbins, and McKay, Matthew. *The Relaxation and Stress Reduction Workbook.* Richmond, California: New Harbinger Publishing Co., 1982.

Demo, D. H., & Acock, A. C. "The Impact of Divorce on Children." *Journal of Marriage and the Family,* 50, 619–648, 1988.

Deutsch, M. *The Resolution of Conflict.* New Haven: Yale University Press, 1973.

Douglas, Merrill and Douglas, Donna. *Manage Your Time, Manage Your Work, Manage Yourself.* New York: AMACOM, 1980.

Drakeford, John. *The Awesome Power of the Listening Ear.* Waco, Texas: Word Publishing, 1967.

Drescher, J. M. "When Opposites Attract." *Marriage and Family Living,* 61 (May 1979), 9–11.

Dyer, Wayne W. *Your Erroneous Zones.* New York: Avon Books, 1977.

Eckman, Paul and Friesen, Wallace. *Unmasking the Face: A Guide to Recognizing Emotions from Facial Clues.* Englewood Cliffs, New Jersey: Prentice Hall, Inc., 1975.

Ellenson, Ann. *Human Relations.* Englewood Cliffs, New Jersey: Prentice Hall, Inc., 1982.

Ellis, Albert and Harper, Robert. *A Guide to Rational Living.* North Hollywood, California: Wilshire Book Company, 1973.

———. *A New Guide to Rational Living.* North Hollywood, California: Wilshire Books, 1977.

———. *Reason and Emotion in Psychotherapy.* New York: Lyle Stuart, 1962.

———. "Rational Psychotherapy." *Journal of General Psychology,* 50 (1958), pp. 35–49.

Emery, Gary and Campbell, James. *Rapid Relief from Emotional Distress.* New York: Ballantine Books, 1986.

Erb, Everett, and Hooker, Douglas. *The Psychology of the Emerging Self.* Pennsylvania: F. A. Davis Company, Publishers, 1971.

Erikson, E. H. *Identity: Youth and Crisis.* New York: Norton, 1968.

Etaugh, C. F. "Effects of Maternal Employment on Children: A Review of Recent Research." *Merrill-Palmer Quarterly,* 20, 71–98, 1974.

Exupery, Antoine DeSaint. *The Little Prince.* New York: Harcourt, Brace and World, Inc., 1943.

Fast, Julius. *Body Language.* New York: Pocket Books, 1971.

Fensterheim, Herbert and Baer. *Don't Say Yes When You Want to Say No.* New York: David McKay, 1975.

Festinger, L. *A Theory of Cognitive Dissonance.* Stanford, California: Stanford University Press, 1957.

Figler, Howard. *The Complete Job Search Handbook.* New York: Holt, Rinehart and Winston, 1979.

Fischer, C. S. "What Do You Mean by 'Friend'? An Inductive Study," *Social Network,* 3 (1982), 287–306.

Forst, Solar. *Alphabet of Love.* New York: The Peter Paupere Press, 1967.

Fowers, B. J., & Olson, D. H. "ENRICH Marital Inventory: A Discriminant Validity and Cross-Validation Assessment." *Journal of Marital and Family Therapy,* 15(1) (1989), 65–79.

Frankl, V. E. *Man's Search for Meaning.* New York: Simon & Schuster, Inc. 1972

———. *Man's Search for Meaning.* New York: Washington Square Press, 1963.

———. *The Unheard Cry for Meaning.* New York: Bantam, 1972.

Freud, Sigmund. *The Problems of Anxiety.* New York: Norton, 1936.

Friedman, Meyer, and Rosenman, Ray H. *Type A Behavior and Your Heart.* New York: Fawcett Crest, 1974.

———. *Type A Behavior and Your Heart.* New York: Fawcett, 1981.

Fromm, Erich. *The Act of Loving.* New York: Harper and Row, Publishers, Inc., 1956.

Frost, Joyce Hocker, and Wilmot, William W. *Interpersonal Conflict.* 2nd ed. Dubuque, Iowa: Wm. C. Brown, 1985.

Gibran, Kahlil. *A Friend Indeed.* Missouri: Hallmark Cards, Inc., 1971.

———. *The Prophet.* New York: Alfred A. Knopf, 1923.

Ginott, Haim. *Between Parent and Child.* New York: The MacMillan Company, 1972.

———. *Between Parent and Teenager.* New York: The MacMillan Company, 1971.

Glasser, William. *Reality Therapy.* New York: Harper and Row Publishers, Inc., 1965.

Glenn, Norval D., and Weaver, Charles N. "The Marital Happiness of Remarried Divorced Persons." *Journal of Marriage and the Family,* 48, 737–748, 1978.

Goodman, David. *Living From Within.* Missouri: Hallmark Cards, Inc., 1968.

Gordon, Thomas. *Parent Effectiveness Training.* New York: Peter H. Wyden, Inc., 1975.

———. *Parent Effectiveness Training.* New York: New American Library, 1970.

Grasha, A. *Practical Applications of Psychology.* Boston, Massachusetts: Little, Brown, and Co., 1983.

Greenwald, Jerry. *Be The Person You Were Meant to Be.* New York: Dell Publishing Co., 1973.

Haas, Linda. "Domestic Role Sharing in Sweden." *Journal of Marriage and the Family,* 43, 957–967, 1981.

Hall, Edward T. *Silent Language.* New York: Doubleday and Company, Inc., 1959.

———. *The Hidden Dimension.* Garden City, New York: Anchor Books, 1969.

Harris, Thomas A. *I'm OK—You're OK.* New York: Harper & Row, 1969.

Harrison, Delyn Dendy. *Some Things Are Said in Black and White.* Fort Worth, Texas: Branch Smith, Inc., 1978.

Harrison, Randall. "Nonverbal Communication: Exploration into Time, Space, Action, and Object," *Dimensions in Communication: Readings,* edited by James Campbell and Hall Harper. Belmont, California: Wadsworth Publishing Co., 1970.

Hecklinger, Fred and Curtin, Bernadette M. *Training for Life.* Dubuque, Iowa: Kendall/Hunt Publishing Co., 1984.

Heslin, R. and Alper, T. "Touch: A Bonding Gesture," *Nonverbal Interaction,* ed. J. M. Wiemann and R. P. Harrison. Beverly Hills, California: Sage Publishing Co., 1983.

Hoffman, Gloria and Graiver, Pauline. *Speak the Language of Success.* New York: G. P. Putnam's Sons, 1983.

Hoffman, L. "The Effects on Children of Maternal and Paternal Employment," in N. Gerstel and H. Gross (Eds.), *Families and Work.* Philadelphia: Temple University Press, 1987.

Hopkins, L. T. *Interaction—The Democratic Process.* Boston, Massachusetts: D. C. Heath Company, 1941.

Horney, Karen. *Our Inner Conflicts.* New York: W. W. Norton and Company, Inc., 1945.

James, Muriel, and Jongeward, Dorothy. *Born to Win.* Boston, Massachusetts: Addison-Wesley Publishing Company, 1973.

James, W. H., Woodruff, A. B., and Werner, W. "Effects of Internal and External Control Upon Changes in Smoking Behavior," *Journal of Consulting Psychology,* 1965, 29, pp. 184–186.

Johnson, David. *Reaching Out.* Englewood Cliffs, New Jersey: Prentice Hall, Inc., 1972.

Johnson, Kenneth. *Nothing Never Happens.* California: Glencoe Press, 1974.

Jones, John, and Pfeiffer, J. William. *Annual Handbook for Group Facilitators.* 10 vols. San Diego, California: University Associates Publishers, Inc., 1973–1983.

Jourard, Sidney. *Personal Adjustment.* New York: The MacMillan Company, 1973.

———. *The Transparent Self: Self-Disclosure and Well-Being* (rev. ed.). New York: Van Nostrand Reinhold, 1971.

———. *The Transparent Self.* Ontario, Canada: Van Nostrand, 1964.

Jung, Carl G. *Psychological Types.* New York: Harcourt, Brace, 1923.

Kavanaugh, R. *Facing Death.* New York: Nash, 1972.

Kelly, Joan Berlin. "Divorce: The Adult Perspective," in Benjamin B. Wolman (Ed.), *Handbook of Development Psychology.* Englewood Cliffs, New Jersey: Prentice Hall, 1982.

Kerschenbaum, Howard. *Advanced Value Clarification.* California: University Associates, 1977.

Kluckhohn, Florence. "Value Orientations," in *Toward a Unified Theory of Human Behavior: An Introduction to General Systems Theory.* Ed. Roy R. Grinker, Sr. New York: Basic Books, Inc., Publishers, 1956.

Krantzler, Mel. *Creative Divorce.* New York: The New American Library, Inc., 1974.

Kriegel, Robert and Kriegel, Marilyn Harris. *The C Zone, Peak Performance Under Pressure.* New York: Ballantine Books, 1984.

Kruper, Karen. *Communication Games.* New York: The Free Press, 1973.

Kübler-Ross, E. *Death: The Final Stage of Growth.* Englewood Cliffs, New Jersey: Prentice Hall, Inc.

Lair, Jess. *I Ain't Much Baby—But I'm All I've Got.* New York: Doubleday and Company, Inc., 1969.

Laird, Donald. *Psychology, Human Relations, and Motivation.* New York: McGraw-Hill Company, 1975.

Lerner, Harriet Goldhor. *The Dance of Anger.* New York: Harper & Row, 1985.

Levinson, D. J., et al. *The Seasons of a Man's Life.* New York: Knopf, 1978.

Lewis, Howard, and Streitfeld, Harold. *Growth Games.* New York: Bantam Books, 1972.

Luft, Joseph. *Of Human Interaction.* Palo Alto, California: National Press Books, 1967.

Mackenzie, Alec and Waldo, Kay. *About Time.* New York: McGraw-Hill Book Co., 1981.

McCullough, Mamie. *I Can. You Can Too!* Nashville, Tennessee: Thomas Nelson Publishers, 1987.

McHolland, James D. *Human Potential Seminars,* Leader's Manual. Chicago, Illinois: McHolland, 1972.

McKeachie, Wilbert and Doyle, Charlotte. *Psychology* (2nd ed.). Reading, Massachusetts: Addison-Wesley Publishing Co., Inc., 1970.

McLeod, Alastair. *Understanding Psychology.* California: CRM Publishing Co., 1974.

McTuade, Walter, and Aikman, Ann. *Stress.* New York: Bantam Press, 1974.

Maltz, Maxwell. *Creative Living for Today.* New York: Pocket Books, 1972.

———. *Psychocybernetics.* Englewood Cliffs, New Jersey: Prentice Hall, Inc., 1960.

Maslow, Abraham. *Motivation and Personality.* New York: Harper and Row Publishers, Inc., 1970.

———. *The Healthy Personality.* New York: Van Nostrand Reinhold Company, 1969.

———. *The Further Reaches of Human Nature.* New York. Viking, 1971.

Marvin, John, *You're My Friend, So I Bought You This Book.* California: Montcalm Productions, Inc., 1970.

May, Rollo. *Man's Search for Himself.* New York: W. W. Norton and Company, Inc., 1953.

———. *Man's Search for Himself.* New York: W. W. Norton & Co., 1967.

———. *Love and Will.* New York: W. W. Norton and Company, Inc., 1953.

Mehrabian, Albert. "Communication Without Words," *Psychology Today,* 9: 53, 1968.

———. *Public Places and Private Spaces.* New York: Basic Books, 1976.

Menninger, Karl. "Feelings of Guilt," *DHEW Publication* No. (ADM) 78–580.

Miller, Sherod; Wackman, Daniel; Nunnally, Elam; and Saline, Carol. *Straight Talk.* New York: Rawson Wade Publishing Co., 1981.

Milton, Walter. "Values Clarification Workshop." Dallas, Texas, 1985.

Montague, Ashley. *Touching.* New York: Harper and Row, 1971.

Morris, W. N. *Mood.* New York: Springer Verlag, 1987.

Nichols, Ralph and Stevens, Leonard. *Are You Listening?* New York: McGraw-Hill, 1957.

———. "Listening to People." *Harvard Business Review,* 9: 28–30, 1957.

Nock, Steven L. "Family Life Transitions: Longitudinal Effects on Family Members." *Journal of Marriage and the Family,* 43, 703–714, 1981.

Nutt, Grady. *Being Me.* Tennessee: Broadman Press, 1971.

O'Donnell, Lydia N. *The Unheralded Majority: Contemporary Women as Mothers.* Lexington, Massachusetts: Heath, 1985.

Odiorne, George. *Objectives-focused Management.* New York: AMACOM, 1974.

Okun, B. F. *Working With Adults: Individual, Family and Career Development.* Pacific Grove, California: Brooks/ Cole Publishers, 1984.

Peale, Norman Vincent. *Enthusiasm Makes the Difference.* New Jersey: Prentice Hall, Inc., 1952.

———. *The Power of Positive Thinking.* New Jersey: Prentice Hall, Inc., 1956.

———. *You Can If You Think You Can.* Connecticut: Fawcett Publishers, Inc., 1976.

Peck, M. Scott. *The Road Less Traveled.* New York: Simon & Schuster, Inc., 1978.

Peplau, Letitia, and Gordon, S. L. "Women and Men in Love: Sex Differences in Close Heterosexual Relationships." in Virginia O'Leary, Rhosa K. Unger, and Barbara S. Wallston (Eds.), *Women, Gender and Social Psychology.* Hillsdale, New Jersey: Erlbaum, 1985.

Peter, Laurence J. *The Peter Prescription.* New York: William Morrow and Company, Inc., 1972.

Pfeiffer, J. William, and Jones, John. *A Handbook of Structured Experiences for Human Relations Training.* 4 vols. San Diego, California: University Associates Publishers, Inc. 1973–1976.

Piotrkowski, C. S., Rapoport, R. N., and Rapoport, R. "Families and Work." in M. B. Sussman and S. K. Steinmetz (Eds.) *Handbook of Marriage and the Family.* New York: Plenum Press, 1987.

Pittman, J. F., and Lloyd, S. A. "Quality of Family Life, Social Support, and Stress." *Journal of Marriage and the Family,* 50, 53–67, 1988.

Plutchik, R. Emotion: *A Psychoevolutionary Synthesis.* New York: Harper and Row, 1980.

Powell, John. *Fully Human, Fully Aware.* Niles, Illinois: Argus Communications, 1976.

———. *Why Am I Afraid to Love?* Chicago, Illinois: Argus Communications, 1972.

———. *Why Am I Afraid to Tell You Who I Am?* Chicago, Illinois: Argus Communications, 1969.

Radecki-Bush, C.; Bush, J. P.; and Jennings, J. Effects of Jealousy Threats on Relationship Perceptions and Emotions." *Journal of Social and Personal Relationships,* 5, 285–303, 1986.

Raschke, H. J. "Divorce," in M. B. Sussman and S. K. Stenmetz (Eds.), *Handbook of Marriage and the Family.* New York: Plenum Press, 1987.

Raths, Louis; Harmin, Merrill; Simon, Sidney. *Values and Teaching.* Columbus, Ohio: Charles E. Merrill, 1966.

Reichert, Richard. *Self-Awareness Through Group Dynamics.* New York: George A. Pflaum, Publishers, 1970.

Ringer, Robert. *Pulling Your Own Strings.* New York: Thomas Y. Crowell Co., 1978.

Rintye, Ed. *Centering a Lopsided Egg.* Boston, Massachusetts: Allyn and Bacon, Inc., 1975.

Rogers, Carl. *On Becoming a Person.* Boston, Massachusetts: Houghton-Mifflin Company, 1961.

———. "The Necessary and Sufficient Conditions of Personality Change." *Journal of Counseling Psychology,* 22: 95–110, 1957.

Rogers, Carl R. *Client Centered Therapy: It's Current Practice, Implication, and Theory.* Boston, Massachusetts; Houghton Mifflin, 1951.

Rokeach, M. *The Nature of Human Values.* New York: The Free Press, 1973.

Rotter, J. B. *Generalized Expectancies for Internal Versus External Control of Reinforcement.* Psychological Monographs, 1966.

Rubin, Z. "Measurement of Romantic Love." *Journal of Personality and Social Psychology,* 16, pp. 265–273, 1970.

Rusbult, C. E., and Zembrodt, I. M. "Responses to Dissatisfaction of Romantic Involvements: A Multidimensional Scaling Analysis." *Journal of Experimental Social Psychology,* 1983, 19, pp. 274–293.

Sabatelli, R. M. Exploring Relationship Satisfaction: A Social Exchange Perspective on the Interdependence Between Theory, Research, and Practice. *Family Relations,* 37, 217–222, 1988.

Salvoey, P., and Robin, J. "The Differentiation of Social-Comparison Jealousy and Romantic Jealousy." *Journal of Personality and Social Psychology,* 50, 1100–1112, 1986.

Saulnier, Leda, and Simard, Teresa. *Personal Growth and Interpersonal Relations.* Englewood, Cliffs, New Jersey: Prentice-Hall, Inc., 1973.

Satir, Virginia. *Cojoint Family Therapy.* Palo Alto, California: Science and Behavior Books, 1972.

———. *Making Contact.* Millbrae, California: Celestial Arts, 1976.

———. *People Making.* Science and Behavior Books. Palo Alto, California, 1972.

Schachter, S. and Singer, J. "Cognitive, Social and Psychological Determinants of Emotional States." *Psychological Review,* 69: 379–399.

Schindler, John. *How to Live 365 Days a Year.* Englewood Cliffs, New Jersey: Prentice Hall, 1970.

Seyle, Hans. *Stress Without Distress.* New York: J. B. Lippencott Co., 1974.

———. *The Stress of Life.* New York: McGraw-Hill, 1956.

Simon, Sidney and Clark, Jay. *Beginning Values Clarification.* La Mesa, California: Pennant Press, 1975.

Skinner, B. F. *Beyond Freedom and Dignity.* New York: Knopf, 1971.

Smith, Maury. *A Practical Guide to Value Clarification.* La Jolla, California: University Associates, Inc., 1977.

Sperry, Len. *Skills in Contact Counseling.* Reading, Massachusetts: Addison-Wesley, 1975.

Stagner, Ross. *The Dimensions of Human Conflict.* Detroit: Wayne State University Press, 1967.

Sternberg, Robert J. "A Triangular Theory of Love." *Psychological Review,* 98, 119–135, 1986.

Stevens, John O. *Awareness.* New York: Bantam Books, 1973.

Stolberg, A. L.; Camplair, C.; Currier, K.; and Wells, M. J. "Individual, Familial and Environmental Determinants of Children's Post-Divorce Adjustment and Maladjustment." *Journal of Divorce,* 11, 51–70, 1987.

Stone, W. Clement. *The Success System That Never Fails.* Englewood Cliffs, New Jersey: Prentice Hall, Inc., 1962.

Stroebel, Charles. *The Quieting Reflex.* New York: G. P. Putnam's Sons, 1982.

Sullivan, H. S. *The Interpersonal Theory of Psychiatry.* New York: Norton, 1953.

Tavris, Carol. *Anger: The Misunderstood Emotion.* New York: Simon & Schuster, Inc., 1989.

Taylor, Dan and McGee, Dan. "Stress Management Workshop Series." Metro-McGee Associates, Inc., Arlington, Texas.

Teachman, J. D.; Polonko, K. A.; and Scanzoni, J. "Demography of the Family," in M. B. Sussman and S. K. Steinmetz (Eds.), *Handbook of Marriage and the Family.* New York: Plenum Press, 1987.

Toffler, Alvin. *Future Shock.* New York: Random House, 1970.

Tubesing, Nancy Loving and Tubesing, Donald A. *Structured Exercises in Stress Management, Volume II.* Duluth, Minnesota: Whole Person Press, 1983.

Viscott, David. *How to Live with Another Person.* New York: Pocket Books, 1976.

———. *The Language of Feelings.* New York: Pocket Books, 1976.

———. *Risking.* New York: Pocket Books, 1977.

Watson, J. B., and Rayner, R. "Conditioned Emotional Reactions." *Journal of Experimental Psychology,* 3, 1920, pp. 1–14.

Weider-Hatfield, Deborah. "A Unit in Conflict Management Skills." *Communication Education* 30: 265–273, 1981.

Weingarten, H. R. "Marital Status and Well-Being: A National Study Comparing First-Married, Currently Divorced, and Remarried Adults." *Journal of Marriage and the Family,* 47, 653–662, 1985.

Weiss, R. S. *Loneliness: The Experience of Emotional and Social Isolation.* Cambridge, Mass.: M.I.T. Press, 1973.

———. "The Provisions of Relationships," in Z. Rubin (ed.) *Doing Unto Others: Joining, Molding, Conforming, Helping, Loving.* Englewood Cliffs, New Jersey: Prentice Hall, Inc., 1974.

Whitman, Ardis, "The Invitation to Live," *Reader's Digest,* 83–87, (April 1972).

Wolock, Isabel, and Horowitz, Bernard. Child maltreatment as a social problem: The neglect of neglect. *American Journal of Orthopsychiatry,* 54, 530–543, 1984.

Woodmansee, J. J. "The Pupil Response as a Measure of Social Attitude," in *Attitude Measurement,* edited by G. F. Summers. Chicago, Illinois: Rand McNally, 1970.

Worchel, Stephen and Goethals, George R. *Adjustment.* Englewood Cliffs, New Jersey: Prentice Hall, Inc., 1989.

Yalom, I. D. *Existential Psychotherapy.* New York: Basic Books, 1980.

Ziglar, Zig. *See You at the Top.* Gretna, Louisiana: Pelican Publishing Co., 1977.

Zimbardo, P. *Shyness, What It Is, What to Do About It.* Reading, Massachusetts: Addison-Wesley, 1977.

GLOSSARY

Acting A process of clarifying values, whereby an individual follows a pattern of taking action on a chosen value.

Active Listening The act in which a receiver paraphrases the speaker's message.

Adolescent Identity Crisis Stage One of Levinson's developmental stages occurring between the ages of 17 and 22; characterized as the period of searching for personal, career, and social identity, along with the need to become independent from parental influences.

Adult Ego State The mature and rational decision-making part of the personality.

Advising Response Responding to others by offering a solution.

Aggressive Moving against another with an intent to hurt.

Alarm Stage The stage where the body recognizes the stressor and prepares for fight or flight, which is done by a release of hormones from the endocrine glands.

Anal Stage One of Freud's Psychosexual Stages of Development, evolving around toilet training and a child's attempts to become a capable, somewhat independent being.

Anger The feeling of extreme displeasure, usually brought about by interference with our needs or desires.

Anxiety An unpleasant, threatening feeling that something bad is about to happen; the basis of the fear is not generally understood.

Assertiveness Response to conflicting situations that involves standing up for yourself, expressing your true feelings, and not letting others take advantage of you; however, assertiveness involves being considerate of others' feelings.

Attitudes Positive or negative orientations toward a certain target.

Attribution The process of labeling physiological arousal as a particular emotional state.

Attribution Theory An explanation that suggests we frequently overestimate the influence of an individual's personality and underestimate the impact of his or her situation.

Autonomy Versus Doubt Erikson's psychosocial crisis at the second stage of the human life cycle; the two- and three-year-old develops independence and self-reliance in proportion to positive parental encouragement and consistency of discipline.

Avoidance Response to conflicting situations that involves being passive and removing yourself from the conflict.

Belief The acceptance of some thought, supposition, or idea.

Blamer A fault-finder, a dictator, and a boss.

Blended Families A family system consisting of stepchildren and stepparents.

Blind Area of Johari Window Information about you of which you are unaware but is easily apparent to others.

Broken-Record Technique Calmly repeating your assertive message without getting sidetracked by irrelevant issues.

Chair of Life An analogy, representing four valuable parts of life. The "chair" (our life) can either be in balance or out of balance, based on the amount of time we devote to each of these important parts of life.

Child Ego State The primitive, demanding, impulsive, playful, creative, and manipulative part of the personality.

Choosing Freely Consciously and deliberately making a value choice without any pressure from significant others.

Classical Conditioning Learning procedure whereby an organism is repeatedly presented with a neutral stimulus (conditioned stimulus) paired with an unconditioned stimulus in a fixed order; the conditioned stimulus eventually elicits a conditioned response that is very similar to the unconditioned response.

Closed Questions   Questions that often result in yes, no, or a very short response.

Cognitive Dissonance   A concept (theory) that accounts for reactions to inconsistencies in attitudes and beliefs.

Cognitive Theory of Emotion   A theory that emphasizes that the emotion we feel will be determined by the explanation we place on the physiological arousal.

Cohabitation   A situation in which couples live together outside of marriage.

Collaborative Problem Solving   The win-win approach to conflict resolution whereby conflicts are resolved with no one winning and no one losing. Both win because the solution must be acceptable to both.

Commitment   A joint decision to begin a relatively long-lasting, more intimate relationship that to some extent excludes other close intimate relationships.

Communication   The process of conveying feelings, attitudes, facts, beliefs, and ideas between individuals, either verbally or nonverbally, and being understood in the way intended.

Communication Barriers   Things that stop, block, prevent, or hinder the communication process.

Communication Channels   The medium through which a message passes from sender to receiver.

Compromise   Agreement reached by mutual concessions, because each side gives something up to end the conflict or solve the problem.

Codependent   A dependency on people—on their moods, behavior, sickness, well-being, and their love.

Conceived Values   Stated values not acted on.

Conditioned Reinforcers   Stimuli to which we have attached positive or negative value through association with previously learned conditioned reinforcers

Conditioned Response   A response resembling the unconditioned response evoked by the conditioned stimulus as a result of the repeated pairings of the conditioned stimulus with unconditioned stimulus.

Conditioned Stimulus   A neutral stimulus that for experimental purposes is presented to an organism together with a nonneutral stimulus (unconditioned stimulus) for the purpose of developing a conditioned response similar to the unconditioned response previously evoked by the unconditioned stimulus.

Conflict   An expressed struggle between at least two people who perceive the situation differently and are experiencing interference from the other person in achieving their goals.

Conflicting Stimuli   Things that are in conflict with your beliefs and values.

Debilitative Emotions   Emotions that prevent a person from functioning effectively.

Decoding   The process in which a receiver attaches meaning to a message.

Defense Mechanisms   Behavior patterns used to protect one's feelings of self-esteem and self-respect.

Delight   The earliest pleasant reaction (emotion), appearing in the form of smiling, gurgling, and other babyish sounds of joy.

Desensitization   Method of behavioral modification whereby the individual's fear of an object or person is replaced by relaxation.

Displacement   A defense used when the person redirects strong feelings from one person or object to another that seems more acceptable and less threatening.

Distractor   An individual who responds in an irrelevant way to what anyone else is saying or doing.

Distress   Negative or harmful stress that causes a person to constantly readjust or adapt.

Divorce   A complete, legal breaking up of a marriage.

Domination   An aggressive technique of resolving conflict, characterized by moving against another with the intent to hurt.

Double Bind in Communication   A situation in which the nonverbal message contradicts the verbal message.

Ego   The rational, logical, and realistic part of the personality that attempts to maintain balance between the id and superego.

Emotional Attachments   Feelings that there is someone around to take care of us or help us out.

Emotional Debt   A condition of imbalance in which feelings are trapped instead of expressed.

Emotional Intimacy Complete emotional and personal communion, based on complete openness and honesty in sharing feelings.

Emotions Feelings that are experienced.

Empathy The ability to "feel with" another person, to sense what that person is feeling in an emotionally arousing situation.

Encoding The process of putting thoughts into symbols—most commonly words.

Esteem Needs The need to feel worthwhile, which is often satisfied by maintaining a healthy self-image, through status, prestige, a good reputation, or titles; also referred to as one of Maslow's Hierarchy of Needs.

Eustress Good stress or short-term stress that strengthens individuals for immediate physical activity, creativity, and enthusiasm.

Exhaustion Stage In a three-phase reaction to stress the phase in which continuous stress will not enable the important resistance step to take place, and an individual will go from step one, alarm, directly to step three, exhaustion.

Exposure Effect A phenomenon which states the more we are exposed to novel stimuli, a new person, or a new product, our liking for such stimuli increases.

External Locus of Control A characteristic of individuals who see their lives as being beyond their control; they believe what happens to them is determined by external forces—whether it be luck or fate, or other people.

External Noise Includes such elements in the physical environment as temperature, a show on television, music on a stereo, loud traffic, or any other external event or distracting influences.

Facilitative Emotions Emotions that contribute to effective functioning.

Fear The feeling associated with expectancies of unpleasantness.

Feedback The process by which the sender clarifies how his or her message is being received and interpreted.

Feeling Dimension The emotional aspects of any conflict situation.

Friend A person attached to another by respect or affection.

Full Value A value that meets all of the criteria that have been established by Value Clarification theorists.

Gay Relationships Homosexual relationships.

General Adaptation Syndrome The stages of chain of reactions to stress.

Generativity Versus Self-Absorption Erikson's psychosocial crisis at the seventh stage of the human life cycle; conflict between concern for others and concern for self.

Genital Stage One of Freud's Psychosexual Stages of Development, beginning at puberty and characterized as a time when a person has to take his or her new found sex drive that cannot be exhibited directly and learn how to control it through some form of socially acceptable activity.

Getting Established Stage One of Levinson's developmental stages occurring between the ages of 22 and 28; characterized by establishing oneself in a career, getting married, and having a family.

Getting Settled Stage One of Levinson's developmental stages occurring between the ages of 33 and 40; characterized as the period of establishing ourselves in society, solidifying our family life, and becoming successful in the world of work.

Goals An aim or purpose—a plan.

Good Grief The process of working through the stages of grief so that it becomes a positive growth experience.

Grief and Bereavement To be deprived of someone or something very important; sometimes referred to as mourning.

Grief-Work The process of freeing ourselves emotionally from the deceased and readjusting to life without that person.

Guilt The realization of sorrow over having done something morally, socially, or ethically wrong.

Hearing   The physiological sensory process by which auditory sensations are received by the ears and transmitted by the brain.

Hidden Agenda   Entering a conversation or situation with a special interest in mind, a grudge that we are wanting to bring into the open, or even a "chip on our shoulder."

Hidden Area of Johari Window   Information and personal feelings that you keep hidden from others.

Honeymoon Period   Anytime from the wedding day to a year or so from that day.

Hyperstress   An overload that occurs when stressful events pile up and stretch the limits of a person's adaptability.

Hypostress   An overload that occurs when a person is bored, lacking stimulation, or unchallenged.

"I" Message   A message that describes the speaker's position without evaluating others.

Id   The part of the personality composed of the basic biological drives that motivate an individual.

Idea-Oriented Value System   A value system categorized by someone who has a zest for knowledge; someone who likes to think, imagine, and intellectualize.

Identity Versus Role Confusion   Erikson's psychosocial crisis at the fifth stage of the human life cycle, in which the 12 to 18 year-old adolescent must integrate his experiences to develop a sense of ego identity.

Impression Management   Our conscious efforts to present ourselves in socially desirable ways.

Individuation   The establishment of one's identity, based on experiences, rather than following parents' dreams.

Industry Versus Inferiority   Erikson's psychosocial crisis at the fourth stage of the human life cycle; the 6 to 11 year old whose curiosity is encouraged develops a sense of industry, as opposed to the child whose curiosity is disparaged and who develops a sense of inferiority.

Initiative Versus Guilt   Erikson's psychosocial crisis at the third stage of the human life cycle; the 4 or 5 year old either is encouraged to go out on his own or is restricted in his activities.

Intangible Values   Abstract values such as knowledge, religious, or spiritual growth.

Integrity Versus Despair   Erikson's psychosocial crisis at the eighth stage of the human life cycle; a response that depends on how an old person remembers his life.

Intense Emotions   Emotions that are debilitative—they disrupt our overall functioning.

Internal Locus of Control   The state in which individuals who feel that what happens to them and what they achieve in life is due to their own abilities, attitudes, and actions.

Internal Noise   Includes such things as a headache, lack of sleep, daydreaming, preoccupation with other problems, or even a preconceived idea that the message is going to be unimportant or uninteresting.

Internal Psychological Filter   A filter through which all information received is processed. This filter consists of prejudices, past experiences, hopes, and anxieties.

Interpretative Response   A response in which the receiver tries to tell the sender what his or her problem really is and how the sender really feels about the situation.

Intimacy   The feeling that one can share all of one's thoughts and actions with another.

Intimacy Versus Isolation   Erikson's psychosocial crisis at the sixth stage of the human life cycle; the young adult either is able to relate to others or feels isolated.

Intimate Distance   One of Hall's four distance zones, ranging from skin contact to 18 inches.

Irrational Beliefs   Beliefs that result in inappropriate emotions and behaviors.

Issue Dimension   Conflicting needs, preferences, values, and beliefs involved in a conflict situation.

Jealousy   The state of demanding complete devotion from another person; being suspicious of a rival or of one believed to enjoy an advantage.

Johari Window   A model that describes the relationship between self-disclosure and self-awareness.

Judging Response   A response that shows that the receiver is making a judgment about the motive, personality, or reasoning of the sender.

Kinesis   The science or study of nonverbal communication.

Latency Stage   One of. Freud's Psychosexual Stages of Development, occurring from age six to puberty and considered to be a quiet time in a child's development.

Learning   A relatively permanent change in behavior as a result of experience or practice.

Listening   An intellectual and emotional process that integrates physical, emotional, and intellectual inputs in a search for meaning and understanding.

Listening with the Third Ear   Listening to what is said between the lines and without words, what is expressed soundlessly, and what the speaker feels and thinks.

Loneliness   A feeling of longing and emptiness, which is caused by the lack of emotional attachments and/or social ties.

Lose-Lose   An approach to conflict resolution whereby neither party is happy with the outcome.

Love   When the satisfaction, security, and development of another person is as important to you as your own satisfaction, security, and development (Harry Stack Sullivan); also referred to as the desire to see another individual become all they can be as a person—with room to breathe and grow.

Love and Belonging Needs   The need to feel loved, included, and accepted; this need usually assumes importance after the safety and survival needs have been met; also referred to as one of Maslow's Hierarchy of Needs.

Lust   An intense physiological attraction for another person.

Marriage   A close union of two people who decide to share their lives, dreams, and goals with each other.

Maslow's Hierarchy of Needs   The arrangement of needs in order of basic importance as established by Abraham Maslow: physiological needs, safety needs, belongingness and love needs, esteem needs, and self-actualization needs.

Matching Hypothesis   A concept that proposes that people of similar levels of physical attractiveness gravitate toward each other.

Midlife Crisis   Occuring somewhere between the ages of 40 and 45; may be characterized by a painful and disruptive struggle with one's identity and satisfaction of personal needs.

Midlife Transition Stage   One of Levinson's developmental stages occurring between the ages of 40 and 45; characterized as the period when individuals realize their life is half over and they reevaluate their life and what they want out of the remainder of their life.

Mild Emotions   Emotions that are *facilitative*—they assist us in preparing for the future, solving problems, and in doing what is best for us.

Mixed Emotions   Emotions that are combinations of primary emotions. Some mixed emotions can be expressed in single words (that is awe, remorse), whereas others require more than one term (that is, embarrassed and angry, relieved and grateful).

Moods   A general feeling tone.

Moral Values   Values having to do with right and wrong, good and evil.

Motive   Something (a need or desire) that causes a person to act.

Move Against   Being aggressive and responding to conflicting situations with the intent to hurt.

Moving Toward   Responding to conflicting situations by moving toward you opposition until you are either closer together or on the same side.

Need   A lack of something desirable or useful; to be in want.

Negative Reinforcement   Anything that increases a behavior by virtue of its termination or avoidance.

Neurotic Anxiety   Anxiety experienced when the quality of the threatening experience is blown out of proportion to the actual danger posed, and to the point that the anxiety hinders daily functioning.

Nonmoral Values   Values having to do with tastes, preferences, and styles.

Nonverbal Communication   Messages expressed by other than linguistic means.

Novel Stimuli   People, places, or things that are new, different, unique, or original.

Observational Learning   Learning that occurs when an individual's behavior is influenced by the observation of others, who are called models.

One-way Communication   Communication in which a receiver provides no feedback to a sender.

Open Area of Johari Window   An area that represents information, feelings, and opinions that you know about yourself and that others know about you.

Open Communicator   One who is willing to seek feedback from others and to offer information and personal feelings to others.

Openness   Trust and mutual sharing of information and feelings.

Open Questions   Questions that provide space for the speaker to explore his or her thoughts.

Operant Conditioning.   Conditioning based on the principle of reinforcement; the consequences of a response determine whether that response will persist.

Operative Values   Real values implemented in our lifestyle.

Oral Stage   One of Freud's Psychosexual Stages of Development that puts emphasis on satisfying the basic biological drives, specifically the need for oral gratification, usually satisfied via sucking.

Paralinguistics   Nonlinguistic means of vocal expression: tone, rate, pitch, and so on.

Paraphrase   Stating the essence of the other person's spoken words in your own words.

Parent Ego State   The evaluative, nurturing, and judging part of the personality.

Parenthood   The role of being a mother or father.

Parroting   To repeat exactly the speaker's words.

Passive   Avoiding or removing yourself from the conflicting situation by leaving, shutting up, placating, concealing your feelings, or postponing a confrontation until a better time.

Passive Listening   *See* One-way Communication.

Peak Communication   Rare moments when you are perfectly in tune with another, communicating with understanding, depth, and emotional satisfaction; further characterized by openness and honesty.

People-Oriented Value System   A value system categorized by someone who truly enjoys working and being with people.

Personal Distance   One of Hall's four distance zones, ranging from 18 inches to 4 feet.

Personality Fit   The process of being attracted to another person because the differences in one person's strengths compensate for the other person's weaknesses.

Personal Self Image   The part of the self that includes physical, behavioral, and psychological characteristics that establish uniqueness.

Phallic Stage   One of Freud's Psychosexual Stages of Development whereby an individual gains his or her identity, specifically sex role identity.

Physiological Needs   Our most basic and fundamental needs, such as food, water, sleep, clean air to breathe, exercise, and sex; also called our primary or survival needs; also referred to as one of Maslow's Hierarchy of Needs.

Placater   An individual who conceals his or her own feelings.

Positive Reinforcement   Anything that increases a behavior by virtue of its presentation.

Pot of Self Worth   Virginia Satir's view of how much self-worth we have at any given time; the amount in the pot is constantly changing based on the different experiences we have, as well as the feedback we get from others.

Prejudices   A preconceived opinion, feeling, or attitude, either positive or negative, which is formed without adequate information.

Preparation Anxiety   Anxiety that helps individuals get energized to deliver their best, such as mild tension before going for a job interview.

Primary Effect   Occurs when the first impression carries more weight than subsequent information.

Primary Emotions   Basic emotions identified by R. Pluchick as joy, acceptance, fear, surprise, sadness, disgust, anger, and anticipation; identified by Gary Emery and James Campbell as mad, sad, glad, and scared.

Primary Reinforcer   A reinforcer to which we respond automatically, without learning (food, drink, heat, cold, pain, physical comfort or discomfort).

Prizing   Cherishing and being happy with the choice (value), as well as being willing to affirm the choice (value) publicly.

Projection   A defense mechanism used when an individual attributes their own feelings, shortcomings, or unacceptable impulses to others.

Psychological Reactance   The tendency to protect or restore one's sense of freedom or social control, often by doing the opposite of what has been demanded.

Psychosexual Stages of Development   Five stages (oral, anal, phallic, latency, and genital) proposed by Freud to explain the biological controls of an individual's behavior.

Public Distance   One of Hall's four distance zones, ranging outward from 12 feet.

Punishment   Anything that decreases a behavior by virtue of its presentation.

Questioning Response   A response that indicates that the receiver wants to probe the sender for additional information and to discuss the issue further.

Rage   Uncontrolled anger.

Rational Beliefs   Beliefs that result in appropriate emotions and behaviors.

Rationalization   A defense mechanism consisting of reasonable, rational, and convincing explanations, but not real reasons.

Reacting to Others   A situation in which the emotional, feeling, and irrational characteristics of a person are communicated.

Reaction Formation   A defense in which impulses are not only repressed, they are also controlled by emphasizing the opposite behavior.

Real Self   The person you really are, not who you think you are; a situation in which the belief system is accurate, rather than distorted.

Reciprocity   The tendency to like individuals who tend to like us.

Reinforcement   The effect of applying reinforcers.

Reinforcers   Pleasant or unpleasant stimuli that strenghten behavior.

Remarriage   Marrying for the second, third, or subsequent time.

Repression   A defense mechanism consisting of the exclusion of painful, unwanted, or dangerous thoughts and impulses from the conscious mind.

Resistance Stage   The period of recovery and stabilization, during which the individual adapts to the stress.

Responding to Others   A situation in which the rational, thinking, logical part of a person is communicated.

Risk   To reach for something you are not entirely sure of but believe is better than what you now have, or is at least necessary to survive (David Viscott).

Role Confusion   An uncertainty experienced by individuals during the ages of 12 and 18 about who they are and where they are going.

Role Expectations   Beliefs about a man and woman's roles in marriage.

Safety and Security Needs   The need to protect oneself from danger and to keep safe from harm; on a psychological level, safety needs might relate to safety and security, such as finding and keeping a job; also referred to as one of Maslow's Hierarchy of Needs.

Self-Actualization   The fulfillment of one's own completely unique potential.

Self-Actualization Needs   The need for self-fulfillment; the need to become all that one is capable of becoming; also referred to as one of Maslow's Hierarchy of Needs.

Self-Disclosure   The process of deliberately revealing information about oneself that is significant and that would not normally be known by others.

Self-Efficacy   Our belief about our ability to perform behaviors that should lead to expected outcomes.

Self-Esteem   An overall evaluation of oneself, whether one likes or dislikes who one is, believes in or doubts oneself, and values or belittles one's worth.

Self-fulfilling Prophecy   A prediction or expectation of an event that makes the outcome more likely to occur than would otherwise have been the case.

Self-Image   A mental blueprint of how we see ourselves and how we feel about ourselves.

Self-talk   A person's beliefs or what they say to themselves.

Semantics   The study of the meaning and changes of meaning in words.

Shyness   The feelings, physical reactions, and thoughts that create a state of anxiety, discomfort, and inhibition.

Significant Others   The important people in our lives.

Significant Stimuli   Anything directly related to another person's needs, wants, interests, and desires.

Similarity   The process of selecting friends because of comparable interests, income level, educational level, beliefs, and so on.

Singlehood   The decision not to marry.

Social Distance   One of Hall's four distance zones, ranging from 4 to 12 feet.

Social Perception   The way we perceive, evaluate, categorize, and form judgments about the qualities of people we encounter.

Social Ties   The feeling that we are part of a group or have an identity.

Stages of Grief Work   The process of freeing ourselves emotionally from a "loss," readjusting to life without the cause of this loss, resuming ordinary activities, and forming new relationships; the stages are identified as denial, replacement or searching activity, anger, depression, and acceptance.

Stages of Psychosocial Development   Eight stages of Erikson's human life cycle; the stages are trust versus mistrust, autonomy versus doubt, initiative versus guilt, industry versus inferiority, identity versus role confusion, intimacy versus isolation, generativity versus self-absorption, and integrity versus despair.

Stepfamilies   Remarriages involving children from one or both spouses.

Stereotyping   A process of making generalizations by categorizing an object, person, or situation.

Stimulus Generalization   Tendency for a stimulus similar to the conditioned stimulus to evoke or to set the occasion for a conditioned response.

Stress   The nonspecific response of the body to any demand placed on it, whether that demand be real, imagined, pleasant, or unpleasant.

Stressor   A stressful event.

Strokes   A special form of stimulation one person gives to another.

Sublimation   A defense whereby an individual redirects their basic desires toward a socially valued activity.

Submissive   An individual who behaves passively in a conflicting situation.

Success   The outcome of setting a goal and achieving that goal, whatever that goal may be.

Superego   The part of the personality that consists of our values, morals, religious beliefs, and ideals of our parents and society; sometimes referred to as our conscience.

Supportive Response   A response that shows the receiver's intent is to reassure, comfort, or minimize the intense feelings of the sender.

Suppression   A defense mechanism in which people are conscious of their emotions, but deliberately control rather than express them.

Symbols in Communication   Such things as the selection of words, tone and pitch of voice, nonverbal method, or even types of supportive materials.

Tangible Values   Specific values such as a car or money.

Thing-Oriented Value System   A value system categorized by someone who works hard and saves money to obtain material objects or even a large bank account.

Thought-stopping Concentrating on the unwanted thoughts and, after a short time, suddenly stopping and emptying the mind of all stressful thoughts.

Timewaster Anything preventing you from achieving your objectives most effectively.

Transactional Analysis A system developed by Eric Berne to teach people a theory of personality to use in becoming more aware of themselves, their interactions with others, and their life patterns or scripts.

Trust Versus Mistrust Erikson's psychosocial crisis at the first stage of the human life cycle; the subsequent response of a person to the way he is treated as an infant.

Two-way Communication An exchange of information in which the receiver deliberately provides feedback to a sender.

Type A Behavioral Pattern A behavioral pattern characterizing individuals who live a competitive, aggressive, ambitious, and stressful life style.

Type B Behavioral Pattern A behavior pattern characterizing individuals who live a more relaxed and less hurried lifestyle.

Type C Behavior Pattern A behavior pattern characterizing people who perform at peak levels under pressure and change, without the debilitating effects of stress.

Unconditional Positive Regard The situation in which love is given freely and does not depend on any specific aspects of behavior.

Unconditioned Response Response that automatically occurs when an unconditioned stimulus is presented.

Unconditioned Stimulus Stimulus that automatically produces a consistent response.

Unknown Area of Johari Window Information about you that is unknown to self or others.

Value The personal worth placed on an object, thought, or idea.

Value Clarification A process that helps people distinguish between full values and partial values.

Value Indicators Partial values, such as desires, thoughts not acted on; opinions, interests, aspirations, goals, and so on, that are in the process of being formed.

Value System The personal blueprint or guidelines for one's life, based upon one's values.

Verbal Communication The expression of words; language.

Wavering and Doubt Stage One of Levinson's developmental stages occurring between the ages of 28 and 33; characterized as the period of evaluating "what we are doing and where we are going."

Win-Lose An approach to conflict resolution whereby one person gets his or her way, and the other does not.

Win-Win An approach to conflict resolution whereby conflicts are resolved with no one winning and no one losing. Both win because the solution must be acceptable to both.

INDEX